WOMAN ON TRIAL

WOMAN ON TRIAL

LAWRENCIA BEMBENEK

HarperCollins*Publishers*Ltd

*Tons of appreciation to editor Marq de Villiers for facilitating communica-
tion so effectively. His hard work, expert advice, experience and humor
made it all not only possible, but a pleasure as well.*

—L.B.

*Cover photo: This courtroom picture was taken during my post-conviction
motion for a new trial. (Milwaukee Journal Photo.)*

WOMAN ON TRIAL. Copyright © 1992 by Lawrencia Bembenek.
All rights reserved. No part of this book may be used or reproduced
in any manner whatsoever without prior written permission except
in the case of brief quotations embodied in reviews. For information
address HarperCollins Publishers Ltd, Suite 2900, 55 Avenue Road,
Toronto, Canada M5R 3L2.

First paperback edition: 1992

Canadian Cataloguing in Publication Data

Bembenek, Lawrencia
    Woman on trial

ISBN 0-00-637915-X

1. Bembenek, Lawrencia. 2. Escapes — United States. 3. Trials
(Murder) — United States. 4. Woman murderers — United States
— Biography. 5. Prisoners — United States — Biography. 6. Fugi-
tive from justice — United States — Biography. 7. Refugees, Political
— Canada — Biography. I. Title.

HV248.B4A3 1992   364.1'523'092   C92-093398-X

---

92 93 94 95 96 97 98 99 ❖ OFF 9 8 7 6 5 4 3 2 1

To my parents, who are the sun and moon in my life. To all my true friends, who have supported me and helped me beyond words.

Now here you see, it takes all the
running you can do to keep in the
same place. If you want to get
somewhere else, you must run
twice as fast as that.

— Lewis Carroll

THE VERDICT

"All rise."

The jury walked in.

I sat down with my hands folded in front of my face, biting my knuckle as I watched them enter, one by one.

My counsel had said to me, "*Watch their faces!* If they look at you, you're home free. If they don't ... you're in trouble."

It was silent, like a death watch. I heard no sound but the shuffle of a single pair of shoes and the sinister, insistent hum of the TV cameras at the back of the courtroom.

The heavy woman with the long, brown hair wouldn't look at me.

The elderly black man watched his feet as he entered the jury box.

"Oh no," I heard my counsel whisper.

More jury members followed in a solemn line. Not one of them returned my gaze. I broke the skin on my knuckle with my tooth.

"God, no," my counsel said again.

The jury forewoman was short, dark-haired, rigid. She had squinted at me through schoolteacher eyeglasses while I testified. She wasn't looking at me now.

"Ladies and gentlemen of the jury," Judge Skwierawski was saying, "have you reached a verdict?"

"We have, Your Honor," her nasal voice replied.

The judge opened the envelope. His ruddy, bearded face did not change expression. He read calmly:

"We find the defendant, Lawrencia Bembenek, guilty of first-degree murder."

I felt my life begin and end in that single instant.

Guilty! The word sliced into my consciousness with the heat of a lightning bolt, slashing like a razor.

Guilty! It made a sound inside my head like bones breaking.

I could taste blood in my throat, and I clenched my jaw shut.

Suddenly, I was standing at the bench, in front of Skwierawski, unaware that I had just walked there.

The judge was saying something. I saw his mouth form the words, his jaw move, I saw the hairs of his beard, but it was all movement and bleakness and silence, and I heard nothing.

"No," I said. "Oh, no."

I felt my pulse hammering. How could there be blood in my heart when there was room only for this pain? Tears welled up.

"I must sentence you to life imprisonment."

I heard sobs behind me. I told myself not to turn around, to try to hang on. *Don't turn around and look at them, or you will die.*

My counsel was speaking, saying something about some kind of appeal bond, which Skwierawski was denying, and my eyes traveled in slow motion to the jurors. I half-expected to see that they had turned into headless demons. Even then, none of them would look at me.

"Laurie?" the bailiff said, and even his eyes were red. My counsel had his arm around my shoulder for a second, and then I was gone, led to my captors, moving slowly, not knowing what I was doing. My purse and coat were two feet behind me, but I couldn't stop for them.

A crowd of deputies surrounded me and cuffed my hands to a chain around my waist. The chain felt big enough to shackle the world.

I felt so very small.

Then I was in a room, on a chair, all alone, and the tears came.

■   ■   ■

When I was a little girl, nine years old, I almost drowned. I was in a swimming pool, on vacation in Canada with my parents. I clung to an inflatable ring, and I accidentally floated into the deep end. The ring slipped away from me. Suddenly I couldn't reach the bottom, and I was under the water. Panicking, I tried to get my face above the surface, desperate for air, but I went down again and again and again, and I started to scream inside my mind. Then my mother's hand came out of the sky and grabbed my flailing arm, hauling me out of the pool, to safety. To safety.

Mom, mom, help me! Please help me! I'm drowning again!

But my mother was behind the wooden courtroom railing, seated next to my dad, her hands rigid and her heart breaking.

And then they came, and they took me away.

1

WHO I AM

I'm the person you don't know. You may think you know me, but you don't. You know only some creature from the media, from the hype and hysteria that surrounded my arrest and trial in 1981 for the murder of my husband's ex-wife.

Bambi, the ex-bunny! The killer! The fugitive!

I'm no Joan of Arc, nor am I what you think. I was a person who trusted too many people too much, who was naive, who made many bad decisions, who has grown up in a way I wouldn't wish on your worst enemy. But I'm not a bad person, and I'm not a killer, either.

I have learned some things I wish I'd never learned. I've learned that the media is sentimental and cruel, feeding on self-serving thoughts of its own lofty role in our system, but in reality filled with lies and lazy ignorance. I have no wish to make enemies of the press; I have more than my share of enemies already. But the press convicted me before my trial, turned me into some kind of crazed killer bimbette in drop-dead clothes, out of a wish for a story that they only imagined was there.

That's not me. None of that is me.

You may have read that I was a cop, once, but did you know I was an artist? You almost certainly have heard that I was a "bunny" for Playboy (as if four weeks as a waitress should define a life!), but did you know that my favorite color is periwinkle blue, and that I love animals, foreign films and jazz? There are articles about my jobs, about my dismissals, about my appeals being denied, about my filing for bankruptcy, but no articles to say I enjoyed books by Marilyn French and John Steinbeck, that I played the flute for twelve years, that I've been painting since I was old enough to pick up a brush, that I used to plant a garden, and that I love the smell of wood and burning leaves. If I was free, I would want to work for Greenpeace. I'm a person, not a headline. I'm a prison-reform activist, a feminist, a lifer. I'm a daughter, a friend, a lover, a sister—maybe like yours.

Jail isn't what you think, either, not in a million years. This is not the late show. This is where women are imprisoned for prostitution while rapists go free; women caged for cocaine use while cops are on drugs; women incarcerated for fraud while witnesses commit perjury. Some women are here for stealing, but they've had everything taken from them: their freedom, their children, their humanity.

No one is safe here. Not your children, your mothers, your sisters.

I was once asked what I miss about the streets. I rambled on and on about the small things that people take for granted—frying an egg, raiding the refrigerator, driving a car. But that's not it. It's privacy. To have my love letters read, my every thought authorized, my property and my very body open to inspection—God! Is there a world without strip-searches, walkie-talkies blaring and the footsteps of the guards?

Privacy, privacy is what I miss.

When I had my freedom, I didn't even know that was all I needed.

I have cruel dreams of being free again. I dream I'm at my mother's bedroom window. My mom! Always calm and fresh, like the rain on the tiger lilies by the backyard swing, her skin cool and clean. I dreamed I saw her at the park, in her sleeveless blouse, with the wind swaying the branches above her. Safe arms to come home to. Only to wake at the sound of the blaring bell, and realize I am still here.

I've been inside for ten years now. My life is passing, my body breaking down. I don't know if there's hope left in me. I try not to cherish the anger, but the anger keeps me going.

Because I did nothing wrong.

I don't know if you can believe that. But it's true all the same.

■   ■   ■

Okay, lighten up, Bembenek!

■   ■   ■

The hoopla that surrounds this case, even now! The circus! So many partisans! So many enemies! When I was on the run, after I escaped from prison and took refuge in Canada, a Milwaukee radio station printed up thousands of Laurie Bembenek masks. All you had to do was call and they'd send you an LB Mask, made from a hideous old picture of me taken at the *Milwaukee Journal* in connection with my lawsuit years before. They blew it up and punched the eyes out so you could wear it. I got a copy later. And a naive friend asked, "But don't they have to have your permission to do that?" Yeah, sure! Permission from me! I've had every ounce of power wrestled away from me.

I was called "Bambi." It was a nickname I acquired at the Police Academy in Milwaukee. Nobody could pronounce Bembenek, though it seemed easy enough to a Polish girl from South Side Milwaukee, seeing as it's pronounced exactly the way it's spelled. Most recruits at the Academy acquired some sort of goofy nickname. It was a paramilitary environment, and to break the tension, there was a lot of horseplay and kidding around. There was a Jones, and we called him Jonestown, after the poisoned Kool-Aid place. Bradford was called Brackley, for some reason. Me they called Bambi.

That was only at the Academy. No one else called me that. I was always Laurie to my friends, or LB. It was the media that picked it up.

There were T-shirts after I escaped. *Run, Bambi, Run!* they said. My friends were baffled. My friend Kathy Braun, my best friend from prison, wrote and asked, "What? What is this Bambi thing?" She thought it was so funny.

My friends tell me that when they're making calls on my behalf, perhaps asking someone to write or do something for me, they'll ask, "Are you familiar with the Laurie Bembenek case?"

Often, the answer is no. Then they'll ask, "You know, the woman they call Bambi?"

"Oh! Bambi! Of course!" They remember that. So, in a way, the nickname is helpful. It's a double-edged sword. Some people say I shouldn't criticize it too much, because it's now used sympathetically and even affectionately as often as not. But it perpetuates a trivial image. A "Bambi" is a frightened little deer in the woods. Not exactly a feminist nickname, is it? It's awfully close to "bimbo."

The media image I was tagged with at the beginning of my case follows me still. Recently, a sympathetic reporter from the *Toronto Star* saw some of my paintings and asked me whether I'd been painting long. He was surprised when I told him I'd worked as a display artist for two or three years and had painted all my life. Yet for four or five weeks out of my life I worked at the Playboy Club, and he certainly knew that, but he didn't know that I'd taken the job because I had been black-listed by the MPD and ordered to pay back the unemployment compensation I'd received.

When I first got to Toronto, after my recapture, the *Sun* ran an editorial saying, "She posed for a Playboy centerfold. Do we want that kind of person here in Canada?" In truth, it was just a waitressing job, but people somehow assume that a centerfold goes along with it. And so the myth is perpetuated, and becomes "fact."

After that, a few of the male guards came running up to my cell-block asking for my autograph.

"Why?" I'd ask.

"You were in the magazine ... *Playboy.* You were a centerfold ...!"

They didn't believe me when I told them I'd never posed for any such thing.

Now, if you rode a horse once, fifteen years ago, would they call you a former equestrian? Of course not.

But a bimbo seems to live forever.

■   ■   ■

Many characters have paraded through my life, for good or ill. Some of them I think of fondly, others I try not to think of at all. Some became friends; others did me harm and caused only pain. You'll meet them in what follows; some will touch you, some will very likely make your skin crawl.

You'll meet the boy I loved, who couldn't abide to see me change. You'll meet the man I married ... I thought I loved him too, but knew nothing of the shadowy world in which he lived. You'll meet the pitbull private eye who became obsessed with my case; the conman and manipulator who tried to destroy me; the convict who "confessed" to the murder for which I was convicted; the armed robber who might actually have committed that murder but who shot himself to death in the middle of a hostage-taking incident years later. You'll meet the members of the Milwaukee Police Department: some good officers and decent people, but too many of them crude and brutal men who were interested only in survival and self-profit. You'll meet the friends I made in jail, the man who helped me escape, the woman who betrayed me, the counselors who helped me, the friends who supported me, the family who loves me, the lawyers who have worked for me, some of whom I have recently learned to trust.

So many people! Some passing through my life and disappearing in a cloud of malice and acrimony; others chipping out a small niche for themselves in the place I keep the good memories, where I keep my family and my friends.

But in the end, I'm the one in jail. It's my life that is slowly seeping away, precious water sucked into the arid deserts of uncaring bureaucracy.

Here they put me, and here I still am.

■   ■   ■

I had a happy childhood, I think, though I was alone a lot. I grew up in a South Side Milwaukee neighborhood that was largely Polish and German. My mom and dad are Catholics, good people. I have two sisters, Colette and Melanie, but they are ten and thirteen years older than me, so we were never kids together.

I used to read a lot when I was a kid, because I was alone so much. I had a best friend in the neighborhood named Lori Schultz who lived just down the alley. She had four brothers, and we used to roughhouse with those kids all the time. But if she wasn't around or was busy, I was alone. I spent a lot of time reading and drawing, and my parents encouraged that.

Like most adults, I keep in my mind only a few powerful memories of those years.

Here's one: I had a bad attack of appendicitis when I was four and a half, and I remember it as if it were yesterday. It was my first disillusioning lesson in breach of contract, too.

That night, I remember, my sister Colette was babysitting—again. She was not too happy about that. We sat at home watching Red Skelton and, being typical kids, had fun chowing down on Malomars, salami and popcorn.

I started to complain about a stomachache. My sister, naturally enough, thought it was the food. I remember squeezing my little bunny slippers together, it hurt so much. I have a high tolerance for pain, and don't show it much. This can be a curse, because if you're not hysterical, people don't believe anything's wrong. My sister told me to stop crying or she'd put spiders in my bed—she was mad! By the time my parents came home I was really wailing. "My side, my side ..." My temperature was raging and they took me to the hospital, flat on my back down a corridor strapped to a table, right into the operating room. I felt really small. My dad said if I was brave he would get me a wooden rocking horse ...

I woke up with a huge scar; it looks like a caterpillar, and I don't like to wear a two-piece bathing suit to this day. Still, I was brave, very brave about the whole thing. But when I got out, my dad decided arbitrarily that I was too old for rocking horses, and he never bought me one.

My mom remembered, though. Years later, when I was married, she bought me a Christmas tree ornament that was a little wooden rocking horse. She looked at me, and I at her, and we both wanted to cry. It was a wonderful moment.

Later, I became interested in playing the flute. I started about the third or fourth grade, and I continued until I was out of high school. I'd practice two or three hours a day. Partly because of so much practice, I guess, I was better than average. When I was thirteen or fourteen, I studied with Professor Israel Borouchoffe at the university; I was the youngest person to study at the University of Wisconsin–Milwaukee. I was a bit of a prodigy, I guess.

Becoming a musician had been my mom's dream when she was young, but in those days parents didn't want to waste that kind of money on a girl, so her brother got to be a musician instead. She wanted to give this gift to me. It was her dream that I join the Milwaukee Symphony some day.

The thing about music is that it consumes your life. You must devote so much time to it. I was with one concert band for four years, and then another for four more years. My whole life as a kid seemed to be music lessons, band practice, playing for one concert or another, field drill. I never saw a parade when I was a kid—I was always in them! I went as far as I could without becoming bored, without losing all other aspects of my life.

I started my schooling at St. Augustine, a grade school. I made some good friends there. When you grow up with kids, you remember so much about them. You remember when John threw up in church in third grade, and all the trivial and wonderful stories that children retain.

Next I spent a year at St. Mary's Academy, a Catholic high school.

Ah, Catholic schools ...! Every morning we had to go to church before school. In those days, the girls had to wear chapel veils. If you forgot your chapel veil, one of the nuns would pull her hankie out of her pocket and you had to sit there with her hankie over your head. It was really humiliating.

Even as a kid, I noticed that something was screwy, really wrong, about organized religion. It seemed to be all about money and was male-dominated. The priests drove brand-new Cadillacs. I was in the rectory only once, and it was like being ushered through the gates of heaven—an awesome place, expensively furnished, with walnut paneling, thick carpeting and velvet drapes. The nuns, of course, had taken a vow of poverty and were not permitted any possessions; their house was spartan in comparison. I was just a kid, but I knew something was terribly skewed. We weren't even allowed to give the nuns small presents for Christmas.

In our neighborhood ... well, Catholics didn't allow contraception, so there were commonly huge families of thirteen or fourteen kids. Another kid? It's God's will.... I felt wealthy compared to some of my friends. I was the last of three children, and my dad was in the construction industry, which was booming at the time. We were comfortable. My friends all wore hand-me-downs.

On the other hand, I was drawn to large families, because their homes were so alive with noise and kids, laughing and playing and roughhousing. Because my sisters were so much older, I was the only child in my little house, and it was always so quiet. My mom would have classical music on, and everything was just so, perfect, and then I'd go over to the house of one of my playmates and there'd be fourteen kids screaming and fighting. It seemed like a lot of fun.

I loved big families for another reason. When you're the only one at home, you're the only object of attention. So if you're five or ten minutes late, they know, they're waiting for you. My parents were strict with me. But heck, at my friend's house we could be an hour late and her mom never even noticed! What a difference! Her mom had ten other kids to take care of. They just didn't get the attention I got, and of course I saw that as an advantage.

The problem with some brands of Catholicism is that everything is a sin. Even thinking about sin is a sin. You grow up guilt-ridden, shame-based. I broke with that as much as I could, but some of it still comes back to haunt me ... it's ingrained.

At St. Augustine, I had an outrageous experience with a priest that has colored my thinking about the church and religion ever since.

This priest taught a catechism class to sixth- and seventh-graders. He told us that among advanced theologians there is apparently a theory that Mary Magdalene was Jesus's mistress. But you don't tell that to sixth-graders! At that time, I was a true believer. I loved Jesus with all my heart. It was blind faith. The way that man talked about Jesus seemed so wrong and dirty and shocking, it made me want to cry.

I started to challenge him—I always had a big mouth. I would look around to see if my classmates were similarly shocked. Oh, over there would be someone picking her nose, and someone else would be sleeping and yawning. Most were not even listening.

I tried to tell my mom all this, but I couldn't understand it well enough to know what was going on, so I didn't explain it well. I just knew something was really wrong.

The priest was also in charge of the gym classes, which were held in the church basement, and he would make more strange comments there. He would say stuff like, "If you girls do enough of this exercise, you'll all look like Marilyn Monroe."

I was thinking, What is this guy saying? Developing girls are so self-conscious as it is. All these references to our body parts? I knew it wasn't appropriate. It gave me the creeps. Everything he did was to embarrass us, to put us down as girls. Some of the girls had their periods already, and when they felt too sick to take the gym class he'd ridicule them for that.

One afternoon, when I was twelve, I was sitting on the basement floor, wearing pants, with my feet up on a bench along the wall. He looked over and yelled, "Bembenek, get your feet off the wall!"

Well, I was a smartass and never did like authority. I lifted my feet in the air but didn't move them. Technically, they weren't on the wall anymore.

He turned around and glanced at me again and lost his temper altogether, and in front of all these little kids, he hollered, "Goddamn it, Bembenek! I told you to get your fucking feet off the wall, you look like a slut!"

I looked at him ... I didn't even know what a "slut" was! All the little girls dropped their jump ropes and stood there with their mouths hanging open at this sight of a priest swearing and taking the Lord's name in vain in a major way.

I knew, however, that whatever a "slut" was it was really bad, and I wasn't that. So I stood up and I said, "I am not a slut!"

And he said, "If you look like one I'll treat you like one!"

Nice man.

"Go back up to the classroom," he shouted. "Get out of my sight. You disobeyed me."

I looked at him, and I just couldn't keep my mouth shut. I said, "Oh yeah, and you know what you are!"

I didn't know what I was saying. I didn't know what "gay" was, never mind "pedophile" or "misogynist." I just knew he was bad. I had to say something, so I said it and started to walk away.

Then I heard my girlfriends yelling, "Run, Laurie!"

I turned around, and this guy was coming after me. There was a tunnel between the church and the school building, and I took off on my spindly little legs and ran through the tunnel. He was a big, oafish guy and couldn't run very well, and I was a little sprinter. To this day I wonder what he would have done if he'd caught me.

I went to the playground, panting against the church wall like a little criminal, then later I hid in the girls' washroom.

I was miserable. I told my mom I'd gotten into trouble at school again, and explained what had happened. My mother was shocked. When my dad came home, I told the story again. I don't want to say anything against my parents, because I love them, but they were brought up not to make any waves, to leave things alone, to clean it up, not make things worse. If that had been my kid, I'd have run right to the *Milwaukee Journal*, and to the first lawyer I could find, and I would have taken that creep into court so fast ... but people weren't sue-happy in those days.

They decided to go and see the pastor. On the way to my flute lesson after supper, we stopped at the rectory, but the pastor was so drunk he wasn't even coherent. He had changed too much water into wine, I guess.

My mom and dad decided I should leave the school, but I refused to go. I said no, I want to graduate, I don't want to leave my friends. If I left, it would be admitting I had done something wrong, and I hadn't.

It was my first really powerful lesson in independence.

■   ■   ■

I went through something of a rocky adolescence, as many teenagers do. My parents, who were very strict, were not ecstatic about my behavior. In the ninth grade I suddenly wanted to stay out as late as my other friends. They could stay out until eleven, but I had to be home by nine. We could not agree on anything. I was a bit of a wild child, I guess. Some of my rebellion was a fascination with the tail end of the sixties, when disobedience was fashionable; we all still wanted to be hippies. My sister had a boyfriend with long hair, and I wanted one too. I thought my two sisters were just the coolest things on earth, and I wanted to do everything they did. I wanted to wear the shirts from India with the little mirrors all over them and burn incense and wear sandals and smoke hash and be like them. And of course I was too young to do any of those things, really.

My mom went through menopause when I was going through

adolescence—talk about raging hormones on Taylor Avenue!

We battled it out all the time. I wanted to wear make-up and she wouldn't let me. I couldn't even get a phone call from a boy. And of course the more they prohibited me, the more I wanted to rebel.

They decided it would be a good idea for me to go to an all-girl school and wear a little plaid skirt. Scholastically, St. Mary's Academy was the best school around; I was reading Keats and Shakespeare and studying Latin. But it wasn't a well-rounded atmosphere—there was no band, the school offered only a few sports and a small Art Department.

When you're an adolescent, you really have no way to meet boys aside from school. In an all-girl school, you're stuck. I guess St. Mary's was a good preparation for prison in that way. But like the prisoner who most wants what she can't have, we were obsessed with boys, because there weren't any. I don't think you can develop normally in an all-girl setting. I remember these dreadful dances, the boys bused over—it was so embarrassing. We were all so shy. Everyone stood on one side or the other of the gym, too scared to talk to anyone, not knowing how ...

Finally my rebelliousness persuaded them they were wasting their money, and they transferred me to the public system, to Bay View High. Then I was bored; we were reading books I'd read two or three years earlier. I lost interest in my studies. But I did other things. I joined the band. And I joined the girls' track team. We were the first girls' track team in the state, which shows you how backward things were. Before that, the only thing for girls to do was cheerleading. I was always long and spindly, but I could run like the wind, and I ran the 110-yard hurdles.

The boys all got to take shop; the girls had to take sewing and cooking. I have a domestic deficiency to this day—I can't cook. (Of course, ten years in prison doesn't help!) I hated being dictated to on that level. I wanted to take woodworking and shop; I loved the smell of wood, making things from wood. I never did understand why I couldn't do these things ... I couldn't understand why women were denied choices just because they were women, and why housework was gender-specific. I was a feminist before I'd ever heard the word.

■   ■   ■

I got my first job when I was sixteen and still in school. There was a program in my senior year that allowed students to work if they didn't need a full load of courses. I had enough credits to graduate early, but who wants to hire a sixteen-year-old? Instead, I decided to take one or two easy credits in my senior year—ceramics was one—and work after school. I went to school for half a day, worked half a day. First I worked for a jewelry store, then as a waitress downtown. What an education! That part of town was full of pimps and prostitutes, drunk sailors, mentally ill people wandering around. Later I was a waitress in a mall department store on the south side and worked for K–mart in the shoe department. I regret now that I didn't go all the way through to university, but I guess I was a typical teenager of the time.

I looked into the job of police aide—this is not exactly a police officer but more like a clerk. But my birthday didn't fall on the right date—I was either too young or too old by a couple of months, so I missed it.

The summer I graduated from high school was the best of my life. I was soon going to be eighteen and able to drink legally. Everything seemed possible. My best friend, Joanne, decided to go to the University of Denver, so it was our last summer together. As a graduation present, I got permission for the first time to go to Daytona Beach for the college madness. Joanne and I went together. It was the first time I'd been to Florida.

I met a guy there who was from Milwaukee, Danny, and I ended up going out with him for four years. I loved him so much! It's too bad we were so young when we met. If we'd been older, it might have worked out, and everything would have been different. But it was too early. I felt I was in transition from one life to another. I wasn't ready. He wanted to get married, but marriage was the last thing on my mind.

On a whim that summer I took a test and won a scholarship to a local business college, Bryant & Stratton, where I took an associate degree program in Fashion Merchandising Management. The hours were peculiar and so I managed to hold down three part-time jobs at the same time. At night I tended bar. In the afternoons, I worked at a pharmacy, as a cashier, and whenever I had a few spare hours, I did inventory for a baby clothing company, Carter's.

It was during this period that I started modeling.

■　　■　　■

Talking about this period of my life is tough for me, even now. So much garbage has been written about me and how I look, as if that's all there is. After my arrest, even local women's groups couldn't seem

*to see past the descriptions of my clothes and my face and my body.
And it still happens. A* Vanity Fair *reporter, speaking to me in jail this
year, denied that I could have been unhappy during this period. "You
were drop-dead gorgeous, you had everything going for you, how can
you sit there and tell me you were depressed?" he demanded.*

*All they ever want to do is ask me about sex. All they ever do is
think back to that one cheesecake calendar photo I did for Schlitz (in
which I was Miss March 1978, but fully clothed, after all), which they
have turned in their minds into some kind of symbol for my life. Why
must they try to imprison me in my body as well as in these grim, gray
places they have put me for the past decade?*

■   ■   ■

When I was growing up, people would often say to me, "You're so
tall, you should be a model!" You hear that often enough and you're
just a kid and you get curious. So I looked into it.

There are so many false, preconceived notions about the life of a
model. I thought it would be really glamorous, and to a certain extent
it was. But you know what? It's not exactly cerebral.

I couldn't understand why I was not happier doing it, this job that
I thought I wanted, but it was completely unsatisfying. I was treated
like a mannequin. Everyone condescends to you. The photographers
are prima donnas of the worst kind.

I was pretty naive around then. I was a teenager, and my politics
weren't really together yet. I was dabbling, not yet knowing what I
wanted, who I was. I wouldn't do lingerie shows and I never did nude
modeling. I knew I had to be able to come home and show my dad the
photos without being embarrassed. The calendar was the most risqué
thing I ever did. I was eighteen when I posed for that thing; it's fifteen
years old. Why do they keep bringing it up? I never did anything like
it again.

For a while, I worked for The Limited, a store that sold better
ready-to-wear fashions. I was selling their designer dresses, at three
and four hundred dollars each. Employees were required to wear their
clothing, but even with forty percent off it was expensive. It was easy
to become addicted to the very latest things—I had all kinds of
clothes. My closet's probably still stuffed with all that junk.

In 1978 I started working for Boston Store, as a display artist. I
really liked that. I was up and down on ladders all day doing displays
and fixtures, that sort of thing, helping to move all the wretched

excess of the capitalist system! I was happy. It was creative, and without the pressure of sales. I liked the store and all the employees. To this day some of them write to me. I also taught a health-and-beauty course to eighth-graders, and worked part-time at Vic Tanny's Health Club.

But I was impatient. I was always impatient. I wanted a little authority, a little responsibility, but I discovered that the store didn't accept anyone under twenty-four into their management program. I was only nineteen, and twenty-four seemed decades away. Then the store was bought out, and there were major changes. I started thinking about police work again.

I had always had police work in the back of my mind. My dad had been a cop for a while, an MP in the U.S. Army and later with the Milwaukee Police Department.

My dad never, ever, told me I couldn't do something just because I was a woman. Never. He was extraordinary that way. My mom doesn't think he's the most progressive guy in the world, and in some ways he's not. But he never treated his daughters in any way but with encouragement.

■   ■   ■

At the same time, my relationship with Danny was beginning to sour. That relationship ... oh, it almost became habit. We couldn't live with one another, we couldn't live without one another. It was difficult. I was living at home. I could barely afford things like car payments. Wages were so low I was working at two jobs, from eight to five at Boston Store and then from six to ten at Vic Tanny's. This wasn't uncommon—lots of people, especially women, worked at a couple of jobs to survive. I couldn't afford to move away from my parents.

Danny and I were not officially living together. Practically, you understand, but not really. I look back on those years with him as perhaps the happiest years of my life. We had no adult responsibilities. We had trivial priorities like learning the latest disco dance step and trying to outdo each other in getting a darker tan. I wish I had such problems now! He had a married brother in Chicago and we'd visit him all the time. We'd go out and have fun there. We'd have fun all the time. When I think of it, ah ... really ...

No, I mustn't think of it, not now.

I became very unhappy. I began to dislike modeling. My other jobs were going nowhere. I didn't know what I wanted. I didn't know why I was unhappy. And it was ridiculous. I had the world by the tail, but I never realized it. I didn't know how really miserable it was possible to be.

I turned twenty-one. It was then that I applied to the Police Department. We know what happened after that.

Very wise decision on my part, right?

2

OFFICER BEMBENEK

Around my twenty-first birthday, I came across a notice in the newspaper that indicated special applications were being solicited for the Milwaukee Police Department. In order to meet federal requirements, women and minorities were being urged to apply. Eagerly I made the trip downtown once again.

■　■　■

Oh God, why was I there? Why didn't the ghosts of the future frighten me off? Why didn't I flee? I would have, should have, if I'd only known ... I'd listened to my dad talking about the cops, telling stories—none of the bad stuff, of course, only the romantic stories. Why didn't I shut my ears?

My dad wasn't a cop for very long, really. Now he says he hated it, hated the corruption and the special pleading and the double-dealing. Maybe he thought it would be different for me ...

By trade he's a carpenter, and an excellent one; he's a big man with big carpenter's hands. I worked alongside him sometimes, and he told me I could have been a carpenter, too. I was good with wood. I'm no cabinet maker, but I'm not shabby either.

I could have been a carpenter, and not a cop. I could have been a carpenter, and not a convict.

But I've been inside ten years now, ten years of watching the branches, the green wood, through small windows, past bars, the green wood against the open sky.

And I know that might-have-beens are a trap for the unwary.

■　■　■

I was scheduled for a short interview with a sergeant at the station in my district. Dressed casually in jeans and a T-shirt, I parked my car and entered the building. I hadn't been there for years.

I sat down on a hard bench and overheard the boisterous cops behind the desk, arguing over who should pick up the fish-fries for supper that night. One of them noticed me and smiled.

"Don't tell me you're waiting for an interview? You mean a pretty little thing like you wants to be a big, bad policeman?"

"Police *officer*," I corrected him. Off to a good start.

Another cop sneered. "Hey! Assign her to my squad! I'll teach her a few things!" An outburst of guffaws followed. These are the kinds of remarks all women grow accustomed to.

To my relief, the sergeant then called me into his small, stuffy office. He was a polite, middle-aged man, the buttons bulging on his blue uniform shirt. He explained that character references would be required and then a background investigation would follow.

A few months went by and I was notified by mail that I was eligible to take a written exam. At the exam, I tried to analyze every question to establish what exactly it was they were looking for. My answers must've been acceptable because I was notified after several months that I'd passed.

A physical agility test was next. It included tests of speed and strength. I read the list of events and it didn't appear to be too difficult, with the exception of a test to scale a six-foot wall.

I searched the city for a similar wall to practice on. I thought a schoolyard or an institution of some sort might suffice, but cyclone fences weren't the same.

The night before the test I couldn't sleep. I kept thinking about that crazy wall as I tossed and turned. As the gray light of dawn began to filter in through my windows, I abandoned the effort to sleep and wearily rose from my bed. My parents were already awake, rinsing out the coffeepot at the kitchen sink and plugging in the toaster. I dressed quickly, saying a silent prayer before leaving the house for the Police Academy where the test was to be held.

"I promise to go to church every Sunday from now on if only I pass ..."

I ran dashes and long distances. I hung in a chin-up position until my eyeballs bulged, and then I had to drag a 150-pound dummy a certain number of feet in under ten seconds. The grip-strength of my hands was tested on a meter. The wall was the last event.

As I stood in line with the other contestants, a young woman behind me began chatting about her progress that day. She was worried about passing. I confessed my fear of the wall. It was a relief to know that I wasn't the only one harboring an insecurity or two. The young woman said her name was Judy.

I drove home happily. I'd passed every test, even going over the wall like a squirrel. I was certain the hardest part was over.

Another month passed. I received notice of a medical exam. All female applicants had to have a pelvic exam. I grimaced at the thought of it.

The next thing I knew, I was standing in a line with a cup of freshly-peed urine, clad in a drafty, white paper sheet, feeling like I had just joined the army. The examining doctor asked me if I was on birth-control pills. Was it any of his business? I answered the question anyway. Later, I realized that the question would indicate whether or not a woman was sexually active—yet there was no similar indicating question for men. I knew the Police Department had in the past dismissed its officers for "sexual conduct outside the sanctity of marriage," and also for "cohabitation." Such things were technically illegal in Wisconsin in 1979 even though no one was ever arrested for "living together."

A few months elapsed, and then I was granted an oral examination before the Fire and Police Commissioners. They presented hypothetical examples, rating each answer I gave.

They asked me why I wanted to become a police officer. Tough question to answer without sounding naive or insincere. I tried to answer honestly. Nervously, I looked at each Commission member for some sign of reaction, but they simply continued silently to write their evaluations.

The last situation described to me was this:

"You are in a squad and you're the senior officer. You get dispatched to a 'man with a gun' call. When you arrive, the scene is a three-story apartment building, and a crowd of people block the entranceway. A woman runs up to your squad and identifies herself as the sister of the man inside with the gun. She informs you that he has himself locked in, has turned on all the gas inside the apartment, has a shotgun and refuses to come out. She adds that he is also presently under psychiatric care. What do you do?"

I thought I managed to answer this complicated question logically, while the Commission members returned my stare, expressionless. I suggested calling for other squads, clearing the crowd away from the entrance, contacting the man's doctor if possible and turning off the gas in the apartment.

"What if every step you took failed?" they countered. "What

would you do if the man still refused to come out?"

"Then we'd just have to go in," I replied, and then thought, "Oh no!"

The Commission thanked me for my time. Later, I found out that I had scored very high, despite my doubts, placing sixth. I was excited. It was now only a matter of time before I got my appointment date to the Police Academy. My last small exam was straightforward, vision testing and a test for color-blindness.

Almost a year had passed since I'd filled out the application.

I had to sit back and wait. Patience was never one of my virtues, and as time went by I grew restless. I was losing interest in my work at Boston Store. I didn't resign, though, because I was entitled to vacation time, and I'd decided to try to synchronize this time off with Danny's spring break from school.

We were having problems. He seemed to be distancing himself from me. We couldn't seem to make it through an evening without a heated argument. He'd been unenthusiastic about my career plans, to say the least. He merely shrugged when I talked about the Academy. Were we just a habit now? But we were in love, we believed. We'd been dating for four years. I loved him, and I thought that if we could just be alone for a while we could save what had meant so much to both of us for so long. We talked about going away together for a week or two.

It wasn't to be. Just after confirming our vacation plans, I was notified of my appointment date at the Milwaukee Police Academy: March 10, 1980.

Danny and I had just returned from a ski trip. I went in the back door of my house, wet skis under my arm, and my dad met me. He had the envelope from the city. He'd been so eager for the news that he'd already opened it. I read the letter and showed it to Danny, smiling and happy.

"March 10?" he exclaimed suddenly. "Laurie! That's right on top of our vacation!"

We argued for a while, fruitlessly, but then he left, slamming the door behind him.

It had taken me so long to get this appointment! I'd worked hard for it. I wanted this career. Why couldn't he understand? Maybe, I thought optimistically, we could squeeze in a vacation before my starting date. I could quit my job earlier than I had planned.

I'd just finished putting away my boots, goggles and ski poles in the hallway closet when the phone in the kitchen rang. It was Danny.

We argued some more, but he refused to compromise. It was impossible for him to get away from school and his part-time job any other time, he said. "Now we face a cancellation penalty from the travel agency."

Half an hour later he called me back to announce that he had a replacement to go with him on our special vacation—a buddy from his neighborhood.

That seemed to be that. He had chosen to precipitate a break.

■　　■　　■

Still, I had three weeks before starting at the Academy and had paid vacation time from Boston Store. I really wanted to go somewhere. I knew it would be another year before I could get away again.

I was at the Police Administration building downtown for some last-minute errand when I ran into Judy Zess, the woman who'd worried so about passing her physical agility tests. We were both quitting our jobs early. I told her I was planning to take a vacation before starting at the Academy.

"I'd like to go on a vacation too. Someplace warm! After this it's going to be a lot of hard work. Did you say you had reservations somewhere?"

"Yeah. I managed to book a hotel in Miami at the last minute—a few days ago. Getting the flight was harder."

"Are you going alone?"

"I guess I am."

"If I could get a flight I could join you in Miami! That is, if you'd like some company. We'd have fun."

"Sounds like a good idea," I said.

A week later I flew down to Florida, and Judy met me there. The weather was a little cool but we still had a pleasant time. Judy's intelligence and frankness impressed me. She spoke French fluently and told me that she'd studied in Switzerland as a foreign exchange student.

Aren't first impressions wonderful? Two years later this woman would testify against me.

There was one odd incident during our vacation, though I didn't pay it much attention at the time. A man staying at our hotel had been meeting Judy for drinks and sitting with her at the pool. He told me Judy had said she was obsessed with the desire to sleep with me. I was shocked. I laughed it off. She must have been joking. I felt it was too absurd to repeat to Judy, so I didn't confront her.

■   ■   ■

Fun ended at the Milwaukee Police Academy doors. I hadn't expected such a military atmosphere. Marine Corps Basic Training couldn't hold a candle to the twenty-one weeks of grueling misery that the Academy put us through. I felt as though the intention was to drain the recruit of identity, of anything that contributed to individualism or personality. We were blue machines, carbon copies of one another. We were programmed into a blind obedience—a selfless dedication.

The Department rules and regulations were originally written for men, since at that time there were no women police officers. At the Academy, unwritten rules for female recruits were arbitrarily introduced and arbitrarily enforced. No make-up, fingernail polish or long hair allowed. It's difficult to ignore years of socialization, so I felt almost naked without all of those things at first. For both men and women, hair could not touch the shirt collar and sideburns had to be cut to reach mid-ear. Hair on the sides could not cover the ears. Inspection every morning allowed our commanding officers to make sure we all appeared perfect. The black shoes we wore had to be shined, our navy-blue uniforms lint-free and our brass buckles polished.

In addition to having our appearance scrutinized at inspection, our memories were tested. We had to memorize the Daily Bulletin, which listed all the crimes that had occurred in the city the previous day, all the felonies, misdemeanors, missing persons and stolen cars. We learned descriptions, the names of victims, the license numbers of cars. It was demanding and at times ridiculous. There were no excuses or exceptions. Our jobs were on the line.

We had strenuous physical training daily, including running, weight lifting, calisthenics, volleyball and self-defense. I threw myself into this because I enjoyed it immensely. I did well. I found myself alongside some of the best guys in the class when it came to running and weight lifting. It was competitive and challenging, and I think some of the male recruits enjoyed competing with me. We were a class of fifty-five, nine of us women.

We studied subjects like Accident Scene Procedure and Report Writing. Our classes included Traffic Law, Criminal Investigation, Search and Seizure Law, Defensive Driving and a course in the Rules and Regulations of the Department. We used shotguns and handguns. We were certified in first aid and Cardio-Pulmonary Resuscitation.

Camaraderie developed. Nicknames emerged. "Bambi" made her appearance.

At noon every day there was a movie—a different lesson each day, different crime scenes and situations. I suffered through an emergency childbirth film—a huge close-up on an eight-by-nine-foot screen, of an explosion birth. The vulva tore.

"Jesus! You could drive a truck through that thing!" laughed one of the male recruits. Typical subtle humor.

I almost made it through the movie, my disinclination to bear children completely reinforced by this time. I cringed at every labor pain. Then the placenta emerged, and I was out the classroom door. When I returned, white-faced, the men teased me about leaving.

"You missed the best part of the film! They showed us how you can use your shoelace to disconnect the umbilical cord by tying a knot around it," a recruit informed me, grinning.

"What?"

"Suppose a lady decides to give birth on a street corner or in an elevator and you don't have your first-aid kit?"

"I'll tell you what I'm going to do," another recruit assured him. "I'm going to take off my shoelace, tie that lady's knees together and go Red Lights 'n Siren to the hospital where she belongs!"

"Thank God cops don't have ambulance duty anymore," I said. Milwaukee had abolished that practice several years before.

The female officers got back at the men a few days later. The noon movie was called *The Mansfield, Ohio Exposé*. A public washroom in Mansfield was the target. To the dismay and embarrassment of the male recruits, we viewed acts of oral and anal sex between men who frequented this restroom. There was a great deal of hand stimulation and hilarious defiances of gravity. The men arrested included married teachers, lawyers, family men and one well-known athlete. The female recruits had a good snicker at the roomful of red-faced men at the end of the movie.

I had another problem with the film, though. It was intended to reinforce the Police Academy's disapproval of a recent bill challenging state law on sex between consenting adults. Like the archaic "illegal cohabitation" standards, there was still a "fornication" law on the state books. The Mansfield film served as a statement from our superiors that legalizing any sex between consenting adults would encourage homosexuals, lesbians and child-molesters—all that they considered "deviant."

During one class, an instructor known for his lurid vocabulary lectured us on street language. His name was Blackburn.

"Now," he began, "assuming that probably all of you officers come from good, God-fearing homes, and that you are all intelligent, educated people, you'll find out when you get out on the street that there are a lot of seedy individuals. You'll have to get used to the language they use, because they'll use it to shock you—to get you to lose your temper. Don't give anyone the satisfaction of knowing that they pissed you off."

He walked around the room. "Especially you female officers! You'll have to resign yourself to being an unusual sight for most people. The public is used to seeing the neighborhood policeman. You might face a bit more harassment on the street."

I watched him pace back and forth. "I'm not saying you have to take whatever anyone dishes out. If abusive swearing disturbs other people, then you can make an arrest for disorderly conduct. But if their comments are not made in front of other people, you have no right to arrest them. They can say anything they want to you. If you lose your temper and a fight starts over something they said to you, you won't have a leg to stand on in court. It will be an open-and-shut case of police brutality."

He stopped in front of a female recruit. "For instance—say two fellas come up to you while you're walking your beat and say: Well! What do we have here? A pussy cop!"

She blushed, but he continued.

"Hey! Why are you carrying around that night-stick? Can't you find a man?"

Her name was Linda Palese. She turned three shades of red and everyone in the class laughed. Then he turned and looked at me. I stopped laughing.

"Bembenek! Is your mother still hooking?"

"Just on weekends, sir," I replied, playing his game.

It was an exercise in self-control, of course, to illustrate what can happen on the street. I understood what he was trying to get across. Blackburn was an excellent instructor, a twenty-two-year veteran of the department. His experience was valuable, his war stories humorous and his intentions basically good.

Palese never came back after that. Maybe she just realized that she didn't like the job.

Blackburn was always looking over my shoulder, always scrutinizing my work, appearance and attitude. He especially liked to catch me in a transgression and make me file what we called a "Matter of " report—a standard disciplinary device. I recognized this immediately, so purposely kept on my toes when he was around.

In April we received our four-week evaluations. I got good marks from all the sergeants and instructors but was told that they were particularly impressed with my physical performance on the track and in the gym. There were only three men who ran faster than me.

After our evaluation, a heavyset guy by the name of Duthie was gone. No one in the class knew if he was dismissed or if he resigned. It put a scare into a few of us.

Meanwhile, Blackburn continued to catch me doing chin-ups on doorjambs in the hallways and threw reports back at me that were written in blue ink instead of the required black ink. He saw even the smallest mistakes, and never failed to come down hard on me for them.

After some weeks, when he'd summoned me to his office for more correction, he sat back in his chair looking at me. I returned the gaze.

"Off the record, Bembenek—you know I've been picking on you to a certain extent."

"Have you sir?" I asked innocently.

"Yes. I think we're on the same wavelength. I was testing you to see what kind of stuff you're made of. I thought I might be able to get your goat, make you lose your temper, your self-control ... perhaps even make you cry. But you're doing all right, Bembenek. You'll be okay."

About a week later, another female recruit officer resigned. Her name was Janet Shadewald. I liked her and thought she was going to make a good cop. Again, no one knew what happened. I passed her in the hallway one morning and could see she had been crying. She was in civilian clothes and was carrying the contents of her locker. I wondered if she was dismissed or if she had resigned.

At home, I was preoccupied with studying and memorizing Miranda, the Carroll Rule, the Plain View Doctrine, the basic circumstances of a legal search, the Fourth Amendment and many other lessons. I had exams coming out of my ears, along with memorizing the Daily Bulletin, the hot car sheet and cancellations of items when suspects were apprehended. I had to ask my mom to help me wash and iron my uniforms because I was beyond help in that department. "What I need is a wife!" I thought cynically.

In the midst of this whirlwind, Danny returned from vacation. He seemed like a different person. I asked him if he'd met another woman while he was away, but he denied it. We argued constantly.

"I hate that dyke haircut," he snapped. "Why do you want that macho job?"

"My hair will grow back. But why do you assume I'm changed? It's only my appearance."

"It's not just that," he insisted. "That job is interfering with us. First it interfered with our vacation and now it's interfering with our social life, because you're always busy studying or too tired to go out. And you've changed. You're swearing too much. It's not ladylike."

Maybe, I thought, I had changed. I wasn't seventeen anymore. Perhaps I'd outgrown him.

"Since when has that mattered? You swear a lot," I said.

"That's different, Laurie. I'm a man."

"You drive me crazy!" I shouted.

Great dialogue, right?

Our fights became more frequent, each one increasing the futility of our efforts to restore harmony. Every time we argued, he would bring up the subject of my job.

So I was forced to choose between the man in my life and a career I wanted.

Mostly what I felt was anger, I had trained on my own for the job for a long time and passed a series of difficult tests. But instead of being proud of me, he was filled with resentment. I wondered if he wasn't jealous because of the high salary I was earning.

I began to examine him through the prism of some of my new attitudes, as well as my older, more feminist attitudes. He seemed so ... outdated. He was hopelessly traditional, conventional, with all the sexist double standards of our time.

He tried to persuade me that a wedding in his church, followed by a marriage with children, was the only life for us. I told him I didn't want to marry, didn't plan to have children, ever, and even if I did eventually marry I'd want to be secure in a career first. I didn't feel it was my obligation to get married in his church, I said, and in any case, I didn't intend to change my name.

Did I love him? If I did, it must have been for physical reasons. We had so many differences, religious and political, and our goals seemed always to conflict. In the end, I just couldn't give up everything that was "me." And so, on a quiet Saturday afternoon, I picked up the phone and we said goodbye.

3

FIRST INTIMATIONS OF TROUBLE

Blackburn continued to single me out. One day he had a lesson in observation to teach the recruits. After his usual class, he walked to the back of the room and ordered everyone to remain seated, facing the front.

"Okay officers!" he shouted. "You've all been staring at a suspect for over an hour now—namely *me*. Officer Bembenek, describe that suspect."

"Shit!" I thought. Facing the front of the room, I stood up quickly and tried to recall what he was wearing. I hadn't paid much attention. But I still had an advantage—my training from the fashion world. I knew that the cheap old goat only owned about three suits. To give myself more time to think, I started with the obvious physical description, starting at the head and going down.

"White male, six feet, two inches and about 170 pounds ... short gray hair, mint-green polyester plaid sports coat ... white shirt and tie, green pants, brown shoes ... and I would say the suspect had to be between fifty-five and fifty-nine years of age," I recited.

"I'll get you for that last one, Bembenek!" he said, and the class laughed. He was only in his forties.

Another time we had an exercise with a film series called *Shoot—Don't Shoot*. It illustrated the minute amounts of time available for decision-making in emergencies. An officer has only a split second to decide whether or not to use his (or her) gun. The film's choice: shoot at a suspect, or not shoot and risk death.

I was told to pick up the imitation handgun and stand before the screen. The film began. The first scene showed a squad answering a family-trouble complaint. I "entered" a yard full of small children. It was very hard to discern movement. There was a sudden, loud **BANG**. A five-year-old kid had a gun that I didn't see, and shot me. The sergeants rewound the film and let the class review it.

"Well, Bembenek—you're dead!" Blackburn declared. "Now,

my question is: would you have pulled out your gun and shot a five-year-old child had you seen the gun in time?"

I was uncertain. "Um. Yes, sir."

"Do you mean to tell me that you would have pulled out a gun and shot a small child?"

"Yes, sir," I answered apprehensively.

"Damn right, officer! Don't sound so unsure of yourself! I don't care if an eighty-five-year-old woman points a gun at you! You don't have time to ask them if they plan on shooting it or not!" He looked at me. "Let's give you the next film to try, Bembenek."

The next situation had me approaching a car stopped for speeding. It was a convertible with the top down, an old woman behind the wheel. As I approached, before I even reached the door, she turned around and—**BANG**! I was shot again. I began to think the situations were downright impossible.

"Watch the hands! Watch the hands!" Blackburn was bellowing. "Officer Bembenek, you don't seem to be doing so well. Shot to death twice today! Why don't we give you one more chance. Let's run the next film and see how you manage this one."

"Damn it!" I thought, rattled. The class was chuckling. I was determined to do well on the next situation.

The film showed a squad car in the area of a bank that had just been robbed. Several people had described the suspect: she was armed and dangerous, a black female, five feet, seven inches. She was wearing a white blouse, yellow skirt and white boots. She was on foot.

The film had me leave my squad. I began walking through a crowded square not far from the bank. A black woman fitting the description was walking straight toward me. When she saw me, she reached into her purse and began to pull something out. Quickly I drew my imitation handgun and—**CLICK**—pulled the trigger to shoot her.

A second later she started to powder her nose with the compact she withdrew from her purse. Everyone laughed.

A replay of the film allowed the class to see that she was wearing a yellow blouse, white skirt and yellow boots—close but not correct. Blackburn explained that the sequence of situations had been intentionally arranged to show how a chain of events can affect observation adversely.

"Every recruit ever tested overreacted the very same way," Blackburn said.

The didactic methods were effective, but I thought they bordered on brainwashing. It took me years to understand the politics behind the ideology being inculcated. We were only presented with one explanation of crime, and we were expected to buy it completely, without question.

Department attitudes towards women were appalling. I tried not to be aggressively feminist when discussing cases of rape, but it was hard—I'd never thought rape was anything to joke about. For several years I'd been a member of various feminist groups: NOW, Women Against Rape, the Women's Political Caucus. I'd contributed money, written letters and marched in protests. I'd even attended a rally against Police Chief Harold Breier for refusing to establish a special sexual-assault unit to replace the hopelessly insensitive, male-dominated Vice Squad. (This was before I joined the force, of course!)

One day in class the subject of a highly publicized sexual assault was brought up. The case involved a young woman who was pressing charges against several members of a local motorcycle gang, the Outlaws. She was the girlfriend of one of the members and had been sleeping with him at the gang's clubhouse one night when the rest of the bikers arrived. Three of the Outlaws repeatedly and viciously raped her.

"It's really a shame the way the law works," was the Sergeant's viewpoint. "Here you've got this broad who's a dancer at some bar—she's got a lousy reputation already but now she's screaming rape. She was sleeping with one of these bums but the way our law works? Even if her choice was Guys One, Two and Three: Yes, but Guys Four, Five and Six: No—she could actually press charges! She could have numbers Four, Five and Six prosecuted!"

Most of the other men in class thought this was funny, but Kocher's attitude outraged me. I couldn't shut up.

I raised my hand. "Sir, there's another way to look at this. Say that there's a man around town who is very rich. Say this man carries a lot of cash on him, which is unwise, and has even been known to flash his money around and give some away to strangers. Knowing all this, would that give you the right to steal from him? No! The same holds true for sexual assault. No one has the right to forcibly take a woman's body."

Kocher raised his eyes and changed the subject. Afterwards he would occasionally comment to me on the progress of certain women's issues. One morning he walked in and smiled. "Did you read the paper this morning, Bembenek? Another one of the states refused to ratify!" He was referring to the Equal Rights Amendment.

"Male-dominated legislature," I simply replied.

A black male officer by the name of Hicks was gone that day. The class was shrinking. There were hushed comments and worried glances.

■   ■   ■

Then I was invited to a party. From where I look now, I can feel that invitation as if it were yesterday, and I want to scream down the years, No! Don't go! Only dire things will happen! But, of course, time is my enemy, and I cannot hear ...

■   ■   ■

It was late April, and the party was given by a recruit called Boville as a housewarming. It had been such a long time since I had been out that I decided to go. I asked Judy if she planned on going, but she hadn't been invited. Later that day, on break, I was talking with a black recruit named Thomas about a new record album. Thomas asked if he could borrow it. I said yes and asked him if he was going to Boville's party. He said he was planning to but didn't know where it was. I offered to drop off the album on my way to the party and give him Boville's address.

"Where are you going to be after work?" I asked him.

Just then the intercom came on and we were called back to class. Over the drone of the speaker, Thomas told me an address. I scribbled numbers onto a notebook cover.

I returned home later that day and my phone rang. A girlfriend was in town for the weekend.

"Can we get together?" she asked. "What are you doing tonight?"

"I've been invited to a party—a guy from work. You can go with me but you won't know anybody."

"That's okay. I'd like to go. Can you pick me up?"

"I have one place to stop first, to drop off an album, but then I can pick you up. Sure."

I changed out of uniform, showered and put on a denim skirt with a striped T-shirt. I found the album and rushed out of the house. The address Thomas gave me was on the North Side of town.

When I arrived, I gave Thomas the record and Boville's address with the nearest intersection listed on the same slip of paper. Another recruit, White, was there. I only stayed a few minutes because I had to pick up my friend.

The party was crowded, hot, blasting with music from the fifties. It wasn't my kind of get-together. I stood in the basement with my Dixie cup of beer, watching someone do "the twist." My friend looked bored. Some of my classmates were there, but we couldn't talk over the loud music. My friend and I decided to leave.

As we stood in line to use the bathroom upstairs, a drunk lurched up to me and announced that she was Officer Tim Klug's wife. With no provocation she began insulting me.

"You work with my husband, don't you? Well! You can't let much more hang out of that T-shirt, can you?" She was swaying badly.

What was this? "Look," I said. "I don't know what your problem is, but why don't you go sit down before you fall down?"

"I saw the way Tim looked at you when you walked in!" she continued. "Why don't you stick that badge of yours up your ass?"

My friend nudged me and whispered, "Let's just go, Laurie."

"I didn't say one goddamn word to your husband tonight, so you got no beef with me," I snapped. I wanted to smack her but I knew better. She was a fellow officer's wife, and I couldn't lose control without hell being raised at work. My friend and I worked our way through the crowd and left by the back door. I needed to cool off.

■　■　■

About a week later, I was summoned to Sergeant Orval Zellmer's office in the Internal Affairs Department. He informed me that I was about to become the subject of a confidential internal investigation. I was confused. For what?

Two sergeants—Zellmer and Figer—read me Rule 29 from the Department regulations. This is the section that deals with untruthfulness. They asked me if I understood it and told me I was being given an order not to discuss what was about to be said with anyone.

I sat with my hat in my lap, nervous and worried. What was going on? This sounded serious. I couldn't begin to imagine what it was all about.

They asked me about my off-duty activities the week before, and Friday evening in particular. I couldn't even remember at first and had to look at a calendar to see that it was the night of Boville's party. I wondered what right they had to ask about my off hours, but they ordered me to answer.

It was either capitulate or lose my job.

I told them about the friend I'd gone with, and supplied her name and address. They asked which recruits had been at the party, and whether they'd been with their wives. What was served to drink? Was marijuana smoked? Did I ever smoke pot?

In the middle of the questioning I suddenly remembered I'd forgotten to tell them about stopping off at Thomas's on the way to the party. But if I brought that up, it would only complicate matters further. It didn't seem important anyway.

They asked a few questions a second and third time, pushing for discrepancies. I was then informed that they were going to search my locker. They escorted me to the women's locker room and poked through my belongings—my purse, my lunch bag and my jacket.

When we got back to the sergeants' office they told me to "Matter of" everything I'd told them. Several hours had passed.

Finally, Zellmer told me that someone had made an anonymous complaint, saying that I was at Boville's party with my badge pinned to my shirt, smoking a joint. The caller said I'd declared that I couldn't be busted because I was a cop. Zellmer said that the description given by the caller was correct—they'd described my red-and-white striped T-shirt and blue jean skirt. That was it—the whole evidence. On that, Zellmer had acted. I couldn't believe it. It was ridiculous. Why would anyone say such a thing, and how could the Department give so much weight to an anonymous complaint?

I repeated what I'd already said: the only disagreeable incident during my short stay at the party had been the one with Klug's wife.

After I was released to return to class, the sergeants called down a few more officers, announcing their names over the intercom. I regretted having told them who was at the party, but no one had done anything wrong. I was sure Zellmer wouldn't find any inconsistencies in our reports, since the truth was the truth. I was sorry I'd bothered to go to that party—it wasn't worth the trouble.

The others were curious to know what I'd been doing in the office all that time, and they began to worry and talk about me among themselves. I got the impression that some thought I was snitching on them—about Lord knows what. A recruit approached me during break and told me that Judy had been saying I was no longer her friend because I couldn't be trusted. I wanted to confront her, but I was prevented from telling anyone what had taken place in Zellmer's office because of the gag order I was given.

A few weeks went by. Judy and a group of her friends had tickets to see Rufus and Chaka Khan at the Milwaukee Auditorium. "The tickets are only seven dollars," Judy told me. "Do you want to go with us?"

"Okay. Are we meeting at your house?"

"We're going out for some Mexican food first. I'm going to change at my boyfriend's house, so I'll call you before I leave."

I met Judy and her friends Norm and Jan at a restaurant for drinks and guacamole. After about the third margarita we left.

Our seats at the concert were terrible; we could barely see the stage. Judy and Jan left to look for better seats. When they returned, they suggested we move to a different section. It was a wild concert, with crowds of people in the aisles dancing and drinking and smoking.

We had just sat down in our new seats when I left to use the bathroom. Norm wanted to get more beer so we left together. He got in line for refreshments as I departed to find the women's room. The drinks had made me a little fuzzy.

The line in the washroom was unbearably long. When I walked past the beer stand later Norm had already gone. I hoped I'd be able to find our new seats.

I strained to see over the people. The smoke was thick and the music very loud. To my surprise, I saw a man standing behind Judy, gripping her in a headlock. At first I thought it was a friend of hers, joking. Then another man appeared and they dragged Judy and Jan out of their seats and down the row. I struggled to get through the crowd, trying to see in the dimly lit auditorium. Near the doorway I saw one of the men take Jan's purse away from her. He pulled out what looked like a small bag and I thought I heard him shout, "You two are under arrest!" but the music was so loud I couldn't be sure.

I sobered up and turned to look back at the seats to see if Norm was there. He was. He appeared to have fallen asleep. I squirmed between bodies to get back to our seats, calling frantically, "Norm! Some guys just took Judy and Jan away—I think they were cops."

Norm started. "What do you mean ...?"

"Well, they were dressed in plain clothes, but I heard them say that Judy and Jan were under arrest—I think. We've got to find them to see what happened."

Norm agreed, but by the time we got back out into the main hallway, Jan and Judy were gone. Searching seemed futile in a crowd that size. Not knowing what else to do, Norm drove me back to my car, which was parked at the restaurant. We both drove home.

I let myself into my house, crept upstairs and got into bed. The phone rang. It was Norm.

"I tried calling downtown to find out where that dingbat and her girlfriend are but I guess they've already been booked."

"For what?"

"Possession, I think," Norm said. "That stupid Jan had a nickel bag in her purse."

"Oh God," I groaned, hanging up the phone. I was sorry I'd gone. My mother had tried to talk me out of it earlier. Shouldn't I reconsider? I was a police officer now and I should be more careful. I just laughed and told her she was being overprotective. What could happen at a concert? I was so naive.

The following day I drove to the Academy with the reluctance of a grade school student approaching the principal's office. Even before roll call I was summoned to Zellmer's interrogation room. The same procedure followed—I was read Rule 29 and the questioning began. It lasted hours this time. They wanted to know every move I'd made before, during and after that concert.

I felt like a criminal—or worse—kept in that tiny office and ordered to repeat my story over and over. The lunch hour came; I was escorted into another room and locked in.

When the sergeants returned, I had to write a "Matter of" report. Zellmer brought up all kinds of irrelevant issues, like my trip to Florida with Judy. Afterwards, I was again ordered not to discuss the interrogation with anyone.

Finally, toward the end of the day, the sergeants allowed me to return to the classroom. To my surprise, everyone knew of Judy's arrest. A couple of veteran officers had in-service classes at the Academy that day and had gossiped to the recruits at lunch. I worried that my superiors would blame me for blabbing. As it was, everyone played "twenty questions" with me, and I had to avoid them as much as I could.

After work that night I headed to the airport. I'd been invited to a friend's wedding in New York. I sat back on the plane and ordered a double Scotch. As we left the ground and Milwaukee disappeared out of view, all I could think of was losing my job. It looked so bad—first that stupid anonymous complaint, and now this!

"God! Any normal person would think I'm crazy to want this insane job," I thought. "I can't even have a private life. Wait till I get back—they'll probably have my dismissal papers all ready for me. And where the hell is Judy? Still in jail? What did she say to them to make them come down on me so hard?"

The weekend in New York was miserable. My friends were concerned. They felt I had changed. They couldn't understand how a job could mean that much to anybody.

On Monday, when I returned, matters proceeded exactly as I had expected. I was summoned to Zellmer's office and the interrogation resumed.

The sergeant asked if I had had contact with anyone over the weekend—namely Judy. They seemed almost disappointed when I explained that I had been in New York. I was ordered to write a report on my trip. I sat there wishing it would all end.

Then an odd issue was raised. Officer Thomas—did I ever smoke pot with him or stay at his house? No, and no, I said. I couldn't understand what they were accusing us of. They ordered me to add more statements to the report I'd just written, standing over my shoulder to make sure I worded everything to their liking.

Everything was being blown out of proportion. They acted as if this was a grand jury investigation.

The next day I was sent to the Captain's office. I was ordered to give a verbatim statement, which was recorded by a stenographer. Everything, the whole story, over and over ... Boville's party ... the concert with Judy Zess.

The Captain asked me if I was aware that, at that very moment, Paul Will, Jr. from the Vice Squad downtown was at the DA's office trying to obtain a warrant for my arrest. I answered no—how would I know that? And for what? I couldn't tell if they were trying to bluff— it sounded so crazy—or if they were really going to charge me with something.

I was too young and inexperienced to know that as soon as criminal charges were threatened I had the right to demand representation. I could have refused to cooperate, under the protection of the Fifth Amendment. But how would I know? I was totally baffled by the whole thing. Criminal charges? What criminal charges? My job was on the line and I was scared, so I cooperated. I thought that if I didn't, it would have looked like I had something to hide.

It was a busy week for Zellmer. Recruit officers were continually being called down to his office—the majority of them female and/or black. I found out that, while I was in New York, Thomas had had a party at his house that was now under investigation. I was glad I'd been out of town or Zellmer probably would have tried to connect me with that in some way, too. I kept my airline ticket stub as proof of my trip.

That night I was surprised to see Judy Zess's photo in the news-paper, along with an article about her efforts to get her marijuana case reopened. She wanted to withdraw her plea. She said she'd been denied an attorney and had been forced to plead guilty.

4

FIRED!

I went downtown to the Milwaukee Police Association office, hoping the union attorneys could answer some of my questions. I didn't know where else to turn. They were glad to talk to me but told me that they really couldn't do anything until my superiors took some sort of action—like dismissal or suspension. Newly graduated officers were officially on probation and had no appeal rights for a whole year.

The other problem was timing. For eight years they'd been working on a Bill of Rights for police officers. It would include the right to representation before interrogation by commanding officers, the right to remain silent until represented and the right to know the nature of the investigation before interrogation—all things I could have used right then. The governor was about to endorse the bill, then it had to be signed into the state journal. It would be in effect in about a week. A week too late for me.

I got the impression that the union was rather ineffectual. They seemed more interested in Department gossip than anything else. Someone at the union office passed on a rumor they'd heard about Boville's party. Naturally, by the time the story got to them it was even wilder than the original hearsay. They were told that a female recruit had been caught walking around the party with nothing on but her bikini underpants—with her badge pinned to them!

The union officials asked me to keep them informed and wait for the Department to make its move. The president added that as soon as he could give me the actual date on which the bill would be signed, he'd tell the union attorney, Ken Murray, to give me a call. He advised me to call in sick until the bill was passed to avoid further interrogations.

"I can't wait for that bill to be passed," Tom Barth, the union president, said.

"Did you ever imagine that cops would have fewer rights than criminals? Keep your chin up—maybe Breier's witch-hunts will cease."

When I returned home, I received a call from Judy. "Judy!" I exclaimed. "I've been trying to get hold of you for days! Where the hell have you been?"

"I've been staying at Bill's until things around my house cool down. Was my dad pissed!"

"I saw the article in the paper. Jesus, have they been giving it to me at work! I've been going nuts. What on earth happened with you?"

"Those assholes," Judy said. "They're trying to get away with charging me on a possession case. Can you believe it?"

"But I don't understand," I said. "You didn't have any pot with you that night?"

"Well ... Jan and I were smoking a joint, but I threw the roach down and they recovered it. They picked up a soda cup from under my chair and used that. There was a roach in the cup. Do you want to hear the ridiculous amount they recovered?"

I said nothing.

"Point zero six of a gram of marijuana! It was just a little tiny butt! My lawyer thinks the whole thing is ludicrous. Especially since the pot wasn't in my possession! They're only supposed to charge people who are in possession. Jan, the dummy, was the one with the dope in her purse."

"Why have they been hassling me at work? Zellmer has been working me over like a homicide suspect!"

"Laurie, I didn't even tell them you were with us that night. Jan might have said something, but she doesn't know your full name. I just told them we were with Norm."

"Then I don't understand their hot pursuit."

"They probably think we were all in on it. You know how they are! Their rules say that even if you're *aware* of a violation, you're just as guilty as the violator."

She was right. Had I simply been aware of the marijuana in Jan's purse, that would have been sufficient grounds for dismissal.

Since I hadn't heard from the union, I went to work the following day as usual, only to be called to the offices again. I was almost getting used to it. This time I was informed we were going to the Deputy Inspector's desk. He was higher in rank than the Captain. I half expected to see the Chief of Police himself sitting there.

The Deputy Inspector hit me with both barrels. "Officer Bembenek," he said, "I've reviewed the reports from your sergeants concerning several different instances, and I'll tell you right now, I'm making my recommendations to the Chief to have you dismissed. You have no integrity or moral responsibility! You don't even have the decency to admit when you've done something horrendously wrong! You obviously think we are playing games here. Well, Officer, we are not playing games."

He stared at me. I sat in front of him, not allowed to say anything. I felt two inches tall. I wanted so badly to say, "No! No! You're wrong!"

He continued. "What we're basically doing here is giving you the option to resign. It would look a great deal better on your employment record to resign rather than to be dismissed by this Department. So you think it over. You really have no choice. You don't deserve to wear the honored badge of this Department! You are nothing but a liar! You were at that party walking about with a marijuana cigarette, wearing your badge on your dress! You've smoked marijuana with members of this class and lied about it when we have affidavits to prove it! You don't have much more time on this Department, Officer Bembenek. I suggest that you simply resign."

I looked at his fat, round, expressionless face. I felt defeated and helpless. The room was silent.

"Respectfully request permission to speak, sir," I asked meekly, trying to establish a courageous facade.

The Inspector nodded.

"I can't imagine what instances you are referring to. I attended a party at a fellow recruit officer's home—but, sir, you've got to believe me! You can ask anyone who was there! I did no such thing! It's got to be a m-m-mistake," I stammered. "All I can tell you is that all my life I've only wanted one thing, and that is to be a police officer. My father was a police officer. I would never do anything as foolish as what you've accused me of. You've got to believe me!"

The Inspector said nothing, just hoisted his plump body up from the chair and announced, "Dismissed."

I stood, returned the salute and left, with the sergeants on my heels like two Dobermans. It was useless.

On my way back to the classroom, Sergeant Zellmer cornered me. I was as tall as he. He scowled and said, "Bembenek, you really had us fooled. You say your father was a police officer? I suggest you tell him what you did and ask him how we adjudicate matters on this Department! I'm satisfied that it will be taken care of in a matter of days. Think seriously about resigning."

Two days passed without another interrogation, but I still jumped whenever the intercom came on. Other recruits were being questioned, and there was still trouble brewing. We were all too scared to talk to each other in the relaxed, friendly way we used to. No one trusted anyone.

I wondered why Boville wasn't in any trouble—it was his party and his house! But then Boville was a white male, just what the Chief of Police wanted for his Department.

I made up my mind not to resign. I wasn't going to give in to those bastards when I hadn't done a damn thing wrong. They would have to take my job away from me.

My marksman scores on the firing range, previously very good, went to hell. Even my performance in the gym reflected my depression.

I called the union and was told that the police officers' Bill of Rights would be in force in three days. I told Murray about the rest of the confrontations that had occurred. He again suggested I call in sick, so I did, for the next three days.

Some time went by with no mention of the investigation. I thought optimistically that since the information on which the accusations against me were based was erroneous, I'd not be dismissed. Some of the tension lifted and the recruits became friendly and talkative again.

My evaluations went from bad to worse, though. It angered me, because some of them bore no relation to my performance. I knew I was being victimized. For example, I'd made a point of trying to raise my hand in class and participate more than before. But the comment in the "Willingness to participate in classroom discussions" section was "Poor."

After some time, I regained some of my fight. One afternoon, we were shown a slide presentation with pictures of the Police Department administration in living color.

I raised my hand.

Sergeant Kocher nodded in my direction. "Officer Bembenek?"

"Sir, why aren't there any women within the administration? I don't see a female above the rank of patrol officer. Not even a sergeant."

"No female officers have been members of the Department long enough," he answered.

That's an understatement! I thought bitterly, but I kept the thought to myself. I wondered why the female cops didn't organize a separate support group, since the black officers could rely on the NAACP or The League of Martin.

Graduation was drawing near and field training assignments

were listed. Field training allowed a recruit to work on the street with a seasoned officer prior to graduation. Each recruit was assigned a Field Training Officer, or FTO, who would submit an evaluation afterwards. Field training lasted three weeks—one week on third shift, referred to as "late," and two weeks on second shift, referred to as "early." It was now July.

I was assigned to District Number Five, which included an all-black neighborhood and some of Milwaukee's East Side, extending to the lakefront. My FTO was Rosario Collura. His squad partner was Michael Jourdan.

Crossing my fingers, I reported for my first day of field training. There was so much to learn. Collura told me to drive the squad car and be on the lookout for any traffic violations. I was apprehensive, because at the Academy they hadn't taught us how to use the squad radios or the walkie-talkie. I bit my lip and hoped I'd get through it correctly. To add to my problems, I was unfamiliar with the district, let alone our assigned squad area in the ghetto.

After driving around for about half an hour, Collura began to tell me where to turn and which streets to take. We ended up in an alley. He turned to me.

"Stop the car. Okay, Bembenek—what's your 10-20?"

He was asking me what my location was in police code. I knew how important location was; they always stressed it at the Academy. If you didn't know where you were, you couldn't call for help. After making all those turns in such an unfamiliar area, I could do nothing but guess. Fortunately, I was correct.

I soon learned that I was training in a very busy district. On my first day we were sent to numerous shootings, armed robberies and other serious crimes that never made the news.

"Take the shotgun and cover me!" Collura told me as we pulled up in front of a house where an armed man had been arguing heatedly with his wife. The shotgun was in a zippered pouch attached to the back of the front seat.

I took a position behind a tree at the front yard opposite Jourdan. Collura went in and arrested the man. No shots were fired.

Half an hour later we responded to an armed robbery of a store. The owner had shot one of the robbers and we chased the wounded man down an alley, following a trail of blood. A car picked up the wounded suspect and tried to make a run for it, but they were apprehended by another squad that blocked the end of the alley.

When we weren't busy, Collura and Jourdan had their fun. I was instructed to write all the reports after each incident. The forms had to be filled out in duplicate with carbon paper, so if a mistake was made, the whole thing had to be redone. I'd be writing an Offense Report or an Accident Supplementary Report in the booking room and Collura would come flying past, saying, "You're not done yet? Finish it at home—we got another hitch. Let's **GO**!" I'd jump up and fly out after him, papers scattering.

Usually I got home from "early" shift well past midnight. I'd sit up until two or three at the kitchen table, writing reports, updating the hot car sheets and Daily Bulletin cancellations, knowing that I had to appear in court the next morning because Collura was sending me to every case he could think of. Although I was earning a lot of overtime pay, I wasn't getting much sleep.

I didn't know how much more I could take.

Collura's vocabulary was worse than Blackburn's. The vulgar verbal abuse was uncalled for. We were standing roll call when the sergeant ordered us to draw our guns and unload for inspection. As we reloaded, I took a second longer than the veteran officers. In the silence, my gun was the last to click as I snapped the cylinder back into place.

The sergeant was aware of that last, late click. "Was that you Jourdan?" he asked.

"Nope—it was the dumb cunt," Collura said. Snickering followed.

Department rules supposedly made it mandatory to treat fellow officers with respect, especially when in uniform. Apparently this didn't apply to Collura or Jourdan. Once, Collura and I were in a squad, driving through an alley behind the station house, when Collura pulled up next to a civilian.

"Hi, Rosie!" the man said, using Collura's nickname. "I see you have a new partner."

"Yeah," Collura smiled. "I was going to let her drive, but I didn't want the seat to be all wet and sticky!" They laughed.

I was furious, but he was the senior officer, so I said nothing. I told myself he was just trying to get my goat and that I'd only have to work with the creep for another week. When I switched to "late" shift, I'd be assigned another FTO.

My stubbornness only provoked Collura. He sent me into situations I was untrained for just to watch me fall on my face in ignorance.

I understood that field training was a period of rigorous instruction that was supposed to prepare recruits for the worst—it was supposed to be tough. But there's only so much a rookie can be expected to know. Instruction was supposed to be a part of the training. Collura apparently preferred the school of hard knocks.

I was lucky I knew how to change a flat tire because that was Collura's next little trick.

We were sent to a family disturbance. We found a woman throwing her boyfriend out of her house, along with everything she owned that was breakable. The street was littered with broken glass. I was glad I wasn't driving, because as we pulled up a sliver of glass punctured a tire.

We stopped the fight and arrested the woman on a Disorderly Conduct charge. After the wagon pulled away from the scene, my FTO told me to open the trunk of the squad.

"You'll find a broom in there."

"A broom?" I blinked.

"Yeah!" Collura snorted. "I figure you'd look more natural with a broom in your hand! Now sweep up all this glass."

The crowd of people that had gathered outside to watch the fight still stood in the street. Sheepishly, I swept the glass into the gutter.

"That's good, Bembenek!" Collura hollered to me. "Now, you want equal rights? You can change that tire next!"

Gritting my teeth, I took the jack out of the trunk. I wondered if Collura had been talking to Sergeant Kocher.

"That's cold-blooded!" a black woman said to Collura, laughing. "Making a lady change a flat tire."

"Hey! She wants a man's job, let her do a man's job," he said.

Later, I called a few recruits to see if they were as exhausted as I was from field training. To my surprise, they weren't. No other recruits had even been allowed to drive a squad. I had more overtime than anyone I knew. One of my friends said that they'd had a flat tire too, but their FTO had called a Department tow truck team to change it. This made me wonder what was going on.

Finally, toward the end of my hellish two weeks, Collura took me aside.

"Bembenek, I'm putting my ass on the line for telling you this, but you've been a good shit, so I figure I owe ya."

"What?" I asked suspiciously.

"Well ... okay, don't let this get around, but I was ordered to give you a hard time—which I did. The stripes were hoping that you'd just give up and resign. Did some shit come down at the Academy or something?"

"Way back in April, or May," I replied. "I thought it had all blown over."

"Oh." Collura glanced around nervously. "Hey—all I have to say is, you took an awful lot these past two weeks. Good luck, kid."

That was the last time I would ever see Collura. Five years later he would be shot and killed on duty.

The next day, I thought about what he'd said. Why was discipline so different for the women and blacks on the one hand and for the white males on the other? Collura and Jourdan always had wine or beer with their lunch, on duty, despite the fact that it was against Department regulations. They overlooked a lot of marijuana, but Judy was arrested with less than a gram that wasn't even in her possession. They made sexist, vulgar remarks to me in front of sergeants, and nothing was done.

Sergeants Eccher and Dagenhardt (nicknamed Dragonheart by Fifth District officers) handed me a good evaluation report at the end of my field training.

Graduation day arrived, and I participated in the ceremony, with my parents attending. I received a basic certificate from the Department of Justice's Law Enforcement Standards Board, and a certificate of completion from the Milwaukee Police Department's Police Academy.

My permanent assignment was Second District, on the South Side of town. At least I would be familiar with the terrain, and I considered this new assignment a chance to start fresh. Still, I'd heard rumors that the lieutenant on late shift had no use for female officers and didn't even try to hide his prejudice. I was warned to stay out of his way.

It was August, and I felt that I had finally made it through my troubles. Who cared about a single hateful lieutenant when I had survived the worst? Or so I thought at that time.

If the Deputy Inspector really felt I didn't deserve the "honor" of a Milwaukee Police Department badge, he could never have laid eyes on the "Finest" of Second District. What a place! What a force! Many of the cops were brutal, lazy, apathetic and corrupt. Second was a slower district with less crime, except in one poverty-stricken Hispanic area, but the less the cops had to do, the less they cared to do. I saw *hundreds* of rule violations. Squads would park in the cemetery at night after the bars closed and sleep away three or four hours on late shift, or drink in "squad parties." Cops walking a beat were getting free drinks at bars. Some were selling pornographic films from the trunks of their cars, or seeing girlfriends on duty while their wives thought they were at work. They used brutal, unnecessary force on suspects already in handcuffs—in the booking rooms, away from the public eye. They used and sold drugs. They demanded and got blowjobs from prostitutes. They paid their informants with drugs. They released drunk drivers from accident scenes to avoid the overtime it took to process, test and book them. What I didn't observe personally, I heard about, because corruption was common knowledge. Rank made no difference. But obviously sex and race did.

In this environment, the rookie is in a precarious position. If I witnessed a rule violation, as I did, I was just as guilty as the violator if I didn't turn him in. So if I didn't make my Commanding Officer aware of it, in the eyes of the Department I was violating a rule myself. And if I did ... I still had to take orders from these veteran officers. Try calling for backup in a life-threatening situation and have nobody show up!

I wasn't going to be their Serpico.

Then, of course, there's the comradeship between patrol officers, the "us against them" feeling. Collura was the first one to tell me: "Never trust stripes!"

"After all," he had said, "if we don't take care of our own, who will?"

At least Jourdan and Collura worked hard, for all their faults.

Despite everything, I began to enjoy the work, and the advantage of having a permanent assignment. I especially liked to walk my beat alone, a duty that appeared more frequently on my schedule. Then I could be my own boss and didn't have to worry about seeing rule violations or being at the command of some shiftless senior officer. I felt I was adjusting very well to police work.

My friends during this period were mostly from the Academy, working the same late shift I was. My old civilian friends worked "normal" hours, and it was getting harder to relate to them. My new friends were all cops.

An officer I will call Suzy, with whom I'd had drinks once before, called me one afternoon. We had a lot to discuss, since she had field-trained at Second District and was now working at Five, where I had field-trained. We swapped talk about how our work was going, the problems of adjusting to the late shift and of losing contact with old friends.

We started meeting for lunch, and once in a while we'd visit Judy to sit poolside with a bottle of wine. Suzy usually got very drunk, and I began to worry about her. Once she took me aside.

"Listen, I don't mind seeing Judy now and then, Laurie. But believe me, Zess is trouble with a capital T."

I wondered what she meant. Judy was working then as a waitress. She hadn't gotten into any trouble since the concert. If there were any signs I should have recognized at that time, I failed.

Suzy was irritable at times; there seemed to be a great deal of anger inside of her, though at what I couldn't say. She was struggling to raise a daughter, who frequently woke her up during the day as she tried to sleep. I felt sorry for her.

She was dating a man named Steve but told me that she was just using him for his money. Her real love was an old flame, Seymour, who lived in Chicago. She told me she'd lived with him years before her ill-fated marriage. She occasionally drove to Chicago to see him, but it was a strain.

Around this time she mentioned that she'd met and was dating a Department detective, but then she quickly changed the subject, as if mentioning him had been a mistake.

Meanwhile, men had virtually vanished from my life. I didn't want to jeopardize my job again, so I didn't go out with any cops, and I couldn't seem to find the time to date men who weren't cops. This hardly helped my reputation at the Department—I got wind of a rumor that I was a lesbian. After all, I lifted weights!

The rumor was reinforced one night when my squad partner decided to drive past the gay bars in the district to harass the patrons. He enjoyed himself, whistling through the squad loudspeaker microphone, making comments. He spotted two women on the sidewalk, embracing. They were just hugging, but my partner turned the squad spotlight on them.

"Youse could be arrested for that, ya queers!" he yelled.

Blinded by the light and embarrassed, they parted and walked to their own cars.

"Why are you doing this?" I asked finally. "Don't we have more important work to do? They aren't hurting anyone, but plenty of people in this city are, right now."

"They're queer," he sneered. "You wouldn't happen to be a dyke, would you?"

I could tell by the look in his eye and the tone in his voice that I was not going to win this argument, so I dropped the subject after assuring him that, no, I wasn't a "queer," to use his jargon.

■   ■   ■

Summer began to pass by quickly. My parents had a foreign exchange student staying at our house from Japan, but I wasn't home much. On my days off I looked at several condominiums in town that were for rent with an option to buy. My birthday was uneventful. I turned twenty-two.

At the end of August, I called my district station to confirm my work schedule. The Captain picked up the phone to inform me, nonchalantly, casually, that the Chief had sent out an order for my dismissal.

The bomb had finally fallen.

They didn't even have the guts—or the courtesy—to do it to me in person.

They'd got me for—what? For being a woman? For not shutting up and taking their sexist garbage? Because I asked too many questions? How could I know?

I knew it wasn't because I had lied or broken rules—clearly cops weren't being dismissed for that. I knew it wasn't because I'd done anything wrong. I knew it wasn't because I wasn't a good cop. I think I was, or was becoming one. I would have been, if they'd let me stay.

The following morning, a day-shift sergeant came to my house to take away my badge and my gun and other Department property.

I fumbled with a screwdriver, trying to take off my newly bought mahogany grips from my Department thirty-eight caliber Smith and Wesson.

When my dad returned home from work that afternoon, I told him the news and cried in his arms.

5

FRIENDS

So much time had gone by since the party in April and the concert in May that the dismissal came as a terrible shock. The charges that had been filed against me were typed on the dismissal order I was handed: untruthfulness and filing a false official report. The order did not list the details of the charges and I could only guess what they involved. When had I lied? In what official report?

I called Suzy and tearfully told her the news. She, too, was shocked.

"Where are you?" she asked.

"I'm at Judy's. I can't bear to hang out at my house. My parents are too upset. They were counting on me ... "

"Stay where you are. I'll be right over," Suzy said, and in half an hour she was knocking on the door with wine, cheese, soup and beef sandwiches in her arms.

"Have you talked to the union yet?" Suzy asked.

"I've got an appointment with them tomorrow," I said. "What's that called? A 'grievance for reinstatement'?"

Suzy nodded. "What are you going to do for money?"

"That's the worst part—this ruins everything. I can forget my plans to buy a condo. I was supposed to close the deal next week, but now that's shot. I have my pension fund and I could apply for unemployment."

"You're lucky you didn't move out already. Think of what a mess that would have been! If you're interested, I need a babysitter for Aimee. Right now, a cop's wife is watching her at night, but it's a real pain because I have to drop Aimee off and pick her up everyday on the opposite side of town. It's hard to find someone to babysit late shift. She's four years old—she wouldn't be a real problem. At least it would get you out of the house and hold you over financially for a while."

I thought it over. I knew I had little experience with or tolerance for small children, but I guessed it would be better than nothing, so I agreed.

The following day, the union attorneys seemed optimistic when I saw them. First, they wanted to review my files, in order to establish the reasons for my dismissal. It took several letters from the union before the seventy-year-old Chief finally agreed to allow me to review my records.

When I appeared for my appointment at the Police Administration building, it was already September. I walked in to see Thomas, Bonnie Avanti and Pat Lipsey there. They had all been dismissed the same week I had, for various reasons. All three were black.

We sat outside the Chief's office for about three hours while the lawyers, Tom Barth and Ken Murray, were in conference with Breier. After waiting all that time, we were told to go home. The Chief wasn't going to allow us to see our files after all.

Several Second District officers phoned me. They wanted to know the details of my dismissal, and some were concerned about a rumor accusing me of turning in my co-workers for rule violations.

"Why would they say that?" I asked a caller.

"Oh, they always say that about anyone who gets fired. They're all paranoid, that's all—afraid the cop that gets dismissed wants to get even."

By now I was babysitting every night and on weekends for Suzy. She was in bad shape. She drank more than anyone I knew: three or four bottles a week of Jack Daniels. She'd drink late in the day—too late to get up for work—so she'd snort a few lines of cocaine to sober herself up.

I knew myself that late shift was hard to get used to. When I was working, I couldn't have a drink any later than lunchtime if I didn't want to feel groggy and listless on the job that night. I could see how hard it was for a single mother, trying to hold down a job.

Suzy was buying her coke from several different people, but the majority from a guy named Jimmy, who drove a white Corvette and occasionally spent the night with her. She was hooked. Despite her constant complaints about money—she was behind in the rent and ate off paper plates—she still spent a great deal on drugs.

I know I should have disassociated myself from people like Suzy and Judy when it became obvious what they were like, but there were many dumb reasons why I didn't. My firing had disoriented me. I was disillusioned and confused, which made me lonely and desperate for friends—even the wrong kind.

I'd also started drinking too much to be in any real control of my life. I don't know why I turned to alcohol, other than the fact that it was so socially acceptable. It was there, I guess, and everyone else did it. I certainly didn't learn to drink at home, because neither of my parents did. All I knew was that when I drank, life didn't seem so cruel. I could feel better about everything and I could believe everything was okay.

■   ■   ■

Toward the end of September, I was informed that Chief Breier had agreed to let those of us who were dismissed view our files after all. About the same time, my unemployment compensation started to arrive. I also received a subpoena to testify at Judy Zess's jury trial on the possession charge.

Again I returned to the Police Administration building with my union attorney, Ken Murray. He told me to take a notebook and write down anything important, because Breier stipulated that I review my papers alone, without Murray's help.

So I sat in front of a detective, Bob Rivers, who handed me my file, page by page. Page by page, he read it! It took me weeks of union negotiation to persuade the Chief to release my own files to me, and this nosy detective had the nerve to blatantly read through it all right in front of me.

I regretted that Murray wasn't allowed to help me, because the pile of reports seemed meaningless and confusing—until the shocking discovery of a signed statement against me by Judy Zess! She'd specifically included me in her marijuana smoking at the concert that night, though of course she knew it wasn't true. It was like getting a knife in the back. Why did she do it? Was she angry that night because she was getting fired and wanted to drag me down with her? Was it as simple as that? I was shocked and furious.

I stopped off at her apartment to confront her. She was her usual cheerful self, asked me to sit down, and began to tell me about the progress of her appeal.

"Judy," I interrupted. "I was allowed to see my records today. Downtown."

"So?"

"How could you make those statements against me? You told me you didn't even say that I was with you! How could you do that to me?"

Judy never skipped a beat.

"Laurie, you don't understand. I was drunk. They told me that if I didn't write all those things down, and sign it, that they were going to wake up the Chief and take me to see him! Jan mentioned your name, and then I was confused. They kept me there all night! I just ... I just wanted to go home."

"Bullshit," I said angrily. "You tell them that I was smoking with you two assholes, when I wasn't even there?"

"You've got to believe me!" she protested. "Why do you think I appealed the damn thing? They had me under the hot lights practically. I didn't know what I was doing! They dragged me in there—I fell down and ran my nylons. Then they stood over my shoulder and told me what to write. My rights were violated! I told them that I wanted an attorney but they said, 'No! This is an internal matter!'" Judy was pleading with me. "You've got to believe me."

I didn't know what to think.

"Judy, what the hell am I supposed to do at my appeal when they fling your report at the Commission? What am I supposed to say then?"

"I'll go with you. If you need my testimony, I'll tell it just like it was. They were interrogating me all night! I didn't leave until 6:00 AM! I just spent four thousand dollars on a lawyer to take this thing back into court, because it wasn't fair! It wasn't right!"

"I got your subpoena," I said. "Now I'm supposed to testify for you? How did I even get dragged into this whole thing? I didn't see anything anyway!"

"Look, I'll even give you a signed affidavit if you want one," Judy promised. "You've got to believe me."

I sighed.

"What else was in your files?" she asked.

"Oh, they had so much crap in there! All unsubstantiated hearsay. None of it is concrete! Then White gave them some statement about the night I dropped off a record album at Thomas's house. White says he thinks Thomas and I were having an affair, and that's the reason I stopped there! How could he say something like that? Why would he? And how could the Department take it seriously? Since when is it a crime to go to a black person's house?"

"What was in it for White? Why would he give Zellmer a statement?" Judy asked.

"Maybe White's job is hanging by a thread, too, and he thought it would help. He's supposed to be Thomas's friend."

"What did the union say?"

"I'm going to file a grievance, but I don't know what good it will do," I said, "seeing as I was still on probation when they dismissed me." I shrugged. "Seems to me the only people getting pounced on by

Internal Affairs are the women and the blacks. Just look at how many are gone so far, from our class alone. The year isn't even over with yet. I bet there'll be more."

"What did Pat Lipsey get fired for?" Judy asked.

"She doesn't know the specifics. Her charges read 'For the good of the service.' Can you believe that? I saw her downtown today. Thomas was there, too."

"I've got a good idea!" Judy interjected in her usual, erratic manner. "Why don't we drive out to the Playboy Club in Lake Geneva and apply for a job out there? A friend of mine knows one of the managers."

"Nah."

"Why not?" she insisted.

"What's wrong with your job at Sally's?"

"They're cutting my hours. I gotta get a different job. I won't be able to pay the rent pretty soon. Hey—why don't you move in here with me? I'd really like to live with you."

"I can't. The way things are going, I'm lucky I live at home. I got a notice yesterday from the unemployment office—the bastards are appealing my compensation eligibility now! The hearing is next month. If I can't even get unemployment, I won't be able to make my car payments, or anything."

"I thought anyone who gets fired is eligible for unemployment," Judy said.

"No. They said they have to determine that the employee didn't intentionally get fired in order to receive benefits."

"That's nuts!"

"I know. I think the city always appeals these things."

That night, Judy and I sat around at Suzy's house with a few of her friends. I was bored with the card game, so I called another cop friend of mine to see if he wanted to stop over. He agreed to come, but explained that he couldn't stay too late because he had to work that night. I fell asleep on Suzy's couch, watching TV, before he left.

The next day he called me. He sounded different.

"Is something wrong?" I asked him.

"Yeah. Well ... something is bothering me."

"Shoot."

"Laurie, I don't want to really get too involved. You know. With you and Suzy."

"What? What about Suzy?" I persisted.

"You seem to think she's your friend, but I'd be careful with her if I were you. Last night, after you fell asleep on the couch, I stayed for a few hands of cards. Suzy and Judy were laughing and getting super drunk, you know, and then when Suzy walked me out to my car, she was saying some really bad things about you."

"Like what?"

"She started out by asking me if I liked you very much, so I told her we were just friends, and then she was telling me some very vicious gossip about you—the real reason you got fired. It was stupid, sexual talk."

I was appalled.

"I know she was really looped, but that's no excuse. She said she heard it from some detective downtown."

"Why would she repeat that crap? If she only knew what they all say about her!"

"I know. Well, I didn't want to tell you, but I wanted you to know. I'd rather not go there anymore."

"Okay. Sure," I said. I hung up the phone.

I dialed Suzy's number but there was no answer. Then I remembered that she'd told me she planned on going to Chicago for the weekend to see Seymour. She had accumulated a lot more time off than the others from my class because she had been on the city payroll previously, as a metermaid.

A few weeks passed before I saw Suzy so I never did get a chance to talk to her about her indiscretion. I decided it was useless to ask her about something she'd said while intoxicated anyway.

One evening I was playing pool at a tavern and called her to see if she'd meet me there so we could talk. Unsure if she was scheduled to work that night or not, I let the phone ring. I was about to hang up when Suzy answered, sounding drunk and upset. I tried to hear what she was saying over the noise of the crowd in the bar.

"Hello? Suzy? This is Laurie. Are you there?"

She was crying hysterically.

"What's wrong? Are you okay?"

"Fuck it!" she screamed. "Fucking men! They're all the same! Assholes!"

"Suzy—get hold of yourself! What happened?"

"No! No! I was supposed to meet Fritz tonight and I had too much to drink because I lost track of time, so big deal! Big deal! So the fucker left! He didn't even wait for me—and now he just hung up on me!"

Then I heard the phone being thrown across the room.

I had no idea who Suzy was talking about. She'd never mentioned Fritz. I didn't know what she'd do next, so I ran out of the bar, jumped into my Camaro and drove to the other side of town. I kept thinking about the time Suzy came over with soup and cheese and wine, the day I told her I was fired. Now she needed me.

I hoped she wouldn't try anything stupid. She once told me that years ago, after a fight with Seymour, she'd taken an overdose of sleeping pills and had to have her stomach pumped.

When I got to her house, the front door was open. She had passed out on her bed, an empty bottle of Jack Daniels on the floor. Her breathing was regular, her pulse normal.

I looked around the room for any prescription bottles, but there were none. I checked her wall calendar to see if she had to work that night, but saw that "Overtime Off" was scribbled in.

I picked up what was left of the telephone, turned off the house lights and covered Suzy with a blanket. I looked in on Aimee and left, locking up the house.

The following day, Suzy remembered nothing. She wondered aloud what had happened to the telephone. I told her about our conversation, but she simply laughed it off.

"Jesus! Sometimes I get crazy when I'm tanked," was all she said.

That month, Judy again asked me about moving in with her, and I again told her it was impossible. She repeated her idea of applying for a job at the Playboy Club.

I wasn't keen, but I was in rough shape financially, especially since my unemployment compensation was being appealed. My life was a mess. It wasn't always pleasant babysitting for Suzy, and I didn't know how much longer I could stand it. Suzy's erratic drinking, moods and rages were more and more disturbing. She began to expect me to show up, with little notice, when she wanted to take off for a few days with a boyfriend. She went to homecoming weekend at La Crosse, Wisconsin with some man, but refused to tell me who it was. She complained about what a mess the house was, as if I was her housekeeper, too. I grew tired of her irritability.

I just didn't feel like my old self. I was directionless. I was drinking too much, applying for jobs all over town without luck. If I lost the unemployment compensation appeal, I'd be ordered to repay almost two thousand dollars to the city. I had no health insurance, and I had car payments. I didn't know what else to do.

I didn't even know what I looked like anymore. My hair had

started to grow back, but my nails remained short and unpolished, and I almost never wore make-up. I usually dressed in jeans and shirts. I had unconsciously adopted a somewhat androgynous appearance, so different from the sophisticated, "feminine" polish of my modeling days. The whole sex and identity issue disturbed and confused me. Nothing seemed to be working for me.

So, on more or less a whim, I decided to return to traditional work and took a waitressing job at the Playboy Club at Lake Geneva for a month.

■　　■　　■

Biiiig mistake!

I waited on tables and learned to do the bunny dip. I wore that stupid little costume for only four weeks, and I collected money to pay back what they said I owed. And I apparently turned myself forever from Lawrencia Ann Bembenek into Former Playboy Bunny Bembenek. It was a waitressing job. Can we let it go now?

■　　■　　■

I had another blow in mid-October. I got a letter from the police union stating that they intended to drop my case. Although I'd paid my dues, it was just too expensive for them to pursue reinstatement. I had not completed my probationary period. Too bad all the interrogations took place before the police officers' Bill of Rights was passed. Most unfortunate. Too expensive. Too bad.

I felt everyone had given up on me.

My unemployment hearing was next. Ken Murray agreed to represent me there, even though the union had dropped my grievance.

I arrived at City Hall to find about twenty-five cops there—four sergeants, some Vice Squad officers, stenographers and others. I felt very small and alone. Finally, Judy and my attorney arrived.

The hearing took four long hours. All kinds of people testified—including the stenographer who took my verbatim statement—whether their testimony was relevant or not. Vice Officer Paul Will took the oath. He said I was arrested the night of the concert, along with the others, but was released after they'd determined that I was not in possession of marijuana.

"There must be some way to prove that I wasn't arrested!" I whispered to Murray. "Can't Judy testify? I wasn't even apprehended!

Wouldn't there be a clearance or an arrest record on me if I was arrested?!"

"Calm down, Lawrencia," Murray said. "Let me handle it."

When it was over, I was informed that the decision on whether or not to grant me unemployment compensation would be mailed to me at a later date.

Judy's jury trial on the possession charges followed. The trial went on for over three days, and my testimony was delayed over and over again. The witnesses were sequestered, so initially I sat outside the courtroom. Finally, I was called to testify and entered the room. I was amused to see that the young court reporter was my ex-boyfriend's buddy, the guy who'd taken my place on the vacation we had planned.

I answered questions from Judy's lawyer, was briefly cross-examined, and was asked to step down. Watching the Vice officers testify, I noticed that their stories varied a lot from the reports they handed in—varying even further from how they had testified at my unemployment hearing. I wasn't surprised. I knew that police officers are encouraged to testify about what would have been correct procedure, not what really happened. It was a technique that was subtly reinforced at the Academy, where officers were not formally taught to lie, but it was suggested that if they couldn't remember exactly what had occurred, then they should describe what they should have done.

I was to watch this technique again and again. Judy ended up with a hung jury.

6

FRED SCHULTZ

*M*onths passed in a blur. I felt as though I was inside a bottle, looking out: fingers pressed against the glass walls, closed off, closed in, suffocating. I felt oppressed by failure. I clung to the few relationships that I had, because they were all I had. By now I knew who Suzy and Judy were. It's true they were amoral—boozing and screwing around and doing dope. It's easy to say now I should have fled, but I was at a loss. And I was lonely. I was mixed-up, confused, miserable about everything.

My life seemed to be falling apart. I tried to pick up the pieces, to stabilize, but I couldn't. Every time I tried to do something, I took one step forward and three steps back. I tried to get work, another job, any job. It was really demoralizing. I applied everywhere. Nobody would hire me.

I sometimes wonder how different my life would have been had I found a full-time job, made new friends and become engrossed in that ...

I discovered that I'd been blacklisted by the police. I almost got a job working as a security guard in a factory. The guy was impressed with my Police Department experience and hired me. But the day I was to start, the job suddenly didn't exist ... the position was mysteriously filled. It happened so many times. There are jobs, but the jobs suddenly don't exist. No one tells you anything. You get jacked around. It was so frustrating.

The police union abandoned me. The unemployment hearing went against me after the police presented their side to the Commissioners, and I was ordered to pay back the compensation I'd earned. Nothing I did helped or worked. The air was thin, and I was panicking ...

So I thought, Okay, that's it, I'm going to give up trying in Milwaukee. I enlisted in the Air Force. But that effort failed, too ...

■　　■　　■

Judy was working as a sales consultant for a local waterbed store by then. Her bills were accumulating because of her court case, so she told me about a devious scam she had thought of.

"I called all the guys I've been sleeping with," she said. "I told them all I was pregnant and needed an abortion! At two hundred dollars apiece, I raked in about eight hundred dollars!"

"That's really low," I said.

"Oh, don't worry!" she said. "I have to make a living. Besides, one of them was that detective's son—Huey. He's a busboy at Sally's. He was scared that his daddy would find out."

"So what else is new?" I asked, wanting to change the subject.

"Oh—I know what I was going to tell you. The DA decided to drop the charges of possession. With a hung jury, they would have had to re-try the case. That's good news, isn't it? Now it's like you were fired for a non-existent crime!"

"True."

"So what are you going to do now? Look for another job? Or try to get back on the Department? You'd have to reapply and go through all those tests again, and the Academy."

"No. I couldn't do that. I've been working part-time at the gym. I'm considering the Air Force," I said.

"The Air Force? You're crazy!" Judy laughed. "What do you have? A uniform fetish?"

■　　■　　■

It was at this time that I met Elfred Schultz, Fred, Suzy's "Fritz." He was at Suzy's house one night, one of those many nights we'd had too much to drink, and I stayed over in Suzy's spare room, sleeping in my clothes.

The next morning I awoke and walked into the kitchen. Fred was sitting at the kitchen table. I was dying of thirst and poked about in the fridge. My head ached. Suzy was still sleeping.

"God," I groaned, "I wonder how many brain cells I killed last night."

"Probably both of them!" Fred said, laughing in a great bray, an outrageous laugh. I disliked him at once.

"You're going to have to trade that laugh in for a smaller model," I told him. "It's enough to wake the dead." Every word was an effort. I decided I had to get away from this guy and go home, so I gathered up my keys and purse, ready to leave.

He was still sitting on the kitchen table. "Will you go out with me?" he asked.

"Save your breath, Schultz. You'll need it to blow up your inflatable date tonight," I said.

"See?" he persisted, following me out to my car. "We have something in common already! I like Rodney Dangerfield, too!"

I drove home, irritated.

More weeks went by. No jobs appeared. I went to parties. I drank too much. I tried to have a good time, but I was miserable. I should have returned to school full-time, but didn't have any money and didn't know how I'd pay for it.

The Air Force seemed more and more like the answer to my problems. I was programmed into a Delayed Entry Plan.

Downtown one night, I ran into an officer from my Academy class. He told me that he had heard about the dismissal and he expressed his condolences.

"Man, we thought you were going to make it. We all had our fingers crossed for you. Then when we graduated, we thought you had made it. It's a damn shame. You were good."

"Thanks," I sighed.

"What are you doing now?"

"I enlisted in the Air Force. I'm scheduled to go in February. I train in Texas but then I get stationed in Illinois at Chanute. It sounds like a good deal. You get trained for a job that you can work at as a civilian when you get out."

"You're crazy! What are you doing that for? You could be doing so many other things."

"Like what? Everywhere I apply, they find out I was fired."

"I can't believe the number of people that have been fired." He shook his head.

It felt good talking to him. He seemed to be on my side.

"I can remember when you first went down for all that shit about Boville's party," he said. "I heard that it was a Police Aide that was smoking pot at that party, outside the house. She had blond hair, too. That's where it all started."

After all this time!

"What? Why didn't somebody say something to Internal Affairs? I got blamed for something I didn't do and all you punks were sitting back when you knew what really happened?"

"We were scared to say anything! Besides, we didn't know you'd take a rap for it! What are we talking about here? Rumor! It was all rumor! Nobody could talk!"

I walked away from him in anger and went inside an East Side club. Suzy's friends Russ and Jim were gathered at one end of the bar, looking at some snapshots with another guy named Eddy. They were photos of naked women standing on picnic tables. The background appeared to be some sort of a public park, with a huge crowd of people, including kids.

"Where was this?" I asked, looking over Jim's shoulder.

"Lake Park."

"Here? In Milwaukee?" I asked.

"Yeah! Don't tell me you never heard of the Tracks picnic?"

"No."

"They have this every year," Eddy said. "A whole bunch of cops were there."

"You mean all these people were taking their clothes off in a public park and no arrests were made?" I was incredulous.

"For what?" Russ asked.

"For what? For indecent exposure! Disorderly conduct! That's lewd and lascivious behavior! It's against the law!" It wasn't hard to think of possible charges; this was Milwaukee, after all.

"Oh. Well, most of the cops there were off duty." Jim shrugged. "Besides, they were all having a great time! Maybe they were paid off. Who knows? They'd have to be crazy to start anything—there were too many drunk fools."

Russ nodded. "See, they always get off to a wild start by having a free beer tent, and then something like a pie-eating contest, and then this Wet T-shirt contest. The crowd always begs the girls to take everything off."

"I can't believe this," I said. "In a public place where everyone can see? Outside? No one was arrested?"

"You think these pictures are good, you should see the ones from last year," Eddy told Jim.

"The Tracks ..." I began.

"It's a bar on Locust. A lot of detectives hang out there," Eddy said. "They had a Wet Jock contest, too. Look at all the crazy guys that took their clothes off."

He showed me pictures of a row of naked men on a table.

"Well, you see one, you've seen them all," I said sardonically. "Anybody could use these pictures to blackmail them. How could they do this?"

"You must know some of these cops," Jim said to me. "Here, look."

■   ■   ■

My tests for the Air Force turned out favorably. I was looking into a program that trained cadets to be fire fighters at airports. They told me that municipal airports only hired people trained by the Air Force. All my friends thought I was nuts to consider the Armed Forces.

"What do you want to be?" one friend asked. "Another Private Benjamin? Sometimes I think you've got a screw loose. You're going to be miserable."

■   ■   ■

Maybe I did have a screw loose. But my dismissal from the Police Department still rankled, and in December, I decided to talk to a representative from the Equal Employment Opportunity Commission, known as the EEOC. Maybe they could do something. I knew it wasn't just me. There were too many things wrong, too many good people getting fired for too many trivial excuses.

After reviewing the records of my dismissal, the EEOC rep said he felt I had a good case for sex discrimination. He explained that I'd have to show how male officers were disciplined differently than females. I told him about all the rule violations I'd witnessed. The key, he said, was to show that the Department administration knew about these violations. I told him about the Tracks picnic photographs, and his eyes lit up. He referred me to an Assistant U.S. Attorney.

The attorney said he was documenting the way that minority and female police officers were handled by the MPD. A pattern was becoming obvious, he said. Federal guidelines made the hiring of minorities mandatory, and these numbers the Department reported. Of course—there was federal funding at stake. The numbers dismissed or forced to resign, however, went unreported and unnoticed. He had come to believe those numbers were substantial.

I couldn't see how the Police Department could possibly maintain they weren't aware of what was going on. But just in case, I was going to make sure they did; I'd push their noses in it. For starters, I borrowed the photos of the Tracks picnic and turned them in to Internal Affairs. Some of the people in the snapshots were wearing T-shirts that said "The Tracks Picnic 1980," which was explicit enough. When Zellmer saw the photographs, his eyes almost popped out.

"Why are you here?" he asked me.

"Because," I said virtuously, "I was fired for little more than rumor, when cops out there are getting away with things ten times worse! I don't think it's fair. You tell me how this picnic could have gotten so out of hand, right out in the open in a public park. Where were the squads?"

■   ■   ■

Suzy called to tell me that she was leaving for a vacation in California with Aimee.

"Have a good time," I said. "How was your Thanksgiving?"

"Oh, all right I guess. I spent it with Fred at his parents' house. But he's my problem. I just want to get away and be alone for a while."

"Why? I thought you two were getting along so well."

"I've been hearing a lot about him from certain people, and I don't like what I'm hearing," Suzy said. "For one thing, he's been screwing almost every female officer on this Department! But he gives me the 'You're the only one I love' snowjob."

"Like who?" I asked.

"Like Pam and Lori, for starters. Then there are a few nurses, a cheerleader, a Karen, an Elaine ..." she said, disgusted. "What I can't figure out is, when does the guy sleep?"

"Who's been telling you all this?" I asked.

"Remember that guy with the deep, gravelly voice that I used to talk to on the phone? Now don't ever say anything, but that's Fred's roommate, Stu. He's a cop, too. Fred's been living at Stu's house ever since his divorce, and let me tell you, our Mr. Buns has been a very busy little boy. I might just tell him where to go."

"What's the difference, Suzy? You're just as bad. You go out with other guys."

"Oh, I know. But guess what Stu said? He said that Fred's divorce was his fault. Fred was fooling around with someone named Karen while he was still married. Stu said Fred's ex-wife is a really nice lady!"

It got really complicated, according to Suzy. After Fred and his wife, Chris, were separated, Stu began dating her. Stu gave Chris Karen's full name, birth date and address and told her that if she really wanted Fred to meet her financial demands, she should threaten to notify the Department about his girlfriend.

■   ■   ■

I know now the whole thing was sordid and I should have stayed out of it. It wasn't as if I hadn't been warned about Fred. But I was drawn in by his overwhelming personality. He was manipulative and consuming, but he was also full of jokes and laughter, the life of any party he went to. In my depression, he seemed fresh and alive and new, a way out.

I've pondered this so much! I've read what people say of me, that I was part of the fast lifestyle, that I dressed like a slut (that word again!), that my protestations of naiveté are a hazy sham and a cover. They all spin these webs of words, but I look into the net and I don't see me there. I see only a creature that others have invented.

Fred was another of my failures. But I didn't know that, then. He allowed me to forget my depression, for a while.

I was so lonely!

■　■　■

One night I was sitting after midnight in my favorite Mexican restaurant with a friend. The door opened and a frigid blast of air hit us. I turned to see two detectives walk in.

"Cops!" I said to my friend.

"How can you tell?"

"By their white socks!"

It was a dimly lit room, but I recognized Fred by his obnoxious laugh. He saw me and walked to the bar.

"Isn't it against Department regs for you to be here on duty?" I asked with a grin.

"Shhhh!"

"I've heard 'Milwaukee's Finest' love to frequent this place," I said. The usual pleasantries were exchanged.

"I'd really like to get together with you sometime," he said. "I hear you're athletic. I need a jogging partner. Maybe you'd like to go running with me? We can talk. Please. I want to talk to you about Suzy."

"I guess so. Give me your number. I'll call you," I said.

I never had to. Fred called me, and we went jogging. It was bitterly cold as we ran in the sand along a frozen Lake Michigan shoreline. We talked as we ran, mostly about Suzy. I wasn't really listening to him.

"How far have we gone?" I asked between breaths.

"Why? Want to quit?"

"No." The air bit my face, it was so cold, but I didn't want to stop running until he did. Running was the only thing I did for myself anymore.

Fred was so convincing—on his best behavior. I began to think that my first impression of him was wrong. He wasn't that bad, and he was right about Suzy. Everything Stu had told Suzy about Fred was no doubt said from jealousy. After all, Stu was dating Fred's ex-wife. We ended our run and hopped back into his van.

"Where to?" he asked.

"I'd really like to shower. We can go to my parents' house and have some coffee. You can wait while I change into some jeans."

Later, we went to a tavern owned by a friend of his. I had a marvelous time, feeling great after the brisk run. Fred was persuasive and charming. I was mesmerized.

"Would you like to go with me to a party tomorrow night?" he asked me on the way home. "I'd be honored to have you accompany me."

"Whose party?"

"It's the annual Christmas party that the Municipal Court throws," Fred explained. "I don't have a date and I'd really enjoy your company."

"I'd love to," I said.

The evening of the party, Fred arrived with an armful of red roses.

"Thank you—they're lovely. Did you read the headline tonight? Here. Take a look." I showed him an article in that day's paper about my sex discrimination complaint against the Police Department. "That's an awful photograph."

"This is great!" Fred said. "But I hope you know what you're up against."

I just smiled. I thought I did know.

After the Christmas party, we went dancing at a local club. Fred made me think we were so alike, so compatible, that I felt I had known him all my life. We enjoyed the same things. He never disagreed with anything I said.

I was growing fond of him. But I'd be leaving soon to join the Air Force, and I was to be a star witness in a sex discrimination suit, so I didn't pay much attention. I was just enjoying myself for a change.

7

ROSE-COLORED GLASSES

How pleasant it is between two people when everything is new! The need for acceptance brings gentle consideration, caution and polite words. No suspicion or accusations; no angry remarks. Fred flattered me, agreed with me, was interested in all my activities. He seemed to want the same things out of life as I did. He didn't want any more children. He wanted an independent partner, a career woman. On top of that, he was a cop. Although he was ten years older than me, I felt that I had found my perfect match. My glasses couldn't have been any more rose-colored.

Still, I was so sure I was leaving for the Air Force that I tried to close my heart—just my luck to meet someone wonderful right before I was scheduled to begin a four-year hitch.

One cold afternoon we sat by the fireplace at his parents' house, drinking wine and talking.

"I think you love me as much as I love you," he suddenly said.

I thought I was in love with him, but this was the first time he'd ever mentioned love, and it startled me.

I looked down.

"Yes, I do. But I'm going away, for four years ..."

"You're not going anywhere," he said softly.

"I am," I said.

"But you can't!" he protested. "We get along so well, we like all the same things, we feel the same way about everything! This past month has been so wonderful since we started going out. Laurie, I feel like—"

"Maybe we'd better go," I interrupted. I felt bad enough.

We walked outside, and as he locked up the house, I climbed into his van.

Approaching the van from the passenger side, Fred put his hand up on my window before passing by. I put my hand up on the other side, lining it up with his on the window, with just the glass in between.

I smiled at first, but then saw that there were tears in his eyes. After a moment, he turned and walked around the van to his door. I wanted to cry, too. How sad, I thought, that just when I finally found a man who was everything I had always wanted, I was leaving.

■   ■   ■

Many years later I cried again, wishing it had ended that way. I don't know who it was who said, "Be careful what you wish for in life—it just might come true."

■   ■   ■

Christmas was happy. It was that year I received the little rocking horse from my mother. It was a tiny, wooden thing, painted bright red and white, with a mane and tail of fine yarn.

Fred and I dated frequently. We went to midnight mass together and he once accompanied me to a NOW dinner. One evening he invited me to Stu's house for dinner; he was a good cook and loved to prepare meals. As we lingered over the food, Fred complained bitterly about Stu, who was not home. He was upset over Stu's affair with Chris, Fred's ex-wife.

"Is he still friendly with her?" I asked.

"Are you kidding? He's sleeping with her! I always see his car there all night. The bastard even answers her phone! In my old house! Right around the corner from here!"

"You'd think Christine would have better taste," I commented. "But really, Fred, what's it to you?"

"Chris is probably just keeping him around to do all her heavy work around the house," Fred said angrily. "I just hate the fact that my kids are around that guy all the time!"

■   ■   ■

In January, a cop friend called me late at night with a warning.

"Laurie, keep your car off the street at night."

"Why? What are you talking about?" I asked, startled. I sat up in bed and rubbed the sleep out of my eyes.

"It's the guys. Boy, are they pissed. We were standing roll call last night, and one of the officers told us that, all because of you, we have to make our marks now."

Beat cops and squads were required to "make their mark" every hour while on duty, which means using a callbox to contact the station. The purpose was to keep track of all officers. If an officer failed to make her or his mark, she or he could be injured or incapacitated, and the station would investigate. At Second District, none of the late-shift officers ever made their marks.

"He also told us to be super careful, because of that discrimination thing you filed. The guys are being investigated."

"You know how unfair it is!" I said. "I had to show that white, male officers get away with violations that females are disciplined for!"

"Laurie, I don't want to know what you said. You're my friend, all right? All I'm telling you is, be careful. They were all grumbling and saying that they were going to shoot you, or blow up your car and all kinds of shit. Square business!"

"It's not my fault that those assholes made corruption commonplace! Then someone tells the whole shift! Christ!"

"Don't tell anyone I called you. In fact, they were getting on me a little bit because we're friends, but I denied seeing you for a long time. I don't know what you're doing, Laurie ..."

"So? The guys have to make their marks now! Just like every other station. Big deal!"

"Don't you get it? You can't make your mark if you're sleeping. You can't make your mark if you're drinking."

I hung up the phone and called Fred, but Stu said he wasn't home from work yet. A few minutes later, my phone rang again.

"Hello?" I thought it might be Fred.

"Bembenek, your mother's dead," a male voice growled. Then there was a click, followed by a dial tone.

I got out of bed and started to dress. Looking out the window through the snow, I noticed something strange about my car. Something was on the hood.

I threw on a jacket and ran outside. There was a big, black, dead rat on the windshield of my car, tucked under the wiper like a parking ticket. Wincing, I pushed it off with a stick and tossed it down a sewer.

"What's wrong?" my mom asked when I got back into the house. Before I had a chance to answer, my phone rang again. My heart pounded as I ran upstairs to answer it. It was Fred.

"Where are you calling from?"

"I just got home," he said. "Stu left me a note that you called."

"Fred! I'm in trouble." I told him about the phone call.

"Keep your car in the garage at night until we straighten this out," Fred said. "It will probably just blow over. Those guys are a bunch of windbags. I've got more bad news. Stu came home from work last night, and we got into a fistfight."

"Are you okay?"

"I kicked his ass! The chump! The only thing is, now I have to be out by the end of this month. I don't know where to go."

"I'll help you move, if you find a place." I paused. "Wait a minute. Judy has been bugging me for months to move in with her. She can't afford that two-bedroom place. You might be able to move in with her."

"I don't think so."

"Well, suit yourself. I just thought I'd make you aware of the possibility."

"Forget all that," Fred said, brightening. "Would you like to take my kids to a movie today?"

"I guess so," I said, still feeling uneasy about the rat.

"Good! We'll have lunch and then go to a matinee."

Later that day we pulled in to the driveway of the large house that Fred built several years before. His two boys came flying out the front door and a huge Great Dane bounded after them. I thought we were leaving so I remained in the van, but Fred went into the house. The boys plopped themselves down in the back of the van by the windows. They were playing with a small electronic game. Sean was eleven years old, with very dark hair and brown eyes. He looked like he had a tan even in the middle of winter. His seven-year-old brother, Shannon, looked just like Fred, with fair skin, blue eyes and blond hair.

Moments later, Fred's ex-wife Christine looked out the front door of the house as Fred left. She smiled, waving at me. Surprised that she was so friendly, I waved back.

The children impressed me with adult manners and polite behavior. I had underestimated them. We lunched at Taco Bell and then sat through a modern version of *Flash Gordon* in a movie house filled with active, screaming children. It was exhausting.

The threatening phone calls continued.

■　　■　　■

A few weeks later, my Air Force recruiter called. He sounded indignant.

"You didn't tell us you had a lawsuit pending," he said.

"Technically, it's not a lawsuit yet. It's still in the complaint stage with the Equal Employment Opportunity Commission," I explained. "Why?"

"Because the Air Force can't accept anyone with any litigation pending. Nothing. Not criminal litigation, not a civil action, a divorce proceeding, a custody petition. Nothing. Not even a complaint or claim with a government agency that involves hearings."

"So what are you telling me?" I asked. "I can't leave for basic training next month?"

"Not unless your complaint is dismissed or decided by then."

I met Fred downtown for lunch and told him the news.

"That's great!" he exclaimed. Then, seeing my frown, he added, "I mean, I'm sorry if you're disappointed, but this means that you're not leaving! That's all that matters to me!"

I didn't know what to do. I couldn't drop the claim, I just couldn't. There was too much riding on it. Also, others depended on me ... I had time, money, emotion and energy invested in the suit.

Some of it, of course, was a thirst for vengeance; I wanted to get back at the department. I'd had more threats: my car tires had been slashed; I had to change my phone number after a number of harassing calls. But there was more to it than that. If I dropped the case, I knew nobody would pick up the ball. They were all scared.

There were other considerations, too. I was organizing a group of ex-recruits to put together a Class Action suit against the Police Department. I was also cooperating by now with a U.S. District Attorney, James Morrison, to be a federal witness against the Chief of Police. All this was going on. How could I just drop it all and go? For four years in the Air Force?

I made up my mind.

I told Fred over a long lunch.

"So I guess I won't be leaving next month. I just have to get my career back on the ground. I have to have a direction. I have to work. I'd be so unhappy if I didn't." It was well after three in the afternoon. The wine made me feel warm.

"You know, Laurie," Fred said softly, "we're so much alike. When are you going to ask me to marry you?"

I just laughed. I was stunned.

"Then I'll ask you. Do you want to get married?"

I was caught in the mood of the moment, and my heart swelled.

"Of course," I finally replied. "I'd love to get married."

So we eloped the following day—a sunny January 31—and were married by a judge in Waukegan, Illinois. On the way back, we stopped at a park and took some pictures.

The rest of that day we spent, prosaically, moving Fred's belongings into Judy's condo. We'd move my things after the honeymoon. I didn't feel any different. I didn't feel "married." I was a little disappointed by my lack of excitement. I wore a gold wedding band that matched Fred's.

■   ■   ■

So there it is. I'd given up a loving relationship with a man I really loved for a job in the police force, then after a year I had neither the man nor the job. I'd applied to the Air Force but they wouldn't take me because I was involved in litigation. I'd given up the Air Force. Again, everything went wrong. I lost everything in the long run. What a series of dreadful decisions!

Several times I'd come to a fork in the road, and I took the wrong turn every time.

I felt that things couldn't possibly get worse. What did I know? It always does.

On my bulletin board in prison I had a cartoon of Garfield the cat. In the first panel, Garfield was up a tree. He was saying, "So I'm stuck up a tree, it can't get any worse." In the next panel it starts to rain, and he's saying, "So it's raining, it can't get any worse." Then, in the last panel, Kaboom! He gets hit by lightning. There it is. That sums it up. That's the way my life was. If I could go back I'd do it differently, but then, I didn't know what to do.

■   ■   ■

When I told my mom and dad that we'd just gotten married, they thought we were joking. Then they were a bit angry that we hadn't told them of our plans, but eventually they relented.

"We're legally married and everything," I said. "We just didn't have a reception, so we might have a little thing in spring."

"You're having a little thing in spring?" my mother asked me facetiously. "Is that why you eloped?"

"Impossible!" I said, laughing. "I married him for his vasectomy!"

"I suppose you insisted on keeping your name," my mom whispered. "You've been pontificating about that for years."

"You know better than to argue with me about that," I said. "Yes, I kept my name. For feminist reasons."

"I hope you know, Fred, you got yourself an independent little cuss here," my mom said, as I groaned at her choice of words. "But I don't understand. Laurie always said that she didn't like the domestic scene!"

"Fred loves to cook, and he can even sew! He just replaced the zipper that I broke in my Calvin Klein jeans! It's a nice role-reversal."

Before we left for our honeymoon, Fred called Christine to tell her the news. Unexpectedly, he handed me the phone.

"I heard you collect butterflies?" I asked, not knowing what else to say.

"I put them on velvet and make wall-hangings," she said.

"Maybe I can buy some tropical butterflies and bring them back for you." It was awkward.

"That would be nice," Chris replied. "Could I talk to Fred again?"

He finished talking on the phone and then hung up.

"I guess Chris felt a little uncomfortable, talking to you," he explained.

"Why did you hand me the phone like that? I didn't know what to say, either!"

"You'll be seeing a lot of each other because of the kids," Fred told me.

"I just don't have any experience with this kind of situation. Give me time."

We spent our honeymoon in Jamaica. On the way back, Judy picked us up at the airport. She told us we were in store for a disappointment. She'd been evicted, so we were out with her.

"Oh, Zess! We just moved in!"

"At least everything of yours is still in boxes," she said. "I'm sorry!"

■   ■   ■

One night, while Fred was sleeping, Sgt. Zellmer paid me a visit, with another cop in plain clothes. They wanted to know if I was willing to testify against the officers suspected of wrongdoing. I explained that I had suffered threats and I didn't want to testify against anyone. I told them they didn't need me anymore in their investigation. I'd given them some leads and made them aware of what was going on. That was the extent of my part in the whole mess. They had photographs! What more did they need? They left.

■   ■   ■

While we were still in the apartment, I had an odd conversation with Judy.

"You'll never guess who keeps bothering me," she told me. "That big hulk who lives on the thirteenth floor. I can't remember his name. I think it's Tom. Anyway, the guy is huge! I call him The Hulk."

"Does he want to go out with you?"

"I think so. I don't want to be seen with him!"

"Is he a bodybuilder?" I asked. I'd seen him on occasion, usually on the elevator.

"Yeah. I was talking to him down at the pool in the summer. He was trying to get a tan for some kind of contest. He told me he was Mr. Wisconsin a few years back."

"Really?"

"He doesn't work out at your club, though. He goes to the Wedgewood gym. That I remember."

"Did you know I bought Fred a membership to my club as a wedding present? We're going to start working out together."

"What *don't* you do together?" she said, with a peculiar whine to her voice. "I still can't believe you two just ran off and got married."

"Why?"

"I don't know if I like this arrangement. When I asked you to move in, I meant just you—not you and a guy."

"Okay. Why don't we give it a try until we have to move. Then, if you really feel that it's not cool, we'll get a place of our own. Don't you like Fred?"

"He's okay," she answered. "He's just ... the way he always brings you flowers and is cooking all the time."

She continued to speak almost as if she was irritated or jealous. I couldn't see why. She had no reason to be.

■   ■   ■

At the end of February, Fred came home one night with an upset look on his face that was becoming uneasily familiar.

"Is something wrong?" I asked.

"I had the property settlement today," he said. "On top of that, Chris sold my dog without even telling me!"

"One thing at a time. What are you talking about?"

"Never mind. I don't even want to talk about it," Fred snarled. He paced back and forth, slamming our kitchen cabinet doors like a child and mumbling, half to himself, "I paid three hundred dollars for that dog! My Great Dane! Too hard to take care of a dog! She's just too goddamned lazy!"

"Whatever you say," I commented, bewildered.

My in-laws were to become my next big problem. I wasn't accepted into the family with the open arms I'd expected. I didn't know it, but Fred's divorce had caused a nasty family feud, and by marrying him I had joined the ranks of the enemy. Fred neglected to explain any of this to me, so the first display of rejection shocked me.

Kathy was his brother John's wife. They lived across the street from Fred's parents. If we dropped in on them to talk to John, Kathy would take one look at me, excuse herself and leave the room to go upstairs. Kathy despised Fred with a passion, and decided I should be treated with hate by association. I didn't catch on immediately, until it got back to Fred that Kathy had been expressing her disapproval to John and to Fred's mother.

"Why does Kathy dislike me?" I asked Fred.

"Well, perhaps part of it is that she's real thick with Chris."

"But so what? Chris doesn't hate me, and I didn't do anything to Kathy! I only tried to be polite!"

My parents, on the other hand, warmed to Fred in the beginning. They gave us many things that we needed and invited us over frequently.

I took on more hours at the health club, and filled out an application to join the Fire Department. Within a few weeks, however, I was turned down. The Fire Department had a rule that prohibited any member of either the Police Department or the Sheriff's Department from applying for a job after being dismissed. Applicants had to wait at least a year after dismissal to apply.

Around that time, I was surprised to learn that a black friend of mine, Officer Darlene Anderson, had resigned. She was in my Academy class—a sharp, streetwise woman. She told me she could no longer endure the harassment that superior officers subjected her to. I wondered how many black or female officers were left from our class.

In March, our landlords at the highrise finally gave us a notice to vacate, and we resumed our search for an apartment. Most of those we saw were either too big, too expensive, too small or outside of the city limits. (Cops must reside in the City of Milwaukee.)

Judy said she wanted to continue living with us. She said that she couldn't afford an apartment on her own.

She had started dating "The Hulk," whose name was Tom Gaertner. He would come up to our floor occasionally and knock on our door, always very late at night, after Fred had already left for work. I found him arrogant, an opinionated boor. He was very aggressive and rude.

He hated cops. They were, in his opinion, "the lowest scum of the earth."

I argued with him. "I know there are some jerks in blue. I myself got the shaft from the Police Department. But you can't generalize like that. What am I supposed to say? My dad was a cop, I was a cop, and I'm married to a cop. You can't say they're all bad. That's just as bad as when people call weight lifters 'dumb jocks' or 'steroid-heads.'"

One night over dinner, Fred talked in detail for the first time about his previous marriage. His version was that he "barely knew" Chris at college in La Crosse. Fred insisted that after a drunken, one-night stand, Chris announced she was pregnant.

"I never could believe it was me," he said. "We just passed out that night! But no! She tells her parents, who rushed to tell mine, and we were both rushed to a church in Appleton! White wedding gown and all!

"We were strapped for money because of the baby, and because of the baby, Chris said she couldn't work!"

He claimed he told Chris he didn't want any more children, but two years later she surprised him with another pregnancy, saying it would save their marriage.

"Why didn't you take the responsibility for contraception?" I finally asked Fred.

"I did! Only too late!" he insisted. "I went for my vasectomy. I couldn't trust her maternal impulses. Then she refused to work because of the kids."

"When did you build the house?" I asked, referring to the tri-level that Chris was living in.

"I was only seven credits away from my Bachelor's degree when I stopped school temporarily to build a house. See, I had a car accident that I got money from. That, together with an inheritance, enabled me to start building.

"I spent Christmas Eve of that year nailing the last of the roof shingles. One day Chris just announced that she didn't love me anymore.

She said she never loved me, and didn't want to sleep with me anymore! Said I should go out and get sex somewhere else! She didn't care! I never beat her, I never gambled, I never cheated on her or drank. All I did was work! So she says I was never home!

"I hadn't even finished installing the skylights yet when she kicked me out. I paid cash for her new bedroom set and it wasn't even delivered yet. I never slept in the damn bed!"

"Fred, you say Chris uses the kids as an excuse for financial dependence now, so it's hard to believe she didn't consider the effect the divorce would have on them."

"Are you kidding? She said that she didn't care. And that the first kid was never really mine to begin with! Look at Sean—he looks nothing like Shannon."

■   ■   ■

The World According To Fred. It was all lies, of course, created from some detached, internal frame of reference. He left himself blame-free, as he would do years later, with me. He conveniently failed to mention that he abused Christine horribly, both physically and verbally, and had many affairs with other women. It was unbelievable that Chris tolerated him for ten years. Still, had someone told me then what he was really like, I wouldn't have believed it. If love is blind, then I needed a seeing-eye dog.

■   ■   ■

For the next few months, Fred was so intense and possessive that he nearly smothered me. He said he was determined to make sure that he spent enough time with me, and as a result he didn't give me enough space. He almost consumed me. I wished I had more time to myself. I wondered why Fred didn't have any friends of his own. Other men I knew needed their "night out with the boys." Not Fred. My friends became his friends. Later, I found out this wasn't exactly true. Fred was "out with the boys" while he was working; it was more like whole aspects of his life were kept secret, hidden from me—he never talked about that part of his life.

After a long search for another apartment, we finally found a place. It wasn't as luxurious as the one we were forced to leave, but it was less expensive and was bigger, with two bathrooms and a large living room, a loft and three bedrooms. I appreciated the spacious closets and the spare room. Judy, who had been bad with money in the past, seemed to have settled down. She was doing well at her job in sales at Wonderful Waterbeds. She promised that in April she'd sign a year's lease with us and pay her share of expenses faithfully.

I was wallpapering our bathroom one afternoon when Fred came home, looking heavy-hearted. He'd finally gotten the decision on the marital property settlement. He began to cry. We were alone; Zess was out somewhere.

"How can one person financially rape another person legally?" he complained, weeping. "What I built with my own two hands and what I paid for isn't even mine anymore! It's all hers! She's using the kids! She's just using them!"

"Calm down," I said. "What are you talking about?"

"The judge said I had to keep paying the mortgage on that god-damned house—$383 a month! While she's allowed to live there, rent free! I also got socked with child support payments of $365 a month! That's almost $800 a month! Out of my pocket!" He was weeping.

His annual income as a detective was about thirty-two thousand dollars a year, which averaged to around twenty-six hundred dollars a month. My job and the carpentry work Fred and I did on the side added to this income, so the alimony and child-support payments were tough, but not that much of a hardship.

"I'm even required to pay her attorney's fees!" Fred complained. "Besides that, she's entitled to my pension when I resign from the Police Department—whether or not she remarries!"

I didn't know what to say to him. The whole matter was so foreign to me. I simply allowed him to continue.

"The hideous fact of the matter is, Chris misrepresented her earnings in court, but there's no way to prove it. She just stood up and said that she can't work full-time because of the children! Again—the children! When I know for a fact that she's been earning almost six dollars an hour and has been working forty hours a week for the past nine months!"

"How do you know this?" I asked.

"I saw her check stub! The last time I picked up Sean to take him to a game after school, I waited for him in the kitchen—"

"And you were snooping?"

"No! I wasn't snooping! The stub was lying right there on the kitchen counter along with a mess of other papers. She's such a slob."

"Can't you prove it? There must be a way to subpoena her wage statements."

Fred shook his head. A tear rolled off his face and fell to the floor.

"I suppose I could. But that would mean I'd have to reopen the case, and that would cost me more in attorney's fees, and all that takes time. Meanwhile, the bitch is robbing me blind!"

He calmed down a bit. "She's just using the kids, Laurie. Two weeks ago, she was trying to make me feel real guilty, asking me if I could give her more money. She said the kids didn't have enough to eat! Can you imagine? Then I find out from Sean that all she did was fill the liquor cabinet for a party she was having! I always fall for it!" He began weeping again.

I was bewildered. How could such a financial slaughter happen? It didn't seem possible. I felt he must be exaggerating. Did my inexperience make me wrong? Both my sisters were divorced, and they ended up with nothing. I thought of Suzy, with her child support payment of eighty-five dollars a month. I couldn't believe there hadn't been some provocation, and I knew already how Fred tended to distort the facts.

In the back of my mind I was annoyed with his sniveling. If he was so poverty-stricken, why did he push me into getting married so fast? Sometimes the things he did made no sense.

The phone rang. It was the manager from the health club where I worked part-time with more bad news. Talk about bad timing!

An odd chain of events had led up to an incident that almost cost me my job. He told me the story.

He was in a laundromat doing his wash when a woman approached him and "came on to him like a bulldozer." He told her he managed the health club. She said she was a cop.

"Oh yeah? I've got a girl working for me that used to be a Milwaukee cop," he said. "Maybe you know her. Her name is Laurie Bembenek."

"I know her," she snapped, suddenly cold. "She's married to my ex-boyfriend!"

"No shit? What's your name?" he asked.

"Pam Fischer," she answered, and left abruptly.

Later, Pam gossiped to an executive of the health club chain that she had worked with me—although I'd never even met her—and that I was dismissed from the MPD for sitting on a married guy's lap at a party, smoking pot. Yet another version of the Department rumor! The wife of this executive phoned and demanded that I be fired. She didn't want someone "of that moral character" working for the club.

I had some difficulty keeping my job because of her.

Later that month, I met with a different representative of the Equal Employment Opportunity Commission, who was even more optimistic about my complaint than the first. I turned in signed statements, supporting my case, that I'd been collecting. The most important was signed by Judy Zess, and described the coercion she was under when she wrote the reports about the concert incident.

The reports dated May 2, 1980 that I filed in regards to the incident on May 1, 1980 were written under coercion and after long hours of interrogation and under mental duress. I was intoxicated and confused at the time.

The written reports dated May 3, 1980 that Lawrencia Bembenek filed in regards to that same incident of May 1, 1980 were factual and truthful.

On Dec. 15 the criminal charges of POCS (Possession of a Controlled Substance) issued against me were dropped after a jury trial within the Circuit Court of Appeals before Judge Patricia Curley during October, 1980. I was represented by Attorney Jack Gimbel.

I feel that both Lawrencia Bembenek and I were discriminated against because we were dismissed on false charges and allegations that were asserted and substantiated by nothing more than hearsay evidence. Harold Breier and his administration opposes women and minorities on the job. White male police officers are afforded preferential treatment in regards to disciplinary action.

Judy L. Zess

The representative wanted a list of police officers from my Academy class who had either resigned or were dismissed.

Meanwhile, a *Milwaukee Journal* analysis of city data produced even bleaker statistics, according to findings that were dated March 31, 1980. Female and minority officers just didn't last on Chief Breier's Department.

From my Academy class alone, the list was grim. With only one year having passed since our appointment dates, five black men, four white women, three black women and one white man were already gone. The white male was considerably overweight and resigned because he couldn't match the physical standards the Academy demanded. Out of eleven female recruits who joined the department when I did, eight were already without a job. Others would follow.

8

SASSON

We were still living out of boxes; Fred had never gotten around to unpacking. One afternoon, when I was irritable and short-tempered from a frustrating afternoon downtown filling out job applications, I began unpacking cartons and labeling the ones that were seasonal. Judy walked in.

"My! Aren't we organized!" she said.

"Look at this mess! Fred told me he'd unpack these things, but he never got around to it—all this stuff has been just sitting here. You've got to get Fred a key to the storage area so we can put some of these boxes away."

"When he comes home, I'll take some of my shit down there, too," Judy said. "I've got Christmas ornaments and a fake tree in a box that's taking up too much room in my closet."

"I wish you'd get a copy of that key made soon, anyway. You keep saying you'll do it."

"Calm down," she said. "I'll go to Sears this weekend. Hey! Tom's talking crazy lately! I think he's in love."

Fred came in the door, bristling with anger. He was upset because Stu Honeck had done some inept repairs to his precious house. Why couldn't he leave them alone? He seemed obsessed with Christine and with that wretched house. I tuned him out.

■　　■　　■

My parents came over to our apartment for dinner on their thirty-sixth wedding anniversary. They'd seen the place several times when they came over to drop things off, but had never stayed long. I wanted to make the evening special, so I bought some slim blue candles, and folded cloth napkins into pretty designs I had learned when I was a display artist. I finished decorating the table with a huge bunch of fresh flowers.

Fred made a salad, soup, beef, fresh vegetables and rolls. I bought a fattening German layer cake for dessert. Judy had made herself scarce and went out with Tom for the evening.

The evening was pleasant and relaxed. The only inconvenience was the toilet in Judy's bathroom. It was plugged and would overflow if flushed. I caught my mother as she was about to use it, and directed her to the apartment's other bathroom. "That's what's wrong with this complex," I told her. "Ever since we moved in here, there's been trouble with the plumbing. And problems always seem to take weeks to fix."

"That's a shame," my mother said. "Especially with the rent you pay here."

"One time I was all set to do a stack of dishes and the landlord called to warn everyone not to run their water! Soap was all over everything. I was so mad. All five apartments had the water shut off. The place downstairs was flooded."

My parents left late, after hugs and warm wishes, taking their cake with them.

■   ■   ■

The day of my Fact-Finding Conference with the EEOC finally arrived. The City Attorney, Ritter, was there, along with Lieutenant Tromp and the Commanding Officer of the Second District Station, Captain Pape. My complaint and the separate charges were presented orally, step by step. The City Attorney was given the opportunity for rebuttal.

I maintained that I was dismissed for reasons of sex discrimination. The report I'd filed the previous May regarding the concert was truthful, I said, and I submitted the signed statement from Zess. I pointed out that the charges issued against her had been dropped. I showed that there were numerous contradictions among the reports filed by the arresting officers—differences in descriptions and some outright falsehoods. One I recalled was in an Offense Report that said, "... cleared by the arrest of Lawrencia Bembenek," when I was neither arrested nor apprehended at that concert.

Ritter denied that, saying he had witnesses to verify my arrest.

Witnesses! Sure! But this one I knew I could prove. I told him to refer to his copy of my Verbatim Statement transcript, given before Captain Beste of the Police Academy. There he'd find the question:

"Are you aware of the fact that at this time, Paul Will from the Vice Squad is downtown right now trying to obtain a warrant for your arrest?"

To which I had replied: "No."

Ritter apologized. Then he shifted tactics. I was correct about not being arrested, he said. But still, my complaint of being subjected to sexist harassment was not "specific" enough.

He wanted specific? What about the names I was called?

"The word 'cunt' refers only to a woman, doesn't it?" I asked. "That was uncalled for and was done to me deliberately."

"You can't prove intent," Ritter said.

"I know it was deliberate because my FTO later informed me that he was told to give me a hard time—per his superiors."

"I ask, then, that you identify your Field Training Officers," Mr. Bronson from the EEOC said.

I told him their names.

Ritter chipped in. "Might I explain to the Commission that Field Training is a vigorous period of training that occurs before the recruit is allowed to graduate. It is only natural that the FTO gives his recruit a hard time. There's nothing sexist about it. It prepares the recruit."

"The name-calling ...?" Bronson asked Ritter.

"Street jargon and bad language come with the job," Ritter said. "Male recruits might be called 'pricks.' Besides, if Miss Bembenek was so concerned about it, she should have made supervisory personnel aware of it."

"I did!" I argued. "I talked to two sergeants about it, but they brushed it off like it was nothing."

"Did you file a 'Matter of' about it?"

"No. But there were times when the verbal abuse occurred in front of a sergeant! One time it happened at roll call. My point is that disrespect for a fellow officer is a rule violation."

"Are you aware of any other females that received similar treatment during Field Training?" Bronson asked me.

"Yes."

"You don't have to name them at this hearing, but would you be willing to identify them at a later date?"

"Yes."

The hearing continued for several hours. The city's final point was to the effect that my basis for a charge of discrimination was unfounded. They said I claimed that male officers were not disciplined for rule violations that got females fired, yet I hadn't presented a single incident involving a male officer that was identical to the action against me.

"Do you mean to say I'd have to tell you about a case exactly like mine, but involving a male cop?" I asked Bronson after the hearing. "Where a male filed a false report but didn't get fired for it? We're getting off the point here—the report I filed was not false!"

"But that would illustrate a clear case of discrimination."

"That's ridiculous!" I said. "I don't have access to personnel files!"

"That's why the City Attorney has such an advantage over you. I know what kind of game they're playing. Even though I'm an impartial fact-finder, it's obvious. Ritter could come up with fifty cases where disciplinary action had been taken against male officers."

"What about all the rule violations by men that I reported to Internal Affairs? They did nothing about all that."

"Laurie, they'd still argue that those are immaterial because it's not a relevant comparison."

"It's relevant by sheer fairness! What if I knew of several cases where male officers filed false reports?" I asked. "Like regarding sleeping on duty? I know they slept on duty. The reports they filed had to be false."

"They could still counter your assertion by saying that the brass didn't know those reports were false."

"This is impossible! They judge whether a report is false or not—even when it's the truth! It's so unfair! That female Puerto Rican from Second District took a rap for falling asleep on duty! They all sleep!" I sighed. "So. It's not enough to prove that a male officer filed a false official report. I also have to show that the commanders knew it was false and did nothing about it. That's impossible."

"I know how frustrated you must feel."

"I have a newspaper article about a Fifth District police sergeant, Clarence Martin, who was dismissed. It was his third offense for filing a false official report."

"They'll defend that by saying that his status accounted for the difference. You weren't a sergeant." Bronson managed a tired smile. "Cheer up. All is not lost."

"What now?" I asked wearily.

"We'll be contacting you soon. A 'Cause' or 'No Cause' determination will be made. If we find cause, the Commission will pursue this matter through the Department of Justice. If no cause is found, then you'll have the right to sue—at your own expense—in the federal court system. So it's far from over."

"Okay. Thank you," I said, picking up my file. I left and walked through the chilly air to my car.

■ ■ ■

The following week, the weather grew warmer. Fred suggested we have a barbecue. He'd go over to the house on Ramsey and retrieve one of his grills. Christine had three, he said.

We drove over to Ramsey Street, and I sat in the van as Fred ran up to the house. Stu's car was parked in the driveway. Sean and Shannon ran up to the van to say hi. They chattered on and on about a game they were playing. Fred returned within a few minutes with no grill.

As we drove away I looked at Fred. I was afraid to ask what had happened this time.

"She's got three goddamn grills and she won't even give me one! And I bought them all to begin with!" Fred complained.

"Did you tell her—"

"I couldn't tell her anything! Stu was right there, sticking his lousy two cents in. I didn't want to start anything with that turkey."

"Oh."

"And she had the nerve to ask me for money for her crummy electric bill, just because I used one of my power saws in the garage the last time I was there."

He squealed the van around a corner. "She kept all those bills in my name, so if she doesn't pay it, my credit rating goes to hell. Let me tell you something. Sean has been telling me that she's been missing work more and more lately. It's always the day after Stu's been over. I think she's starting to get too hungover for work. That's why she wants more money. Well, I'm not paying for her parties with Stu. She can go to hell!"

"So what about the grill?" I asked.

"I'll wait until she's not home and go in and take one," Fred snarled.

So much for the calm, fun-loving man I thought I'd married. He was always complaining about Christine, though he'd rarely even mentioned her before we got married.

Judy was not home much anymore. She spent most of her time with Tom, who was training for a bodybuilding contest in California. She told me he was on a special diet and was working out all day. I asked her what Tom did for a living, but she simply replied that he was a bodybuilder. I wondered about her answer, briefly, since he drove a Corvette and owned a boat. Later, she changed her story and said that he was living off an inheritance.

Soon she began to drop hints and talk idly about Tom asking her to move in with him. I reminded her about the lease.

■   ■   ■

A few days later, after I'd been doing laundry at my mother's house, she found something at the bottom of the tub. It was Fred's wedding ring from his earlier marriage, inscribed from Chris to Fred. I went back to the apartment. Fred and Judy were eating lunch when I let myself in.

"I have something of yours," I told Fred crossly, pulling the ring out of my pocket. His mouth opened slightly.

"Where did you find that?"

"My mom found it—at the bottom of her washing machine. Why were you carrying that around?"

"You're overreacting to this," Fred replied. "I don't know how it got there."

"Get real," I groaned.

"I don't! You don't believe me? Your mother must have got you all riled up."

"She was angry when she found it. As a matter of fact, so am I. Wouldn't you be?"

"Who cares what your mother thinks? You're married to me now!"

"Am I?" I asked. "It sure doesn't feel like it! It's always Christine this and Christine that. She has more to say about the things you do than you're willing to admit!"

"Bullshit!" Fred yelled.

"It's true! You always say you're going to do something but you never end up doing anything."

"You don't understand!" Fred claimed.

"All I understand is that she must have something on you and it must be something good, because when she puts her pretty little foot down, Fred jumps! You couldn't even get a grill from her."

"What do you want me to do?" Fred argued. "I've done all I can do. That's just the way the divorce laws are set up in this state!"

"I've been talking to some friends of yours and they told me that you just gave everything away without a struggle. A goddamn surrender! Goddamn it, why? What has that woman got on you?"

Fred sat down in a chair, looking tired and defeated.

"You just don't know, Laurie. She had me by the balls. She could've had my job." He wouldn't explain further.

He looked up at me, slowly. "Do you know what I'm going to do with this?" he asked, holding up his old wedding band. "I'm going to get rid of this right now." He tossed the ring into a bag of garbage.

"I'm sorry," I said.

"I'm sorry, too."

To make up, Fred suggested we visit friends of his in Florida, Dennis and Karen. He figured he could even make some money while we were there, working with Dennis, putting up aluminum siding.

"When do you want to go?"

"How fast can you pack?" Fred asked, grinning.

■　■　■

On the way to Florida, I learned a curious piece of information. I'd brought up the subject of Judy's mysterious boyfriend, Tom.

"You know," I said, "he says he hates cops so much, yet the other day Judy was telling me he used to have a best friend who was a Glendale officer."

"Really? What was his name?"

"His name sounded like those designer jeans—Sassoon? Sasone?"

"Not Sasson!" Fred exclaimed.

"I guess so. Why?"

"I shot and killed a Glendale cop in 1975 named Robert G. Sasson," Fred told me. "Don't you remember reading about it in the newspaper?"

"No. I was in high school then."

"It turned out that he was a bad cop who was dealing drugs. I was in a squad on that side of town when a call came over the radio: officer needs assistance, 10-17. The location was vague. They said somewhere on Silver Spring Road. We kept listening. The dispatcher came back and confirmed the location as a tavern called The Northway Tap. So anyway, we arrive, and a woman in the parking lot waves to us. She tells us to go in through the back door because the front was locked. It was Sasson's wife, Camille."

"Who locked the front door?"

"Wait. Let me tell it. This woman is pretty sloshed. I had a rookie with me, so he followed me in through the back entrance of the bar. There was a frosted, glass partition right by the door. Rounding the partition, all I see is a guy in a yellow baseball uniform kneeling over a black dude on the floor. This is about six feet away from me. As soon as we approach him, he stands up and puts his semi-automatic to the rookie's chest!"

"Holy shit!"

"That's what I said! I pulled my piece and loaded four slugs into the baseball uniform. It all happened so damn fast. Then the broad is screaming: 'That's my husband! He's a cop!'"

"What ...?"

"We found out later he was trigger-happy. That wasn't the first time an incident of that nature involved him. He drank too much and usually got in trouble with his gun."

"Wow."

"He had connections in after-hours places. It all came out during the investigation that followed his death."

"Why did you handle a call outside Milwaukee?" I asked.

"Oh. The Northway is in Glendale but the guy who called the cops was from out of town—so, by mistake, he called the Milwaukee Police instead of Glendale."

"What happened at the inquest?"

"I went before the DA who reviewed the case and ruled it justifiable homicide."

"Was that the end of it?"

"Camille Sasson filed a lawsuit against the county and was granted seventeen thousand dollars."

"Sasson is Tom's friend?"

"Could be," Fred said. "Pretty big coincidence if it isn't the same guy. This is going to be ticklish, living with Judy, if Tom is around. Don't say anything about it."

■   ■   ■

Here's a pretty kettle of seafood! Many rumors have swirled about over Sasson's death. Why were the Milwaukee cops called? Why are there rumors of cover-up? Why were the stories floated about Sasson's bad habits? Where is the proof that drugs were involved? What about the witnesses who said Sasson did not have a gun to anyone's head? That Fred must have known he was a cop? That he was trying to wave to Fred? What did Chris know about this? Was she holding some secret knowledge over Fred's head?

No one knows the truth to any of this, except that there is nothing straightforward about what the Milwaukee Police Department (or some of its officers) were up to. The whole thing smelled very bad. But I didn't know that then.

■   ■   ■

Of course, Fred messed up our vacation, too. He insisted on surprising Dennis and Karen instead of calling to let them know we were on our way. When we arrived, we found Karen's parents staying with them; they had no room for us. Nor did Fred do any work. He was gone every day with Dennis, leaving me alone with Dennis's mother.

We had to hurry back to Wisconsin so that Fred could return to work. We arrived home weary from all the driving, and noticed that some of Judy's appliances were missing from the kitchen. When I asked her about it, she said she was letting Tom borrow some things he needed, because he'd left the girlfriend he was living with.

■   ■   ■

The following week, Fred and I were invited by Christine to a party for Shannon's first communion. Fred was opposed to going. He said Christine's parents, Alice and Earl Pennings, would no doubt be there, and there were still too many hard feelings from the divorce. On the other hand, Fred's mother insisted that we both attend, because of the children.

I suggested that Fred simply go alone.

But Fred called Christine to say he wouldn't be going. He blamed me. He said I'd told him I'd be "too uncomfortable" around her.

I was furious.

"Damn it, Fred! Why did you have to put it all on me? I wasn't eager to go, but you didn't have to say I'm the reason we were refusing the invitation! It's just not true!"

"What was I supposed to say?"

"Why use me as an excuse? Why don't you just be honest—"

"Don't talk to me like I'm a child!" he interrupted.

"But he's your kid! Why won't you go?"

Fred pouted in silence.

But then I knew. Of course. Stu would be there!

"You're jealous! Why do you care so much?" I asked.

As I suspected, Fred never did call Chris back to straighten things out.

■   ■   ■

One morning, on my way out the main entrance of the apartment building, I checked the mailbox. To my pleasant surprise, my income-tax refund had arrived. Happily, I stuffed the envelope into my purse. I knew what I would spend it on.

I called Judy from work to ask her about a jeweler she was acquainted with. "Can you still get me a deal on a diamond ring?"

She said she could, and told me to meet her at Tom's. I called Fred to tell him that I'd be late.

"I'm going jogging with Judy at the lake."

"Good!" said Fred. "I'm going, too!"

Not wanting to ruin the surprise, I put him off.

"Look, Freddy. Remember that talk we had? You can't be with me twenty-four hours a day. You're smothering me. I need time away from you. Okay?"

"Well ..."

"I'll see you later," I said firmly.

"Call me as soon as you're through jogging," he demanded.

"Yeah," I placated him.

"How long will you be?" he insisted.

"You sound like my mother!" I groaned. "Lighten up!"

"Sorry," he mumbled.

Judy and I were gone longer than I'd expected, because when I arrived to pick her up at the high-rise, she wasn't ready to leave. She was alone, and she told me to wait in Tom's kitchen while she changed clothes. She had already started keeping some jeans and shirts there.

The kitchen looked just like the kitchen in our old place. I was thirsty and I poked about for something to drink. I opened the refrigerator door and quickly slammed it shut. It was either full of large bags of marijuana, or Tom was storing a year's supply of oregano for the U.S. Army.

So that's what he did for a living.

I said nothing to Judy, and we set off for the jeweler on the other side of town. I bought Fred a diamond solitaire ring for less than half of what was marked on the price ticket. I thanked Judy for arranging the deal. Fred's birthday was in June, and I wanted to surprise him— I'd never given him more than a simple wedding band. We were a little better off now. My hours at the club had been doubled and Fred had gotten a raise, so I didn't feel it was an extravagant purchase.

During our drive home, Judy began to talk about Tom.

"I really don't think I should move in with him. He's really so much older than me. What I want to do is go to California next summer. Besides, Tom's landlords aren't too thrilled about seeing me because I got evicted from two different condos at the high-rise. Ha!"

"What are you talking about? You signed a year's lease with us. By the way, the rent is due in a few days."

"Oh. I'll be a day or two late with my half," Judy said airily. "I don't get paid until after this weekend."

"We'll send our half with a note saying that you'll be late."

When I dropped Judy off at the high-rise, I ran inside to use Tom's phone and called Freddy. I felt like a stupid seventeen-year-old. As it rang, I thought with disgust, "I hope I don't get grounded for being late."

"Where are you?" Fred was furious.

"I'm on my way home now," I explained. A little more than two hours had gone by. He had the nerve to hang up on me! I drove home thinking that it was a mistake to have bought him the ring.

As I walked in, Fred bombarded me with accusations. While I was gone he had broken some things in anger and thrown them about. In the middle of his rampage, I calmly produced the ring box, tossing it down on the table in front of him. Instantly, he stopped. A pained expression replaced the rage.

"I feel about two inches tall," he whispered. His eyes lit up as he pried the top open. Blushing, he slipped the ring on, next to his wedding band.

■   ■   ■

A few days later, Judy called me at the gym. She was frantic.

"Laurie! Tom found out!"

"What?"

"Did Freddy kill a Glendale cop back in 1975?"

"Yes."

"That was Tom's best friend! We were at a dinner party the other night. The guy's widow was there. What was his name?"

"Sasson."

"Yeah! Camille started talking about it for some reason, and then she mentioned how the cop who killed her husband had been promoted to detective, and then she said Fred's name! I almost shit! Why didn't you ever tell me?"

"Judy, I just found out about it myself. Fred told me on the way to Florida. What did Tom say?"

"Oh! First, he just looked at me. Then he asked me what Freddy's full name was. He knew anyway. He is pissed!"

"I don't know what to do! It all happened before my time!"

"I don't know what to do either," Judy said. "You know how Tom hates cops to begin with."

As a result, Judy began to move out, presumably at Tom's request. But she did it in a sneaky way; she'd come by when neither Fred nor I were in the apartment and take a few things. She knew our work schedules. She knew I was always gone all day Saturdays. I knew she was avoiding us. Every time we returned, something else was missing. We had no real way to reach her, because she kept Tom's phone number a secret, and she was never available at work when we called. She still owed us her half of the rent for May, and we started to wonder how we'd find another roommate. The two of us didn't need three big bedrooms. I was worried.

I was also worried about Tom.

"That guy scares me," I told Fred. "He's so huge! He looks like he could squash your head like a melon."

Fred agreed. "Leave it to Judy to get involved with a creep like that. You didn't have to tell me he's a drug dealer. I had a funny feeling about him right from the start. I think I'll have to start calling you at night after I leave for work to make sure you're okay. Don't ever forget to lock the door."

"Judy still has a key," I told him. "Can't we change the lock or something?"

"She still has her damn furniture in the apartment and she'd go complain to the landlady. I don't think we can change the lock."

"What else can we do?" Fred asked. "Judy also still has the key to our basement storage-cage. She was supposed to make copies of that key and never did. If we do move, we have to get our boxes out of there."

We didn't hear from Judy again until she came home one night with Tom. Fred had already left for work. It was after eleven when I heard the door. I had to release the chain on the door for them. I was civil, thinking that it would do no good to start an argument. But Judy started in on me anyway, which led to an argument about the lease. I followed her to the door.

Tom stepped between us. I stopped talking in the middle of my sentence.

"Listen," he demanded. "We don't give a good goddamn about your finances. All I know is that your husband is nothing more than a scared, motherfucking punk that killed my best friend! The trigger-happy pig!"

I blinked. Tom was six feet, two inches, 250 pounds. But I just glared back at him, irrationally fearless.

"That all happened a long time ago," I said. "Before I met Freddy. Before I met you. Before you met Judy. So I'm not going to stand here and discuss Sasson. There's no point to it. I wasn't there when it happened, and neither were you. So who are you to judge?" I turned to look at Judy. "Get the rest of your shit. And get out."

After Fred got home from work the next day, I told him what had happened the night before, and we once again began looking for another apartment. Luckily, the landlady didn't care; she knew three young people who needed a place. I was sad that none of my friends had seen the apartment—somehow they never seemed able to find the time to visit. Years later, they said they'd kept refusing to visit because they disliked Fred so much.

We found a one-bedroom efficiency across from a park, not far from where my mom and dad lived, and we quickly signed for it. It was just the right size for the two of us.

About a week after Judy moved out, I read in the newspaper that Tom had been arrested by federal agents and charged with Possession With Intent to Deliver Cocaine. I woke Fred.

"I hope Tom doesn't think that you or I set him up. We didn't exactly part friends."

"How would we have done that?" Fred said. "We only had a hunch as to what he was up to. Oh well, it serves Judy right. I'm surprised she wasn't with him!"

A few days later, Judy arrived. She'd been crying. She came to drain her waterbed and retrieve the rest of her property. As I helped her hook up a garden hose, Fred went into our bedroom to use the phone. He'd been calling Chris. He was irritated because he'd heard that she'd taken the kids out of town without telling him, in violation of the divorce stipulation. I heard him shouting at her.

"What pisses me off is that I've asked you three times now to let me know when you take the kids up to your folks' house. If one of my boys needed emergency surgery, they'd have to have their father's permission to operate. What if you got in an accident?

"And another thing! My goddamn family won't accept Laurie because I remarried, but they sure are accepting that lowlife bastard you've attached yourself to." Fred paused. "Yes, I mean Honeck. Don't you see he's only dragging you down? That rotten guy spends time with my kids? Then you come bitching to me that you need more money! Listen, I know how often you take off work when you're too hungover to go in ..."

There was a silence, and I heard Fred laugh angrily.

"Yes! I know how often you call in sick. How I found out is my own business. We haven't settled this matter about my visiting rights." He paused again. "Ten miserable years and I'm paying through my teeth! Don't give me that crap, Chris. I know how much you make. I intend to expose your income to a judge just as soon as I can! I'll see you in court!"

I closed Fred's door and looked in on Judy while she drained her bed. I wanted to make sure she wasn't getting water all over the rug. Also, I was curious to know what had happened to Tom and if she intended to stay at his apartment. She still looked upset.

"Boy, is Fred having a good fight," she said. "Christine?"

"Yes. I'm bored to tears with all these arguments of his," I told her. "I'm just glad it isn't my problem."

"What's she like?"

"I've only met her a few times. She seems all right." I changed the subject. "Are you moving back home?"

"No. I'm staying at Tom's."

I left to sit outside on the porch. Fred came out after a while, smiling.

"Guess what?" he asked.

"I hate to ask." I squinted in the sun. Auto chrome in the parking lot gleamed.

"Chris is mad because someone turned in Honeck for sleeping with her."

"Really?"

"Yeah! And you know what's even funnier?"

I waited for an answer.

"They're both sure it was you!"

"Me?" I gasped.

"Ha ha! Isn't it hilarious?" He sat down with a smirk on his face. "I'm sure it wasn't you."

"What do you mean?"

"Because it was *me*!" he said, and started to laugh.

I could think of nothing to say. It was like the time when Fred told Chris he wouldn't go to the party for Shannon because of me. I refused to talk to him for the rest of the day.

9

MURDER

The following day, I went to several job interviews. When I got back, I checked our answering machine to find out if anyone had called. A peculiar voice started to growl after I pushed the Play button.

"Fuck you, motherfucker," the voice said.

I stopped the tape and rewound it for Fred to hear. He walked over to the phone and a look of disgust came over his face.

"Who is that?" I asked.

"Don't you know? It's Honeck."

"How did he get our number? What's going on?"

"The asshole is probably drunk. I'm sure Chris cried on his shoulder about the little fight we had," Fred said nonchalantly.

"How did he get our new phone number?" I demanded angrily. "This is a brand new, unpublished, unlisted number!"

"I don't know." Fred shrugged.

"You gave our new number to Chris, didn't you, and Stu got it from her!"

"So?"

"So? I thought you said you wouldn't give our number to her again! Didn't we have enough weirdos calling us and threatening us at our old place? Damn it! Honeck's got our new number."

Fred continued dressing for work, strapping on his shoulder holster.

"Stop it, Laurie. I refuse to argue about this. We've been through this all before. I had to give our number to the boys the last time I saw them. They're my kids! They have to know how to reach me!"

"You told me that they could call you at work in the morning— but you gave them our number!"

"I had to give it to Chris, and that's final."

"First you said you gave it to the boys. Now you say you gave it to Chris! I hate it when you lie to me! The phone is in my name, and I get the bills. You'd think I'd have a right to know who the hell gets my number!"

"So we got an obscene phone call! Honeck's not going to do anything. Why weren't you as indignant when your 'friend' Judy came by yesterday? How could you even talk to her after what she did to us?"

"That's irrelevant. But if you must know, I was fishing for information about Tom's arrest. I was being nosy."

■　　■　　■

The next day was taken up with more fruitless job interviews. After the first one, for a security firm, the interviewer told me I'd seemed unenthusiastic or disinterested. I guess I was becoming disillusioned; I no longer really expected anyone to hire me. Then I went to a different place and spent two and a half useless hours in a room, scratching in answers with a lead pencil to a computerized psychological exam.

I returned home around five. After dinner, my parents came over as planned, with some empty cartons, and my mother stayed to help me pack. Fred sat around for a while, watching us wrap things in newspaper. He grew tired and excused himself to get some sleep before work.

I packed in a rather half-hearted way. My mother, always able to sense my moods, tried to reassure me.

"We'll get this all done tonight. It certainly is a job, isn't it? But it will be so much better, living without Judy. You'll see, hon."

"Oh, yes, I'm sure it will be," I replied. "But we just unpacked, and now we have to pack again! I feel like a tumbleweed."

"What's your new place like?"

"It's small. It faces a nice park. Good neighborhood."

We packed for a while, and it grew warm and dusty in the room. I opened a can of beer. My mother looked around the apartment. "What's left?" she asked.

"The spare room. Most of that stuff is Freddy's junk—four hundred socks, ninety-eight T-shirts, all that sort of stuff. I told Fred that even Ripley wouldn't believe it! Would you like the honor of packing that room? I'll finish up here."

"Sure."

"It's a good thing I didn't bring my bench and all my weights over here. I was going to set them up in that spare room and start bench-pressing again on a regular basis. That would have been heavy stuff to move."

"You can leave it in our basement. There's plenty of room for it. That way, whenever you feel like working out, you can come over," my mom told me.

After we finished packing, I woke Fred for work. My dad arrived to drive my mom home, and I hugged them both, thanking them again for all their help.

Fred sleepily wandered out of the bedroom, half-dressed,

"I'm surprised you managed to pack everything tonight!" he said.

"You slept for about four hours," I told him.

He glanced at his watch. "Are you still planning on going out with Marylisa tonight?"

"No, I don't think so. I'm too tired and dirty. Besides, I have to work tomorrow morning."

"Did you call Marylisa?" Fred asked.

"Yeah. I tried her apartment earlier, but her roommate told me she went straight to Jeff's after work, and I don't have his number. So she must have forgot about our plans anyway. It doesn't matter."

Fred finished dressing, straightened his tie, and I walked with him to the door. "Are you on a South Side squad tonight?"

"Probably," he replied. "We'll stop by again for some coffee if we're not busy. Otherwise, I'll call you. I still worry that Judy and Tom might pay you a visit after I'm gone."

Some nights, Fred would drive past our apartment if he was in the area, to see if a light was still on. I'd usually keep the coffee warm until I went to sleep.

I put some jazz on the stereo and got ready for a shower. I was a bit disappointed that I couldn't reach Marylisa, because we had planned to see a special show at a club called The Tropicana.

■   ■   ■

Oh Marylisa, why didn't you call? That night, of all nights, I should have gone out. I should have stayed up to party, enjoyed the fast life, stayed out late in the company of friends, been seen drinking in a bar, in many bars, made a noise, danced, done anything. But how could I have known I would need an alibi? Instead, I listened quietly to jazz and went to bed.

Someone, somewhere, was thinking of murder that night.

■   ■   ■

I'd just stepped out of the tub and was brushing my teeth when the phone rang. It was Fred. Turning off the stereo, I asked him to call me back. I was dripping wet and my mouth was full of toothpaste.

He called me back after roll call. We talked for a few minutes, but his lieutenant approached his desk so he was forced to hang up abruptly.

I was reading a novel in the dim light of a small bedside lamp when my eyelids grew heavy. Again the phone rang and it was Fred. The fleeting thought went through my mind: Does he call so frequently out of concern, or to check up on me? We said good night. I turned off the light, and fell asleep.

Much later, I heard the phone ringing again. I had no idea what time it was. Still in bed, I reached over to pick up the receiver, dazed from sleep.

"Hello?" My voice wouldn't work.

The voice on the other end sounded like something out of a dream. Clutching the phone, I began to drift off to sleep.

"Laurie! Are you awake?" I recognized Fred's voice.

I nodded, forgetting that he couldn't see me. The tone of his voice sounded so different that it alarmed me slightly.

"Are you awake? Wake up!"

"What's wrong?" I asked, sitting bolt upright.

"Laurie, Chris has been shot. She's dead. I'm going over to the house now to see if the boys are okay. Are you all right?"

"Of course." But it really didn't register. I hung up, rolled over and fell back to sleep. I didn't fully understand what was going on; I thought it had been some kind of dream. Then the ringing woke me again. At once I remembered the previous phone call and jumped out of bed.

"Laurie?"

"I'm awake now. Freddy, was I dreaming, or ...?"

"No. Chris is dead. Somebody broke into the house—two guys, we're not sure. Maybe burglary. There was one guy—Sean saw one guy."

"My God."

"The kids are fine. They're next door here at the neighbors. Billy is coming to pick them up after the police talk to them."

"God, I—I don't know what to say."

"The stereo and the strongbox were moved, so we think they were in the process of stealing them. We don't know. Maybe Chris tried to struggle with them." Fred was talking rapidly, but with no emotion in his voice.

"Are you coming home? What should I do? Should I call your mom and dad?"

"Just get up and make some coffee. My partner and I will be coming over."

"Okay." I hung up the phone and quickly pulled my furry robe over my shoulders. For a second, I felt as though the whole thing was a joke, but I dismissed the thought. Fred wouldn't joke about such a matter. But it was so hard to believe ...

I stumbled down to the lower level of our apartment, squinting as I turned on the overhead light. I groped for the coffeepot, but suddenly realized that everything was packed in boxes, and I couldn't begin to guess where it was.

I plopped down on a box next to the table in the kitchen and tried to clear my head. None of it seemed real. It didn't make any sense. What was I going to do about work in the morning? Should I call in sick? How could I make coffee with everything packed? I wished Fred would come home and tell me that he was mistaken, that perhaps Chris had been injured, but not dead.

Not dead.

Not ... murdered.

What was I going to do with the two kids? What about moving? My head spun. It was all so complicated. I felt like crying. What a nightmare. I picked up a bottle of brandy from an open box near the table and took a swig, grimacing at the taste.

For what seemed like an eternity, I stared out the dark window and jumped at every headlight that drove up, thinking it was Fred and his partner. I called my mom and dad. I was hoping Fred might have called them and told them when he'd be coming home. Fred had just talked to them but hadn't said where he was calling from. My dad asked me if I'd like to wait for Fred at their house, but I decided I should stay at the apartment.

The sun began to rise. It was about four o'clock when I heard the buzzer downstairs. I ran outside, onto our second-floor balcony, hoping that it was Fred, but when I looked down I saw two detectives.

"Could we come in? We have some questions."

I left the apartment and hurried down the stairs to the main entrance to open the door. They followed me back upstairs, introducing themselves as Detectives Abram and Templin.

We sat down by the table in the lower-level kitchen. They explained that they hated to disturb me, that it was routine. One lit up a cigar.

"I'll do anything to help," I said.

They asked about Stu Honeck, and whether Fred was jealous of Stu's relationship with Christine. I told them about the obscene phone call, saying that it sounded just like Stu's voice. The phone interrupted us several times, and I had to leave the room to answer it. My mother called back, and Fred's mother called to see if her son was there.

Finally I asked if they knew what was keeping Freddy. "He called me a long time ago and said that he'd be coming right home. It's been over an hour, I think."

"He's probably talking to the cops at the scene."

A message came over their radios.

"Negative," he answered into it. "We're 10-6 at the same 10-20." This meant they were still busy at my address. I got the feeling that they were being evasive, and I wondered if Fred was in some kind of trouble.

The phone rang again. It was Freddy. "Something's weird," he said. "They're trying to keep me at the scene. Is anybody there?"

"Yeah."

"Are they asking you questions about me?"

"Yeah."

"Well, don't worry. I'll be home soon."

I walked back down into the kitchen. A hazy, gray light washed in through the windows. The detectives stood up.

"One more thing. Did you buy an off-duty weapon when you were on the Department?"

"No. All I had was a Department issue."

"Did you buy a gun once you got off the Department?"

I shook my head, no.

Why were they asking me about guns?

"Okay," one of the detectives said. "That about wraps it up." Then a smirk crossed his face and he asked an even stranger question. "By the way, you don't own any green jogging suits, do you?"

"I own a sweat suit. I work for a health club," I answered, puzzled. "Two sweat suits. A gray one and a red one."

"Mind showing us?"

"Well, they might be packed. Let me just check the hall closet," I said, as I led them upstairs. "I was supposed to work today. Should be one here. Here it is." I held the red suit up for them to see.

"Fine. We were told to ask. Routine, you know? Thanks again."

They were told to ask me about jogging suits? Why?

After they left, I went back down to the kitchen to wait for Fred.

Another half hour passed. I was restless and upset. I needed someone to talk to, so I made a few phone calls to pass the time. I called my friend Joanne and told her what had happened. Remembering that the call was long distance, and afraid that I was tying up the line, I ended our conversation.

I heard a noise and rushed to the window. No one was there. I sat back down again. It was dreadful. If someone could break into Christine's and kill her, they could just as easily break into our apartment. Irrational fear filled me. I wondered about all the threatening phone calls I had received.

Where was Fred?

I went back to the phone. Who else could I call? Judy. I knew she was accustomed to phone calls at all hours of the night. I got Tom's number from Judy's mother. Judy was alone in his apartment.

"First Tom gets busted, and now this! What's happening to us?" she said. "Now you have two kids to take care of?"

Finally, I heard a car pull up, and within a few minutes the buzzer downstairs rang. I hurried down the stairs to let them in.

"Laurie, this is my partner, Durfee," Fred said, smiling. He didn't appear in the least upset. It was as if he was treating the murder of his ex-wife like any other homicide.

I almost tripped on the hem of my robe as I led the way up the two flights of stairs to our apartment. I went into the kitchen, assuming they were right behind me. I turned, however, and saw that when they came in the door they had immediately begun walking down the hall toward the bedrooms. I thought Fred was showing Durfee to the bathroom, but when I retraced my steps and reached the top of the stairs, I saw that they were in the doorway of our bedroom. Their backs were to me.

Durfee had Fred's off-duty revolver in his hand, chamber open, checking the rounds and dumping them into his hand. He smelled the barrel. "Nope," he said, nonchalantly. "This gun hasn't been fired. Fred, why don't you clean this thing once in a while?"

"Yeah," I heard Fred say. He turned to look at me. "I just wanted to check out this gun right away, and make our report on it. That way there'll be no questions asked. Get dressed, we have to go downtown to ID the body."

"Right now?" I asked.

"Yeah."

"Besides, Fritz," Durfee was saying to Fred, "we think the guy used a forty-five tonight."

I gathered up some clothes and went into our bathroom to change. I was still taken aback at Fred's composure. It was pretty odd of him to march in and have Durfee check his off-duty gun. Wasn't it?

We got into the squad and proceeded downtown because Fred's car was still parked across from the Police Administration building. It was cool outside, and I shivered in my cotton shirt. Durfee chatted with me about the Department; he seemed like a nice guy.

When we arrived at the morgue, Fred and I were alone with the body. He approached the cold, stainless-steel table. It was dreadful. Chris was dressed in a pair of panties and a T-shirt with an Adidas logo. Her lifeless hands had been tied at one time, but someone had untied them and long strands of rope hung loosely at her wrists. A blue scarf was around her neck, and Fred explained that it had been used as a gag. She was about five feet, eight inches and 145 pounds. Fred rolled her body over to look at the bullet wound in her back. It was huge. I wondered if she had been sexually assaulted, since her legs weren't bound together, but I said nothing.

Fred motioned for me to come closer.

"Look at this. This is called radial expansion. See how the muzzle of the gun left its imprint in the skin? That gun was right up to her skin."

I bent over the body to see what Fred was referring to. Various scientific terms I'd learned at the Academy came to mind. I remembered being taught that all body fluids settle into the lowest parts of the body after death, giving the skin a bruised appearance in those places.

My mind was numb. I was exhausted. That was Christine in there! That had been Christine!

We walked up the stairs. Fred talked with the coroner while I waited in a small office with Durfee. He was writing notes in his memo book. I paged through a newspaper that was left on a desk, listening to Fred answer questions about Christine.

"How would you describe her, physically?" a man asked.

"Very athletic!" Fred quickly replied. "Oh yes—very athletic. She was on the swim team at college. Very athletic."

Fred's answer echoed in my mind, because it contradicted what he had often told me. Very athletic? He once told me he couldn't even get her to go jogging with him. He'd told me Chris was lazy, fat, unmotivated. Now he told the coroner just the opposite. Then I heard him say, "It was common for her to run around the house in nothing but a T-shirt and panties."

We walked to the cafeteria. Fred asked me to wait for him there while he punched out his time card and reported to the top floor. Durfee had informed him that some inspector needed to see him. Before he and Durfee left, Fred popped open his briefcase to toss in his memo book. I noticed that his off-duty gun was in his briefcase, even though he was still wearing his service revolver.

Sipping weak coffee from one of the machines, I sat at a table looking through the windows. I knew that the Police Chief's office was on the same floor that Fred had been summoned to, and I recalled the day I'd waited there with my lawyer from the union.

It was still too early to call the gym. I glanced through a magazine that I'd picked off the rack near the cashier. To pass the time, I read my horoscope: "June for Leos is going to be a great month! A newness; finances good."

■　　■　　■

A newness! Is that what it was? June 1981 was the beginning of something new, all right. The beginning of a series of events that made my previous problems look like blessings. The beginning of the end, for me.

Or so I thought, for so many years.

10

THE HOUSE ON RAMSEY STREET

After spending a day with Fred's parents, we took Sean and Shannon home to the apartment, which was still filled with cartons. The boys seemed fine, to my surprise, chattering about the murder as if it were nothing more than a television cops-and-robbers show.

A description of the suspect sought by the police was announced on the evening news. Channel four reported that Sean had described his attacker to the police as a white male with a six- to eight-inch ponytail, five feet, ten inches to six feet tall, wearing a green jogging suit.

"But it *wasn't* a green jogging suit," Sean protested to me and Fred. "It was a green army jacket, without camouflage."

"Sometimes the news gets things wrong," Fred explained to his son.

Numerous calls poured into the police stations. People claimed to have seen a white, male jogger frequently in the area. Others called to say that there had been a substitute mailman in the neighborhood fitting that description.

"Dad?" Sean began with difficulty. "We were all standing there, after it happened—the policemen, and Stu ... well, Stu said 'I bet Freddy did this!' But I know you didn't, daddy!" Sean burst into tears.

I looked at Fred, now hugging Sean, and he returned my angry gaze.

"That wasn't right," I whispered. "To say something like that, in front of a kid."

Later that day, Fred began frantically rooting through the boxes in the spare room. I was irritated that he was making the room a shambles, and asked, "What are you doing?"

"Trying to find my leather jewelry box. Where is it?"

"I have no idea," I told him. "My mother packed this room, so she packed all of your things. Why? You're making a mess."

"It's got to be here," he persisted.

"Why do you need your jewelry box?"

"Because! I have a ring of keys in there, one of which is the key to the house on Ramsey. I wasn't supposed to have a key to the house at all—Christine didn't want me to have one. So, one day when I picked up the boys I made copies of Sean's house key. I hid one in my jewelry box."

"One?"

"I had one on my key chain with my car keys, but I had to give it to the police, so they could get back into the house to dust for prints."

I was disturbed at Fred's easy admission of the sneaky way he'd obtained keys to the house, against Christine's wishes. He tore open another box.

"Here it is! Now we have to get more of the kids' clothing. Some pajamas and toothbrushes. Let's go."

While Fred and I went over to the house on Ramsey Street, the boys had supper at my mom's house. I told Fred that it might be unwise to bring them along, thinking that it would traumatize them. When we opened the door, I was almost bowled over by the odor of dog piss in Chris's house.

"Christ!" Fred exclaimed. "Does it stink! That dog has been gone for almost four months now. She should have used rug shampoo. I was so embarrassed when the cops were in here—a brand-new home and it's a regular pigpen!"

I stared at Fred, confused by his animosity and shocked that he wasn't more tolerant, considering the fact that Chris was no longer there to defend herself or her house. We left the first level and walked up the stairs. Pointing to the boys' bedroom, Fred complained further.

"This room is such a mess that the cops assumed a big struggle took place here. But Sean said no, that's the way it always looks!"

We stepped over piles of game and puzzle pieces, paint brushes, dirty underwear and toy trucks. I started to pack some of their clothes into a paper bag. Fred paced like a mad tiger, and I assumed he was either stirred by memories or still disgruntled by the condition of the house. Crayons were ground into the carpeting, and one Mickey Mouse sheet on the bunk bed was stained from bed-wetting. I opened a window for some fresh air.

"Don't let this scare you," Freddy said. "The boys were never allowed to live like pigs when I was living here! You have to discipline kids!" He walked out of the room like an incensed landlord, running his hand over the door and looking around for possible damage to the walls and furniture.

I followed him into a den.

"This strongbox is right in the middle of the room for some reason," he commented. "But there are only papers and documents inside. The stereo was moved, too, but I really don't know if that necessarily means anything."

"Burglars?"

"The cops didn't find a point of entry. The patio door is a possibility, but who knows? One lieutenant told me that a detective caseknifed the door in back, just to see if it could be done. Knowing Chris, she probably didn't even lock the damn door. That was one of her bad habits." Fred sighed. "Honeck claims that when she drove him home, he asked whether or not she locked the back door, and she told him no, because she was going to be right back. So maybe it was open long enough for someone to get in."

"But what time was that?" I asked.

"He claims that it was around 9:30 PM."

"Then that doesn't make any sense, because the shooting was so many hours later."

"True, 2:00 AM. Unless Honeck's lying about the time that Chris dropped him off."

"Why would he lie?" I asked, noticing Fred's preoccupation with Honeck.

"Well," Fred said, "if they were fooling around that night. Let's say they went to his house when Chris drove him home. If it was later, around midnight? She spends an hour or so over at his house, comes home, and someone is already in the house."

"But you told me that Stu had spent the night here before, so why would they bother to sneak off to Stu's house?"

"That was before I turned Stu's ass in," Fred said. "If Internal Affairs was watching her house, they'd want to leave."

"I thought Stu worked early," I said, referring to second shift.

"He does, but he had that night off or something." Fred went into the bathroom to retrieve the boys' toothbrushes and bathtub toys. I followed him cautiously, disliking the feeling of going through someone else's drawers and closets.

"Why would Stu lie about what time she drove him home?" I asked again.

"To look better in front of the Department, so he wouldn't take a rap for sleeping with her. How much more innocent can you get than a wholesome curfew of 9:30? Unless he couldn't remember what the hell time it was. What really pisses me off is that she left my kids alone in the house. Even if it was early."

"Why would Chris drive Stu home at all? He lives right around the corner. It would be more trouble to pull your car out of the driveway and then park it—I'd just walk home, wouldn't you?"

"Who knows."

I stared at a wad of unraveled gauze draped down the side of an open cabinet. This was the remains of Sean's attempt to administer first aid as his mother lay bleeding on her bed. He'd tried to pack the wound with gauze, before calling for help. Chris had died so swiftly that his efforts were futile. Why hadn't the cops taken it away?

Fred pushed back the shower curtain and stared at the tub.

"Do you see why I couldn't live with that woman? I built a perfectly good clothes hamper, right into that cabinet. It leads to the laundry room. But no! She had this filthy habit of filling the bathtub with dirty clothes! To hide it, she'd pull the shower curtain closed." He stopped, and felt the clothes in the bathtub.

"What?"

"They're not wet."

"So?"

"So ... something doesn't make sense. Do you remember what Stu and Chris were doing during the day?"

"No."

"They were working in the garden." Fred pointed out a window. "See that? Stu brought over his Rototiller, to rework the ground, and they were putting in railroad ties as patio steps."

"Which means?" I asked, tired of Fred's riddles.

"You were with me at the morgue—Chris was perfectly clean. Her hair was freshly shampooed. It shone under the lights. She didn't look like someone who had been working in the garden all afternoon. When I saw Stu, he was cleaned up, too. They both showered somewhere, and it wasn't here. Don't you see? If Chris had showered here, these clothes in the tub would be on the floor. She wouldn't put them back into a wet tub. I bet she spent some time at Honeck's house for a shower and a roll in the hay, and he's not saying."

"What if they don't find traces of semen at the autopsy?" I asked. "I don't think you should jump to conclusions. There might be a few holes in Honeck's story, but it doesn't spell homicide. Besides, Orval Zellmer lives right across the street from Honeck. He's the king of Internal Affairs. If Honeck was under suspicion for sleeping with Chris, I doubt if she'd frequent his house."

"When I lived with Stu, you were there quite a few times. Zellmer can't tell who's coming or going. Too many people live there. I'm tellin' ya—Internal Affairs had a car on Christine's house. I just don't know when," Fred insisted.

"Then they must have been asleep if they didn't see anyone break in that night!"

I followed him down into the kitchen. He opened a cabinet that squeaked loudly.

"I can see where all the money was going," he snapped, continuing his macabre post-mortem critique. "Just think! The bitch was telling me that she didn't have enough food for the boys. She's got more booze in here than the corner bar. Damn!" He slammed the door shut. I watched in disbelief as he whirled around to open the freezer. "Not enough goddamn food?" he repeated, his face red.

Chris's small, suede purse lay open on the kitchen counter. Fred picked it up and noted aloud that her bank book showed a total of three thousand dollars. There were several checks, still uncashed, in a brown envelope. Her leather wallet held sixty dollars.

"Do you realize she's got more in this purse than I have in the bank?" Fred demanded. He continued to rummage through the purse and pulled out a pack of birth-control pills. "Look at this!" he bellowed, waving them in the air.

"Stop snooping!" I said finally. "Let's just go. You're getting yourself all worked up over nothing. If I didn't know any better, I'd say you're actually acting jealous. My God, Fred, she's dead!"

He ignored me, studying Christine's kitchen calendar. I got up from the chair and walked out of the house. Fred caught up with me and pointed to some wires that ran parallel with the roof.

"At one time, this was an excellent alarm system. But right after Chris kicked me out, the garage door interfered with one of the circuits, which knocked out the whole system.

"Why didn't she have it fixed? It might have saved her life. Why? Why? Why did she sell my Great Dane? That dog could have saved her life, too! All for a lousy buck. I think I'll hand her purse over to the police. Maybe they can go through her address book to list people to interview."

■　　■　　■

We spent the following days talking to landlords. The efficiency across from the park was too small for us now that we had two children. A two-week extension at the three-bedroom apartment was a relief, but we couldn't stay there, because that building didn't allow children.

Christine's parents, Alice and Earl Pennings, insisted that her body be buried in Appleton, where she'd been raised.

The weekend of the funeral I was miserable. I felt entirely out of place. Fred neglected me. He never introduced me to anyone. He'd rise from his metal folding chair next to mine to shake the hand of another relative and stand in front of me, leaving me to stare at his rear end. I was the only person wearing black, and wondered if this old tradition was no longer followed. Kathy arrived with John, dressed in a short, orange, sleeveless dress and a white, crocheted poncho. She sobbed hysterically while she leaned on her husband. Christine's mother, Alice, graciously attempted to comfort Kathy, saying, "Come on now. We must be strong."

Fred's children were the only ones who sat with me during the buffet. Fred had disappeared into the bar and his family filled a different table. The two kids laughed and played with their food until I asked them to behave. I guessed that, unlike their father, they were too young to understand what had happened. Finally, Fred returned to our table with a drink in his hand.

"Did you get me a drink?" I asked.

"I forgot. I mean, I didn't know you wanted one."

"Daddy," Sean interrupted, "I wanna go swimming."

"Later."

"Can I get a soda?" Shannon asked, his blue eyes round and large.

After the boys scampered away, I turned to Fred. "I thought you'd never come back! Not to sound self-absorbed, but thanks for leaving me all by myself."

In the main room of the funeral parlor sat a huge bunch of pink roses, as big as a bush. It was so large that it dwarfed the other sympathy bouquets, and we wondered who had sent it. When we got close enough to see the card, we read: "To My Chris, Love, Stu."

"There have to be over two hundred roses on this thing!" I exclaimed. "It must have cost a fortune."

"Honeck sure is playing this to the hilt," Fred said in a whisper. " 'To My Chris!' Yuck! Methinks he doth protest too much!"

You, too, Fred, I thought.

The coffin was as pink as the bouquet of roses, which struck me as particularly poignant. Fred and I knelt before the body, respectfully silent. Simultaneously, we noticed an engagement ring sparkling on

Christine's hand. After we returned to our seats, Fred turned to me. "You saw it, too? That ring wasn't on her hand when we saw her at the morgue! She only had a small pinkie ring on. And it wasn't in her jewelry box, because I went through that to see if anything had been stolen. I don't know how that ring got there, but I bet it happened today.

"Chris never said a word to me about getting married again! That would have been the first thing she would have thrown in my face—if it were true! Especially since I remarried! But this is the first I've heard of it! The kids weren't even aware of it. Of all people, the kids would have known." Fred paused, looking around the dimly lit room. "Let's find Stu and see what he has to say."

Honeck, when we found him, began telling us about two detectives who'd arrived at his house to warn him that he was going to be questioned about his relationship with Chris. He said he was told that the Department was going to want to know whether or not he was having sex with her. I decided I had heard enough. I went outside.

■   ■   ■

During the drive home from Appleton, Sean and Shannon asleep in the back seat, Fred announced that he had agreed to allow Attorney Kershek to handle the problem of the estate paperwork.

"Isn't that ... wasn't that Christine's divorce lawyer?"

"Yeah, but I talked to him today. He's cool."

"Cool?" I thought, bewildered at Fred's capriciousness. He had previously complained that, because Kershek was related to Christine, his representation of her throughout the divorce had been much more vigorous than that of an ordinary lawyer. Now Fred said, "He's cool."

Fred suggested that we move into the house on Ramsey. I disliked the idea. Not only was it the murder scene, but it held all the memories of his past marriage—wedding gifts, baby pictures, all the work he'd done during their days, months and years together. He continued to argue about it, even as I tried explaining my point of view. His solution was to delay the matter until we could reach an agreement. We still had another week to stay at the apartment. After that, we would stay at my parents' house while they were on the west coast. Meanwhile we could discuss it further, even though I was set against the idea.

■   ■   ■

I was at work at the gym one afternoon the next week when two detectives arrived to talk to me. They were trying to persuade everyone involved with the case to take lie-detector tests—Fred, Judy Zess, Stu Honeck, me—in order to "clear" everyone.

My first impulse was to agree, since I had nothing to hide. Then, something about their smiling faces made me think twice. I didn't put it past them to dig for information they could use against me at my discrimination hearings.

I talked to the cops about the test. I told them about a recent experience I'd had with a similar test—I'd taken one for a security job I'd applied for. The results had been confusing and inconclusive, which made me reluctant to try again with a far more serious matter at hand. Finally I said I'd call them back after seeking the advice of a lawyer.

I phoned Fred's lawyer, Reilly. "Absolutely not! I wouldn't advise it. They can misconstrue the results," he said. "Don't trust them. They can't force you to submit to a polygraph either."

Fred disagreed with this advice. "I'm going to take the damn test," he said.

"That's foolish," I said. "Reilly said—"

"I've got to do it," he said, interrupting. "For the children. The Department promised that anyone who agrees to the poly will be cleared if they pass. They won't bother me any more."

"Judy's not taking one either," I said. "Who knows what they'll ask you once they have you strapped in that chair? You could get fired."

Fred went ahead. He returned that evening, exhausted, unnerved and looking pale. They'd watched him via a video camera while he took the test. The questions they'd asked him referred to experiences he'd had as far back as age sixteen. He told me he'd admitted smoking pot in college at La Crosse, and lying on a traffic accident report once, by saying that he was wearing a seatbelt when in fact he was not. He claimed they asked him numerous questions about his temper—if he had ever physically abused Christine, or if he had ever used excessive force while on duty.

"I told them I punched Christine ... once," Fred told me.

■   ■   ■

The next day, I dropped Sean and Shannon off at my mom's house on the way to the gym. When I returned to pick them up that afternoon, I was happy to see my mother in a good mood. She liked children so much.

"How did the kids behave?"

"Fine! They're at the playground."

We talked about our apartment. "We canceled the efficiency place, for obvious reasons," I said. "Four of us couldn't live there. But I don't want to live on Ramsey. Fred just can't understand why not."

"I know how you must feel. That was his house from a previous marriage, for heaven's sake!"

"Maybe only women feel this way," I said.

"How was the funeral? I thought about you all weekend."

I shrugged. "Fred's mother came up to me, hugged me, and cried, 'You're all he has now'!"

"Now?" My mother blinked. "What an odd thing to say. Like as if when Chris was alive, Fred had her, too?"

"That's how it struck me."

"Oh well, don't dwell on it. It was probably said in grief."

I brooded for a while. There was something I felt awkward about, even with my mom.

"It's this situation," I finally said. "Suddenly having two kids dropped in my lap."

"So?"

"I didn't want children."

"I know that ... but these are two small boys that went through an awful, a terrible ordeal! They need a home with their father."

"But—"

"Laurie, stop being so selfish."

"But I married Fred! I didn't marry his kids!" I protested. "I like Sean and Shannon, they're nice kids. But I know what kids mean. It means babysitters and money for school and chauffeuring them all over and chocolate fingerprints on everything!"

"You're scared. Give it a chance! You don't know it will be all that bad!"

"They're not my kids! I'm still trying to adjust to being married—now I'm an instant mommy. Sean is only about ten years younger than me. It was different for you, mom. You had a marriage that was like a World War II novel. You got engaged, dad was drafted, and you waited faithfully for him for four years. He came back, you got married, you had kids. Simple and acceptable."

"It wasn't that simple," she said quietly.

I said nothing.

"I'll help you as much as I can with the boys. They can stay here when you're at work." I saw Sean and Shannon opening the gate of the white picket fence that enclosed the back yard.

"Thanks," I said.

To be honest, I resented the kids. Two children tagging along after me made me feel suddenly older—too old. I wasn't ready for this. It got ridiculous. I peered into the mirror, expecting to see wrinkles around my eyes.

One morning, Fred was playing in a baseball game at a local park. I fed the boys breakfast, got them dressed and piled them into my car to go watch the game. The children and I walked past some men from the other team when we entered the park. I was wearing a plaid T-shirt and cotton shorts, and I was mortified to hear wolfish comments directed at me.

"Mommy! Mommy!" one of the men panted, and the others whistled. I bit my lip and kept walking, telling myself not to let it bother me. But it did.

At the same time, I felt guilty about not being more compassionate, so I decided to try harder to put my needs aside. The boys insisted they loved me, and it was such a pure, unconditional response that it touched me deeply.

I was strict, seeing to it that they ate a balanced diet and picked up their toys. They, in turn, interpreted my discipline as a sign that I cared, according to the child psychologist they were seeing. His name was Ken Ploch.

The two boys had been suffering from recurring nightmares, so of course my first instinct was to wake them. Ploch disagreed. He said they should be left alone to dream undisturbed; it was the only way they could release what was bottled up inside them, to dream it out. With Fred working nights, the kids would often crawl into bed with me because they were so frightened. I would wake up in the morning to discover Sean and Shannon under the covers. I'd done the same thing when I was a child, and it touched me.

To my dismay, however, Ploch also recommended that we move into the Ramsey house—just the opposite of what I had expected (and hoped) that he'd say. He said it would get the kids back into familiar surroundings and routines, with their pals; that it would make the transference of a maternal figure easier for them. This was a suggestion I didn't want to hear. I still didn't want to live there.

Meanwhile, the constant arguments with Fred, the continual bickering, went on. He couldn't seem to let that house—or Christine—alone.

One Saturday, I pulled a pair of jeans over my black leotard and threw on a light jacket, getting ready to leave for work at the gym. Fred told me that he had to go over to the house on Ramsey. He said Christine's mother, Alice, had called and asked if she could come into town to pick up a few of her daughter's personal belongings. Fred had told her that he would meet her there at ten.

According to Fred, when he pulled up in front of the house, a crowd was already in the driveway. He said that Alice and Earl Pennings stood there, with the lawyer Kershek, Christine's brother Michael, Christine's sister Barb and Barb's husband Bruce Christ, and Stu Honeck. Fred claimed that Stu had already used his house key to let everyone into the house. Fred said that, despite his frantic efforts to get the situation under control, he was outnumbered. The family quickly loaded up their cars. Stu even unhooked the HBO unit and removed the antenna. They even loaded up Chris's car and were planning to drive that away, too.

Fred made the incident sound more like grave-robbing than retrieving personal effects. He claimed he told Kershek that no one had given Honeck permission to unlock "his" house, and that as far as he was concerned, everyone was trespassing, to which Kershek allegedly snorted, "So call a cop." Fred said Kershek informed him that Alice planned to petition the court to be appointed co-representative of the estate. He said he tried explaining that he was planning to sell Chris's Mercury Bobcat to start a college fund for the boys, but someone drove away in it.

The following day, Fred said he'd stop at the Ramsey house to clean and disconnect the kitchen appliances.

"Probably half the food in that fridge is spoiled already. We have to move this weekend, remember?"

He paused, waiting for a response from me. When there was none, he said, "What I'm trying to get at is, we have no other recourse than to move into that house."

"Why?"

"We've been through this."

"Why can't we rent a place until you sell the house?"

"Rent? Again? How many security deposits have we lost so far? Besides, we're paying a mortgage on a house we're not living in. We have my sons to consider. We're worse off financially, now, than we ever were. And the house is close to their school—St. Roman's."

"Wouldn't a public school be cheaper? Do you know what tuition is at a private school?"

"We'll talk about that some other time. Right now, all I'm telling you is that we have no other choice but to move into my house," Fred said.

I felt cornered. Fred seemed to have a strange, almost frantic obsession with the house. I wondered if he'd ever part with it.

Still, I did look forward to leaving that troublesome apartment. We'd often tried to contact the landlady about maintenance problems, but the complex of buildings was so large that we were easily avoided. A repair person was always "coming," but this phantom never appeared. The heat vents in the apartment were blasting ninety-degree air into an already warm living room, so we ran the air-conditioner for relief. The hallway closet door had come off its hinges, and the toilet in the bathroom formerly occupied by Judy, had been out of order since the time my parents came over for dinner on their anniversary. Water was running inside the tank. I taped a small sign on the door so the children wouldn't forget to avoid it.

Just before we moved out, into my parents' house, a young woman from across the hall knocked on the door, asking if she could borrow a plunger.

"You're lucky you're moving out," she said. "These places look so nice, but they're falling apart!"

■ ■ ■

During this period, I finally had some good news. I'd taken a physical agility exam as part of the application process for a job as campus guard, or Public Safety Officer, at Marquette University. During the test, I'd run into a former Milwaukee cop who'd been in my Academy class. We'd had a beer together after the test at a bar nearby.

A few days later, I learned I had the job—Marquette University wanted to hire me! I was to start working second shift, which meant I could still keep my other job at the gym. The pay was very close to what I had made as a city cop.

I told Fred the good news about my job when he returned home. Shortly afterwards, he disappeared in his van. I thought nothing of it—I guessed he'd just gone to park it elsewhere, but when he returned, he proudly displayed a shiny, new bicycle.

"Purple!" he said. "Your favorite color!"

"What?"

"It's for you—to celebrate your new job."

Fred always went out and bought things on impulse. It wasn't great for budgeting, but I could hardly complain. It was a nice gesture.

■   ■   ■

The following week, Fred went to the Ramsey house to retrieve something, only to discover that Christine's mom, Alice Pennings, had had all the locks changed.

"That's Criminal Damage to Property! Trespassing! Breaking and Entering!" he yelled, speaking in Police Department capitals. "So Alice doesn't want us to live there? Fuck her. I know how to get into my own damn house," Fred told me. "Hell, I'm a carpenter."

He went back, broke in and changed the doorknob on the back door. He said that he noticed Honeck drive by. Although I'm not sure how Fred knew this, he said that Stu promptly drove away and called Alice in Appleton, to report that despite having hired a locksmith, Fred was back in the house.

Fred told me that the Pennings called Kershek, who was vacationing in California. Kershek called Fred's lieutenant, attempting to persuade him to press charges against Fred for breaking and entering. It was a civil matter, the lieutenant said.

Why were the Pennings so vehemently against Fred? What did they have against him? What did they know that I didn't?

Then Alice insisted that Fred make an offer to purchase the estate's half of the house.

"In other words," Fred complained, "they expect me to buy half of my own house from my children!"

Still, he couldn't leave the house alone. One day he was taking apart the bed in Christine's bedroom. It was a massive, cannonball-style headboard made from walnut. As he began to lift the mattress from the box spring, a penis-shaped vibrator fell to the floor.

"I can't believe the police didn't discover it!" he said. "But it's no wonder, the crime scene that night was a regular circus, with almost every squad on the South Side climbing over one another in the house."

At Fred's request, two detectives arrived to write up a report about the vibrator, but didn't seem interested enough to confiscate the thing.

"They could have taken it to the Crime Lab, and tested it for traces of pubic hair or semen," Fred explained. "But they acted like, 'Who cares'?"

Sean complained that an envelope containing almost one hundred dollars was missing from his room. The money was part of a fund-raising effort for baseball uniforms for St. Roman's. Fred reported this to the police as well.

Although there was no mention of it in the newspapers, Fred told me the police were pestering a man they considered a suspect in Christine's murder. He lived across the street from the Ramsey house.

"He's been described as sort of a nut," Fred explained. "A strange guy, living alone ... history of emotional problems."

"Seriously?" I asked.

"It looks pretty suspicious. I heard that right after the shooting he reported that a thirty-eight caliber revolver had been stolen from his garage."

"But the gun used on Chris was a forty-five, right?"

"No—ballistics determined that it was a thirty-eight."

"Then why was the bullet hole so huge?" I asked. "We saw it at the morgue—remember?"

"They said the wound was that large because of the close proximity from which the gun was fired. Right up to the skin."

"So this guy reported a gun of the same caliber stolen, even before the police knew it was a thirty-eight?"

"Yeah. He also made a statement to a neighbor that he's missing his green jogging suit."

"He must be crazy."

Fred agreed. "He works second shift at a factory, has long brown hair. He paints cars as a hobby, so he'd also have a painter's mask."

"The murderer was wearing a mask?" I asked.

"Well, according to Shannon he was. But then Shannon also says he saw a silver six-shooter with pearl handles."

I shook my head. "He's the one who saw a green jogging suit, too. I think Sean is more credible. He's older, and he's a smart boy. Sean said he saw an army jacket. That's more plausible."

Fred nodded. "The guy consented to a polygraph. The first two were inconclusive, but he passed the third time. He claims to have an alibi." Fred grew silent and appeared moody.

"What's on your mind?"

"Honeck. The whole thing is so goddamn goofy. That surprise engagement! I just re-read Sean's police report at work. He told the cops that on that night, when Chris tucked him into bed, she looked upset about something. Maybe Stu asked Chris that very night if she would marry him, and she refused. Maybe that's why she was upset. You know, Stu was so positive that Chris wasn't seeing other men. He even told the police that she wasn't dating anyone else. But that's not true! Sean told me that she had lots of other male visitors. And I found some cards and letters hidden away in her knitting basket—letters and greeting cards from different guys, signed Bob, Frank, George ... and a Mother's Day card from Stu. A real corny one.

"Know what I think? I wouldn't be surprised if Stu was turned down that night, went home, got one of his guns, let himself back in with his key. Who knows? He only lives a minute away."

"Except Stu claims Chris drove him home," I said.

"Sean says that Stu went home by himself! He knows how loud his mother's car was, because the muffler on Christine's Bobcat was so bad. He told me that Stu and Chris left the house earlier, to return the Rototiller, but that was around dinner. It was still light outside. Sean is positive that Stu left later by himself."

I could only take Fred's word for all this. "I don't get it," I said, puzzled.

"There are too many things that aren't right. Honeck claims he had one vodka gimlet with Chris, while he was there for dinner. Yet there was an empty gallon of wine in the kitchen on the counter, with two wine glasses right next to it."

"Did they dust the glasses for prints? Maybe Chris had drinks with someone else after Stu left."

Fred snorted. "The assholes didn't dust those glasses until I asked them to—the same day they came over to look at the dildo I found. What kind of police work is that?"

"That bottle of wine could have been left there from some other day," I said. "What if it was an old bottle?"

"There was a sales receipt from the liquor store in a bag on the floor. It was dated May 27 and listed a price that matched the price-sticker on the bottle."

"Did the autopsy discover alcohol in the blood?" I asked.

"I don't know yet. Besides all that, Stu says in his police report that just after he got home Chris called him and they spent another hour or so on the phone. Why would you call someone just after spending almost the whole day with them?"

"Unless you were ironing out a disagreement."

"Another thing—they never determined the time of death. They were supposed to use a rectal thermometer at the scene. Everyone's going on the assumption that her death was close to the time that Honeck called the paramedics. It could have been earlier."

■   ■   ■

At least on the job things were going well. I loved the work. Our uniform was a white shirt and blue pants, with Public Safety Office patches and badges. The security force used a couple of squad cars—the campus was large—and we followed usual police procedures, with which I was well acquainted.

All the men on the job were experienced. I was the only female officer on my shift. My lieutenant was a former state trooper, and there were ex-police officers from other cities as well. The person I liked most was the director of the department, the person who had hired me. Her name was Carol Kurdziel. Her opinions were feminist, and she didn't mince words. She showed some sympathy for my dismissal from MPD; she said she was "aware of the chief's ways."

I adjusted well to the new job and was happy to be busy working again. Kurdziel showed me what I'd scored on the psychological exam I took when I applied. The results described me as being confident, assertive and independent, but also indicated that my feelings were easily hurt. As I read the exam results, I told Kurdziel about my situation with two new children. She sympathized, urging me to call her anytime if I wanted to talk. The business card she handed me listed her home phone number.

But off the job ... there was Fred. One day he came home from work, to my parents' house, where we were staying, looking frazzled.

"They're questioning me at work," he blurted out.

"About what?"

"They asked me if I had a key to the Ramsey house. I told them that I gave it to a cop that same night. Then they wanted to know how many keys I had. So I told them: two. One on my key ring, and the other one back here."

"They must know Honeck had a key, too?"

"I don't know. It was like they were trying to establish whether or not you or I had access to the house, because there was no sign of forced entry." Fred looked worried.

"You or *me*?" I replied, in disbelief. "Why? I didn't even know you had a key! The first I heard of a key was when you started tearing open all those boxes, looking for it."

"I know. I kept it a secret, because I wasn't supposed to have a key to that house."

"Did you explain that to them?" I asked.

"No. That would make me look bad."

"You? Jesus Christ! What about me? You make it sound like I

had a key to the place! Why did you even tell them that you had the extra key?"

"I couldn't lie," Fred replied, piously. "If the police saw us in the house later on, I would have had to explain how we got back in, anyway."

I wanted to believe him, but this thing of his volunteering information and letting the blame fall on me for so many things kept repeating itself, and I grew angry.

"No wonder they were hassling me to take a polygraph!" I said. "It's all your fault. First you tell Chris that we wouldn't go to Shannon's communion because of me! Then you drop a dime on Honeck for sleeping with her and let them both think it was me! You were just too chicken to take the blame yourself!"

"Bullshit!" Fred shouted at me.

"Bullshit, nothing! It's been nothing but trouble ever since we got married!" The months of stress caught up with me, and I started to yell. "My mother told me divorced men were nothing but trouble. I should have listened to her! I thought you were different!"

"What are you telling me?" Fred snarled.

"I'm telling you I'm tired of being your fall guy and I want out of this whole nasty situation. I'm not moving into that house on Ramsey! I'm not playing Susie Homemaker to kids who aren't mine! I'm tired of being treated like dirt by your family and I'm tired of this whole thing."

"Either you come with me to live on Ramsey in my house, or I'm leaving you," Fred threatened.

"Fine!" I replied. "I'll live right here with my parents. Go to your damned house."

Fred stood up, as silent as a stone. I was sitting on a lawn chair in the yard, my arms wrapped around my knees. As I watched him walk back into my mom and dad's house, I began to regret my words.

Fred came back out with Shannon. He knew I had a soft spot in my heart for the child, because he looked just like his dad with his large, blue eyes and shaggy, blond hair.

"Kiss Laurie goodbye," Fred announced. "We have to go."

Shannon looked puzzled, because my face was red from crying. Then he smiled and leaned over to hug me, which really affected me, as Fred had intended.

"You really disappoint me, Laurie," Fred whispered, taking his son's hand and walking away.

■   ■   ■

I remember going inside and sitting down with my sketchbooks. For a few hours I worked on a drawing of my mom and dad. As I drew the familiar faces, I remembered wishing so often that I was the oldest child instead of the youngest. I drew lines of weariness around the eyes of my beloved parents, then quickly erased them—only to draw them in again. The lines were real, the worry was real, the age was real. If only I could take away the worry as easily as I brushed away the lines!

■   ■   ■

I heard feet on the stairs. My mother entered the room with a cup in her hand. She'd been in the basement, canning quart jars of dill pickles. A kitchen towel was thrown over her shoulder and she wore a crisp gingham apron.

"I heard the fight, Laurie," she said. She smelled of dill and brine—good smells. "I had the windows open because of the steam. Is there anything I can do?"

We talked for a while, until it grew dark. Then we walked downstairs and sat at the table in the kitchen. A little while later Fred came home, Sean and Shannon following him in the door.

My parents took Sean and Shannon for ice cream so Fred and I could be alone. He begged and pleaded that I change my mind about living on Ramsey. He promised a regular babysitter, a housekeeper, a guard dog, a burglar alarm. He was bursting with his usual optimism. Soon my determination weakened; in another half hour I found myself apologizing.

I agreed to live in the house on Ramsey for the time being. We wouldn't move in until after it was cleaned and redecorated, and while we lived there, the house would be put on the market to be sold. It was a last resort. It was all I agreed to.

11

THE BOMBSHELL FALLS

I was on campus with Thomas Conway, my sergeant at Marquette, when I got a radio message to report back to headquarters for a phone call. It was Fred's lawyer, Reilly.

"Hi, Laurie," he began. "Fred wanted me to call you. He's at the Crime Lab. He wanted me to let you know—they found blood on his service revolver."

"Thank you," I said slowly, hanging up the receiver.

How could that be? Fred had at least two guns. His off-duty gun was a small Smith and Wesson, thirty-eight caliber with wood grips and a two-inch barrel—a very common style. His service revolver, also a thirty-eight, had a four-inch barrel and big, black rubber grips. He always wore the larger gun to work. Now the Crime Lab had found blood on his service revolver. Why? Why had they even looked? Throughout the remaining hours on my shift I wondered about it, thinking that there had to be a logical explanation.

Fred met me at the door when I returned home. He looked frantic.

"What's this all about?" I asked him.

"It was type A blood. I'm type A. But so was Chris," Fred said. I had no idea whether or not this was true. "The only difference is, mine is negative and Christine's was positive."

"Which ...?"

"They can't tell a subgroup like that from dried blood."

"Fred, this ... has to be a frame." I didn't know what to say.

"Maybe it's my blood on that gun, from a fight I got into at work. We got dispatched to a disturbance at Montreal's ..."

"You didn't tell me you were hurt at work."

"I wasn't hurt that bad. But I picked a scab on my arm. That must be it. They've been crawling all over me since we were at the lab. They might as well be accusing me—but I was on duty that night! Then they were ridiculous enough to suggest that you might have been able to switch guns with me that night. Isn't that stupid?"

"*Me*? What are you talking about?" The conversation began to take on an unreal quality.

"You didn't have an alibi that night ..."

"Are you crazy? This is a homicide! An alibi?"

"I know, but ... the way they were questioning me."

"It's your gun! They found blood on the gun you were wearing that night. Why would they be asking questions about me?"

"I passed the polygraph. You refused to take one."

"But—"

"Maybe I'm overreacting, Laurie. All I know is that Reilly told me not to cooperate with them anymore. They'll see that it's my blood on that gun."

I looked at him, trying to make some sense out of what he'd said. The only logical explanation in my mind was that it was his blood on the gun. I didn't like the fact that I was under suspicion, but I thought that it was because Fred was on duty that night, so when they found the blood, it was only routine for them to question my whereabouts. The detectives had talked to me that night. They would find out it was Fred's blood. They must!

That weekend we had the task of cleaning the house on Ramsey before moving in. Several friends of ours came along to help, and so did my mom and dad. The children did all they could. It took six of us over ten hours to finish.

While I was wiping the dust from some kitchen cabinets, I found a coffee mug containing a handful of Fred's old bullets. He said he hadn't even known they were there.

We packed away all of Christine's personal possessions. There were about fifteen different macramé wall hangings, pictures, lamp-shades and plant hangers that must have taken hours to make by hand. Fred wondered out loud why Alice and Earl didn't come and get her artwork and take it home with them.

■   ■   ■

It was only a few days later, just after Fred's birthday (I remember the boys and I got him a pet hamster as a present) that the next and most devastating bombshell landed. I'd been on duty for several hours when I realized I'd left my radio at the station. I'd been using the squad car radio. Back at headquarters, I noticed the sergeant's door was closed, which was unusual. I stared at the lettering that read "Public Safety Department" and knocked. When Conway opened the door, he had an odd look on his face.

"What's wrong?" I said. "I just came back for my radio."

Beyond Conway was Fred's lieutenant and another huge man. They pulled me inside and flashed their badges.

"Of course, you know Lieutenant Ruscitti. I'm Detective Frank Cole. You're under arrest for first-degree murder."

What? I couldn't believe I'd heard him. What was going on? I stood in shocked silence as they handcuffed me and stripped me of my badge, cap and ring of university keys. I was in handcuffs! It was totally unreal. I couldn't react. Murder! Me?

"Is there any other property you'll be needing from her?" Cole asked Conway. Conway looked like he wanted to cry. He shook visibly. I was still in shock. "Just, just her uniforms," he stuttered. He looked at me like he wanted to die.

"They're in my locker," I said to him. "Want to write down the combination?"

As I told him the number, he wrote it down wrong and I had to repeat it. "I'm sorry, Laurie," he said.

When I was a kid, I'd always managed to appear calm and composed, even when I felt hysterical inside. It was some kind of defense mechanism, I suppose; my feelings were so easily bruised! I guess it had become second nature. I must have seemed unnaturally composed to the two cops. Apparently they were taken aback by my calm, because Ruscitti said, "You aren't even surprised, are you?"

"Actually, I'm shocked!" I said. I knew they'd try needling me, and I knew enough not to make any statements at all.

"Well, you knew it had to be—right?" Ruscitti nodded, and he spoke with the comforting tone of voice a priest might use.

"I don't know what you're talking about," I said.

"Suit yourself. Let's go." They walked me outside to an unmarked squad car. Cole had to be at least six feet, seven inches tall and three hundred pounds. I never saw anyone so big. I didn't understand why this was happening, but I was sure it was all a mistake. When we got to the Police Administration building, instead of taking me to the booking room, they marched me into the Deputy Inspector's office and removed the handcuffs. They were unusually nice.

"We really hate to do this," Cole explained, "but it's our job. You're such a beautiful young lady. We're going to have a department photographer come up here in a minute to take your mug shots. That way, we'll have proof that we didn't beat you up or anything. Is that okay with you?"

I nodded, my stomach in knots.

"Would you like a cigarette?"

"I don't smoke."

"All right. Now then, Lawrencia ... we think your husband set you up for this. You know he did it. We can make it easier for you. We know you were both in on it."

"I don't understand," I replied, thinking, Fred? He wouldn't. He didn't. They're crazy!

"If you won't go for that, let us just tell you a few things," Cole said matter-of-factly. "We have evidence, Lawrencia."

I said nothing.

"Enough evidence to lock you up for the rest of your life."

I couldn't believe what they were saying.

"First of all, we know how much alimony your husband Elfred had to dish out to Christine every month. We know what his salary is—after all, he worked for us. That didn't leave you very much to live on, did it? We don't blame you."

"We also know you threatened Christine," Ruscitti said.

I never threatened anybody, I thought.

"We also have the ballistics on Freddy's gun. It all points to you," Cole added.

That blood on the gun? I thought.

"Our theory is, you two cooked up a plan to scare Chris but you fucked up, and killed her instead."

"That's ridiculous!" I blurted.

"You wanted to scare Chris out of that house so that you and Elfred could live there."

I stared at them. How could a grown woman be scared out of her own house? If they only knew about the fights Fred and I had about that damned house.

"We have your shooting scores from the Academy," Cole said. "You're an excellent marksman. Why don't you just admit it?"

"Don't you think we can prove it?" Ruscitti asked. "Hey, you better start talkin', 'cause we're the only friends you have in the world right now! If you tell us what happened, we can talk to McCann and recommend that the charges be knocked down to manslaughter." They opened their memo books, ready to write.

"It's my right to remain silent until I get an attorney," I said.

My lack of response angered them. Cole slammed his pen down on the table.

"Okay, Bembenek. No more games. You want it? You got it. But know this: since you refuse to talk to us, I'm planning to see to it that you also get charged with attempted murder for what you tried to do to that little boy."

That was like a slap across the face. The murderer had struggled with Sean the night of the shooting, trying to strangle the child in his bed. What kind of monster did they think I was?

Frank Cole stood up; he towered over me like a human sequoia. Three years later he would collapse and die of a heart attack, just before Thanksgiving, at the young age of fifty-one.

They left the room as a matron walked in to search me. After that, a photographer took pictures. I was about to take my hair down when Cole said, "Just a minute," approaching me with a ruler. I had about a two-inch blond ponytail in my hair because I needed a neat appearance in uniform for work at Marquette. Cole made a big production out of measuring my ponytail, though the ponytail on the suspect was described as being about six inches longer than mine.

A Hispanic man walked into the room. "I'm a friend of Elfred's," he told me, smiling. "I'm here to give you some advice. Mr. Cole and Mr. Ruscitti aren't bullshitting you when they tell you they can knock this thing down to manslaughter. The DA listens to us. All you have to do is cooperate."

I just looked at him.

"You're only twenty-two years old," he said. "Do you want to spend the rest of your life in prison with all them queers?"

I said nothing.

"We talked to your mother. She's very nice."

My mom had told me that two detectives stopped by the house to question her, about a month ago. She said that she told them she didn't have time to talk to them.

"What do you think she's going to say when she reads the headlines about you?"

"My mom and dad are on vacation," I said. "Can I call a lawyer?"

He frowned. "So. You're a tough cookie, huh?"

"No."

"Look, why don't you just tell us what happened? You don't have the kind of money it takes for a criminal attorney. You'll get some crummy Public Defender and end up in the slammer for the next eleven-three."

"I know I'm allowed a phone call, so may I make one?"

Cole walked back into the room, and the Hispanic cop shook his head at him.

"We've dispatched a squad over to your house on Taylor Avenue, to inform your husband of your arrest."

■   ■   ■

On day two or three they were taking me to booking, and I heard somebody say "Laurie!" I looked and I couldn't see because they had taken my glasses, but there was a tall figure and he said he was Richard Reilly. That was Fred's divorce lawyer. Fred had obviously hired him in a panic when I got arrested.

"Hi!" he said. "Hi! I'm Richard Reilly, and Fred retained me to represent you ..." Reilly took me aside. "Did you make any statements in there?"

"No. This is all a mistake, isn't it? They're going to let me go home now, aren't they?" I pleaded with him. I couldn't think straight.

"They didn't have a warrant for your arrest," he told me. "It certainly appears to be a mistake, but they mean business. Look, just hang in there right now, and don't say anything to them. Do you understand? Not anything! I'll get back to you as soon as I can."

The next thing I knew, I was in a small, dimly lit cell in the City Jail of District One, which was designed to be used as a twenty-four-hour "holding cell." The matrons kept my glasses, and I didn't have my contact lenses, so everything was blurry. I had been to the jail many times when I was a police officer, but never like this. I hoped I wouldn't see any cops I knew from the Academy.

I lay down on the metal cot, still in my Marquette uniform. There were no bars on the cell, just a heavy metal door with a tiny slot. It felt claustrophobic. I stared at four cement walls, a steel toilet and a tiny ceiling light, its bulb enclosed in a wire cage.

There was nothing to do but think, sleep and look out the door slot by pressing the side of my face against the door. I could see nothing but the wall opposite my cell door, as the hallway out there was not very wide.

Late at night there was a great deal of noise. Hundreds of arrests had been made at the beginning of Milwaukee's Summerfest lakefront festival. From what I could hear, the talk in the cellblock described arrests for smoking pot. Most of the other prisoners were from Chicago.

I knew something was wrong, and I worried that Reilly hadn't contacted me as he'd promised. I was stiff and tired. I tried doing some floor exercises just to stay limber, but there was little room to do anything.

Having been in the same clothes all those days without a shower, I felt dirty and smelled of perspiration. There was constant crying and screaming from the other women prisoners. I wondered what day it was, and heard the matron walking down the hallway.

"What day is it, please?"

"Friday," came the answer. I'd been there since Wednesday.

■   ■   ■

I was arrested without a warrant. I was sitting there in jail in this bullpen in my uniform for three days before a complaint was sworn out. I was sitting there thinking, Naaaah, this is crazy, they're gonna see that this isn't right. For three whole days I sat there, in a panic, not knowing what to do. They took away my glasses; I couldn't see anything. All the time I was thinking, This is wrong, they're gonna come now and let me go and say, You know, we made a big mistake, you know what I mean? I didn't even know what day it was, whether it was day or night. It was horrible. The only way I knew another day had passed was when the matron came to the door with a cup of coffee and a bologna sandwich at five in the morning; that's all there was all day. I didn't know what to do. I knew I could make a phone call, but who should I call? I'd never even thought about being arrested before! I didn't want to waste it. I was confused, thinking of calling James Shellow, a prominent lawyer who had overturned the conviction of a man charged with shooting two cops. The case had caused a big stink, and after that the cops changed the rules about carrying guns. Shellow got this guy off ... should I call him? Or Fred? I didn't even know whether they had notified Fred. Should I call him, or Shellow? I didn't know what to do.

■   ■   ■

Finally, my cell door opened with a grinding, mechanical noise. The matron announced that my lawyer was in the visiting room.

"Can I go home now?" I asked Reilly as I sat down anxiously behind the clear partition.

"You've been charged with first-degree murder," he said in a droning voice. "Our next step will be to go before a judge, who is going to set your bail at ten thousand dollars. That amount is a gift. Bail for most murder cases is set around one hundred thousand dollars. Or more."

"Why is mine so low?"

"Well, they have an extremely circumstantial case. Perhaps the judge considered that, and this low bail is his comment on the case. Also, I've proposed that the conditions of the bail stipulate that you live at home with Elfred or your parents, and the children will stay out of town with their grandparents. Fred is at some bank right now. He wanted me to tell you he loves you. He's been trying to get in to see you. He said he's behind you 100 percent. Your parents are on vacation?"

"Yes."

At least they won't see the newspapers. You've been all over the front pages for the past few days."

"Oh, no."

■　■　■

The media circus had already begun. The bunny bimbette killer—this walking metaphor, this person who wasn't me—made her first appearance. I was sitting in shock, waiting for them to admit they'd made a horrible mistake, and on the streets they were selling newspapers crucifying me.

■　■　■

"Okay, like I said, I appeared before the judge for you, but we're going to have to go again. You'll have to be brave and face the cameras. The judge will ask you if you wish to waive your right to a preliminary hearing within ten days. It is my advice that you waive that right, because it will give us more time to prepare."

My mind spun with legal terms unfamiliar to me then.

"Incidentally, Fred was sent home from work for a few days. He went to Marquette to pick up your car. Oh, and Carol Kurdziel gave me a call. You've been suspended with pay."

"Oh." Only half of what he was saying was registering.

"Now, I have several questions for you. Are you all right?"

I nodded.

"Okay. Do you now, or did you ever, own a wig?"

"Yeah. I had two short, blond wigs that I wore when I worked at Second District, instead of getting my hair cut. I sold one of them to my friend Suzy."

"Where is the other one?"

"Somewhere. Either at the house on Ramsey, or at my mom's house—I don't know. We've moved so many times."

"Did you make the statement 'I hate those fucking kids' in regards to Fred's children?"

"Of course not!"

"How do you feel about Sean and Shannon?"

"At first, I wasn't thrilled about the whole idea. But it's working out. I like them. Why are you asking me these things?"

"We'll talk about it in detail, later. Did you ever tell anyone that you'd like to hire someone to kill Christine?"

"No!"

"Okay. That's it for now. I'll be back to accompany you to the hearing. For now, just sit and watch TV and try not to think about too much. You look very upset. I'll see you later."

As I left the room, I thought of his last recommendation: "Sit and watch TV?" What TV? Of course I'm upset!

Before my appearance in front of the judge, I was placed in a bullpen outside of the courtroom. Every few seconds, someone opened the peephole on the bullpen door to peer in at me, out of curiosity. I refused to look up, feeling like a caged animal on display, but listened to the door on the peephole slam over and over again. I was still in my Marquette uniform.

Just as Reilly had predicted, there were a lot of cameras in the courtroom. I felt just terrible after being locked up for three days without a shower or comb. My hair was a head of tangles and my mascara was smudged under my eyes. Everyone in the room was a fuzzy blur, because I still didn't have my glasses.

My preliminary hearing was scheduled for a day a few weeks away. The next day, I was transferred from the City Jail to the County Jail. An emotional paralysis overwhelmed me as I was instructed to change into a light cotton dress issued by the jail. I longed to go home.

I had wondered whether County Jail was like prison, but it was much worse. The cellblock was filthy, with garbage strewn haphazardly in the corners—cigarette butts, moldy bread crusts and dried vomit. An obviously insane woman sat in a corner and sang continually.

There was a small television set against one wall. I watched the six o'clock news. Pictures of me flashed across the screen. All I could hear was "ex-Playboy Bunny." I cracked my knuckles nervously, wondering if my mom and dad were home yet. I felt I was drowning.

One of the deputies walked into the cellblock and asked me whether I was going to be able to post bail. I asked if I could call my husband, since I'd never received permission to make the one phone call I was allowed. When I finally reached Fred, I cried. He said no bank would lend him much, even though he had collateral. He said my parents weren't home yet. The deputy instructed me to hang up the phone.

I sat down on the floor, trying to reconcile myself to the fact that I wasn't going anywhere. The whole thing still felt like a bad dream.

Suddenly, the sheriff motioned to me, and I walked to the door again. "Do you want your relatives to post bail?" she asked.

"Of course!" I cried, wondering who had come to rescue me. I changed back into my Marquette uniform, my face wet with tears.

My Aunt Mary and Cousin Julie came to get me, and we rushed down a back flight of stairs and left the building. I was never so glad to see anybody in my entire life. I'll never forget the family's kindness.

Finally, home. Fred sobbed as I walked in the door. We embraced in the middle of the kitchen and stood that way for a long time; I was afraid to let go. I said the first thing I wanted to do was take a long, hot shower.

Fred told me that the night of my arrest he'd gone to work as usual, but they'd already assigned a replacement for him. They told him he was too emotional to work and that he should go home. They considered his status "on medical leave without pay." Fred didn't know when he'd be allowed to return.

That night, we sat up and watched the late news. None of the stations realized I was out on bail. I watched in disbelief as Channel six did a story on my life, showing my yearbook photo from high school and some pictures from my days as a fashion model. It was unreal. But it was just the beginning.

"You think the TV was bad? Wait until you see the newspapers, Laurie. Are you strong enough to look at them? I saved all of them."

I looked at the huge front-page photographs and headlines and winced. I threw the papers in a corner.

"My God! Did you see this? They're giving me a press trial! How can they do this?"

Fred handed me a drink. "Half of it's just not true. They say that police recovered a red wig from the plumbing of our three-bedroom apartment. That's not true. It came from the apartment across the hall. They say that we moved into my house on Ramsey—we aren't living there yet! Then they say that you were also charged with attempted murder, which isn't true."

"They keep quoting 'a source' but don't say who the source is. 'A source says she owned a green jogging suit!' A source says this, a source says that," I said. "Who is this source? It's so unfair! People read this and believe it!"

"There's nothing we can do about it. Reilly doesn't want you to say a word to the newspapers."

"Why not?" I exclaimed, outraged. "Why can't I tell my side of the story?"

Looking through another paper, I gathered that the police were basing their whole case on the ballistics report that said the murder weapon was Fred's off-duty revolver. It was impossible! Fred and Durfee checked that gun that same night! What about the blood on the service revolver? Did they mix up the guns?

"The papers even mentioned the fact that you refused to take a lie-detector test," said Fred. "So did Judy. So did Stu."

"It says here that a wig hair was found on the body," I said.

"There were at least two female police officers at the crime scene that night," Fred claimed. "They were probably wearing wigs."

"I can't deal with this anymore," I said. "I'm going to bed. This isn't real."

"The department had so many other suspects," Fred said. "Every one a man! Then they arrest you out of the clear blue. It's like they had blinders on—the investigation scope grew more and more narrow. They didn't want to listen to a thing I had to say. I could see it coming, but I thought maybe I was mistaken."

He came over to me and held my hand. "You must promise me."

"What?"

"I've never seen you so distraught. You must promise me that no matter how depressed you get, you'll never do anything stupid. You'll never do anything to yourself."

I nodded.

"We're going to beat this thing," Fred was saying. "It's wrong. But we have to do it together. Your parents will be back tomorrow."

"Oh God! Freddy! I'd rather die than tell them!"

"We must. Do you want me to?"

Feeling helpless, I nodded again.

My parents took it very badly, but I was barely aware of the events around me. I walked around like a zombie, a ghost. All I could do was sleep. Even small tasks seemed insurmountable. It was nightmarish.

Letters began to pour in from all over. Old friends, classmates, neighbors and former boyfriends sent letters of support, prayers and money. A friend in Madison said she was trying to organize some women's groups to help me.

The biased newspaper articles still continued, and in my anger, I granted an interview with a female *Milwaukee Journal* reporter. She had treated me fairly when she wrote the story about my discrimination claim the previous December, so I felt I could trust her. The article described me as a feminist. I raised the possibility that I was being framed and I detailed the harassment I'd undergone after filing my discrimination suit.

Reilly was furious, but admitted the article was not bad. I explained to him that I couldn't stand it anymore—standing by and watching all the lies being printed about me. He scolded me as if I were a child, and made me promise I wouldn't talk to any more reporters.

Soon we discovered that the police had searched my locker at Marquette, without a warrant, confiscating everything. They labeled everything "evidence," including my purse. I needed my purse, because it held all of my money, credit cards, bank books and identification. The police refused to release any of this.

Reilly was making me nervous. Something about him made me uneasy. My preliminary hearing was fast approaching, and he was talking about waiving it entirely. When we finally met, Fred had insisted on sitting in on my meetings with Reilly. After all, he was Fred's lawyer, too.

I didn't have a good rapport with Reilly. In a way, I guess it was a personality conflict; maybe it was me. But his partner was on the Police Commission, and that made me uncomfortable. And then my parents got the feeling that Reilly might be in conflict of interest in representing me after representing Fred during Fred's divorce—after all, the police considered Fred a suspect, too. Still, I was in shock after my arrest, plummeted into this ... depression ... and I couldn't act on my feelings. I knew I wasn't comfortable with him, but somehow I couldn't do anything about it. My parents went to see him and were also uncomfortable with him. They thought he already had me convicted. I don't know whether he thought I was guilty or what. It was hard to communicate with him.

Eventually, Reilly informed me that my preliminary hearing had been postponed—a request that came from District Attorney McCann, who said he was going to Florida on vacation. He gave the case to an assistant named Kraemer. Of course, the newspapers promptly reported that I had requested the postponement.

At that point I gave up on Reilly and started looking for a new lawyer. My parents and Fred helped me with the search. They decided it would be easier to get someone from out of town who couldn't have a conflict, so they went to Don Eisenberg, in Madison. Initially, I was impressed with his personality and style. He was confident, friendly and informative—the complete opposite of Reilly. My heart fell somewhat, though, when he informed me that Reilly's fee was only a fraction of what his own representation would cost—a twenty-five thousand dollar retainer fee, for starters.

I told my family that the fee was out of the question, but they insisted they'd raise the money, even if they had to mortgage their house. Fred agreed. I phoned Reilly to tell him I'd hired a different attorney. He sounded irritated, and with a tinge of sour grapes, he ended our conversation by saying, "Good luck. You'll need it."

Reilly turned over a set of files to Eisenberg's office, all of which were labeled and alphabetized, and all of which were empty.

Eisenberg was pleased that McCann had requested a postponement, since it would give him more time to review the facts. He said it was the most absurd thing he ever heard when I told him Reilly had planned on waiving my preliminary hearing.

"We are going to get this case dismissed at the prelim," Eisenberg said. "You won't even be bound over."

Sean and Shannon were staying with Fred's mom and dad, having a good time because their cousins lived right across the street. Fred said that the boys complained to him that they missed me. They tried calling me on the telephone and mailed me cards.

Fred's dad was very understanding. He stopped at my parents' house to give me a hug and expressed his support and belief in me. It meant very much to me, and I thanked him sincerely. I wondered how Fred's mother felt.

Then Carol Kurdziel called. She'd called a couple of times before, more or less as a friend, I thought, to see if I needed someone to talk to. This time she called to tell me that she was having budget problems. One of her officers had resigned to begin classes at the Milwaukee Police Academy. Several others were studying, and state law wouldn't allow them to work overtime, so they were unavailable. My salary was being tied up, because I'd been suspended with pay. She wanted to apply my salary to a body that could be there. That left me with two options: either I could resign, or request a leave of absence without pay. The latter choice, she explained, would allow me to return to work when it was possible. Eventually I decided on the leave of absence, composed a brief letter to Marquette and mailed it quickly before I changed my mind.

I made a brief appearance before a judge, with my new lawyer, to arrange for another hearing date. There was a small crowd, and, to my surprise, the judge refused to allow television cameras in the courtroom. A preliminary hearing was scheduled for September.

Sean and Shannon were unhappy that they couldn't live with us, but since those were the conditions of my bail we didn't dare question it. Sean remembered that my birthday was coming up in August and asked Fred if they could buy something for me. They chose a red-and-blue blouse and a stuffed dog. I was touched, but also frustrated, because I couldn't thank the boys in person. Instead, I wrote them a short note on a Thank You card, enclosing a snapshot of me wearing the new blouse and holding the dog. I mailed the card to Sean and Shannon, at John Schultz's address in Pewaukee.

Kathy and John turned my letter over to the District Attorney. But Sean sent a card saying, "Laurie we love you no matter what happens."

Eisenberg finally managed to persuade the DA to release my purse from the evidence bureau. When I got it back, all the items were separated into small plastic bags.

■　■　■

With nothing to do and too much time on our hands, Fred and I made plans to go camping with friends from my Boston Store days, Wally and Donna.

Just before we left, Donna appeared with that day's newspaper and pointed out a front-page article. A familiar face peered at me—it was Judy Zess. I read the small print under the headline. She had been attacked by two men, who had robbed her at gunpoint. The robbery took place in the parking lot of the highrise where we'd shared an apartment. The article speculated that the men might have been after money and drugs left behind in Gaertner's apartment after his arrest. I didn't know she was still at Tom's. I wondered how she could afford it.

Judy's description of one of her assailants struck me at once—it was incredibly similar to the suspect described by Sean and Shannon. The man had been wearing a wig, used a thirty-eight, and had handcuffed her. His name was Fred Horenberger. All weekend I wondered about it, weighing the possibility of these two men being tied in with the murder of Christine. Fred suggested that the whole thing might have been fabricated by Judy. I couldn't decide what to make of it.

The weekend was a disaster. It was intensely hot and humid, the woods thick with huge mosquitoes and biting flies. Several times Fred blew up at me for trivial reasons, and once at Donna and Wally.

Once we were back on the road, with Fred driving in silence, Donna whispered to me.

"Look. We planned this weekend for you, Laurie, because we figured you needed it. But this guy!" She pointed a thumb at Fred. "Where on earth did you meet such a jerk?"

When we returned from camping, we moved all of our stuff out of the house on Ramsey and stored it in the basement of my mom and dad's house. Fred and I set up reasonable living quarters upstairs. With half of our belongings still in boxes, I felt disorganized and scattered, but I was glad all of our property was finally under one roof.

Fred's friends Dennis and Karen called us from Florida. They'd been interviewed by police, who asked them if Fred and I had been plotting anything openly. They were appalled. Then my best friend, Joanne, gave me a call. Two detectives had driven to Stevens Point, Wisconsin, over four hundred miles, to question her. They asked the same questions.

"I was so mad!" she told me. "They kept acting like I was lying or something! I told them I never saw you in a green jogging suit—I don't think you own anything green. They knew we were on the track team together in high school."

An acquaintance of Fred's called to tell us the cops had asked him if I'd bragged recently about buying another handgun. This baffled me. Why would the police still be asking about another revolver if their report indicated that the murder weapon was Fred's off-duty gun? Could the ballistics report on the gun be incorrect?

After persistent urging from me, Fred filed for unemployment benefits. It was obvious that it would be a long time before he would be allowed to return to work. The city, naturally, wasted no time denying him benefits, and Fred demanded a hearing to appeal the denial. I told him not to worry.

"I've been this route before. You have to file a written rebuttal, disproving their reasons for denying the benefits."

Living with my parents was difficult. They went to bed very early and woke up early to get my dad off to work. Fred and I liked to stay up late and sleep in the morning. Everyone was frustrated, full of stress. No one was acting normally.

■   ■   ■

Normal? How could anything be normal? I was to stand trial for killing the ex-wife of my husband, a husband I was coming to bitterly regret marrying, supposedly over a house I had no wish to live in, with kids I had never asked for. They were poisoning my friendships with ugly questions. I had been forbidden contact with the children—not my children, but children I cared about all the same. Wigs and jogging suits and guns ... it was all crazy. It meant nothing. I didn't do this dreadful thing!

And I was angry, too. People were telling lies about me. What gave them the right?

I watched Fred fall asleep in front of the television set. Outside, the branches scraped against the window. I fingered my wedding ring.

The nightmare cannot last forever.

I told myself that.

It cannot, it cannot.

12

THE PRELIMINARY HEARING

The night before Fred's unemployment hearing, Fred's tax attorney called Darryl Laatsch phoned. He'd just received a notice announcing a custody hearing, scheduled for the following day.

"Alice Pennings has petitioned the court for custody of Sean and Shannon. But the law requires at least five days' written notice. They can't just plop this in our laps the night before. You have to be served. You weren't, were you?"

"This is the first I've heard of it!" Fred replied.

"From what I gather, Alice is petitioning the court as an extension of the divorce stipulation that gave Christine custody. But Alice wasn't a party to the divorce, so I don't know what she's doing," Laatsch said. "I wouldn't worry about it. It's next to impossible to take children away from a natural parent. It doesn't happen overnight."

We got other legal opinions as well. They all said it could never happen, and we were relieved—until Fred decided to call Sean and Shannon at John and Kathy's house.

I was on the extension phone as Fred talked to Sean. The child told his father that a strange man had been at John Schultz's house that week to talk to him and his brother, Shannon. He didn't know the man's name or where he was from. Fred immediately thought: reporter.

"I told you not to talk to anyone without my permission, son! Was the man from a newspaper?"

"I don't know, dad," was Sean's tearful reply. "I mean, no."

"Did the man give you his name?"

"No, but Uncle John told me to talk to him," Sean cried.

"Calm down, Sean. I'm sorry I hollered at you. I'm not mad. I'm angry at Uncle John for not telling me about this. It's just that I don't want any reporters interviewing you or Shannon."

"Okay."

"What did he ask you?"

Left: Taylor Avenue, Milwaukee, 1961. I was three.
My sister Colette took the picture.

Right: First communion, 1966. I was ten, in the second grade.
My mother took this one.

I was twelve or thirteen here, I think.
I know my mother made this outfit—she was always making me clothes.

Both of these pictures were taken when I was seventeen, for a portfolio I was putting together to launch a modeling career.
The photographer, I remember, wanted a rural setting to set off some of the other, more elegant clothes that I wore.

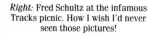

Above: In my Milwaukee Police Department uniform at Taylor Avenue.

Right: Fred Schultz at the infamous Tracks picnic. How I wish I'd never seen those pictures!

Above: In my Marquette uniform, just after my arrest.

Below: Judy Zess, the prosecution's star witness, who later recanted what she said, claiming she'd been bullied into it.

Above: Young Sean Schultz crying on the witness stand at my preliminary hearing. He said very clearly that the person he'd seen was not me. I was greatly moved by his strength and his bravery.

Here I am with Don Eisenberg. This was when we returned to court after the preliminary hearing and the judge bound me over for trial.

Left: Here I am with Fred at my preliminary hearing. This was before he accepted immunity from prosecution and testified against me.

Right: Fred Schultz on the witness stand at my trial. He is holding the gun—the one that was "proved" to be the murder weapon.

Above: Judge Michael Skwierawski,
the trial judge.

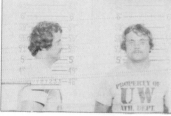

Left: Mug shot of Frederick Horenberger.
There is considerable reason to think
that he might have been the
one to have pulled the trigger.
He committed suicide in
Milwaukee late in 1991.

This is one of the many pictures of me in court. This one isn't from my trial
but from a later appearance, I think about 1986.

Above: This was a meeting of the *Inmate Output* "editorial board." It was held in the Home Ec room at Taycheedah, for lack of any other space. That's Kathy Braun on the right, and Judy in the background.

Left: This is my mom's favorite. She has it hanging on the wall in her home in Milwaukee.

Left: A group of friends in Taycheedah. We all won trophies for something. Mine was for poetry, I think, though Kathy Braun entered me as a joke in a spelling bee and, to her surprise, I actually won! As you can plainly see, we're not all hard cases and crazies. Actually, we look rather ordinary, don't you think?

Center: This was my graduation day. I received an Associate of Arts degree from the University of Wisconsin at Fond du Lac. The ceremony was held at a men's prison called Kettle Moraine, in 1986.

Right: This picture was taken in the visitors' room at Taycheedah. It was just after the "cosmetology department" was closed, and all the bottle-blonds were going "Eeek." I cut my hair short—didn't want to look like a calico cat.

Left: Taycheedah, 1990.

Above: This was a wonderful moment during my brief months of freedom in Canada. It was taken in September 1991 in a park just outside Thunder Bay, Ontario. The Kentucky Fried Chicken bag is full of popcorn— one of the forgotten little pleasures of freedom.

Right: My Thunder Bay counsel. Dave Dubinsky was doing pro bono work the day I needed a lawyer. His partner, Ron Lester (now a judge), picked out a refugee claim as a possible defense.

PHOTO BY DENNIS HILL

Left: With my mom and dad at a Canadian immigration hearing, 1991.

Below: Ira Robins, my very own personal pitbull.

Above: Here I am with my Canadian attorney, Frank Marrocco, at an immigration hearing. I've learned to trust his judgment —he's always thinking four moves ahead, like a chess player.

"He asked us about the night mommy was killed, and he asked us if you or Laurie ever spanked us or hit us."

"Where is Uncle John?" Fred asked, his concern growing.

"At grampa's," Sean replied. "Oh! The man gave Aunt Kathy a little card and I think she put it on the refrigerator door. Do you want me to get it?"

"Yes!" Fred said. "That's good, Sean. Now listen—this is important. Hang up the phone, get the card, and call me right back. Don't run off and play or forget to call daddy back."

About twenty minutes passed. Fred paced back and forth in the kitchen, waiting for the phone to ring. I sat at the kitchen table and finally suggested that he try to call back. Sean answered.

"Why didn't you call daddy back?" Fred asked.

"Because Aunt Kathy wouldn't let me!" the child wailed.

"Is she there right now? Let me talk to her."

There was a long wait. Kathy wasn't coming to the phone. Fred looked at me, and I felt sick. Something was wrong.

"Hang up, Fred!" I whispered. "Go down there! You'll never get this straightened out over the phone. Go!"

Fred hung up the phone. He ran out of the house and jumped into his van. I wished I could go along.

He came back about three hours later. He plopped down on a chair and told me what had happened.

"I think John has had a nervous breakdown!" he said. "When I got to Pewaukee, I pulled the van into my mom's driveway because Sean told me that John was across the street. The boys' bikes were in the yard, so I thought they might all be having supper. Here we were, sitting around the table—"

"Who?" I asked.

"My dad, my mom, me and the kids. Anyway, my brother comes flying in through the door of my dad's house with the Pewaukee cops! He was like a madman!"

"What?"

"I'm not kidding! Remember when Kathy wouldn't come to the phone? She went running to John and told him that I'd threatened to kill her and her whole family! She said I was on my way!"

"You did not! I was right here!"

"So, when the cops arrived, they could see nothing was wrong. John was hysterical. He was screaming that I'm not his brother anymore, and that he didn't want my kids in his house ever again—you should have heard him."

"God."

"You know what they've been doing? John and Kathy have been conspiring with Alice to take Sean and Shannon away from me. They were cooperating with this custody action all along. Kathy panicked when she knew she was about to be discovered."

"Not your own brother!" I couldn't believe it.

"Yeah! Oh, was my dad pissed! He demanded that the police leave his house and told them they had no right to come storming in without a warrant. But fucking John just led the way! My dad told John that he was taking him out of his will and everything!"

I was staring at Fred with my mouth open. What a melodrama! "Did you ever find out who that guy was who talked to the kids?"

Fred nodded. "Lee Calvey."

"Calvey? He's the 'Guardian ad litem'! He's supposed to be the impartial party—"

"I know," Fred said, rubbing his temples with his fingers. "I'm going to take a couple of aspirins and go to bed. I've got to get up early tomorrow and go downtown to see about this custody hearing."

I walked into the den, where my parents were watching television. My dad was cleaning some coins for his collection. He looked up and put his magnifying-glass down.

"What's going on with Fred?"

"Don't ask," I said with exhaustion, sitting cross-legged. How could I explain what was going on when I barely understood it myself? There was a lawyer for the estate, a lawyer for the kids, a lawyer for me, a lawyer for Fred, when just a few years back I didn't even know what a lawyer looked like! Life had begun to seem like one big courtroom.

■   ■   ■

The next day, it rained like it was the end of the world. It was dark and humid all morning. After Fred left for the courthouse, I went to the basement recreation room and stayed there all day, painting and listening to the radio over the loud crashes of thunder.

I was just making a fresh pot of coffee in the kitchen when Fred walked in, soaking wet. He was weeping.

"They took my kids away from me," he said. "I have to turn them over by three."

So much for the lawyers and their advice.

"I can't stay. I have to pack some of their clothes and go back out to Pewaukee."

When he got back, he explained what had happened. When he'd got to the courtroom, Alice and Earl Pennings were there with Barb and Bruce, John and Kathy and Stu Honeck. Fred met Darryl Laatsch inside the court. They were about to approach the bench when the Pennings and Stu Honeck's father went into Judge Curley's chambers. Fred and Laatsch were not allowed to follow them. When they came out, the judge announced his decision. Laatsch's objections were over-ruled. His motion to dismiss was denied.

The newspaper article about the hearing later quoted Laatsch as saying, "It was utter lawlessness."

"They said they wanted to take the boys up north, for their own safety," Fred explained. "They thought you were trying to influence them."

"I haven't seen Sean or Shannon since before my arrest. Those are the conditions of my bail!" I said resentfully. "How could this happen? Was your brother there?"

Fred sneered. "Yeah. Well, at least now my mother believes me. She was so busy being palsy-walsy with Kathy that she wouldn't even believe me when I told her I thought something was going on behind my back. Now that the kids are gone ... now reality has slapped her in the face.

"I was a bit late dropping off Sean and Shannon. I wanted to buy them ID bracelets before they had to go. Stu actually called the Pewaukee police, saying that he represented the MPD and that there was a 'hostage situation' going on! They sent a squad."

"How were the boys taking it?" I asked.

"Crying. Said they would run away."

"What are you going to do now?"

"I already called Eisenberg. He referred me to Joe Balistreri. I know Joey. He's a good attorney. Darryl has enough on his hands with the estate. This was a temporary order. The permanent custody hearing will be in February."

■   ■   ■

The following day was my birthday. I turned twenty-three. At the ripe old age of twenty-three, I felt as though I should already stop celebrating birthdays.

There didn't seem very much cause for celebration.

Time ticked on. Only joy stopped.

■   ■   ■

A few days later, I was going through our mail and noticed that a Denial of Benefits notice had arrived for Fred from the Unemployment Compensation office. He had forgotten to attend the hearing.

I shook my head in disgust and began the paperwork required to request an appeal of the denial. Later, I berated Fred for his failure to attend the hearing.

"To make matters worse, I found all your benefit claim cards piling up on your desk! All you have to do is fill out those cards on time and mail one out every week so that it can be processed by the Tuesday of the following week! This is something you can't procrastinate about. You have to be prompt."

"Don't nag me about this!" Fred snapped.

"Fine!" I replied sharply, and left the room.

Fred came upstairs and tossed his key ring onto the dresser. "When I come home, all I want to do is relax. I don't want you running up to me and nagging me about all kinds of shit."

"Just when do you want to be informed about things?" I asked, hurt by his accusations. "You run around here and there, and days turn into weeks, and appointments come and go—forgotten. After I took care of all that paperwork for you, because you can't even mail anything on time, and then you forget about that hearing! The hearing was the result of all my efforts!"

"How could I remember, with all the bullshit going on?"

"Get yourself a damn calendar or appointment book, then."

Fred was finally allowed to return to work, assigned to a desk job in the Detective Clerical Warrant Division. He saw his children every Sunday between noon and six PM. Barb was ordered to bring Sean and Shannon to Pewaukee and leave them at Fred's mom and dad's house. The custody order included these visitation rights. I struggled to occupy my time alone every weekend; I was not allowed to accompany Fred. I had grown dependent on him, much to my dismay.

■　　■　　■

The day of my preliminary hearing arrived. It was to last two days. The courthouse halls were filled with people. One of my sisters and her boyfriend arrived, taking a seat with my parents and Fred's father. Much to Fred's annoyance, his mother did not show up.

I sat with Eisenberg at a small table, dressed in a gray gabardine suit. It was warm in the room, and I nervously tugged at a wisp of hair that had lost its curl due to the humidity. The judge presiding over the case was Ralph Adam Fine, a young man with dark hair. Police Department witnesses took the stand first and testified about the procedural aspects of the case.

Then the State called Fred's squad partner from the night of the murder. Durfee was as vague and as noncommittal as possible. Eisenberg quietly commented to me on his nervousness. His original report on the events of the night in question had been mysteriously rewritten two weeks later, against Department policy; reports were always required the day of the incident.

Durfee failed to explain why his report was dated two weeks later. It was inconsistent with his first report and conflicted with Fred's. He stuttered and stammered. It was a ludicrous performance. I regretted that a jury was not present to see it.

He denied having ever made any judgment regarding Fred's off-duty revolver. He denied having ever made the statement that it had not been fired, which contradicted his first, written report. He now contended that it would have been impossible to come to any conclusion about the gun, because he was not a ballistics expert.

He did admit that he failed to record the serial number of the revolver he examined that night.

When Eisenberg requested to see his memo book from that night, Durfee informed the court that he had either lost it or thrown it out. That was also a violation of Department regulations.

The court recessed for several minutes, so I left the courtroom to find the women's room. Judy and her mother were sitting on a bench in the hallway, and as I passed by, Judy said hello.

"Oh, hi," I said, stopping to stand in front of them. "I almost didn't recognize you with your new haircut. Cute."

"Thanks!" Judy smiled. "Do you know how long this is going to take today?"

"I'm not sure."

"Look!" Judy thrust out her left hand to show me an antique ring. "Tom and I got married."

"Really?" I raised my eyebrows, because Tom was in prison. "Where are you living now? The return address on your letter was a post office box."

Judy seemed to have trouble answering. Before she could say any more, Eisenberg came out into the hall and motioned to me.

Fred sat down in the witness box and informed the court that he intended to plead the Fifth. I turned to see Fred's lawyer, Joe Balistreri, approach the bench. Once Fred was granted immunity, he began to testify.

Fred explained that on the night of the shooting my mother had arrived at our apartment to help me pack. He said he'd gone to bed, and when he awoke we had finished packing everything.

Fred stated that it was his understanding that I had intended to go out later with a girlfriend, but had trouble getting in touch with her.

He went on to say that he called me several times once he got to work, and that I told him I was going to sleep because I was tired. He then testified that he got a message to contact his captain, who told him about the murder. Immediately afterwards, he telephoned me and woke me up to tell me the news.

Fred got to the part about examining the gun with Durfee, and I was impressed by his testimony on ballistics; his detailed explanation of the presence of dust on all parts of the gun made him sound like an expert on the subject. He emphasized the absence of blood and the absence of traces of lead or carbon.

Then Fred's testimony led to the part where he had to describe his arrival at the scene of the crime, and he stopped suddenly, too emotional to continue. The court had to recess so Fred could regain his composure.

I looked at Eisenberg. "He can't talk about her death, but to me all he does is criticize Christine horribly—even now! I don't get it!" I wondered if it was an act.

Eisenberg put his hand on my shoulder. "Goddamn it! If I'd known Fred was going to do that, I wouldn't have called him!"

I wandered out of the courtroom, feeling hurt and confused. Fred had just told the whole world that he still loved Christine, completely contradicting what he insisted in private.

Alone in the washroom, I leaned up against the sink as my head spun. Splashing water on my face, I squeezed my eyes shut. I couldn't understand what he was doing.

My mom walked into the washroom and stood next to me.

"What was that all about?" she demanded. "What's wrong with Fred? Does he still love her? It sure looked that way to everyone in the courtroom!"

She was right. My mother was always right.

"Please!" I blurted out. "Just leave me alone for a few minutes."

She turned and left, her heels clicking across the tile floor.

After a few minutes, I headed down the corridor toward the courtroom. Stu Honeck stood in the hall with Alice Pennings. I wanted badly to say something to her, to run to her and beg her to believe that I did not do this to her daughter. I knew that I didn't dare say a word. I glanced at them numbly, but remained silent as I passed by.

"She looks stoned," Stu said, loudly enough for me to hear it.

You should know, I thought bitterly. How swiftly they had turned to playing God! Clearly they'd already passed judgment on me and found me guilty.

Honeck took the stand. He slumped in his chair, chewing a wad of gum. He couldn't recall many of the details of his activities on the night in question, nor his whereabouts at specific times. His testimony differed from what Sean had told us. He testified that he was driven home by Christine that evening. He denied that he had ever had a drinking problem. He did, however, admit to having a key to her house.

Then Stu went into a dramatic rendition of the times Chris told him I hated her. He said that Chris had told him I had made her stand outside in the hallway one evening when she'd brought me a blender as a gift, and that I had refused to invite her in.

"That's not true at all!" I whispered.

Eisenberg shushed me, handing me a yellow legal pad to write my comments on.

"**NOT TRUE!**" I wrote in large, black letters.

But nothing shocked me and my friends more than the Judas performance of Judy Zess. I sat in stunned disbelief as she took the stand and testified that I had made many verbal threats against Christine. She also claimed that she'd seen a green jogging suit in our apartment when we lived together.

"Did you say that you had occasion to talk with the defendant in the hall outside the courtroom today?" Assistant District Attorney Kraemer asked Zess.

"Yes," she replied.

"What did the defendant say to you, if anything?"

"She told me that her lawyer would probably not call me to testify ... and she said she could not understand where the police got this green jogging suit nonsense."

"I never said that!" I wrote.

Our turn for cross-examination arrived. Eisenberg attacked Judy's testimony without mercy.

"Okay, Miss Zess," he began. "Let's go back to this party where the defendant allegedly made threats against Christine. What month was this party held?"

"February."

"Did Laurie and Fred get married on the last day of January?"

"Yes."

"Then this party was a happy occasion? A celebration?" Eisenberg paced back and forth.

"I don't know," was Judy's answer.

"Well, Miss Zess, was this party a happy occasion or a funeral? Fred and Laurie just back from their honeymoon. You picked them up at O'Hare Airport. Isn't that correct?"

"Yes."

"And you were at this dinner party, laughing and having a good time?"

"Yes."

"And what exactly did Laurie allegedly say?"

"We were talking about the cost of living, and she said that it would pay to have Chris blown away."

"How did you respond?"

"I don't remember."

"Did you call the police? Did you laugh it off? What?"

"I ... we ... the conversation was dropped."

"Did you think she was joking?"

"No."

"Would it refresh your memory to read a report that you gave the police last June, where you told the police then that you thought, 'It was said in jest,' and you thought Laurie was joking?"

Eisenberg walked up to Zess and handed her a copy of the report.

"Yes."

"You thought Laurie was joking?"

"Yes."

"But, for the purposes of this hearing, you decided to say that you thought Laurie was not joking?" he asked.

"Objection!" shouted the prosecutor. "The witness has already answered this question."

"Sustained," Judge Fine said calmly.

"I'll withdraw that last question, Your Honor," Eisenberg said. He then asked Zess to repeat her description of the green jogging suit.

"What exactly was the occasion on which you first became aware of this green jogging suit in the Schultz apartment?"

"It was when Fred and I were loading some boxes into a storage locker in the basement. I saw the pants in a box as I was helping him."

"What color were these pants?"

"Green."

"Was it kelly green? Forest green? Light green?"

"It was dark green."

"Was it a baseball uniform?"

"No."

"How could you be so sure?" Eisenberg pressed on. "You just testified that you only saw a pair of pants folded up in a box. How could you tell what it was?"

"It was a jogging suit," Zess insisted.

"Did you ever see Laurie jog in it?"

"No."

"Did you ever see Fred jog in it?"

"No."

Eisenberg attempted to uncover the reason for Judy's damaging, fabricated testimony, but he was restrained by the State's constant objections. She had caught us all completely by surprise. I just couldn't see why she would stab me in the back like that. She'd sent me a sympathetic letter; she'd chatted with me in the hall only a few minutes before being sworn in.

"The witness may step down."

I stared at Judy from my seat at the defense table, but she would not return my gaze. She sauntered past, avoided my eyes and looked at the floor.

Eisenberg leaned over to whisper to me. "What the hell happened with Zess? I thought you two were friends! She's digging your grave."

"I can't understand it, for the life of me. We had our minor differences in the past—I told you about them—but it wasn't enough to warrant these lies. How could she do this to me?"

"I want a copy of her last letter to you."

"She talks to me out in the hall, and then tells the DA that I made a remark about the jogging suit? What—?"

"You should never have said anything to her. Next time, no conversation in the halls of this courthouse."

"Don, all I said was that her haircut was attractive, and then she showed me her ring and told me that she and Tom got married."

"Married? She just testified that Tom was her fiancé! Now what the hell is he?"

"Who's next?" I asked, referring to the witness list.

"Fred's oldest boy."

Sean answered questions directly and with a brave maturity. He smiled at me and sat up straight, trying to fill in the large chair in the witness box. At one point, he began to cry, and I felt so bad for him. Genuinely moved, I wanted to comfort him but had to remain seated. Eisenberg offered him a cup of water.

Several times, Sean stressed that the person he witnessed could not possibly have been me, because the intruder was too large—the size of a big man, he said.

"It couldn't possibly be Laurie," Sean repeated. "Even if she had been wearing shoulder pads, like a football player—it still couldn't have been her, because then her body would have to form the shape of a 'V.' This body was big and came down straight on the sides." Sean used his hands to illustrate his meaning. "Besides, I know Laurie. Laurie always smells good 'cause she likes to wear perfume, and I didn't smell any perfume."

The direct examination continued as Sean recalled the terrifying events of that night. "He was wearing a green khaki army jacket," he said firmly. "It wasn't a green jogging suit. I know because when he or she ran down the stairs, I saw the sides of it flap. You know—an army jacket without the camouflage."

Kraemer didn't miss the fact that Sean used the phrase "he or she" and jumped on this chance to confuse the child. Fortunately, Sean was bright enough not to be fooled.

"Tell me, Sean," Kraemer asked with a sly smile. "Why did you just say 'he or she'?" Is it because you're not really sure if it was a man or a woman?"

Sean looked thoughtful. "Well, I said 'he or she' because those are the only two sexes there are." A chuckle was heard throughout the courtroom.

"Sean," Kraemer asked, "you know that your daddy loves Laurie very much, right?"

"Yes."

"Isn't it a fact that your daddy told you that Laurie didn't do it?"

"No," Sean answered.

"Did your daddy talk to you at all about it?"

"Yes."

"What did he tell you?" Kraemer beamed.

"He told me just to tell the truth," Sean said firmly.

Frustrated, Kraemer turned away from the witness stand. "No further questions, Your Honor."

Eisenberg approached the child for several more questions.

"Honey, I know this is hard for you. I just want to clear a few things up, okay Sean? There seems to be some question of whether or not someone told you what to say today. Did anyone tell you what to say?"

"No."

"Did I ever tell you what to say, Sean?"

"No."

"Did Laurie ever tell you what to say?"

"No."

"So, what you told the police that night after it happened, is that the truth?"

"Yes."

"You know the difference between the truth and a lie?"

"Yes."

"Right now, are you telling the truth?"

"Yes," Sean replied. "There was one thing I forgot to tell the police that night, and then I remembered, so I told my dad a couple of days later."

"What was that?" Eisenberg asked. I wondered what Sean would say next. I didn't know there was something else.

"I remembered that the man growled that night. He growled at me. That's the only thing I forgot to tell the police."

"Okay. And am I right when I say that you had enough good, common sense that night to try and administer first aid to your mommy to try and stop the bleeding?"

"Yes, I did."

"Sean, did Laurie kill your mommy?"

"No."

"Do you love Laurie?"

"Yes."

After Sean, my mother was called to testify. Unaccustomed to the courtroom atmosphere, she appeared frail and nervous as she took the stand. I felt a rush of compassion and love for her as she testified. She described the events that took place that same evening, explaining that she'd been with me at the apartment.

"How many hours did you spend with your daughter that night?" Eisenberg asked my mother.

"I'd say about four hours, because my husband dropped me off right after supper and I stayed until around ten."

"What did you do while you were there?"

"I helped Laurie pack, because she and Fred were supposed to move that weekend. So I remember asking Laurie if I should start on the spare room. It wasn't exactly a bedroom. It was a room full of

Fred's books, extra clothes and sports equipment."

"Did you pack all of that up in boxes?"

"Yes, after wrapping everything in newspaper."

"Objection," Kraemer interrupted. "This is irrelevant."

"Your Honor, I believe in a second you will see the relevance."

"Objection overruled. Proceed."

"Mrs. Bembenek," Eisenberg continued, "do you remember packing Fred's jewelry box that evening?"

"Yes."

"In view of your daughter?"

"No. She was in another room."

"Objection! I fail to understand this line of questioning, Your Honor," Kraemer again interrupted.

"The relevance," Eisenberg explained, "is the fact that a bit of circumstantial evidence in this case is the theory of the State that the defendant had access to the Ramsey Street house by using a key, a key that her husband kept in his jewelry box, of which the defendant denies any knowledge. Mrs. Bembenek just testified that she packed away all of Fred Schultz's belongings that night, including the jewelry box that contained the house key. If the key was packed away in a box, by Mrs. Bembenek, before the murder, and if its whereabouts were unknown to the defendant, and if, as Fred Schultz testified, this same key was found still packed away when he had reason to look for it after the murder, the Court will see the thin line of reasoning used to create this theory. The relevance? No access."

"Proceed," Judge Fine said.

Eisenberg resumed his questioning.

"Had you ever been to your daughter Laurie's apartment before that night?"

"Yes."

"When was that?"

"On April 14."

"For what reason were you there?"

"Laurie and Fred invited me and my husband over for dinner."

"Did you notice anything unusual about the plumbing then?"

"Yes. I asked Laurie if I could use the bathroom, and she warned me not to use Judy's bathroom, because the toilet was overflowing."

"So am I correct in saying that this apartment had plumbing problems as early as April 14?"

"Yes."

"Okay. Let's talk about your daughter. You know her as well as any mother knows her daughter, isn't that a fact?"

"Yes."

"On the evening of May 27, when you spent four hours with Laurie ... Strike that. Incidentally, do you know where Fred and Laurie were going to move?"

"Yes. They were moving into an apartment closer to our house, across from a park."

"Did you know why they were intending to move?"

"Because Judy Zess broke the lease."

"Okay, Mrs. Bembenek. Now, going back to that night, was Laurie acting strange?"

"No."

"Was she acting nervous?"

"No."

"Was she acting like a girl who was planning on committing a murder that night?"

"Objection! Speculation!" Kraemer shouted.

"Overruled. You may answer the question." The judge looked at me, as if to analyze me thoughtfully.

"Would you repeat the question?" my mother asked Eisenberg.

"Sure. Knowing your daughter as well as you do, did she, that night, seem like a girl who was planning on committing a murder?"

"Of course not."

"Was she drunk?"

"No."

"Was she on any drugs that you know of?"

"No."

"Did she have any plans for that night, that you knew of?"

"She said—"

"Objection! Hearsay!" Kraemer shouted.

"Overruled. Hearsay from the defendant is admissible."

My mother looked at the judge to see if she should answer.

"You may answer the question."

"Laurie mentioned that she was planning on going out with a girlfriend from work. She was waiting for the girl to call, but she said she might not go, because she was getting tired."

In cross-examination, Kraemer badgered my mother about her testimony. He hauled his heavy body out of his chair and lumbered toward the witness stand in his Hush Puppies.

"Mrs. Bembenek, would you lie for your daughter?"

"No."

"Have you rehearsed your testimony?"

"No."

"Mrs. Bembenek, I find it rather odd that you recall the exact date of the dinner at the Bembenek-Schultz apartment. How do you happen to know it was April 14 when you had dinner there?"

"Because that is the date of my wedding anniversary."

"No further questions, Your Honor."

At long last, the hearing was over. But instead of announcing a decision on whether or not to bind me over for a jury trial, the judge informed us that he wanted both attorneys to file briefs.

My parents and Eisenberg and I left together to have a drink. Fred needed to attend an important engagement elsewhere and told me he'd see me later at home. I was still brooding over his emotional display during his testimony.

"I feel it's important that you at least had plans to go to a bar the evening of the shooting," Eisenberg said. "I mean, it makes no sense. Who would say, 'I can't go out, so what the hell—I'll go out and kill somebody instead'?"

We ordered a round of drinks.

"Don't be too cross with Fred because of his emotional performance," Eisenberg told me. "Ex-wives have a unique way of throwing an enormous amount of guilt on men. I should know—I have two of them!"

"How soon will we be informed of the outcome?" my dad asked.

"In October," Eisenberg replied. "I'm optimistic. It's somewhat unusual for a judge to request additional time to decide on a bind-over. He could dismiss the charges."

"What do you think will happen?" I asked, sipping my Scotch.

"The only thing that the State had to prove at that hearing was probable cause for arrest. It's a probability issue. It's nowhere near as tough to prove as in a jury trial, where the State has to prove guilt beyond a reasonable doubt. The burden of proof is different at the prelim. Here all they had to prove was that it would be reasonable to assume that the defendant 'probably' did it—you know about proba- ble cause?"

I nodded.

"I think we did a hell of a job!" Eisenberg beamed. "We exposed a number of different suspects. The children insisted it wasn't you."

"Honeck denied that he had a drinking problem."

"Simple," Eisenberg said. "All we do is subpoena his employ- ment records with the MPD."

"That suspect that lives across the street from the house on Ramsey—whatever happened to him?" my mom asked.

"He refused to testify. I think he's a fruitcake," Eisenberg said.

"I still can't believe what Judy did," I said sadly.

"I wonder what makes her tick," Eisenberg said. "Somebody must be playing games. The biggest piece of evidence that the State has is the ballistics report on the off-duty gun. I objected to that being submitted, because I didn't have the opportunity to cross-examine the Crime Lab technician, but Fine let it in anyway."

"Do you think it will be dismissed?" I asked again, hoping against hope.

"Don't be devastated if it's not. Of course I hope it will be. It should be! But a lot of judges allow politics to influence their decisions. They have to worry about re-election. You've had an enormous amount of publicity. Fine might just bind you over, to let a jury decide."

The Scotch had relaxed me. I pushed off my tight gray pumps and let them dangle from my toes underneath the glass-topped table.

"I just thought of something," I told Eisenberg. "Judy claims that she saw a green jogging suit in a box when she and Fred were loading some boxes into the storage space? She's the only one who had keys to that locker! She had promised to make copies of the key for both of us but there was no great rush because the boxes were full of seasonal items. She never did give us a key. I remember Fred saying that he had to break the lock on that door when we were ready to move."

"Do you think Fred owns a green baseball or football uniform?"

"No. Not to my knowledge. The pants to his team uniforms are white. I always think it's absurd to wear white since they get so filthy. I have to soak them in bleach for days after a game. His jerseys are maroon and I think he has a yellow one with black letters, but not green."

I paused and then continued talking. "That's just it, Don! I don't own anything green. Not a thing! I just don't like the color. My clothes are either purple or lilac or fuschia, with some blue jeans and three-piece suits that are brown or blue. This is so unreal!"

"I know." Eisenberg nodded. "We've been over all of this before. It wouldn't make much sense for a murderer to wear something so unique. I mean, the guy might as well have worn a yellow chicken suit! The army jacket sounds more realistic.

"Well, let's be on our way. You've had a few tough days."

■　　　■　　　■

Too right, I thought. But worse—much worse—was to come.

13

THE APPROACH OF WINTER

*O*nce home, I fell prey to serious doubts about Fred and what I
really meant to him. There was such a contrast between what
he would say one day and what he would do the next. He kept
me hopelessly confused and longing for reassurance.

What was I to do? How was I to deal with this? I couldn't begin
to believe then that Fred was devious enough to frame his wife for
murder. How could I believe that? I wanted reassurances, not further
anxiety. It's hard to remember now how confused I was—now that
there is no more confusion, only anger; now that I know what the lies
were, and who the liars are; now that my life has become a simple
thing, a drive to Get Out into the free air.

But in those bad days I was young and confused and didn't know
where to turn.

■ ■ ■

I picked up a pile of letters for mailing and I told Fred I was going to
walk to the drugstore. I left the house wearing a plaid blouse and
cotton shorts. The temperature had dropped several degrees since the
afternoon, but I paid no attention to the weather. In my depression, the
chill seemed only natural.

Too many people in Fred's world and in my world liked to lie
and stab and hurt. It was more than I could bear. I hadn't led a shel-
tered life—I thought I was wise, streetwise—but nothing had prepared
me for this. I thought of calling a women's crisis line for advice, but
when I reached the drugstore, someone was using the pay phone. I
looked down the street and saw an open tavern. Almost half an hour
had passed since I'd left the house. It was getting dark outside.

There was only one customer behind the bar. The bartender was a
heavy man with thick glasses and lambchop sideburns. I asked him for
change as I put a dollar bill on the bar and ordered a glass of beer.

The phone was in a dark corner of the tavern. As I dialed the number of the crisis line, I realized I didn't even know what I planned to say, or why I was calling. All I knew is that I needed someone to talk to. A woman answered and explained that all the lines were busy at that moment. They would call me back in ten minutes. I returned to my seat at the bar and sipped my beer. I wanted to run away.

But where to?

The streetlights blinked on, glowing greenish yellow against the eerie color of the sky. On top of the bar, the television blasted the news of my hearing.

"Hey!" the bartender exclaimed, walking toward me. "I knew I seen you someplace before! That's you on TV—ain't it?"

Wincing, I nodded silently. My expression made the bartender apologize.

"Gosh, I'm sorry. I never seen such a bullshit case in my life. They gotta let you go. I can't understand it! At first, the cops were asking citizens to help them find the murderer, and they was looking for a man! Then they arrested you? That don't make no sense."

I smiled a weak smile and shrugged. I couldn't escape it.

"You don't look like no man," he continued. "Besides, that little boy seen who done it, and he said it wasn't you."

The door opened and in walked Fred.

I'm being followed like a child, I thought angrily.

Fred sat down next to me as the pay phone began to ring, unanswered. I fought a choking sensation in my throat.

"Laurie—your dad started to worry about you when you were gone over half an hour. You left in those shorts and it got cold out. It started to get dark—"

"I just wanted to be alone for a while! I just wanted forty-five minutes to myself! I just wanted to mail my letters and go for a damn walk!" I tore apart my cocktail napkin. I was near hysteria.

"Well ..."

"You followed me! I'm a grown woman and I can't even go somewhere by myself! You spoil everything! Do I follow you?"

"What were you going to do? Sit in this gin-mill all night?"

"No!" I was practically hissing.

"Look. Your dad started to put on his coat to look for you. I thought it would be better if I went instead. So I took your car." I found out later, dad wasn't involved at all.

"How did you know I was in here? I just stopped in to use the phone."

"I drove past the drugstore and I saw your blond head in the window. Look, I knew you'd be pissed, but I couldn't let your dad run off looking for you," Fred said.

I gulped the remainder of my beer and held the empty glass tightly.

"By the way, who were you trying to call that you couldn't call from home?" Fred asked suspiciously.

"That's my business," I replied, heading for the door.

"I know why you're mad," Fred said, as we got to my car. "I saw your face after I testified about Chris. It was a very emotional incident!"

"How strange! And after such an emotionless marriage, according to you!" I blinked angrily. "Where was the emotion the night it happened? You didn't cry at the morgue. You didn't cry at the funeral. Did you have to wait to cry on cue in the courtroom for the whole world to see? You claim repeatedly that you never loved Chris. You say one thing and do another."

"I'm not going to try and explain it to you," Fred said.

Because you can't even explain it to yourself, I thought.

For the next few weeks, I clung to the hope that the judge would dismiss the charges for lack of probable cause. Eisenberg had always said that the complaint was no good. They didn't even have a warrant for my arrest.

My mother left for the west coast. We'd been arguing, squabbling over trivia; the tension in the house had spilled over to this most secure of relationships, and I felt a mixture of guilt and relief at seeing her go. I didn't blame her for needing to get away from the tension—I wished I could have gone. I knew it wasn't rational to resent her leaving, because I practically drove her out of her own house, but at the same time I missed her and felt abandoned. I was acting like an emotional infant, so I merely feigned indifference.

Boredom consumed me. I had nothing but housework to occupy my time, and the less I did, the less I wanted to do. I lost weight, had trouble sleeping and stopped exercising at the gym.

Fred and I stopped discussing my case altogether.

He would return home after work tense and irritable, claiming his commanding officers were harassing him: people in the office had been ordered not to talk to him; he was constantly reprimanded and spied on.

One night he was sitting at the kitchen table, with his tie loosened and his vest unbuttoned, busily wolfing down a cold beef sandwich. I had my feet up on another chair and picked at the sandwich on my plate, having lost interest in food. I asked him a question, but he didn't answer.

I thought he was in another of his moods. I was almost afraid to talk to him. I felt resentful.

Then there was a noise in the hallway. I glanced up.

A small, furry, adorable puppy crept cautiously around the corner of the kitchen cabinets. It stopped in fear when it saw me.

I shrieked. "Freddy!" I leapt from my chair and got down on my hands and knees to approach the little rascal. He was a German Shepherd about six weeks old. I scooped his tiny body into my arms and hugged him tightly.

"Do you like him?" Fred smiled. "I bought him for you."

I started to cry as the dog's trusting eyes looked up at the sound of our voices. A tiny, pink tongue licked the skin on my bare arm.

"He's so cute! Look at these huge paws! Where did you get him?"

"A breeder on the North Side."

Once again Fred had spent money we didn't have, once again on me. I couldn't be angry. I so needed someone, something, to love me!

I named the puppy "Sergeant."

■　　■　　■

For the next few weeks, Sergeant was all I clung to. After years of disagreeing with my mother over my habit of sleeping late in the mornings, I began to wake up early. Each day at sunrise, I was unable to do anything but toss and turn restlessly, and I had no choice but to get out of bed as early as 5:30 AM.

I'd make a pot of coffee, let Sergeant outside and read the morning paper until Fred and my father got up to get ready for work. I scanned the want ads and ached to find some kind of employment, but it was useless. I was beginning to feel as though no one in Milwaukee would ever hire me again. My time was occupied with training the dog and getting a few projects around the house finished, but my life felt pinched and mean. Without a job, I felt I was without value. Some days were so bad, I could barely get up enough strength to get myself dressed. When Fred asked me why I didn't change out of my nightgown and robe, I asked, "Why should I?" and really meant it.

My artwork lay untouched. My notebook of free verse was stored on a shelf in my closet, forgotten. I stopped jogging and weight lifting.

As my depression grew worse, attacks of wrenching anxiety began to hit me.

I was twenty-three. I desperately needed help.

I went to a psychiatric clinic to find a friend.

■   ■   ■

I remember a sparrow circling a slice of sky as I walked through scattered leaves down an East Side street. I remember the noise of my high heels clicking against the pavement. I remember the massive front door. I remember pushing open the door, folding my coat carefully so its tattered inner lining wouldn't show. I remember a brief encounter with the receptionist and some brightly colored chairs, and a handful of other people, *normal* people, sitting quietly and waiting. I don't remember what I told the receptionist, but I remember being ushered into the counselor's office.

I had pictured some bearded Freudian. I got Joan.

Her office was dimly lit, comfortable and warm. Lush plants filled the corners.

She was a small woman with a kind face behind large eyeglasses. She made me feel ... comfortable.

"First of all," she said, "I'd like you to know that we deal with everyone here on a first-name basis and keep conversations completely confidential."

"All right," I said. "Thank you. I'm pleased to meet you."

After I'd answered some preliminary questions, Joan told me to relax and untie my fingers. I guess my nervousness was obvious.

"I'd like to start by asking you why you've come here today," she inquired softly.

"Well, I guess I don't want to end up in a rubber room somewhere," I answered facetiously. As usual, I used my sense of humor as a buffer, a defense mechanism. "Honestly though," I added, "I'm struggling with depression."

"Do you know why?"

"What do you mean?"

"Have you been depressed for a long period of time or has some recent tragedy caused you to experience this?" Joan asked carefully.

I had trouble replying at first. "Recent tragedy? No. Not really. I mean, sort of ..."

"Okay. Back to my original question. Why did you come here today?"

"Because I'm afraid—" I suddenly said, biting my lower lip. Tears filled my eyes and I lowered my gaze to my lap. Crying always embarrassed me.

She moved her chair a bit closer to mine and bent toward me. "What are you afraid of, Laurie?"

I started to speak but failed to finish, my throat closing like a vise. I began again. "I'm afraid that someday soon I'll start screaming and never stop."

"You feel overwhelmed?"

I nodded.

"What has led to this?"

"The past few years ... my life ..." my voice trailed off again.

"Begin anywhere you'd like," Joan said.

I thought for a moment. Begin? Where? My experiences as a police officer? My difficult marriage? The arrest?

"I think I know who you are," Joan said. "And believe me, what you tell me won't leave this room. So you can relax and begin when you're ready. Okay? Take a deep breath."

I started in 1976, the happy summer I graduated from high school. And somehow I never stopped talking.

■　　■　　■

In time, counseling helped. I learned to accept the emotional help I needed instead of hiding all the pain I felt.

Joan was a warm, empathetic, middle-aged woman who listened to my problems and taught me to seek answers to difficult questions. I was harboring a great deal of anger, a consequence of the injustices that I couldn't fight—the negative publicity, the regret after rushing into a marriage that had more than its share of problems. She taught me that the depression that strangled me was a delayed reaction to the traumatic experience of the arrest, coupled with a lingering fear that remained as a result of the continuing legal process. I felt guilty for feeling resentment after my mother left. It was crazy. I had no right to feel forsaken. I knew these feelings were unjustifiable, but I could not change.

"Your biggest problem," Joan told me, "is that you insist on being independent and bearing this burden alone. You never talk to Fred about your feelings. You never let your dad know what's bothering you. You just try to keep up appearances, keep a stiff upper lip. Your load is too heavy. You must learn to lean on someone.

"My God—look what's happened to your life in less than a year! You got sucked into a whirlwind romance, because everything else in your life was a mess at that time. Your marriage is one that Fred's family won't accept, you had to move from apartment to apartment, and now you've been forced to live in your parents' house. Then you get two small children dumped in your lap and everyone expects you to welcome them with open arms. There are estate problems, custody problems, and then you get arrested for a murder you didn't commit. You've had best friends turn on you, lie about you and stab you in the back. And you wonder why you're depressed? Laurie! Give yourself a break!

"You've had to sit back and watch all of Milwaukee read and believe the worst publicity I've ever seen on TV, radio stations and newspapers, you lost two jobs that you enjoyed, and now you're home, waiting for a decision from a judge. It's like watching your future dangle by a thread. There's a limit to what anyone can take. Can't you let Fred share some of these burdens?"

"He's got enough to worry about. I have to do everything, or he'd never get anything done."

"You might be surprised to find out that, if he had to do certain things, he could. With you doing everything for him, why should he even try?"

I explained the incident involving the unemployment claim cards that I found piling up on Fred's desk.

"I swear that Fred intentionally refuses to do a lot of things that I remind him about—as if to spite me. The trouble is, how do you find the happy medium between a simple reminder and downright nagging?"

"Through communication," Joan replied. "Before you leave today, I'm going to show you some small ways to communicate more effectively."

I looked down and nervously chipped the fingernail polish off my thumbnail.

"When you first met Fred, you admired him, and now that that illusion has worn off, you're pretty disappointed, am I right? Do you still love him?"

"I think so. But I don't like him very much," I said.

"That's probably the best thing you've admitted all day."

Walking from the center to where my car was parked down the street, I pulled my jacket closed against the wind. Bare, spindly tree branches were silhouettes against the dreary, gray sky. I dreaded the approach of winter, and considered the fall season a gloomy prelude to the cold.

■　■　■

I received several cards from my mother, who explained that she was too despondent to write letters. My father missed her very much, biding his time until his retirement date when he could fly out west to join her.

Troubles came in bunches for my friends, as well. My former employer from the gym told us that his father was in critical condition with a serious heart ailment. My friend Ginger's ex-husband put a gun in his mouth and committed suicide over financial difficulties and some bad investments. Other friends were out of work or laid off from their jobs. Another friend of ours, a veteran, found it necessary to commit himself to a hospital for depression. He asked Fred to hold onto a suitcase that held his gun collection.

The night Chris was shot, I was supposed to go out with a friend from the gym, Marylisa. She had started dating one of Freddy's brothers, Billy, after I introduced them at a football game. She told me that her father had been convicted of embezzling a large amount of money and was being sent to a federal penitentiary. Her ex-boyfriend, Jeff, had been involved in a drunk driving accident while leaving a wine convention in Lake Geneva. Jeff was in a coma. A female friend who accompanied him was killed in the accident. Marylisa had almost accepted Jeff's invitation to go along. Jeff was given five years' probation for homicide by intoxicated use of a motor vehicle.

Fred appeared at his unemployment compensation hearing, after he was granted a new date. He won, was reinstated and received compensation. Small victories like that were dear to us at a time when everything else was going wrong.

The real estate market continued not to favor us, however, and the house on Ramsey Street remained empty. Fred decided then to rent it out.

■　■　■

It's pointless to recall all the fights I had with Fred, all the disagreements, all the times I couldn't understand him. Twice, at home, Fred became so threatening that I called the police, but, as I knew, they could not make him leave the house. That was the law. Once, however, our dispute was violent enough to make the newspapers.

It started because of a football game. Fred had bruised his ribs rather badly in the first game of the season, and I suggested that he sit out a few games, since he had no sick days left to pay for an absence from work. He'd fought so hard to get reinstated in his job—it would be foolish to lose it over a stupid game.

Even though he was hurt badly and winced every time I hugged him or even touched his ribs, he insisted he'd continue to play.

"Don't worry about it," Fred said.

The next game turned out to be a wet, cold, muddy event. Afterwards, Fred ran through the thundershowers back to the van, where I sat watching the teams play. He was irritated not to find me sitting in the bleachers.

"That dedicated I'm not," I told him. "I'm not going to sit there in the rain!"

Fred stripped off his soaked football pants and pulled on a pair of dry jeans. The humidity in the van made the windows cloud with steam.

"Billy and Marylisa want to shoot some pool. Do you want to go? Have a few beers?"

"Okay. Sergeant can sleep on his blanket here in the van."

We found a table at the tavern and began drinking as the rest of the football team walked in, covered in mud and soaking wet. A pool table was free so we started a game. I won twice in a row. Fred became frustrated.

As a joke, he bumped my pool cue just as I started to shoot. I tolerated his mischief at first. The second time was not so funny. After the third time, some balls moved on the table and I became angry.

"You don't know when to quit," I said, putting my pool cue back on the rack. "Cheater."

"So what?" Fred laughed. "Let's just play."

"No. It's almost midnight anyway. Let's go."

We left the bar and began walking to the van. We were drunk and we started fooling around, pushing each other back and forth, like we usually did. It was all in fun, and we were feeling our beers.

"Cheater! Cheater!" I teased, lightly punching Fred's shoulder.

"Quitter!" he sang back.

The horseplay suddenly lost its humor when Fred came around with a flying side kick that knocked me clear off my feet and into a rain-filled gutter on my tailbone. Before I knew what had happened, I was sitting in water and pain shot up my spine.

Fred was grasping my hand and trying to pull me up. I wanted to sit for a few seconds while the pain subsided. As Fred tugged at my arm, I burst out crying.

"Come on! Get up before somebody sees you!" he said.

"Wait!" I screamed. "Are you nuts?"

"The sidewalks are wet. You must have slipped."

"Leave me alone! You kicked me too hard!"

Fred pulled me up as we argued, and we struggled. He tried pushing me into the van.

"Shut the fuck up and get into the goddamn van! You'll wake the whole neighborhood."

I was angry and my back hurt. "I'm not getting into the van!" I cried, shocked because Fred was suddenly acting like a stranger. "I'm not going home with you!" I kicked him in the groin.

An old man walking by tried to break up the fight, but Fred told him it was none of his business. "I'm calling the police," the elderly man said, walking away.

Within minutes, a squad arrived. Since we were outside the city limits, it was not a Milwaukee car, but one from the suburb. I sat down in the back seat of the squad while the cops talked to Fred for a few minutes. I couldn't hear what was being said, but the first question that the police asked me when they got back into the car was, "Are you presently seeing a psychiatrist?"

"No," I lied, sobbing. I felt totally betrayed. How could Freddy tell them that? He's trying to get out of this by telling them that I'm crazy or something!

"Take a deep breath and try to stop crying," one cop told me. "Do you want to file a battery complaint?"

"No. But I want to go to a women's shelter."

In the morning, I thought about what had happened the night before, and I was confused about whether or not to return home. The sobering light of day suggested that I should consider it a drunken scuffle that got out of hand. I wondered if I had reason to believe that it was more. I'd promised myself long ago not to put up with any violence or physical dominance. Yet, if we split up, it would be in the newspapers and that would have a negative effect on my case. I didn't know what to think.

I stepped inside the telephone booth in the hallway of the shelter and made a long-distance phone call to my mom.

■ ■ ■

My mom. Always as calm and fresh as the rain-drenched peonies by
the backyard swing—her skin cool and clean. She would tell me what
to do, and then everything would be all right again. I could picture her
at the park, in her sleeveless '50s blouse, the wind swaying the tree
branches above her. Safe arms to come home to.

How I missed her!

■   ■   ■

When she answered, I was overcome with emotion, once more a
child. My throat closed tightly as my hand gripped the receiver. It was
difficult even to get two words out.

"Where are you, baby?" my mom asked, her voice as comforting
as an embrace.

A few hours later, my dad picked me up about two blocks away
from the shelter. I got into the front seat of his car, forgetting about the
bruise on my back, until I winced and shifted my weight. My father
was anxious to hear my side of the story, since Fred had already given
his version, which of course was completely different. Fred told my
dad that I was so drunk that I passed out and fell down. I was disappointed that he had lied to my father.

When I walked into the house, Fred begged tearfully for my forgiveness.

My dad stood by. "I may be sixty-one years old, but I'll be the
equalizer the next time you pull this," my dad said. "I have two other
daughters that had abusive husbands, and I won't stand for it a third
time."

Fred humbly nodded in silence.

Later, I received a call from Don Eisenberg.

"How are you?"

"Okay," I replied, acting cheerful, "except I feel as though I've
already been sentenced to six months of daytime television. What's
up?"

"You had an altercation with Fred. Anything I should know
about?"

"Boy, you don't miss a thing in Madison. No. It's all just about
settled now."

"Okay. Anything else?"

"No. Why?"

"Well, Judge Fine wants to see both me and Kraemer about
something and I just thought you might know what it's about."

"No."

"Look, as soon as I know anything, I'll call you," Eisenberg promised.

I hung up and watched the yellow phone cord twirl back into the usual tangled mess. Now what? Was the judge going to let me go?

I couldn't have been further from the truth. Judge Fine did not have good news to announce.

Fred's brother, John, had written to the judge, who was obligated to make both the defense and the prosecution aware of the letter. As usual, it caught the attention of the local newspapers, and again a sickening headline appeared.

In the letter, John described his feelings of certainty, saying that he "knew" I was guilty. He had of course no evidence to offer. Somehow he worked in that Fred had been "forced" to marry Chris because of the illegitimate pregnancy; he failed to explain why that was relevant, or had anything to do with me.

The letter alleged that Sean and Shannon had not seen the intruder, as they had told police that night, and said Sean had been "brainwashed" by Fred and me. It said that Sean told John that he did not see the murderer because he ran and hid, too scared to see anything.

He then brought up the incident at the Ramsey house when the Pennings had arrived to collect Christine's personal belongings. Fred had interfered and treated them all "like grave-robbers," he said. And he hadn't even been there!

Later that day, Fred's three other brothers apologized for John and offered their support.

■　　■　　■

Before the decision on my preliminary hearing was reached, Eisenberg asked me to drive over to Madison to see him; he had something he wanted to discuss with me. When I arrived, he told me the DA was willing to accept a plea bargain. Kraemer didn't want to try the case. He seemed to believe either that Fred had hired someone to kill Christine, or that Fred and I together had conspired in some way to do it. The prosecution was willing to knock my charge down if I would give them a statement telling them "what I knew."

I was insulted. "Are they crazy? Why should I make up some ridiculous story? Why should I admit to something I didn't do? Do they actually think I would cover up something for Fred?"

"Obviously, Kraemer can't figure this case out, and would be delighted with an explanation from you."

"Don," I protested, "no way would I be stupid enough to be a party to a murder. If Fred hired someone to do it, don't you think he would have had the murderer use a different gun? Or don't you think Fred would have gotten rid of it? He had over two weeks to lose it or report it stolen! Whatever!"

"I'm in the process of talking to my own ballistics expert about this whole thing. A gunshot wound like the one that killed Christine was so close to the skin that the barrel of the muzzle actually penetrated the tissue. According to my expert, both blood and tissue would definitely have blown back into the barrel of the gun. You would have had to clean that gun before Durfee and Fred looked at it. And, if you had cleaned it ..."

"There would have been no dust," I said.

Eisenberg nodded. "Especially since the gun was placed in a holster, back into a closed duffel bag. It doesn't make sense. Well ... this all may be premature. Meanwhile, I should tell Kraemer no plea bargain?"

"No plea bargain," I replied firmly. "I'm not pleading guilty to something I didn't do!"

■   ■   ■

But I'd be out by now, wouldn't I? That's the justice system for you. Stand up for your rights and lose. Cop a plea and win.

If I'd lied and said I did it, I'd be a free woman today.

I'd be sleeping in my own bed now.

I could lock the door from the inside, and keep Them all out.

If I'd known then what I know now, what would I have done?

What should I have done?

What would you have had me do?

I'm thirty-three now, and I've spent a third of my life in a place where guards can strip-search me any time they want to. What would you have done?

■   ■   ■

The day arrived when I was to report to Judge Fine's courtroom for his decision. I wore a brown suit and leather pumps.

A friend rushed up to me as I stepped off the elevator.

"Hi! My—you're dressed to kill. Oops. Wrong choice of words."

"You can't quote sarcasm," I warned.

Judge Fine began reading a prepared statement to a hushed courtroom. He began by saying that the evidence he reviewed was both "questionable" and "contradictory," and that this was the most circumstantial case he had ever seen. I held my breath.

"However ..." He paused, and my heart fell. "I see fit to bind the defendant over for a jury trial, finding probable cause for arrest since the defendant was the only one to have access to the murder weapon the night of the homicide."

Leaving the courtroom, I tugged at Eisenberg's sleeve.

"That's not true!" I whispered hoarsely. "I'm not the only one who had access to that gun! And how do we know that the gun they have now is even the same gun that was in our apartment the night of the murder?"

"Take it easy," Eisenberg told me. "Let's go someplace where we can talk."

I was bound over by Judge Fine because he'd decided that I was the only person who had access to the gun. Yet many months later, at my jury trial, Assistant District Attorney Kraemer would stand up in front of a blackboard and write:

ACCESS TO MURDER WEAPON?
1. Bembenek
2. Schultz
3. Zess
4. Gaertner

The defense party dodged the barrage of cameras and reporters and left the courthouse.

14

A NET OF LIES

I n the early part of November, I had a short appearance before a new judge, Michael Skwierawski. Because it was a brief matter, I intended to go alone, but my father insisted on taking me there.

■   ■   ■

I stood before the bench in a plain dress with a drawstring waist. The judge was a young, small man with carrot-red hair and a serious face behind wire-framed glasses. He arranged a trial date for the end of February, leaving three weeks open on his court calendar.

The usual number of cameras and reporters were present at the back of the courtroom. They seemed almost disappointed when the whole affair lasted only a few minutes.

"Much ado about nothing," Eisenberg whispered as we scurried past the press. I nodded.

The following day I finally heard from the Department of Labor, Industry and Human Relations on my sex discrimination complaint. They said they found no cause for a complaint, which meant they weren't going to follow up for me. They said I could go ahead with a case, but with my own lawyer and at my own expense. Thanks.

I had other things on my mind right then, so all I did was mail the information to one of Eisenberg's partners.

After getting the letter, Eisenberg phoned me. He had another subject he wanted to discuss with me.

"Where did you get married to Fred?" he asked when I went to see him.

"Before a judge," I answered.

"What county?"

"It must have been Waukegan County, I think. Anyway, it was in Illinois. Why do you want to know?"

"What was that date?" Eisenberg asked.

"January 31, 1981."

"I think we have a problem. Why did you get married there?"

"Because Fred suggested it—I don't know. We eloped. It seemed romantic, I guess. Why all the questions?"

"I'll have to do some checking, but I don't think you two are legally married," Eisenberg told me.

"I don't understand. That can't be. We have a marriage certificate. We had blood tests done and everything!"

"Right. And it may be that your marriage is recognized in the state of Illinois, but it's not legal in Wisconsin. This state has laws restricting people from remarrying less than six months after their final divorce hearing. When was Fred divorced?"

"I was under the impression that it was in 1979. I'm not really sure because Fred mentioned something about getting a 'bifurcated' divorce—whatever that means. So which hearing would you start counting the six-month period from?"

"He may have been separated from Christine in 1979, but perhaps the divorce wasn't final until much later. It takes a long time. There are property settlements and numerous appearances. Have Fred call me so I can get the facts straight. If your marriage hasn't been legal, the DA will swoop right down on that fact and accuse you of cohabiting. I don't want your credibility attacked."

"What on earth do we do, if it's not legal?" I asked.

"Get remarried in Wisconsin."

When I spoke to Fred about the possibility of our marriage being invalid, I received the usual screwy Fred explanation. He claimed that he had specifically phoned Reilly for advice on the matter of getting remarried and was assured that it would be a legal marriage. He said Reilly told him it might not be recognized in Wisconsin, but that it would be a legal marriage. I stared at Fred in disbelief as he led me through all this.

We planned to remarry in Madison at the end of the month.

■   ■   ■

I was doing my best to pull myself together. I felt I needed a library book, a "How To," maybe "How To Fight Depression While Waiting To Be Tried For First-Degree Murder!" There were certainly no fairy godmothers or ruby slippers to save me.

Maybe the solution was to return to school. Registering at the University of Wisconsin–Milwaukee for the spring semester to study art was my next brave plan. I'd already cleaned and organized every closet, attic and basement space in the house and needed something to occupy my mind.

I'd also lost interest in sex, which didn't help. I guess it went along with my lack of enthusiasm for life in general. I tried to shrug it off as a passing mood, but Fred was not as patient. One night, he and I were upstairs in bed, watching reruns of "The Odd Couple" on TV when my eyelids grew heavy and I found myself fighting sleep. I turned on my side with my back to Fred.

"Are you going to sleep?" Fred asked with irritation. "This is the third night in a row!"

"So?" was my tired response. "I'm falling asleep."

"You don't love me anymore," Fred insisted.

"Don't be ridiculous. I just don't feel like making love. That doesn't mean that I don't love you. Go to sleep."

"No, damn it! Sex was the first thing that went to hell in my last marriage, and I'm not going to let it happen again!"

"Why must you constantly compare me with Chris? You're over-reacting."

"No, I'm not!" Fred raised his voice. "You've been so callous these past few months, I don't think you even love me anymore! And now this!"

"Would you be quiet?" I asked Fred. "My dad went to bed a long time ago and he's right beneath us, downstairs. You'll wake him up if you don't lower your voice, and he has to work tomorrow." My temper was rising, and I whispered harshly, sitting up in bed. My father's rhythmic snoring had stopped.

"No! No! I won't be quiet!" Fred said. "It's always the same thing, over and over, living in this house! 'Be quiet or you'll wake up my dad! Don't do this! Don't do that'!" He mimicked me savagely. "Well, I'm sick of it! You always refer to everything as yours. It's your house, your bedroom—"

"This is my mom and dad's house. They are nice enough to let us live here. Now will you shut up?"

"I'm not going to shut up! Living in this house is like living in prison!" Fred snapped.

I threw back the covers and scrambled out of bed, whirling around to look at Fred in the light of the small television screen.

"That's a terrible thing to say! How ungrateful can you get? If you think that living in this house is like living in a prison, then get the fuck out."

"Fine!" Fred bellowed, stomping over to the closet and turning on the overhead light. I watched with anger as he pulled on a pair of jeans and hard-heeled Frye boots, stomping across the polished wooden floor.

"Will you stop making so much noise?" I asked again. Fred ignored me and continued gathering his clothes. I got back into bed and pulled the blanket over my head. As I lay there, I heard his footsteps clatter across the bedroom and go downstairs.

To my dismay, I heard my father get up and open his door, which is just what Fred wanted. He wanted my dad to beg him to stay.

"Freddy? What on earth is going on?" I heard my dad say. "Oh no. Don't do this. Talk things out." My dad suddenly called up the stairs. "Laurie?"

I hopped out of bed and hung over the balcony, shouting, "Let him go! You can't talk to that man. He's crazy!"

■   ■   ■

And so it went. Fights all the time, fights over little things and fights over nothing at all. Fred left, and came back, and left again. Back again, back and forth—but who is to say if he really ever came back?

■   ■   ■

One morning, while Sergeant was preoccupied with his food bowl, I went to the front door to see if there was any mail from my mother. Instead, there was a letter from my attorney, enclosing a statement he'd received from a witness who was willing to testify that Judy Zess had committed perjury.

The house was silent, except for the sound of the wind in the trees outside. I sat down with the papers in my hand, staring at the words, and my mouth fell open as I read it.

This is what it said:

Sometime during the last two weeks of the month of June, I came to know Judy Zess. I had been introduced to her by a mutual friend of her boyfriend and myself. One night in June (I don't know the exact date right now) I had called Ms. Zess and asked her if I could come over to look at a car that she was selling for her boyfriend. Ms. Zess said I should come over around 8:00. I had been to her house a previous night for a short while to view the car, also. This particular night, I arrived about 8:30 or 9:00 PM. Ms. Zess invited me into the apartment again. She escorted me into her dining room and offered me a drink. We talked about Tom Gaertner at great length. I told her about myself and she knew that I was a friend of Tom's. Some time into the conversation, I was told by Ms. Zess that Tom G. was to call her about 9:45 PM or so, as this was a practice of his. That night at approximately 9:45 Tom did call collect from the Federal Jail in Chicago. Ms. Zess and myself went into the bedroom—her and Tom's bedroom. She cautioned me to be quiet while she talked with him. According to the first part of the conversation, they were discussing what Zess had accomplished that day. Zess reported that she had done what he had instructed her to do and went down to the detective bureau and viewed several items that were in evidence in the Schultz murder case.

Of course, this was of considerable interest to me. Judy said, "Yes, I did. Yes, I did," several times, responding to Tom G. After several minutes into the conversation, Zess asked me to listen in on the conversation. Zess asked Tom about the car they were selling and several other items that included jewelry, some dope, etc. Tom was talking about the car. The rest of the conversation centered on his property and romantic concerns. After Zess hung up the phone, we both returned to the dining room and continued to discuss Tom G. and several other topics fell into place. Of course, I during this conversation asked her how she was involved with the Schultz murder case. Zess at this time said: "I guess you are a close friend of Joey and Tom, so I guess I can trust you." She told me that she was going to be a witness in the murder trial of Schultz. She told me and demonstrated how the police had given her a phone tape recorder in case she had any threatening phone calls. Several times when the phone rang, she picked up a device and attached it to the end of the phone, saying later that it recorded what the person was saying on the other line, depending if the caller was friend or foe. Incidentally, she did the demonstration when Tom first called her. She went on to say that she and Tom had been working on some sort of an agreement with the local authorities and federal authorities, whereby they could exchange information about Elfred Schultz's present wife, Lawrencia Bembenek. At that time, apparently the investigation was being centered around Bembenek. I asked her what she might be able to say to them that could possibly help Tom. She said she had that afternoon been down to the Detective Bureau, concerning the identification of articles that Police said were used in the murder. Zess told me that they showed her a wig and a length of cord to identify. She said that the police told her that these items were used and found at the scene. Zess said again that if she cooperated, that this could have a positive effect in Tom's case, according to the police. At this time, I believe she smiled at me and got up from the couch to pour us some wine. She returned and continued to talk about the Schultz case. I asked her about the identification itself. I asked if she could identify these things. She said that as far as she was concerned, the wig could have belonged to her mother. (In jest.) What mattered was if she was willing to say it was in the shared apartment before she moved out. She went on to say that she really didn't remember any wig like this one, but that she had remembered seeing a blond wig or other wigs when the three were living together. I said: "In other words, you are not sure of the wig?" Her reply was: "What do you think, dummy? Saying that it was in the apartment was far more helpful than telling them I never saw it before. I told them that it was the wig." At that time, I said: "Don't you think it is being a little bold to make that identification when there could be a lot of problems with lying and following through?" She said: "Honey, I'm good at it, and other things as well." We later went to the bedroom and while in bed, she received another phone call. She attached the gadget that Frank Cole gave her, and answered the phone. I don't recall who was on the other end, and in fact, the conversation was not the sort that I attempted to remember. She told me she was having sex with Frank Cole because Tom G. had told her to do anything to cooperate and do anything for the police. The next morning, Zess and myself woke up and took a shower together. She received another phone call from Tom G. that I overheard because I was nibbling on her ear. As I recall, they were again talking about Tom's situation, and also how Zess might help him get a deal from the federal authorities. After the conversation was over, I asked Judy what was up. She said Tom had been working on another story that could be what the police want in the Schultz case. Judy told me that she was thinking that if she would say that Bembenek had been asking her to ask Tom about having Schultz's wife taken off, meaning bumped off. She went on to say that they (her and Tom) wouldn't really do anything firm until Tom's trial or after he's tried on the drugs. She said: "Then if he's acquitted, and found not guilty, then we won't have to do shit for the police." She said that they wanted to at least have a story together in case they needed it. I said again: "Aren't you getting a little bold?" She said: "I'm doing it for Tom! Wouldn't you do the same?" I said: "I suppose I would." I again asked Judy if she seriously thought that this would get Tom off the hook with the Feds. She said she thought so. I told her: "What if the Feds want to prosecute a convicted dope pusher more than the State wants a police officer?" She said the bitch probably did it anyway. Tom never killed anyone, and that she loved him. She said: "Don't think I don't love Tom because I slept with you." I said: "I never asked for your love." We both smiled and went back to bed. We were getting dressed and the discussion continued. We talked about several things, but again, the subject that had paramount consideration was the issue of Tom G. and how they could bargain for his release. I said several times to her that I thought that this Federal case had more thrust than the State case, or more importance, and that I didn't think the Feds would let Tom go for the shit that her and Tom were putting together. She appeared to get upset at this time. She said angrily: "Look. The bitch is probably guilty and as far as I am concerned, she's no good. If I have to think up something else, then I will. I want to see them nail her ass to the wall." She then said: "Whatever it takes, Freddy, whatever it takes. Tom never killed anyone." I said: "How do you know she did?" She said: "I don't have to know. I just have to figure out a way to help them prove it." I said: "Damn, what if she really didn't do it?" She said: "Who gives a fuck?" I said: "Maybe Elfred Schultz cares."

She said that Elfred is just as guilty as her or his wife. She then asked: "Whose side are you on?" I told her that going to jail for murder was different than going for dope. That night I again stayed with Judy overnight. While in bed, Judy and I talked about more of her relationship with Bembenek. Just prior to her talking of Bembenek, we were discussing sexual fantasies. I had disclosed to Judy that I didn't mind if two women "got it on" at one time and that I would enjoy going to bed with two such women. Then Judy said one night she had been sleeping in the same bed with Bembenek, just sleeping. Judy admitted that she had always had strong homosexual desires for other women of course to her taste. She said that Bembenek was a very beautiful woman. Judy went on to say that while Bembenek was sleeping, Judy tried to go down on her and when Bembenek woke up, she said she was shocked to find Judy doing what she was doing. Judy told me that after that night, the friendship was not the same and very soon after both Elfred and Bembenek ordered Judy to move out. There are other things that were said, but these things I believe are more relevant to the reason for this statement.

Signed, Frederick Horenberger Dated the 27th day of October, 1981. 6 pages; subscribed and sworn before me on this date 10/27/81, Brian H. Blacker, Notary Public, State of Wisconsin Permanent Commission.

Everything fell into place. Things I was unable to understand before now rang clear. Zess's sudden about-face on the witness stand, her lies—it had all been planned ahead of time, in cooperation with the cops. She'd been waiting for me to call her, to see if she could tape our conversation, hoping I'd say something incriminating.

The impact of the statement was paralyzing.

Even the letter that I received from Zess after my arrest, wishing me the best of luck—it was all part of her game, watching for my next move. If I'd sent her a card in return, she would have turned it over to Frank Cole, the detective who arrested me. I cringed at the thought of her sleeping with Cole. It was despicable—sex as a simple fringe benefit. Horenberger had attached a letter to his affidavit, which described the time he'd bumped into Cole on the way out of Judy's apartment. Cole had been alone, on duty, and arrived in an unmarked car. Horenberger said Cole was not pleased to see him there, and threatened to have his parole revoked.

Waves of sadness washed over me. Parts of the statement echoed inside my head. What had I ever done to Judy? Had she wanted a lesbian relationship with me? If so, I never knew it. She was lying to Horenberger about making a pass at me. It was just one of her fantasies. She never tried anything with me or did anything out of the ordinary.

■   ■   ■

Of course, I could say she did and so help discredit the prosecution's star witness, couldn't I? I could admit to what she had already told Horenberger ... that I woke up in bed with her squirming against me? But it would be a lie. I wasn't going to start lying now.

■   ■   ■

The more I thought it over, the more certain unexplained occurrences acquired new meaning and began to make sense. Certain incidents played in my memory like frames of film, fragmented and out of sequence: Judy's mysterious anger when she found out that I'd married Fred; her over-demonstrative, physical mannerisms; the way she'd collected pictures of me; the way she'd always insisted on wearing my clothes, until she gained too much weight and couldn't get into them.

There was also that first vacation we'd taken together, when a male acquaintance of hers told me that she'd confided in him about her lesbian desires. I'd thought he was joking. True, a lot of cops I knew called her a "dyke," but then they called all the females that, especially those who wouldn't sleep with them.

The thought that someone could feign friendship in hopes of acquiring evidence was sickening. It was also sinister—I even started to suspect that the police were in on her plan. I wished Fred would hurry home so I could tell him about it.

After supper, I filled him in.

"You were so suspicious of Honeck? Take a look at this."

Fred read silently for a few minutes, occasionally raising an eyebrow. When he was done reading, I told him: "There's a transcript even more detailed than the written statement. It says that Horenberger tried contacting several different lawyers with this information, but nobody wanted to have a thing to do with it! One lawyer told

Horenberger, 'I don't want to touch it!' I'm just so angry that they knew about it and didn't want to help!"

"That's because it's a heavy thing. The authorities are involved. Nobody wants to get mixed up in it. How did Don finally get hold of it?" Fred asked.

"I guess Horenberger tracked him down. Don told me he plans on subpoenaing Horenberger to the trial, to expose Zess's perjury. The only thing he's worried about is that Horenberger's affidavit involves hearsay, so it might be inadmissible.

"This explains everything, Freddy! For months, it's all been like some impossible puzzle. I couldn't understand why Judy was saying those things! I kept racking my brain, trying to remember if I actually said the things she claimed I did. You know what I mean? I thought that maybe I was drunk so I didn't remember, or that I was joking around—I felt like I was losing my mind!"

Fred nodded. "I know. If people keep insisting that you did something you know you didn't do, there's always that tiny doubt that perhaps you have forgotten, that you're wrong, that it's all a misunderstanding. But these issues are too crucial. They spell intent. They spell motive. Either you had that frame of mind, or you didn't. Now—you see? You weren't going crazy. It was all a pre-planned story, testimony that the police could use, in exchange for a deal Gaertner would be interested in. I knew Zess was no good."

A few days later, Fred and I drove to Madison in my car, to get remarried in Eisenberg's office. We had applied for the new marriage license in Milwaukee County Courthouse, and we were somewhat unenthusiastic about the second ceremony. I felt that the first time we married was our real wedding, and that this event was just a legal requirement forced on us by the system. I'd not even bothered to buy fresh flowers or a new dress for the occasion; I wore the same outfit I'd worn for Thanksgiving. There was a brief ceremony—just enough to catch the attention of the newspapers—and we were on our way out the door. Fred suggested that we go to Lake Geneva for lunch, since it was a pleasant drive.

"You said some type of good seafood was served at the Playboy Club's café?" Fred asked.

"It's a seafood quiche," I replied. "It's about four inches high and stuffed with scallops, shrimp, crabmeat and tiny mushroom caps. Very, very good!"

We arrived at the Club, only to discover that there was a convention in progress and the dining rooms were crowded. So we were seated at a bar to wait for a table. I ordered Scotch and watched Fred drink his whiskey too fast. Glancing around uneasily, I thought about the police having been there, questioning my former co-workers. I knew that I'd probably been a major topic of gossip here, like everywhere else.

Fortunately, no one recognized me. Employee turnover at the Club was high. A year had passed, and I had changed.

Midway through lunch Fred told our waitress I'd once worked there.

"Oh, we were just talking about Laurie's days here at the Club!" Fred said as she returned with our check. She didn't seem to make much of his comment, and I quickly changed the subject. She walked away.

"I wish you hadn't said anything about me working here," I said.

"Then you should have said something before we got here!"

"I thought you'd have more common sense."

"Do you have something to be ashamed of?" Fred asked.

"No! I'm not ashamed that I worked here, although I wouldn't put it on my resumé. It was something I had to resort to for a few weeks. I'm ashamed that the police were here, questioning everyone about me!" My quiche lay half-eaten on my plate, turning cold.

The argument went on, circular, useless, depressing. I tuned him out.

■   ■   ■

It seemed to us then that nothing was going to work. Fred was still holding a desk job and feeling harassed at work, so he filled out an application for a job with a suburban police department that had several openings. The next day, an article appeared in the newspapers noting that Fred had applied. Subsequently, he was not hired.

"Damn it!" Fred swore, throwing the *Journal* to the floor. "We can't do anything without it appearing in the paper! Do they have to report everything I do?"

I agreed. "What makes us so important or interesting? They've been on our backs for months."

The following day, I'd just finished a load of laundry and fed Sergeant his supper when Fred walked in. He was early, and clearly upset.

"Sit down. We've got to talk."

I pulled one of the wooden chairs away from the kitchen table. Fred didn't bother to take his coat off.

"If I don't resign tonight, Laurie, they're going to fire me. I knew it was coming. I just didn't know when." Fred pulled on his gloves nervously. "I wanted to come home and talk to you about it first. What do you think?"

"What are the charges?"

"Cohabitation," he claimed. I took his word for it.

"You've got to be kidding."

"It was no secret when we got remarried, thanks to the *Journal.* I can do carpentry work until I get something else. Plus, they're giving me hell because of your pending case ..."

"All those years, and they just kick you out, as if you're nothing but a rookie."

"But if they fire me, they'll have to pay me unemployment," Fred said.

"No way. Look at the fight you had just getting compensation out of them for those few weeks! You spent more money on shrink bills for evaluations than it was all worth."

Fred said he'd resign. He said he felt as though a huge load had been lifted from his shoulders.

Around that time, my dad took his well-earned retirement. I threw a small, inexpensive party for him at a local tavern. His friends, co-workers and brothers came. There was a sandwich buffet, and a cake in the shape of a hammer.

The next morning, while I was still nursing a hangover, the phone rang. It was a friend, with interesting news.

"That Zess character is going out with Stu Honeck now. I saw them at a restaurant last night."

"Were they alone?" I asked.

"No. They doubled with another couple."

"I'll tell my lawyer about it," I said. I hung up the phone and pulled my blanket up around my chin, closing my eyes.

When the time came for my dad to leave for the coast to join my mom, Fred and I dropped him off at the airport. He packed a large suitcase and wore a big, quilted jacket. We parked the car in the lot and accompanied him to the gate. I fought back tears—I didn't want to make a scene as he was leaving. He hugged me, picked up his suitcase and disappeared through the door that led to the ramp. As I started to walk away, I glanced at Fred and saw that tears were streaming down his cheeks, too. I was surprised to see that he was as moved as I was.

"Aren't airports terrible places?" he asked.

I was unable to answer and my chin trembled. I had an irrational fear that my dad was leaving, never to return. I knew it was silly, and I tried to ignore my anxiety. I knew my mom and dad would fly back for my jury trial.

During this time I suffered from disturbing, recurring dreams. In one such dream, I was in Florida, moving boxes and furniture into a beach house with several friends. I was embarrassed in the dream, because several of my chairs were tattered and shabby. I joined a crowd of people at a picnic area by the shoreline, when suddenly the tide began to advance rapidly, with great speed and frightening power. The crowd ran up the hill, away from the water, and I ran after them, alarmed because I can't swim. When I reached the top of the hill, I was stopped by a chain-link fence. I was about to hurl myself over it, but it was electrified and the shock threw my hands off. I looked over my shoulder, panic-stricken at being cut off. The waves approached, faster and faster.

I would suddenly wake up, drenched in sweat and gasping for breath, Fred lying next to me asleep, undisturbed.

In another dream, I was in a strange city, applying for unknown jobs and climbing dirty stairways that led into small, old offices. After a short while, I became confused and lost. I walked down the street, searching for a phone, when I heard an ugly, mechanical noise behind me. It was a terrifying grinding, a horrid, rhythmic clicking. When I turned, I saw a robot-like creature following me, with the head of a skull, wearing an Uncle Sam hat. Its jaw opened and closed jerkily. I ran. I found a telephone in a hallway, but before I could call, strange people were strapping me down on a stretcher and injecting something into my arm. I struggled with them, pleading and begging to be allowed to call my husband.

I would wake up, clutching the bed covers and too scared to move an inch or even open my eyes.

Life went on. The days passed. Fred suggested we go to Vegas, and we did. We visited our friends in Florida. But none of it meant anything, not really.

■   ■   ■

I remember a woman we met in Vegas, who recognized me. "I'm so glad your case is over," she said. "I always thought it was bullshit."

"But it isn't," I said.

"Oh," she said, "but I thought the little boy, the eyewitness, said it wasn't you?"

"He did," I said, "but they don't seem to care."

"I'm so sorry," she said. "I think you're adorable."

I didn't know what to say. I never know how to take compliments like that.

And of course it wasn't over, not by a long shot.

■   ■   ■

After we'd returned from Florida, I casually glanced through the Sunday paper and saw a piece about Fred Horenberger, who'd sent Eisenberg the statement about Zess. He and two other men, Danny Gilbert and Mark Eckert, had been convicted of armed robbery against Judy Zess. I was distraught. Horenberger had pleaded not guilty but was convicted by testimony from Zess, who maintained that, since he'd been to Gaertner's apartment several times, he'd had plenty of opportunity to arrange the robbery. I grabbed a pair of scissors and cut out the article.

"Convicted?" I said. "Tied in to that robbery and convicted! My God—there goes my witness! He knew too much. That's why he's gone. He saw Frank Cole at Judy's. She told him about the deal she and Tom were making with the cops. She told him about her plans to lie on the witness stand. She told him about her affair with Cole. Now Horenberger's gone!"

I showed the article to Fred. "Now that he's in prison, he can't testify for me—can he?"

"Sure he can. But his credibility is shot. Now it'll look like he's just testifying against Zess to get even with her."

"But Horenberger gave us the information *before* all of this!" I said. "I've got to call Don, first thing in the morning."

■   ■   ■

My confidence deteriorated. First, my counselor Joan's husband had a heart attack and she had to leave the center, canceling our weekly sessions. I never saw her again. Then my mother phoned to break the news that she was going into the hospital for an emergency hysterectomy. Her doctor said she would not be allowed to travel for at least eight weeks after the operation, which meant that she couldn't be home for my trial. The tidal wave dream occurred more often. I grew afraid to fall asleep, knowing that I'd only have another nightmare. I had spells of overpowering anxiety.

One morning I was sitting in a drawing class at the university, completing an assignment. When I was done, I was allowed to take a break. As I left the room to buy a cup of coffee from the machine in the hall, a terrible feeling washed over me. I felt frightened, but I didn't know why. I didn't want to be where I was, yet I had no idea where I wanted to go.

I had to talk to someone. I almost ran down the hallway between the rows of green lockers. When I reached the pay phone on the first floor, I dialed home and prayed Fred would answer.

He was home! Thank God!

"Fred?" I began to cry and could barely talk.

"What's wrong?"

"I don't know." I tried to explain what I was experiencing, without sounding like I was losing my mind. I didn't understand it myself.

"Do you want me to pick you up?"

"Yes ... no! I've got to try to make it through the rest of my classes, otherwise I'll never be able to come back. Let me try."

I made it through the day.

For days, I felt like a child, afraid to be alone. I stayed awake all night, unable to sleep. At last, a doctor prescribed an anti-depressant drug for me; he assured me it was non-addictive, because I was afraid of drugs.

One by one, I dropped my university classes. My days were colorless, endless.

I got very drunk one night and burned three books of my poems in the incinerator, my tears sizzling and hissing in the fire. I tried to burn the pain, but it wouldn't go away.

The bad news kept coming. One morning a headline on the front page of the morning paper caught my eye. At first reading it seemed meaningless. I read it again: "JUDGE ORDERS SCHULTZ TO PAY $6,600 TO SONS."

Wincing, I read over the article. A hearing had just been held in front of Judge Curley, who had ordered Fred to hand over half of his pension money to the children.

According to the original divorce stipulation, Christine was entitled to half of Fred's pension when he retired from his job on the police force, whether or not she remarried. As a result of her death, the boys inherited this money. The Pennings petitioned the court for the money, and they got it. The court was told by Kershek that Fred was also delinquent in his child-support payments. Child support? Fred wasn't required to pay the Pennings or Barb and

Bruce Christ child support. Or was he?

The article reported that Fred was shirking his visitation rights, since the guardians had dutifully brought the children from out of state to see their father, only to be told he was vacationing in Florida. I wanted to scream.

Vacationing in Florida? *They* had failed to bring Sean and Shannon down for three or four weeks in a row—including the week Fred and I were in Florida! I felt the lies strangling me. I called Fred over.

"Look at this! Look at the way they make it sound!"

He just tossed it to the floor.

"How can they print any of this, without bothering to verify it?"

"We can't fight it," Fred said calmly.

"We have to!" I cried.

"No."

A few days later, I lost my wedding band at the health club. I'd been working with Fred, who was installing a sauna. We had already arrived home when I noticed it was gone. Although we made every effort to recover it, it seemed to have vanished. I guessed it had gone down the drain when I washed my hands.

Our anniversary arrived. Fred and I had been married only one year. It was overcast and reasonably warm outside for the end of January. We went shopping on the East Side and ended our afternoon with a tour of an art gallery. I didn't feel much like celebrating.

■　　■　　■

The trial was drawing nearer. A letter from my mom arrived. Her doctor was impressed with her recovery and was willing to allow her to travel. I smiled at the good news, knowing that she'd return with my dad for my trial.

I drove through the snow to the airport to meet them. Their flight had been delayed because of the weather. Fred waited in the car while I walked through the sliding glass doors of the terminal.

As soon as I spotted my parents, I broke into a run to embrace them, my face wet with tears.

"Don't cry. We're home now," my mom said softly.

■　　■　　■

Within a few days, Eisenberg called. He'd filed a Motion for Discovery and was given copies of all the police reports. He was finally able to review everything the prosecution was planning to use against me. The trial was one month away.

The police had turned over stacks of reports that filled four huge boxes. The subject matter varied from the utterly irrelevant to statements given by potential witnesses.

There was a report from a member of my Police Academy class, Boville, who told them that I once said I felt I could do anything a man could do. Another report simply confirmed that Fred and I had gone to Florida in May. There were various interviews and interrogations with about twenty different suspects, their mug shots included— all of them male.

Many reports were from concerned citizens, who called to say that they had seen a male jogger in that neighborhood on Ramsey Street. Another pile of reports made up the Judy Zess statements. Some reports were from the Crime Lab. The stack of paper was enormous.

Then Eisenberg pulled out a report involving a woman named Kathryn Morgan. "Where was your mother on June 18?" he asked.

Quickly I looked at my pocket calendar and flipped to the month of June. "It was a Thursday ... were my parents on vacation that week?"

"I hope so. The State has a witness named Mrs. Morgan who claims that she saw your mother going through the garbage at your old apartment complex. She says your mother took something home with her in a garbage bag."

"What!"

"Morgan says that on June 18 she was sitting outside her apartment across the yard from your old place when a woman pulled up in a car. She said the woman was about five feet, seven inches tall, forty-five years old, about 130 pounds, with brown hair. Wearing shorts and a tank top. Morgan claims the woman got out of her car and approached her to inquire if the green bins were the trash containers for the apartments. She then claims the woman went to the garbage bin, pulled out a bag, put it in her car and left."

Eisenberg looked up from the report. "How tall is your mother?"

"Don—no way. She's five-seven, but she's fifty-eight-years old! Impossible. Morgan's either crazy or a liar. If my mom and dad weren't on vacation, then my mom must have been babysitting for Sean and Shannon, because I used to work every Thursday until 3:00 PM."

"Does Virginia drive?" Eisenberg asked, using my mother's first name.

"Not much anymore ..."

"What color is your dad's car?"

"Metallic gold or bronze."

"Is it new?"

"Yes."

"Four-door?"

"Two-door. But Don! My dad always takes the car to work! My mom wouldn't have the car at 2:30 on a weekday. Did Morgan get a license number?"

Eisenberg showed me the report.

"Well! The license number is wrong! My God! I can't believe this! Do you know how huge those garbage bins are? I'm tall, but I could never reach into the bin outside the building. The opening was just high enough for me to flip the door open and toss the garbage bag in. My mother wouldn't be tall enough to reach down inside it."

"The State is probably trying to prove that you threw out some evidence and had your mother retrieve it for you," Eisenberg mused. "Is there any way we can prove your dad had the car that day?"

"I'll find out. Maybe his boss can remember. It's all so ..." I paused as something struck my memory. "Remember when my mother testified at my preliminary? Something happened that was strange. Just before Kraemer was finished with his cross-examination, he asked my mom to remove her glasses. Obviously, she complied, and then he told her to put them back on. Let me see that report again."

I scanned the typewritten lines with the aid of my fingernail.

"Here! It says that Mrs. Morgan identified Virginia Bembenek on September 2, 1981, as the woman she saw on June 18, 1981. Morgan identified my mother only after she removed her glasses! The description Morgan gave the police does not include glasses. My mom can't drive without her glasses. She can barely see without them. Her eyes are so bad that she doesn't dare drive at night or on the freeway anymore."

"This is good," Eisenberg agreed. "We're going to have to bring all of this up at your trial. If by chance your parents were on vacation that week, then we're safe."

"I find it so incredible that all these crazy people come forward with all of this bullshit!"

"I know," Eisenberg agreed. "It always happens with a widely publicized case such as yours. People are thrill-seekers. They want to get in on the act. Bored housewife plays detective. And who knows?

Maybe there was some loony digging around in the garbage that day. Cities are full of bag ladies."

"Not bag ladies driving new cars, Don! It's an absurd lie, I'm sure! Would someone who wanted to remove evidence go up to a local resident, chat in broad daylight, the car sitting right there?" I was disgusted.

"Well, Mrs. Morgan certainly doesn't help us. Circumstantial evidence by itself is nothing, but it's like little building blocks. You have this witness, and that statement, and this, and that, and pretty soon you build yourself a case."

"But none of it is true!" I protested.

"There are many reports about Fred in here. Many of Christine's friends told the police that Fred physically abused her. There's one from Jo Anne Delikat."

"Dennis's ex-wife. Dennis who now lives in Florida."

"And one from a woman named Polka, and a report from Attorney Kershek. He says Fred threatened Chris the last time they argued. He claims that Fred stopped paying her alimony."

"That's not true. Kershek represents the Pennings."

I flipped through another stack of reports. "Most of these statements were taken in July, after my arrest."

"When did you last see Christine's babysitter?" Eisenberg asked.

"At the funeral. She's about fourteen or fifteen."

"This report says that she claims you and Fred were at the house on Ramsey sometime in May, to pick up Sean for a game, and Fred gave you a tour of the house. She says you talked to the children in front of her—what's her name? Tammy. Tammy says she heard you ask where the dog was."

"No way. Fred never gave me a tour. Plus, I knew that dog was gone in February. Why would I ask about the dog in May?"

"May seems to be the month of interest, obviously. Were you ever at the house before the murder?" Eisenberg asked.

"Yes, but I never went through the house. Once I waited in Fred's van, and once I waited in the entranceway at the front door."

I carted the remainder of the reports home with me. Eisenberg told me to read them all carefully—an exhausting job.

My mother was appalled when I told her about the Morgan woman's allegations. The vacation she and my dad took was ill-timed—the week following June 18.

I sat down in a chair to read the rest of the reports. Then I came across Fred's statement from that night. Fred wrote that after the shooting, he and Durfee arrived at our apartment, and Fred felt the hood of my car, to determine whether it had been driven recently, but it was cold. I thought that was an extremely odd thing to do.

Another report in the pile was written by Fred's lieutenant, Ruscitti, who said Fred had approached him to report finding some of his bullets out of place—again, conveniently, in May.

The report said that Fred claimed to have questioned me about the bullets, but I denied knowing anything about it. The style in which the report was written gave the impression that I had clearly been tampering with Fred's ammunition. I leaped from my chair and stomped into the kitchen, where Fred was eating a sandwich at the table. Dropping the page in front of him, I stood with my arms folded.

He read the report and looked up at me, blank-faced. I stared back silently.

"What?" he asked.

"What on earth did you tell your lieutenant?"

"I didn't tell Ruscitti anything! I mean, what I told him isn't written down here. It was misconstrued."

"Why would you tell him something like that? It's not true! I feel so betrayed! What are you trying to do to me?"

"Laurie, I was telling him about the time when I found that bullet on the floor by my clothes tree."

"By your clothes tree, in your corner of the bedroom, where you used to hang your ammo belt and gun and everything else! I remember the incident! We already had the boys, Fred! Sean and Shannon were right there. And you accused them of playing with your bullets, when the damn bullet probably just fell out of your pouch to the floor. That happened in June! After Christine's death!"

"So?"

"So the report says May. And it says that you claimed to question me about it. This report wouldn't exist if you hadn't gone to Ruscitti about it in the first place! A bullet falls out of your ammo pouch, amidst all of your junk in the corner, and the next thing I know, my husband runs to his commanding officer about it!"

"What I told Ruscitti was that it would have been possible for Judy Zess to have been looking over my ammunition. That's what I told him. I don't know why he wrote that other shit."

"You turned an innocent incident into a condemning one!" I said. "You of all people should know how the police misconstrue reports. And you felt the hood of my car that night? Why, for God's sake?"

"I did that in front of Durfee on purpose! I did it to show him that it was cold! That way, they couldn't turn around and—"

"But Fred! Why would you do that? Why would you even *do* something like that, unless you were suspicious? How could you?"

Then I mentioned the police reports that alleged Fred had physically abused Christine.

"Those people have as much credibility as Mrs. Morgan!" Fred argued. "They're lies! Just like the report about your mother is a lie. Just like the reports about you are lies. Did I ever doubt you for even one second? I don't believe any of the lies about you—why should you believe the reports about me?"

There was something to that.

■　　■　　■

Something, but not everything. So many little lies, so many "innocent mistakes," misconceptions, misconstruings. Was I being paranoid when I wondered, miserably, why people never misconstrued anything my way?

I could feel the net of lies tightening about me.

15

WOMAN ON TRIAL

The first few days of my trial were uneventful, even boring. There was a lot of legal mumbo jumbo. Most of the time was spent picking a jury, an intricate process full of challenges, counter-challenges and eliminations. Finally, a jury was chosen. Two alternates were added in case of illness. Seven women and five men held my fate in their hands.

Few of the prospective jurors cared to do more than glance furtively at me as we sat in the small annex room adjacent to the judge's chambers. I studied them intently. A retired, old black man with an extreme underbite who wrapped himself in a gray cardigan sweater sat next to a large, solemn woman with a double chin. She said she was a homemaker, sitting erect and folding her hands in her lap. Another woman had the appearance of a schoolteacher as she squinted through thick eyeglasses. There was one young woman, who wore jeans and a simple hairstyle. The male jurors were all older men.

Eisenberg whispered to me during the lengthy process, "By the way, on several occasions now, I've attempted to contact the Pennings or the Christs through Calvey. I wanted to interview Sean Schultz before he testifies again, but I think there is going to be a problem. I sense some resistance on their part."

Before the jury was allowed into the courtroom, the court dealt with several motions Eisenberg had filed, and held a "suppression hearing."

The issue at hand was the legality of the warrantless search of my locker at Marquette. Long after my arrest, two detectives had confiscated my purse from my locker, later contending that hairs from my hairbrush matched a hair found on Chris's body at the morgue.

"This evidence was seized after a warrantless search, and so should be ruled inadmissible," Eisenberg told me.

He began to flip rapidly through the heavy stacks of folders on the table. All the police reports had been arranged and bound alphabetically.

He found a page that listed Crime Lab findings and underlined a section that referred to hair and fiber analysis. Several blond hairs were found that "presumedly" matched Shannon Schultz's hair, but samples from his head were never obtained to verify this assumption. Other hair discovered on Christine's bed was unidentified and ignored. Eisenberg underlined the sentence that listed "one color-processed blond hair" that was found "consistent in characteristics" with the hairs from my hairbrush and "could be from the same source."

"This is the sloppiest police work I've ever seen!" Eisenberg said to me. "Could be? Could be? You might be convicted on 'could be's or could not be's?' Jesus Christ! And to top it off, it was an unconstitutional search!"

Thomas Conway, who'd been my sergeant at Marquette, took the stand. He was at that time unemployed. He testified that after my arrest I gave him my locker combination so he could retrieve my extra uniforms. The police had then removed me from the premises.

As he'd opened the locker, two detectives had appeared and asked if they could be present during the examination of the locker contents. Conway had found a variety of items inside—personal articles and Marquette property. As he began lining them up on a bench, the police snatched up my purse and told him, "We'll need this."

To my surprise, Eisenberg informed me that he wanted me to testify briefly about these events in Conway's office.

I walked to the witness stand, nervous and self-conscious. I was overly warm in the sweater dress I wore, and my slip clung to my stockings from static electricity.

A few minutes later, it was over. I had explained that I gave Conway permission to collect the extra uniforms, but not my personal property. I thought I did all right. I was glad of the chance to testify so briefly. It was good practice for the lengthy testimony I would give at the end of the trial.

■   ■   ■

The court recessed and I wandered out into the hall. When I returned, the judge, Michael Skwierawski, ruled on several of the motions that Eisenberg had filed.

"Motion to dismiss this case due to lack of probable cause: denied. The issue of probable cause was dealt with at the defendant's preliminary hearing before the Honorable Ralph Adam Fine, and I don't choose to usurp another judge's decision," Skwierawski began.

"Why even file a motion if you know it will only be denied?" I asked Eisenberg. It seemed foolish to me.

"For the record," he whispered.

"Likewise," the judge continued, "motion to dismiss due to the inadequacy of the complaint is denied. Motion to suppress the hair evidence, seized from the defendant's locker, is also denied. Although the police did not secure a warrant for this seizure, I don't feel that one was necessary in this situation, because it is my opinion that the police were not there acting as a governmental body."

The police were not there acting as a governmental body? What were they? A glee club?

Skwierawski droned on in the esoteric jargon of judicial decisions, quoting several state statutes. I wondered why judges and lawyers couldn't use plain English. Eisenberg argued and made his objections, and I listened to the proceedings until I heard a noise in the back of the courtroom. Turning my head slightly, I saw the District Attorney, E. Michael McCann, walking next to Police Chief Harold Breier.

Eisenberg had subpoenaed the Chief of Police, along with an order for discovery that included access to Department records on Stu Honeck and Judy Zess.

Kraemer immediately objected. "Your Honor! I must object to the defense's request for these records! I also object to Mr. Eisenberg's strategy. His intentions are focused upon pointing the finger at other suspects, and that is not his job! His job is to defend Miss Bembenek, not identify other possible defendants!"

"Your Honor," Eisenberg protested, "may it please the court to understand that the defense's sole purpose in subpoenaing this information is to inform the court that previous testimony by these witnesses was perjury. At the preliminary hearing, Mr. Honeck denied having any problem with alcoholism, and I believe these records will show that he does indeed have a problem, which may be relevant to his recollection of the events on the night of the murder. If he consumed a great deal of alcohol that same night—"

"Your Honor!" Kraemer interrupted. "Whether Mr. Honeck is an alcoholic or not bears absolutely no relevance whatsoever to this case, and I see no reason why it should be admissible!"

"Gentlemen!" the judge finally exclaimed. "If you'll stop for a moment, I'll tell you that I intend to review the records of both Miss Zess and Mr. Honeck in the privacy of my chambers, and decide whether or not they in fact have any relevance to this case. I will announce whether or not I shall deem them admissible. The court will recess approximately one half hour."

While we waited, Eisenberg asked, "Did Fred see Sean and Shannon this past Sunday?"

"No. There was a hassle. Fred tried to see the boys after their appointment with the child psychologist, but he said he fought with Barb. So he called a police sergeant and showed him a copy of the visitation stipulation, but even that didn't work. Fred says the Pennings are afraid that if he has the boys for the afternoon, he'll meet with you and let you talk to them."

"What the hell are they afraid of?" Eisenberg grumbled. "I talked to those children before, and they had no objection. I have every right to talk to witnesses before they testify. It makes them less nervous because it prepares them for the types of questions that will be asked."

"All stand," the bailiff commanded as the judge returned.

Skwierawski, consistent with his pattern of denying all our motions, announced that he chose to suppress the records of both Zess and Honeck.

Half the week had already slipped by.

Kraemer's opening argument, in which he began to lay out the framework of the State's case, was enough to warrant an Emmy award. Solemnly he asked the jury to think of him as Christine Schultz's lawyer. He spoke with a false piety that was dismaying in its transparent pretense.

The jury listened intently as Kraemer laid out his bizarre theory. Apparently, money had been the motive. We hadn't wanted to kill Christine, not really. We just wanted to scare her out of her house, "so that the defendant and her husband, Fred, could move in."

I was sitting next to Eisenberg at the wooden table behind the prosecution. I crossed my legs and couldn't help fidgeting. Finally, I pulled the cap off a felt-tipped pen and began scribbling on a long, yellow pad of paper Eisenberg had again provided for my comments.

"If Kraemer says there was no intent to kill, then why was I charged with first-degree murder?"

For the rest, I couldn't even comment. How idiotic to think a grown woman could be scared out of her own house! How farfetched! Why wouldn't she just change the locks or buy a guard dog or have someone stay with her? Why would she just move out? Christine's boyfriend was a cop, after all. Besides, Fred and I had had a terrible fight over moving into that house. The theory struck me as a patchwork, pieced together for lack of anything credible.

Kraemer's little drama continued. "Ladies and gentlemen of the jury, I believe the evidence will prove that once Christine Schultz heard the cries of her children, her maternal instinct told her to fight for those children—even if it meant she would risk her own life, which she did. The defendant realized she would have to shoot Christine, when Christine got up, turned around and recognized that it was, in fact, Lawrencia Bembenek who was in her house that night ..."

I was supposedly disguised in a wig and whatever else. How would Chris recognize me? She got up and turned around—yet she was shot in the back? How could he say these things without blushing?

"You see," Kraemer continued, "Ms. Bembenek likes to live life in the fast lane. She wears designer clothes, likes expensive vacations, and has even said that she married Fred for his vasectomy, since children would only burden her extravagant lifestyle.

"Another burden for Ms. Bembenek was the amount of money her husband Fred was forced to pay his ex-wife: in excess of seven hundred dollars a month! Allowing Christine Schultz to live in the luxurious tri-level house on Ramsey, rent-free. A house that Ms. Bembenek wanted to live in desperately. A house that Elfred Schultz built with his own two hands and then was forced to give up—to a woman he no longer loved."

My lawyer made several objections to the style in which Kraemer's argument was delivered. Skwierawski was seemingly already so irritated by Eisenberg's objections that he called them improper. However, he did advise the jury that the statements being made by the District Attorney were not to be considered "evidence"; they were to be considered theory only, which Kraemer would try to prove.

Kraemer continued: "If only Christine Schultz had had her head down, like a good girl, I think Ms. Bembenek would have grabbed the jewelry box and fled. But Christine didn't. She didn't because of the screams she heard emanating from the bedroom shared by her two little boys. Sean and Shannon are attacked by the defendant, and Shannon begins to kick about at the person who is on top of his brother. You can just imagine, ladies and gentlemen, what went through Christine's mind when she heard her children calling for help. You can imagine the sound emanating from that bedroom—"

"Well, now, Your Honor! I object to this! This is not an opening statement!" Eisenberg exclaimed.

"Sustained," the judge said dryly.

"Would the court instruct the jury to disregard Mr. Kraemer's last two or three sentences? There is no way for Mr. Kraemer to know if the children screamed, or if Christine heard screams. There is no evidence of that. There is no evidence that anything went through Christine Schultz's mind!"

"Just proceed, Mr. Kraemer," the judge commanded. "Sit down, Mr. Eisenberg."

He sighed and returned to his seat, shaking his head.

"There were screams coming from that bedroom," Kraemer said. "Screams heard across the hall by Christine Schultz, the mother of those two children."

"I object!" Eisenberg said again. "If it please the court, there is no way in the world that this man can prove that Christine Schultz heard anything!"

"Overruled."

He refused to be silenced. "Also, Your Honor, I believe it is prejudicial and I'd like to approach the bench."

"Request denied," Skwierawski replied.

What was going on? I felt that Skwierawski was acting more like a prosecutor than a judge! If this continued, it would be impossible for the jury not to be influenced by it. I threw a puzzled glance Eisenberg's way.

After my lawyer's opening argument, the State announced its intention to call Sean Schultz to the stand first—obviously to minimize his testimony. Eisenberg explained that Kraemer remembered how strong Sean had been at the preliminary, and wanted to weaken the impact he'd have on the jury. The jury would be ultimately less affected by Sean's testimony if it was heard first and several weeks of testimony followed it. It's only human nature to remember what one hears last with more intensity.

I realized for the first time that a trial was like a poker game. Because Eisenberg had insisted on having witnesses testify at the prelim, perhaps we had shown too much of our "hand."

Before the bailiff was instructed to summon the jury back into the courtroom, Eisenberg informed the court that he had not been allowed to interview Sean since the previous August.

"Your Honor, it has been about five months since the child last testified. Because of his age, his memory is bound to fade faster than an adult's. I have requested several times of the temporary guardians to interview Sean, and have subsequently been faced with blatant opposition."

Kraemer quickly stood up. "Your Honor! The grandparents of

Sean have told me that Mr. Eisenberg has influenced the boy's testimony, and that the last time he was allowed to question Sean, the child became extremely upset and cried all the way home."

"Your Honor!" Eisenberg's voice angrily boomed throughout the courtroom. "Please excuse my choice of words, but the grandparents are nothing but liars! At no time would I stoop to something as despicable and unethical as to attempt to influence a child's testimony! I'll stake my professional reputation on it! I talked to Sean last August at my office in Madison, in the presence of the guardian ad litem! Where's Lee Calvey?" Eisenberg turned to see if Calvey was still in the courtroom. "He will vouch for me. Subpoena him if you wish. I object to Mr. Kraemer repeating such slanderous accusations in open court and I maintain that I have every right to talk with Sean Schultz before he testifies! The children have asked if they could talk to me. They want to talk to me. I attempted to communicate with Barb Christ on a conference call, and she ended our conversation by hanging up on me!"

Kraemer said nothing further. Maybe he realized that the Pennings had exaggerated. Perhaps, in their grief, they viewed all of us with suspicion and hate, which I guess was understandable.

Judge Skwierawski paused and blinked his eyes. "Let me advise both counsel that it is neither a right, nor a violation of any kind to interview a witness prior to testifying. If the children do indeed wish to speak with Mr. Eisenberg, but have been prevented from doing so, then I think it is the court's obligation to intervene. I will allow the interview to take place. However, I think it is necessary to ask the children again, before any decision is made regarding this matter. The court will recess. Mr. Kraemer and Mr. Eisenberg will meet me in my chambers in twenty minutes, if all parties can be contacted."

While the court was in recess, I made for the restroom in the hallway. I was followed by my sister-in-law, Bob's wife Chris. As we went in, Judy Zess came out, and although I glared at her, she refused to return my gaze and passed by me in silence.

"She'll probably run to Kraemer and tell him that I threatened her in the bathroom," I told Chris. "You're my witness that nothing was said."

Fred's brothers were in the courthouse hallway, with his father and uncle, talking to my mom and dad. All potential witnesses had to remain outside the courtroom because of the sequestration ruling. I could tell that my mother was already exhausted.

"You won't be called to testify, mom," I said. "Why don't you go home and lie down?" She was still recuperating.

"I don't understand why we can't go inside," my mom said, with emotion in her voice. "It's driving me to distraction to sit out here and wonder what's going on in the courtroom!"

"I know." I nodded, feeling helpless. "Are you going home?"

"No," she said. "We're not leaving you."

I returned to the courtroom and followed my lawyer into the judge's chambers. Fred and I sat down on a couch against the wall as reporters filled the hallway that led into the annex and the offices of the court reporters.

A scraggly plant sat on the windowsill, its dry branches tumbling down toward the floor. Kraemer and Eisenberg discussed something off to the side. Skwierawski sat back in his chair, waiting. Several pictures, drawn in crayon by children, were taped to the paneled wall behind the judge.

Barb Christ entered the room with Sean and Shannon, her husband Bruce following her. I looked at her, seeing the resemblance she bore to her sister Christine, but her eyes avoided me entirely. Her bleached hair hung thin and straight, framing her jawline. Hovering over the boys, she instructed them to sit down in front of the judge.

"Hello, Sean. Hello, Shannon," Skwierawski said, trying to ease their nervousness in a room full of strangers. "I have a few questions to ask you today. The first question is whether or not you want to talk to Mr. Eisenberg today, before you testify. You can talk to him, if you want to. Or you don't have to talk to him, if you don't want to.

"The second question is whether or not you want to talk to Mr. Eisenberg alone, or in front of anybody. Do you understand?"

Both boys nodded. Shannon glanced at his father.

"Okay." The judge nodded back. "Would you like to talk to Mr. Eisenberg? You don't have to if you don't want to."

"Yes," Sean replied. "I want to talk to Mr. Eisenberg."

"Would you mind talking to him in front of your aunt and uncle?"

"That won't be necessary," Sean responded.

Suddenly Barb asked, "Don't I have any say so in this matter? I'm the guardian, and I think that if Mr. Eisenberg has anything to ask them, he can do so in front of my lawyer and me."

The judge paused after this abrupt comment. "Taking into account the fact that these boys are still just children, I have decided that if the defense counsel still wishes to interview them, he will do so in the presence of Mr. Kraemer and the temporary guardian."

Fred and I left the courtroom. "Barb should talk about influencing the boys!" Fred said heatedly. "Sean said that every time he refers to the murderer as 'he,' Barb always corrects him by saying, 'You mean, she.' Now what kind of shit is that?"

Eisenberg came out of the judge's chambers and I returned to the defense table. "That kid is super," he told me. "I asked him right in front of those assholes if at any time I ever told him what to say, or if I made him cry, and he said '**NO**.' Then I said, 'Did I question you the last time just the way I'm talking to you now?' and Sean said, '**YES**.' I can't believe those Pennings!"

"I told you they were difficult."

Skwierawski returned and told the courtroom that since it was late in the day, the court would recess until the following morning.

After dinner with Eisenberg and his wife, Sandy, I drove home.

■   ■   ■

The days of my trial were merging together like waves on a shoreline. The whole affair had a strange, unreal feeling about it. I felt detached, as though I was merely standing in the wings of a theater stage, viewing a play, watching myself perform, unable to move or shout or cry out against those who were hurting me intentionally, against those who were lying viciously, for reasons unknown to me.

In the evenings, my parents and I would play a game of cards or Scrabble, look at photographs or watch a movie. Sergeant would lie on the floor in the middle of the room and demand everyone's attention, tail wagging furiously. Fred would usually read in another room or do paperwork.

Every morning, I awoke long before the sound of the digital alarm clock. Its red numbers glowed in the gray light of dawn. Then it would be a hurried scramble to get dressed and ready to leave—sleepily standing in front of my closet, trying to find something clean to wear, finding a run in my stockings just before leaving the house.

■   ■   ■

But nothing prepared me for the press coverage of the trial. If I didn't break down and cry, they said I was an ice maiden, cold and unemotional, a hard woman from the fast track. If I sniveled at all they accused me of playing to the gallery. If I answered in monosyllables (which I did a lot, out of fear and nervousness and ignorance), they said I was unhelpful and uncommunicative. If I rambled they said I was trying to confuse the court. They wrote about my "style," about my hair, about my looks, about my clothes ... oh, how they wrote about my clothes! They covered the trial like a Paris runway fashion show. No matter what I wore, they crucified me. One day I wore a frilly blouse, and they sneered that it was my "Little House on the Prairie" look, and said I was dressing for acquittal. If I wore something less conservative they accused me of sexual manipulation, and revived the "Playboy bunny" label. On one of the many days I arrived in a three-piece suit, a Chicago Tribune reporter, angry because my mom and dad had declined a courthouse hallway interview, wrote that I wore "see-through dresses with no slip underneath" and titled his muck "Beauty or Beast?" If my clothes had style they said I'd always been obsessed with fashion. No one asked me why I wore what I wore. (I had no time to clean or press anything, and I wore whatever was on the next hanger in my closet, until the closet was empty—but that was too simple a truth for them.) The only thing they didn't write were the unadorned facts. They didn't write about the leaps of faith and logic the State was asking the jury to make. They didn't even try to write about what was going on in that courtroom.

I was always the bitch, cold and emotionless—but how could they see the pain?

■   ■   ■

At the courthouse, I saw the crowds of excited onlookers push their way in, trampling others to get to a seat. The minute the courtroom doors opened, they gathered like vultures. Every chair in the spectator section of the courtroom was always filled.

I watched them in disbelief. Once, numbly, I dreamed I could make them all go away—I would tap my heels together three times and they'd vanish. I was nervous and sweaty, sitting through day after day of testimony, objections, motions and recesses. The jury rarely looked at me, fixing their gaze instead upon the judge or the witnesses.

The elderly black juror dozed off occasionally.

Courtroom bailiffs were kept busy with a mentally disturbed woman named Mrs. Bursar who constantly interrupted the proceedings. She wandered in from the street, cried out loud during questioning and demanded to be allowed to approach the bench, to file her motions. I wondered if she had gone mad during a stint at law school, it wouldn't have surprised me. She was physically restrained and removed from the courtroom more than once. On one occasion, as she was being escorted away from the bench, she stole my purse off the defense table and its contents went flying across the floor. The judge threw her in jail.

I wished we could have videotaped Sean's testimony at the preliminary, because the children, as expected, remembered far less now than they did then. Sean was still firm, but his testimony was not as detailed at my trial as it had been the previous September. Kraemer didn't seem to pressure Sean much, but he brought up the fact that my mom and dad took Sean to Great America Park for his birthday. Kraemer insinuated that my mom and dad did this to bribe Sean. The boy denied this. The same line of questioning followed regarding Fred and me. Kraemer asked Sean if we had influenced his testimony, which Sean refuted. My heart went out to him, and I wanted to hug him for being so brave, but I had to remain seated, less than ten feet away from the child.

Judy Zess approached the witness stand, unusually meek. Her bold mood from the prelim had disappeared. Her testimony varied yet again, not only from the police reports, but even further from the story she'd told in September. So far, she'd returned her apartment key to the landlord on three different dates. When Eisenberg made her aware of this, she became confused and wasn't even able to recall the correct month, if indeed she'd turned the key in at all.

She claimed she could recognize Fred's handgun by some grooves or scratches in the handle. I'd seen the gun more than she had, but even I didn't know what she was talking about.

Christine's babysitter, Tammy, faltered in her story about my alleged question regarding the dog in May. She was a shy teenager. Clearly the police report had colored her story.

Kershek testified that before Christine was murdered, she had complained to him that Fred had stopped paying his alimony—again in the month of May. Eisenberg objected, saying that Kershek's testimony was hearsay. It could not possibly be verified because she was dead. The objection was overruled.

"Your Honor," Eisenberg began, "I would like a clarification, if I so strenuously disagree with one of your rulings, may I ask for a clarification or at least ... I don't mean more argument, but—"

"Well, apparently you do mean more argument, Mr. Eisenberg," said Skwierawski. "And you have a habit of objecting after I make a ruling. You also object after you have previously objected on a point and made your argument. I am advising you, now, what the appropriate procedures are in this branch of this court and I expect that counsel will conduct themselves accordingly."

Eisenberg then mentioned that two uncashed alimony checks had been found in Christine's purse after the homicide.

Kershek went on to testify that Christine had complained to him that Fred threatened her in May, saying that he would "blow her fucking head off" if she continued to argue with him. Again, this could not possibly be verified since Kershek had not reported it to the police at that time.

The Milwaukee County Forensic Pathologist (or coroner) took the stand and testified that she had performed the autopsy. Dr. Elaine Samuels was a very precise, intelligent woman, and she explained that the bullet, which she referred to as "the missile," had entered the back of the right shoulder and made a direct, diagonal path to the center of the heart.

Eisenberg asked her opinion of the "blow back" issue, when Kraemer objected.

"'Blow back' is a subject meant for a ballistics expert. I don't think Dr. Samuels is qualified to testify about that subject."

"Your Honor, would the court ask Dr. Samuels if she thinks she is qualified, and not depend on Mr. Kraemer's assumption that she is not?" Eisenberg suggested.

"Dr. Samuels?" the judge asked.

"I think it is directly within the realm of forensic pathology," Elaine Samuels stated, enunciating every word very clearly.

I was irritated by the prevailing attitude that Elaine Samuels was "strange," not so much because she worked in the morgue, but because of her appearance. She didn't meet the socially defined standards of what doctors are supposed to look like, primarily because of her sex, and secondly because she had short hair and wore no make-up. She was heavy and wore black-rimmed glasses, giving her a masculine appearance. For such shallow reasons, her credibility was apparently questionable. But she was obviously competent enough to work for the County Medical Examiner's Office!

"Then allow me to continue with my line of questioning, Your Honor," Eisenberg said, glancing at me. "Dr. Samuels, would you explain 'blow back' please? For the jury."

"'Blow back' is an event that takes place when a gun is fired at close range to the body. Blood and tissue explode from the missile entering the body, and splash back into the barrel of the gun." She frowned in intense concentration. Usually, she explained, microscopic traces of blood or tissue were found, even if no visible traces were discovered. Tiny striations inside the barrel of a gun spun the bullets from the barrel, and it was these striations that held blood residue.

"Did you observe the bullet wound on the body of Christine Schultz?"

"I did."

"Would you describe that bullet wound?"

"The wound itself was quite large. The skin around the wound held the impression of the gun's muzzle in a visible, circular pattern."

"Would you say the gun was at close range?"

"Yes. It had to have been touching the skin."

"Dr. Samuels, to a degree of medical, scientific certainty, would it be your opinion that 'blow back' would have occurred?"

"Yes."

Eisenberg made a point of tediously repeating this to the jury, because the gun that the Crime Lab identified as the murder weapon had no traces of blood or tissue inside the muzzle or the barrel, nor traces of cleaning solvent. Just traces of dust.

Fred's brother John arrived as a witness for the prosecution. Under direct examination by Kraemer, John maintained that Sean hadn't, after all, seen the intruder. John said Sean told him he was so frightened by the event that night that he ran and hid. It was only because Fred and I had influenced him that he said he'd seen someone, John said. After all, I had sent the boys several photographs in the mail.

Under cross-examination, he grew emotional.

Eisenberg asked, "Isn't it a fact that you took it upon yourself to write a letter to the judge who presided over the defendant's preliminary hearing, the Honorable Ralph Adam Fine, in hopes that it would influence his decision to bind the defendant over for jury trial?"

"Yes."

"And isn't it a fact that you state in this letter that you know Lawrencia Bembenek is guilty of murdering Christine Schultz, when in fact you have absolutely no evidence to support this opinion?"

"I ..."

"Do you have any evidence?"

"No."

"It's opinion?"

"Yes," John meekly replied.

"Yet you took it upon yourself to write a damaging, accusatory letter that received considerable publicity, ending up on the front page of the *Milwaukee Journal*?"

"Yes."

"John Schultz, are you aware that your whole family is present today in support of the defendant?"

"Yes."

"Out of five brothers, you are the only one who has a different opinion about the defendant?"

"Yes." John's face turned blotchy and he nervously folded his hands over and over.

"Tell me," Eisenberg continued. "Isn't it a fact that your wife, Kathy, and the deceased were like sisters, they were so close?"

"Yes."

"And isn't it also a fact that your wife hated Laurie because of the fact that Fred remarried Laurie?"

"Well ... we were trying to work that out."

"But, at the most, your wife merely tolerated Laurie?"

"That's true," mumbled John.

"I'm sorry, I didn't hear you."

"I said, that's true," John repeated.

"If the court would allow me to show the jury the photographs that the State has introduced into evidence, in trying to insinuate that the defendant tried to influence the children," Eisenberg asked. He picked up a small pile of pictures. There was one of Fred, a few of the boys at the apartment, and one picture of the four of us at the Brady Street Festival. One picture of me was included, wearing the blouse that Sean and Shannon had bought me for my birthday.

"Now, I'm assuming that either you or your wife, Kathy, turned these photographs over to the District Attorney?"

"Yes."

"There's a small notecard that the snapshots were enclosed in, with a short letter printed inside from the defendant. Would you read out loud, to the jury, what that letter says?"

John opened the card as tears filled his eyes. He began reading with a weak voice. "It says: 'Dear Sean and Shannon, I am enclosing some pictures of you and your daddy and me. Don't lose these. There is one of Shannon, with a noodle hanging down his chin, and one of your silly daddy, who put popcorn up his nose. Remember'?"

John's voice broke, but he continued. "'In the picture of me, I am wearing the shirt you bought me for my birthday. Thank you! I like it a lot. The dog too! I wish I could thank you in person. Remember Stan and Suzy from the gym? They went to California on vacation. They have a lot of nice pictures. I love you, Laurie.'"

"Now," Eisenberg said, his hands clasped behind his back, "is there anything in that letter that you would consider unduly influencing?"

"No."

"Did Laurie say, 'Please lie for me'?"

"No."

"Did Laurie say, 'Say I didn't do it'?"

"No."

"Does that letter sound like it came from a woman who hates children?" Eisenberg shouted.

"Objection!" Kraemer interrupted.

"Sustained."

"I'll withdraw the question, Your Honor. Just a few more questions, Mr. Schultz. You lived with Sean for a period of time, did you not?"

"Yes."

"Do you know him to be an extremely bright child?"

"I'm not sure what you mean."

"You have a son who is Sean's age, do you not?"

"Yes. Marshall."

"Well, would you say that they are equal in intelligence, or is Sean a little more advanced than Marshall?"

"I'd have to say that Sean is more advanced."

"Are you aware of the fact that Sean was bright enough, considering the circumstances, to attempt to administer first aid to his mother, while she lay dying?"

"Yes."

"Do you mean to tell this court, then, that a child who had enough composure to administer first aid after the shooting occurred was the very same young man who allegedly told you that he was 'so scared that he ran and hid and that he didn't see the intruder'?"

"Objection!"

"Your Honor," Eisenberg asked, "I'd like this witness to answer the question, please?"

"Sustained," the judge replied.

"Then answer me this, John Schultz," Eisenberg countered. "How do you explain the original reports that Sean gave to the police, immediately after it happened, if Sean, like he told you, didn't see anything?"

"Objection!" Kraemer announced again. "Your Honor, Mr. Eisenberg is obviously asking the same question in a different form. It calls for speculation! And he's badgering the witness."

"I have no further questions," Eisenberg quickly interjected.

"Sustained! Obviously improper," the judge insisted. "The jury is instructed to—"

"No further questions, Your Honor," Eisenberg repeated.

"—to disregard the remarks of Mr. Eisenberg again!"

Eisenberg sizzled with irritation. "If it please the court, I would like to make a comment for the record. I object to the court. I have no problem with the court saying to the jury that they should disregard a statement of mine, but I do object to the court adding the word 'again.' If I make a mistake, I am entitled to have it disregarded by the jury without the court implying that I am repeatedly at fault. I think the court's word 'again' is highly improper, and I object to it."

Skwierawski sighed. "You may object to it. Your objection is overruled. When counsel continuously pushes the limits of admissibility, in terms of questions being asked of witnesses, bordering on and verging on improper conduct in front of the jury, I will take every step necessary to stop it and I will continue to stop it throughout this trial, regardless of how often it happens! And if it happens again and again, then you will be stopped again and again. I don't need any further argument on the issue! The issue is closed!" The judge turned to the Assistant District Attorney. "Wish to redirect?"

"No, Your Honor."

"The witness may step down."

■   ■   ■

It was Friday evening. Eisenberg asked me to meet with him—one of the few "attorney-client privilege" meetings I had with him without Fred being present.

"What I have to show you is very important," he said. We were at a downtown restaurant, in a secluded booth. We always seemed to meet in restaurants or bars. His office was in Madison and he didn't want to come to my house. Maybe he thought it would seem improper.

"What is it?"

We ordered drinks and waited until the waitress left our table. The large diamonds on his cufflinks, rings and tie tack glittered in the candle light.

"This is serious." He was solemn. "I've been investigating this case for about nine months now. In the beginning, I made you realize how important it is for you to be completely honest with me, because I have to defend you. I know you have been. Like I told you before—I don't care what you've done. I wouldn't care if you did commit the murder, because it's not my job to pass moral judgment on you. I've defended people for every crime you can imagine.

"Okay, we've gone over this before several times and you have told me that you didn't do it and I believe you."

"So, what did you want to show me?" I asked, impatient.

"First, I want to ask you something. This is very important. Is there anything you're not telling me?"

"No! What do you mean?"

"About Fred. Are you covering up for him in any way?"

"No!"

"Are you afraid of Fred?"

"No!"

"You've told me everything?"

"Yes! Why?"

"I have some information from my investigators. This guy may be a quack, but I'm not so sure. I can't leave any stone unturned. I have the transcript here. While you're looking it over, I'll summarize. It says Fred hired a hit man out of Chicago to kill Christine. A lot of what he says jibes with the case, but then again, he may have been able to piece it together from the newspapers.

"He says one thing that makes a lot of sense. That there were actually two guys in the house that night. I've always wondered how one person could tie Christine up and hold a gun on her at the same time—or why she didn't resist at all against only one man. There were no signs of a struggle. She was a good sized woman—not some weak female.

"Also, it says one of the men woke up the kids on purpose so that Sean would see it wasn't his father."

I read the transcript as fast as I could. "This guy that gave us this statement is a convict?" I asked, noticing the address.

"Yes."

"But I thought someone incarcerated has little or no credibility in court ..."

"Do you have any idea what this could be about?" Eisenberg interrupted. "If you do—please, tell me right now. We're talking about a life sentence now. We're not talking about going away for a few months."

"I don't have any idea. I don't know what this is all about. Honest to God! I wouldn't cover up for a murder ..."

"Are you positive? If this is true, Fred is using you."

"I don't know what to think," I said. "I find it hard to believe that some guy sitting in prison calls you out of a clear, blue sky ..."

"All I'm saying is ..."

"All you're saying is that either I could crucify Fred to save my own neck, or keep things the way they are and take my chances?" I looked at him. "It's either Fred or me? This evidence is so shoddy to risk all that! What if I tell you to use this guy, and it turns the jury against me? What if it makes them think Oh wow—now she's even trying to pin it on her own husband?"

I stopped talking as the menus were placed on our table. Fred? Was it possible? I recalled that Fred had said I had a key to the Ramsey house, when I didn't even know he had a key. How did blood get on his on-duty revolver? Why did he burst into tears at the Prelim? Why didn't he write the times that he called me that night in his damned report? Why did he want to move into that house?

I ordered an appetizer, since I wasn't very hungry, and asked for another drink.

"I don't know what to do," I said. "I have to think about this. If we had better proof that Fred hired someone ... but it's such a big risk to take, considering how flimsy the evidence is. Can't we verify this somehow?"

"Speaking of flimsy evidence, I don't see how we can lose this case," Eisenberg assured me. "It's nothing but a collection of contradictory facts, and speculative theory!"

Soon our lunch ended, he climbed into his Jaguar and I drove home. I didn't want to believe Fred hired someone to kill Christine and then made it appear as if I did it. How could I believe that? This was the man I had chosen to marry!

What was I to do? This was Friday and Fred was due to testify on Monday morning!

Fred had the perfect alibi—he was on duty that night. Maybe, I thought, he expected me to keep my date with Marylisa? That way, I would have had an alibi, too ... But there was no *time*! No time to even attempt to verify this statement—a statement from a convict, no less ... I didn't want to think about it anymore. I believed in Fred, still. He'd stuck by me through this whole thing. He lost his house, his job, and his children. No ... I couldn't turn on him. If I did, I wouldn't be able to live with myself.

I called Eisenberg. I told him I didn't want to use the convict's statement.

■   ■   ■

As he did at the prelim, Fred's former squad partner, Durfee, arrived to testify as a witness for the prosecution. His story had changed a bit. This time he included a part where he said Fred and I talked for a few minutes after they arrived at our apartment. He said Fred and I were alone, and he could not hear what was said.

I wondered why Durfee would add this part to his version of what transpired on the night in question. It certainly cast a note of suspicion our way, but it wasn't logical. If Fred and I had had a moment or two alone, like Durfee said, and if I were guilty, I would have told Fred to do anything but examine the gun! Fred could have said it was lost or stolen. Instead, the two of them entered the apartment and walked directly to the bedroom to examine the gun.

Durfee admitted that he failed to record the serial number of the gun he examined that night, a bizarre piece of misprocedure. He said he'd lost or thrown out his memo book from that night. He responded vaguely when Eisenberg questioned him about the Department policy to save all memo books and about the date of his second report.

But at least Durfee maintained that the revolver he examined that night could not possibly have been fired.

I'd supplied Eisenberg with a list of my Police Academy class members to prepare him for the next witness. An officer with tinted glasses and a trim mustache named Keith Faubel was the only one out of over fifty people who claimed to remember that I wore a green jogging suit at the Police Academy.

Faubel admitted that he'd come forward with his story just before my preliminary hearing. When Eisenberg asked why he waited so long to tell the DA about his recollection, Faubel claimed that just after the murder he'd informed his sergeant.

"When did you go to your sergeant?"

"In May or June," Faubel said. "Of last year."

"Who was the sergeant?"

"I don't know his name."

I stifled a groan. Being aware of your sergeant's name was not only mandatory, it was a basic survival tactic. Needless to say, the "mystery sergeant" was never found.

Eisenberg asked Faubel another question. "What shade of green was the jogging suit?"

"Forest green."

"Interesting, Mr. Faubel. You are sure of this?"

"Yes."

"Okay. I'm going to read a list of names to you, and you tell me if these people were your classmates at the Police Academy. Ready? Darlene Anderson, Douglas Boville, Michael Koszuta, Jackie Hawkins—"

"Objection!" Kraemer said.

"—Linda Palese, Michael Stoychavich, Linda Reeves, Samuel Thomas, Robert White—"

"Objection! Your Honor, what is the purpose of this?"

"—Klug, Bradford, Duffee, Wedemeyer—"

Losing his temper, Kraemer flew at Eisenberg, pointing to him and thrashing the other arm about. "Objection!"

Eisenberg calmly lowered the paper from his eyes.

"Mr. Eisenberg?" the judge asked.

"Your Honor, my intention is to ask this witness if he is aware of the fact that out of all these people, out of over fifty people, he is the only one who seems to remember the defendant in a green jogging suit at the Police Academy."

The State subpoenaed a firearms instructor from the Police Academy. I remembered him. He'd always talk and joke with me at the firing range. "That's right, Bembenek!" Marcellus Cieslik would say. "Get 'em right in the ten ring!" He'd been on the police force long enough to remember when my dad was a cop. I was polite to him and he in turn was pleasant, quick with a joke.

Cieslik testified that I was a good marksman. What was the point? Christine was shot at point-blank range.

Eisenberg asked him about the cleaning of revolvers.

"What do you train your recruits to clean their handguns with?"

"We have an oily substance that is standard gun-cleaning solvent."

"Does it have an odor?"

"Yes. A distinct odor."

"Do traces of this fluid remain on guns for long periods of time?"

"Yes, I suppose that inside the barrel, in the striations, traces of this fluid would remain."

I found it odd that answers from a State witness were advantageous to the defense. I turned to look behind me, but realized Fred was still sequestered from the courtroom.

"Now, Sergeant Cieslik—the prosecution has inferred that a gun could possibly be cleaned with soap and water. Is that possible?"

"Yes."

"But, as an instructor, wouldn't you be upset with one of your recruits if you found them cleaning their service revolver with soap and water?"

"I suppose."

"In fact, wouldn't it cause a gun to rust?" Eisenberg asked.

"Not this gun," Cieslik said suddenly, holding Fred's snub-nosed Smith and Wesson.

"Why not?" Eisenberg asked.

"Because this gun is aluminum, sir," Cieslik replied. There was a chuckle throughout the courtroom, yet the judge did nothing to maintain order. I thought he would be pounding his gavel, like judges do on television, but he remained motionless. I was embarrassed for Eisenberg, and of course the *Milwaukee Sentinel* reported the "aluminum" testimony word for word.

Eisenberg remained calm and acted as though nothing had happened.

"All right. Would it be reasonable to conclude that if a person used a gun to kill someone, and if that person had been one of your recruits, and if that person knew that bullets can be traced back to guns, which is what you teach your recruits—would it be reasonable to conclude that that person would want to get rid of the murder weapon?"

"Objection!" Kraemer stood up. "I ask that the court instruct the jury that the comments and statements made by Mr. Eisenberg are not evidence in this case!"

"I haven't made any comments or statements, Your Honor."

The judge stared at both lawyers grimly, saying, "The jury has been so instructed on several occasions throughout this trial, and is again instructed to disregard the last question asked by defense counsel."

When I told Fred about Cieslik's answer, he was furious.

"Why the hell would Cieslik say that? Tell Don that the only aluminum part on that gun is the frame! The rest of that gun sure as hell *would* rust if someone cleaned it with soap and water! Especially the barrel! Jesus! Tell Don to ask the ballistics expert when he's called."

Fred's turn on the witness stand was similar to his testimony at the prelim, except that this time, he didn't lose his composure.

Kraemer spent considerable time belaboring the Waukegan marriage license. He went so far as to bring in a transcript of Fred's divorce hearing. I couldn't see the point.

Fred claimed that he was unaware of the fact that he couldn't by law remarry at the time he married me. Kraemer contradicted Fred by saying that explicit instructions were given to Fred by Judge Curley regarding the issue of remarrying. I began to wonder who was on trial.

Then Kraemer questioned Fred about his finances. Fred told Kraemer that the amount earned from the carpentry work we did in our spare time supplemented Fred's regular salary and my wages. The prosecution's painting of bleak financial despair began to brighten considerably.

In an attempt to support his "life in the fast lane" theory, Kraemer asked Fred about our "exotic" vacations, which ended up sounding like nothing more than a honeymoon and a Florida visit with friends.

Fred explained that it was a Police Department regulation to save memo books, and produced an entire briefcase full of books dating back to 1970. This made Durfee's testimony about losing his memo book sound negligent at best.

Kraemer asked Fred to produce the memo book that held the serial number of his off-duty revolver. After hunting through the briefcase, Fred found the memo book from the year when he purchased the gun.

Kraemer was trying to confuse our "switched gun" theory by asking Fred to verify the serial number, which he did. Of course, it was identical to the handgun in evidence. That wasn't the point. Eisenberg was putting forward the theory that, because Fred and Durfee neglected to record the serial number of the gun they examined that night, the gun they examined might or might not be the same gun that the Crime Lab identified as the murder weapon. Along with the physical appearance of the gun that indicated it had not been fired, there was also the fact that Fred's guns had been confiscated so many weeks later. Some time in between, the gun Fred and Durfee examined that night was taken and replaced with Fred's gun. That was the only logical explanation, because the gun Fred and Durfee had looked at that night had not been fired, and Fred's gun had. As usual, the newspapers confused this issue.

Fred's description of the gun's appearance that night was detailed, and his knowledge of ballistics sounded impressive, but his testimony turned into what Eisenberg called a "two-edged sword" when Kraemer used his knowledge against him.

"So, Mr. Schultz, what you're telling this court is that, even with your extensive familiarity with handguns, you weren't even sure that the gun you and your partner examined that night was yours?"

"No. Not without checking the serial number. The gun itself has

quite a common appearance. The grips were standard. I thought it was
my gun. But I can't be sure."

Eisenberg surprised everyone when he presented his own snub-
nosed revolver. He wanted to show the jury how similar guns appear.
Later, at the defense table behind Kraemer, Eisenberg began clicking
the barrel release nervously. Kraemer again lost his temper and angrily
instructed him to "stop playing with that gun behind my back!"

Eisenberg just chuckled. Kraemer then requested that the court
order him to remove his revolver from the jury's view, and Skwierawski complied, adding:

"Well Mr. Kraemer, you probably ought to take the same self-
help action that Mr. Eisenberg has taken in this case about four or five
times, in terms of just getting up and grabbing onto the exhibits and
waltzing them over and putting them in a box somewhere, getting
them out of sight. I am not going to let this case be resolved by self-
help."

Detective Ronald Krusek had been seated at Kraemer's left
throughout the trial. He began testifying about the day Kathryn
Morgan identified my parents' car.

"What did you observe Mrs. Morgan do?" Kraemer asked.

"She proceeded east on Ramsey."

"And how long was she gone?"

"Three to four minutes."

"When she returned, did Mrs. Morgan tell you anything about an
automobile?"

"Yes. She said—"

"Hearsay objection!" Eisenberg quickly interrupted. Even I knew
by then that a witness was not allowed to testify as to what someone
else said. The only hearsay that was allowed was when a witness testified as to what the defendant said. The judge, however, disregarded
the rules of evidence.

"Overruled."

I gave Eisenberg a worried look. When Conway from Marquette
had wanted to tell the court that he heard me call the murder of Christine Schultz a "tragic, unfortunate event," Kraemer raised a hearsay
objection and it was sustained, which I didn't understand, because
hearsay from the defendant is admissible. Now this detective wanted
to testify about what Mrs. Morgan told him, my lawyer raised a
hearsay objection, and he was overruled? Not for the first (or last)
time, I wondered what was going on.

The notorious Kathryn Morgan finally told the court her fairy tale about my mother digging through garbage bins. Eisenberg's cross-examination was fierce.

"Isn't it a fact that you identified Mrs. Bembenek at Lawrencia Bembenek's preliminary hearing?"

"Yes."

"After requesting that Mrs. Bembenek remove her glasses?"

"Yes."

"The woman you saw on June 18 was not wearing glasses?"

"No."

"Are you aware of the fact that Virginia Bembenek is almost blind without her glasses?"

"No."

"Are you aware of the fact that Virginia Bembenek cannot drive without her glasses?"

"No."

The prosecution had done its homework. They introduced into evidence a copy of my mother's driver's license, but it was to our advantage, since it listed a restriction for correctional lenses.

"Mrs. Morgan," Eisenberg asked, "are you telling this court that you saw a woman once in June of 1981 and identified this woman four months later?"

"Yes." Morgan was in her thirties, with shoulder-length dark hair. She had a cleft chin and a bad underbite, so when she talked I became aware of her "S's." I wondered what made her go to the police with such a story. I had never seen her before.

"Would you like to review the police report to refresh your memory?" Eisenberg walked up to her and handed her the white copy. "Now, you describe the woman you saw as being about forty-five years of age, according to this report?"

"Yes."

"Are you aware of the fact that Mrs. Bembenek is almost sixty?"

"No."

"Are you also aware of the fact that Virginia Bembenek almost never wears shorts, because she's embarrassed about her varicose veins?"

"No."

"Do you really expect this court to believe, Mrs. Morgan, that a woman who was allegedly trying to recover murder evidence from a large trash container would come up to a perfect stranger in broad daylight, ask you about the trash containers, and then take a bag out of them and drive away?"

"Objection!" Kraemer said in a tired voice.

"Sustained! Sustained! We don't need any more of Mr. Eisenberg's editorializing. Defense counsel is instructed just to ask questions the witness can answer."

"All right, let's use this blackboard behind you, Mrs. Morgan," Eisenberg continued. "And write the license number you gave the police. Next to that, I'm going to write the license number of the Bembenek family car."

Mrs. Morgan turned in her chair to see the blackboard.

"Not the same number, is it, Mrs. Morgan?"

"No."

"Are you aware of the fact that the Bembenek family only has one family car and that Mr. Bembenek uses it to drive to work, where he works until 4:00 PM?"

"No."

"You said that you saw the woman digging through the garbage at 2:00 PM on June 18?"

"Um."

"Well, that's what you told the police, Mrs. Morgan. It says so right here in this report. Let's talk about the car you saw on June 18. How did you come to identify this car?"

Eisenberg paced back and forth in front of the witness box. The witness swallowed hard.

"A detective came to my house," Kathryn Morgan replied, "and asked me if I would go with him to identify the car."

"When did this take place?"

"About a month later."

"Who was the detective?"

"He's right there." She pointed at Krusek.

"What exactly happened?"

"Well, I got in his police car and we drove to that house on Ramsey Street, where I saw a brown automobile in the driveway."

"And then what?"

"I told him that it was the car."

"Mrs. Morgan, it says in this report that your exact words were, 'It looks similar to the car I saw on June 18.' Now, I hope you're not getting confused in the excitement of the trial and the TV cameras and everything. Didn't you say that the car looked similar?"

"Yes."

"Not that it was the same car?"

"No."

"How many other cars were parked at the house?"

"I think another car and a van. I think."

I remembered a police car watching the Ramsey Street house when my parents and Fred and I were cleaning. It was either that time, or when we moved our boxes into the house to store them there.

"Were any other cars parked on that street?"

"No."

"On that block?"

"No."

"Mrs. Morgan, do you mean to tell me that Detective Krusek took you to a house that had exactly two cars parked in its driveway, plus one blue van, and asked you to identify the car you saw on June 18?"

"Yes."

"What did he say? Isn't it a fact that he took you over there and said, 'That's the car, isn't it'?"

"Objection! Leading the witness!" Kraemer bellowed.

"Sustained," Skwierawski said firmly. "Argumentative. The jury is instructed to disregard the last several questions."

"The last two questions?" Eisenberg asked.

"That's right. Two is several," the judge replied.

"Two is several?" Eisenberg asked again.

"Yes." Skwierawski nodded. I could see Kraemer shaking his head.

The next trick the prosecution pulled was a fast one indeed. The State claimed to have four witnesses—two cops and their wives—who said they remembered bumping into me and Fred at a movie the previous winter, in 1981. They said I was wearing the infamous green jogging suit, of course.

All four were on the witness list, but when it came time to call them to the stand, Kraemer informed the court that one couple was in Colorado and would not be available to testify. The other cop had since been promoted to detective.

"This is so they don't all have to corroborate their damn story," Eisenberg whispered. "What the hell is this one about? You were at some movie with Fred?"

"Yeah. It was a cop movie, too! Good grief—*Fort Apache: The Bronx*, with Paul Newman."

"Forget Paul Newman, Laurie. What were you wearing?"

"Probably jeans and my ski jacket, as usual. I remember Fred talking to two couples in the lobby. Isn't winter a cold time of year to be wearing a jogging suit?"

"They've already covered that argument," Eisenberg said. "This report says that that's the reason they remember the green jogging suit so vividly—because it was so cold to wear something like that."

"Tricky."

"We'll see how tricky they are when I cross-examine them."

As it turned out, the detective and his wife disagreed about what I was allegedly wearing a year previous to their testimony. The husband, Gary, said it was a green jogging jacket with stripes on the side. His wife, Darlene, said it was a whole jogging suit, including jogging pants. They both disagreed about what type of jacket Fred was wearing.

But they were sure about the date. After the show, they'd dined at the Captain's Steak Joynt and charged the meal on a credit card, which recorded the date.

The whole subject of the green jogging suit had been blown totally out of proportion. The police had neither confiscated this nonexistent suit, nor submitted one into evidence.

Of course, the State was hand-picking its evidence. Fred's younger boy, Shannon, who by now admitted that he remembered absolutely nothing, was the one who originally claimed he saw a green jogging suit. This was the boy who also claimed to have seen a silver revolver with pearl grips.

Sean, on the other hand, was an older and more credible witness, and he said the intruder had worn a green khaki army jacket.

Two young women from the apartment across the hall from where we had lived were subpoenaed by the State. They testified about the plumber finding the wig in their toilet. They also told the court that they'd twice let Zess into the building when she pressed the buzzer. They saw her open our apartment while we weren't home and go in for some time. Those dates were in May, right before the murder and right after.

Whenever the court recessed, I managed to spend a few minutes in the hallway with my mother, who kept her vigil with my dad on the wooden bench. It must have been nearly unbearable to spend all those hours in such an uncomfortable place after an operation. The pace of the trial was hard to judge, and I wasn't sure when she would be called to testify.

The State then summoned a photographer from the *Milwaukee Journal*, Robert Goessner. He claimed to have remembered me from two years before—December 1980. That was the month the paper took a picture to print with a piece about my sex discrimination complaint. Goessner admitted he himself did not take the picture—he only passed me in the hall as I walked to the photo department. It was pretty hard to believe that anyone would remember such a fleeting glance, but he said he remembered me because I was "so beautiful."

Kraemer then produced the black-and-white photograph from the *Journal*, and Goessner testified that it was a picture of me in the green jogging suit he remembered me wearing that day. What I remembered having worn was a red warm-up jacket!

I began writing furiously on my legal pad as Kraemer questioned his witness.

A friend of mine had worked at a photo lab, and had once explained how to tell the color of objects in black-and-white photographs. Through spectroscopy, she'd said, you could determine which end of the spectrum an object was in. Green would be on the opposite side of the spectrum from red. I had no idea if this was true, but I passed it on to Eisenberg.

So he asked Goessner about the process. Fortunately, the witness admitted that such a process, and other tests, could have been used to prove the color of the jacket. No such tests had been done.

"Of course the police didn't test the negative," I scribbled to Eisenberg, "because it would have proved that the jacket I am wearing in the photograph is red!"

Eisenberg nodded, whispering, "If I was Kraemer, I would be ashamed to introduce such cheap, ridiculous evidence."

"Did you ever attempt to test the negative of this photograph to determine the color?" my lawyer asked Goessner.

"I don't have that equipment."

"But that type of equipment is available, isn't it?"

"It might be," Goessner nodded reluctantly.

"And it is available to the County of Milwaukee and to the District Attorney of this city, isn't it?" Eisenberg persisted.

"Objection!" Kraemer shouted.

"Sustained."

"No further questions," Eisenberg added.

Two officers from Marquette arrived to testify. Conway returned, followed by Lieutenant Pileggi. They rehashed the events that led up to my arrest.

When Conway had testified at the suppression hearing concerning the evidence taken without a warrant from my locker, Eisenberg had tried to question him about statements I'd made that referred to the murder in a sympathetic manner. Kraemer raised a hearsay objection, and it was sustained—even though much of the State's case was hearsay.

Now that Pileggi was on the stand, Eisenberg again tried to ask questions about my statements describing the murder as unfortunate. This was perfectly admissible, ordinarily. But Kraemer again objected and was again sustained.

Eisenberg was outraged. "Your Honor! This testimony is hearsay evidence from the defendant, and therefore should be admissible."

"Mr. Kraemer's objection is sustained. Mr. Eisenberg—"

"Your Honor, with all due respect, I must say for the record that I feel justice has done an about-face in this courtroom!" Eisenberg said in frustration.

"One more comment like that, Mr. Eisenberg, and you will be found in contempt of court."

Armed with a thick textbook by Charles O'Hara, Eisenberg began cross-examining Arthur Varriale, a fiber analyst. O'Hara's book was a fundamental text and was on the required reading list for the Milwaukee Police Department Detective Exam. Varriale wouldn't dare quarrel with it.

The expert was forced to admit that fiber analysis was not a science. The closest analysis he said he'd be able to make between two synthetic wig fibers would be "similarity in characteristics," not positive identification. He tended to use the word "consistent" in his analysis, and referred to characteristics like color, chemical composition and structure. Eisenberg raised the issue of the millions of wigs throughout the world that are all composed of the same material. Varriale admitted there was considerable doubt in his "identifications."

"So what you are now telling this jury is that the fiber you examined, found on the leg of Christine Schultz, and the fiber that made up the wig taken from the drain pipe could be the same, or they could not be the same. Isn't that correct?" Eisenberg asked Varriale.

"Would you repeat the question?"

"The two fibers you examined. You cannot tell this jury that, beyond a reasonable doubt, with a degree of scientific certainty, those fibers are identical, can you?"

"No, sir."

"You are only able to tell us that they could be the same, or they could not be the same?" Eisenberg repeated, emphasizing every word.

"That's correct," was the reply.

The next witness for the prosecution was an alleged "expert" in hair analysis named Diane Hanson. In his examination, Eisenberg forced her to admit that her Bachelor's degree was in the field of bacteriology—totally removed from the study of hair analysis. Her knowledge of hair was gained piecemeal, in six weeks at various seminars.

The reluctant admission of her true field of study and the usurpation of her authority upset Hanson. She became evasive and uncooperative. Eisenberg's cross-examination lasted two hours. As he led her into disagreeing with the facts written by O'Hara, she began to appear confused and unsure of herself.

Hanson admitted that hair analysis was even less accurate than fiber analysis, which Eisenberg had already reduced to nothing more than a guessing game. Hanson's temper finally overwhelmed her common sense when she slipped and revealed that she had violated the court's sequestration order. She had discussed Varriale's testimony with him.

This is how she came to admit it:

"So, what you are saying, Miss Hanson, is that you disagree with the statement that I have just read?" Eisenberg asked, an incredulous look on his face. "You disagree with O'Hara?"

"You're not reading the whole paragraph!" she retorted. "That's only part of the paragraph that you've just read!"

Eisenberg's eyes narrowed. "How do you know that, Miss Hanson?" A hush fell over the courtroom.

"Um, is it a part of the paragraph, I'm asking?" She flushed.

"I'm asking you, when did you read this paragraph in O'Hara's book? Today?" Eisenberg asked.

"Today," Hanson quietly squeaked.

"I suppose Mr. Kraemer told you about this? When? Over lunch?"

"No."

"Did any member of the Milwaukee Police Department advise you to look over Charles O'Hara's book today?"

"No, they did not."

"How did you come to know about it today?" Eisenberg refused to back down, as Hanson's reluctance increased.

"I knew that you had asked Mr. Varriale a question," she mumbled.

"How did you know that?"

"He mentioned that you had referred to O'Hara's book."

"Gentlemen," the judge interrupted, "I feel that it is in order at the moment to excuse the jury and look into this matter."

Hanson remained seated, her hands in her lap. Embarrassed, she only glanced at the judge. After further questioning by both counsel, the court found that Hanson had violated the sequestration order by discussing Varriale's testimony while driving him back to the Crime Lab. Eisenberg made a motion to strike Hanson's testimony because of this.

"Denied," the judge said. "It is not substantial. And let me advise you that you are also denied any further argument, Mr. Eisenberg."

"Your Honor, I think Mr. Varriale should be recalled to find out what he will testify to, regarding his conversation with Miss Hanson."

"No. Request denied. All right—I don't require any further argument on this issue. There has been a violation of the court order. The request made by defense counsel to strike this witness's testimony is denied."

"Your Honor—"

"No further argument, Mr. Eisenberg."

"I'm not—"

"I have made my decision."

"I want a request, if it please the court."

"What is it, Mr. Eisenberg?" the judge hissed.

"I would request that you instruct the jury as to what you have just said," Eisenberg asked finally.

"I'm going to ... I object!" Kraemer stammered.

"No! No!" Skwierawski said vehemently. "Request denied!"

■   ■   ■

I remembered what our instructors at the Police Academy had drummed into us: the law protects the criminal. Any tiny technical flaw in an investigation would void a prosecution. Civil libertarians were everywhere, with power to throw out any case on any minute error, no matter how harmless.

It was all nonsense, paranoid nonsense, and I'd known that even then.

I was even more sure now.

16

THE SKYLINE DARKENS

The end of the list of State witnesses was drawing near. Finally I'd be able to see some allies on the witness stand.

The last person to testify for the prosecution was Monty Lutz, the New Berlin Crime Lab's ballistics expert. As we expected, he testified that the bullet removed from the body of Christine Schultz came from Fred's off-duty gun. During cross-examination, however, my lawyer used Mr. Lutz to our advantage, by inquiring whether or not Fred's revolver was made of aluminum, as Sergeant Cieslik had testified.

"No. Just the frame is aluminum. The barrel, and the other parts of the gun, are not. I don't know how detailed you would like me to get ..."

"Thank you, Mr. Lutz. If soap and water were used to clean the gun, would rust appear over a period of time?"

"Definitely."

"If cleaning fluid or solvent was used, would the lab detect traces of it?" Eisenberg asked.

"Yes."

"If cleaning fluid or solvent was used, would dust be present?"

"I suppose over a period of time."

"Over a period of a few hours?"

"It depends where the gun was stored."

"If it was in a holster, stored in a closed compartment, like a gym bag with a zipper?"

"Oh. Then I'd have to say no. Dust would not be present if the gun had been cleaned and then put away."

Eisenberg emphasized this line of questioning because we already knew that Fred's gun had not been cleaned. So if that were the murder weapon, where was the blood? The carbon?

The first six witnesses the defense subpoenaed were former members of my Police Academy class. They testified briefly, as character witnesses, and also to say that they never once saw me in a green jogging suit. I appreciated their cooperation and support, especially since I had not seen any of them in such a long time.

After two weeks of being restricted to the hallway of the courthouse, my parents were finally allowed into the courtroom to testify.

My mom raised her right hand, her face pale and tired. I crossed my fingers and hoped Kraemer wouldn't upset her. Her testimony hadn't changed from the preliminary hearing. She talked about helping me pack on the night of the murder. She denied Morgan's allegations that she had been digging through the garbage bins at the apartment complex.

I knew that her every word meant the world to her, and she was trying painfully to answer every question with care. I had cautioned her that Kraemer found it easy to turn around an honest word to suit the State, and she was more scared than I was. After her testimony, the court recessed and I found her in the hallway, crying.

"Don't, mom!" I said, hugging her. "You were fine. It's over."

"I was so scared that I'd say something wrong! You know how those police can confuse a person who is just trying to tell the truth! So much depended on my testimony today. I'm so afraid for you!"

"I know," I said. "Don't worry."

When we returned, my father's testimony was brief. I'd been even more apprehensive about his testifying, because he had difficulty hearing. But he was fine. He simply explained that he was using the family car the day Morgan claimed she saw my mom pull up in a car. The cross-examination by Kraemer was not rigorous.

Afterward, my parents found a place to stand at the back of the courtroom, since all of the seats were taken. At last they were able to listen and watch the proceedings. Typically, The *Milwaukee Sentinel* suggested that they hadn't cared enough to arrive until the very end, not explaining that they actually hadn't been allowed in.

Fred's father, Elfred Schultz, Sr., testified about the incident that took place the day Fred uncovered the custody conspiracy. He's a highly emotional man, like the rest of his family, and he burst into sobs in mid-sentence. The court had to recess. Afterwards, he contradicted his son John's innuendo about the incident in which John had called the police. John had tried to maintain that Fred had been calling to bully Sean about his testimony in the murder. Not at all, Fred's dad said. The incident was related to the custody battle. Fred's father also served as a character witness for me.

Fred's mother never testified. She never even came to the trial.

It was so easy for the State to make insinuations! For example, while the defense was subpoenaing some last-minute witnesses, Fred had stopped at Marquette's Public Safety office to return my uniforms. He'd talked to Carol Kurdziel, who'd asked him if there was anything she could do. Fred asked her if she'd be a character witness for me. She agreed. He had a few blank subpoenas in his pocket and handed her one. This is common practice. Anyone, with the exception of the defendant, can serve subpoenas.

Fred returned home and told me that Kurdziel would testify. But a few days later, Kraemer began, "Before we proceed, I would just like to inform the court that I have gotten several complaints from people who have called my office, informing me that Elfred Schultz, Jr., is running around delivering subpoenas. One woman from Marquette University in particular does not want to testify."

Eisenberg looked at me curiously, checking the last page of the witness list. "Who is he referring to? Carol Kurdziel? I thought she was a friend?"

"I thought so, too."

"Your Honor." Eisenberg stood. "It is not unlawful for Fred Schultz to serve subpoenas. In any event, the defense has not intended to subpoena someone against their will. We do not want a hostile witness, as I'm sure you realize."

Another witness lost.

The next day, we called three people to the stand. A former neighbor with two children testified that she'd known me for more than ten years; I used to babysit for her son and daughter. She believed in my innocence.

My friend Joanne, who lived in Stevens Point, Wisconsin, told the jury about the phone conversation I'd had with her the night of the murder. She and I had attended the same grade school and high school. We were in the band together and on the track team. We had belonged to the same parish. She had moved away from Milwaukee to go to college, but I drove up north to visit her about once a month. She, too, had known me for over ten years. She believed in my innocence.

My former employer from the gym testified that I had worked for him for about four years. I'd been employed there at the time of the homicide. He praised my work and said he would hire me back if he could. He was someone else who believed in my innocence.

■   ■   ■

The next day, I was to take the stand.

It was a snowy morning as Fred and I drove to the courthouse in his van. Movement was slow in the street because it was so slippery.

Eisenberg opened the proceedings: "The first witness we intend to call this morning is the defendant, Lawrencia Bembenek."

"Bring in the jury." Skwierawski nodded to the bailiff.

"Just a minute," Kraemer said. "There is another matter, Your Honor. There are names on the defense witness list that I object to, and I move that they be stricken from testifying based on their irrelevance to the case." He paused. "One of these names is Frederick Horenberger."

I froze. The DA was attempting to prohibit the testimony of the one person who could discredit the statements of Judy Zess, the prosecution's star! Zess had simply verified anything the State wanted her to. Now her testimony would go unchallenged.

"If Mr. Eisenberg insists on calling this witness to the stand—I understand Mr. Horenberger has been transported from Waupun Correctional Institution to the Milwaukee County Jail—then he should be willing to tell us why his testimony is relevant," Kraemer said.

"Mr. Eisenberg? Would you care to give me an offer of proof?" asked the judge.

"Your Honor," Eisenberg said slowly, "I cannot tell you the relevance of Horenberger's testimony without giving away my whole defense to Mr. Kraemer."

Several minutes of arguing continued, until Skwierawski was able to establish that Horenberger's testimony was hearsay evidence. Subsequently, it was suppressed as inadmissible, despite Eisenberg's objections.

"Even if it's evidence of perjury?" I wrote on the pad.

Eisenberg shrugged. The last speck of optimism that remained inside of me shriveled.

"Bring in the jury," Skwierawski said again.

"Are you ready?" Eisenberg asked me.

"Yes. I think, I'm a bit scared of Kraemer."

"Don't be." Eisenberg grinned. "You're smarter than he is! Laurie, if you're scared, don't be afraid to show it. You usually appear a bit too calm. Probably your police training."

"I'm not an actress."

"Then be yourself."

In total, I spent five hours on the witness stand. The cameras that had stared at my back for over two weeks now faced me like cannons. Beads of sweat rolled down my back.

Eisenberg asked me about my experiences as a female police officer, and the reasons for the complaint I'd filed against the department. He asked about my schooling, my childhood and my ambitions. I told the jury about the details of my marriage to Fred, and the problems we'd had with Judy Zess. The members of the jury stared back at me, expressionless. I looked into their faces for some sign of their reactions, but they were as stoical as the mannequins I used to dress at the Boston Store.

The court recessed occasionally, and I was keeping a fairly stiff upper lip, until my testimony reached the part about Fred's diamond ring. Eisenberg asked me about it to illustrate the point that, if we were as financially devastated as the State contended, I certainly would not have spent fifteen hundred dollars on a ring for Fred. For some reason unknown to me, the subject made me want to cry.

"I understand that in May of last year you took your tax return and bought your husband an expensive diamond ring, did you not?"

"Yes."

"Why did you buy that for him?"

"Because he never had anything like that ..." I said, my throat closing. I was unable to say any more. I didn't burst into sobs but tears filled my eyes. The bailiff brought me a paper cup of water.

I wrung my handkerchief and allowed the emotion to pass.

"How do you feel right now?" Eisenberg asked.

"Scared to death," I replied.

After lunch, Kraemer was scheduled to begin his cross-examination. I nervously tossed down three glasses of wine, remembering how throughout Eisenberg's direct examination Kraemer had sat next to Krusek, smiling and shaking his pudgy head. He acted as if my testimony was so unbelievable it was funny, scoffing at my replies. If I saw his body language, surely the jury did, too? I had to remind myself not to lose my temper with Kraemer and be sarcastic or flippant. He was so easy to dislike.

Kraemer immediately attacked my description of my Police Department experiences. "Miss Bembenek—does the alleged harassment you encountered on the Milwaukee Police Department have anything to do with this trial?"

"I don't know."

"And do any of the things you have just spent the entire morning telling this jury have anything at all to do with this trial?"

"I don't know," I repeated, wanting to say, "You tell me!"

"Ms. Bembenek, let's go into the reason why you were dismissed

from the Police Department. Isn't it a fact that you were seen by Milwaukee Vice Squad officers smoking a marijuana cigarette at a rock
concert?"

"I object!" Eisenberg shouted. "The subject of Ms. Bembenek's
dismissal is not supported by any evidence from the State, and is
immaterial."

"Well, Mr. Eisenberg," Skwierawski smiled, "the State was planning on restricting mention of that particular subject, but you are the
one who opened that door, during direct examination. Overruled."

I could see Eisenberg scowl.

"Wasn't this concert the one you attended with your former
roommate, Judy Zess?" Kraemer asked.

"Judy Zess was arrested for marijuana, but I was not present."

"You were required to file a report about that incident?"

"Yes."

"And isn't it a fact that the report you filed was false?"

"No. It was the truth."

"Weren't you identified by a Milwaukee Vice Squad officer,
arrested and then released?"

"No! I was not! Another friend of Judy's was."

"Who?"

"Her name was Jan something. She was Judy's friend, not mine."
I looked at Eisenberg. He winked at me and smiled. I knew that I had
the statement from Judy Zess, sitting on the table next to my lawyer, if
the issue went any further.

Kraemer caught me off guard by changing the subject.

"Let's talk about the marriage license that you and Fred signed in
Waukegan. Isn't it a fact that you knew Fred was not allowed to
remarry?"

"No. I had no idea."

"Then why did you leave the state of Wisconsin in order to get
married? Wasn't it because you could not obtain a license in this
state?"

"No. Not at all. I went to Waukegan to get married because Fred
suggested it. We eloped."

"That's the only reason?"

"And I thought it was romantic."

"Oh. You thought it was romantic," Kraemer said sarcastically.
"But isn't it a fact that you signed that marriage license, knowing that
you two were not free and clear, by law, to marry?"

"No! I was free and clear to marry."

"You didn't know Fred wasn't?"

"No. How could I know?"

"Didn't you discuss his divorce?"

"No."

"Oh. Okay. Did you discuss money?"

"In regards to what?"

"Money. You know—what his salary was, what his alimony payments were, his child support, his house payments. Did you discuss that?"

"No."

"Before you were married, you had no discussions about money?"

"No. We were in love. We talked about what we had in common. We didn't discuss money."

The questioning continued. Then Kraemer got to the subject of Chris.

"Ms. Bembenek, isn't it a fact that you hated Christine?"

"No!"

"You didn't have any problems with her at all?"

"No."

"Did you ever talk to Christine Schultz?"

"Yes. A few times. Over the phone and in person."

"Where?"

"One night she came over to pick up the children ..."

"Were you ever inside the Ramsey Street house before May 28?"

"Yes."

"Isn't it a fact that Fred gave you a tour of that house?"

"No."

"But you were inside?"

"I stood in the front hallway by the door on the landing. I did not go in any farther," I explained. "Fred was picking up Sean."

"Was Fred proud of that house?"

"Yes."

"Fred built that house?"

"Yes."

"Fred built that house, but he didn't want to show it off to you?"

"Objection. That question has been asked and answered," Eisenberg said.

"Sustained."

"Ms. Bembenek, did you know that the Schultz family owned a dog?"

"Yes."

"Isn't it a fact that, in May, you asked Shannon, in front of his babysitter, where that dog was?"

"I had no reason to. I knew the dog was sold in February."

"How do you know the month it was sold?"

"It was around Valentine's Day. Fred was angry about it."

Eventually, the subject of my clothes was introduced by Kraemer.

"Ms. Bembenek, how many diamond rings do you own?"

"Objection!"

"Overruled."

"I own facsimile rings. But it's cosmetic jewelry, not genuine."

"I noticed you wore your rings every day, throughout this trial. Yet you're not wearing them to testify. Did you just decide to leave them at home today?"

"Yes."

"You just decided not to wear them today?" Kraemer smiled that same cynical smile.

"That's right," I said. I wanted to explain that my fingers were swollen, and that actually my mother suggested I not wear them, but I failed to elaborate. I was afraid the judge would say, "The witness is instructed to answer the question *yes* or *no*." I wondered why Kraemer was making a federal case out of my rings, anyway.

"Do you own any designer clothes?" he asked.

"Not originals."

"Originals?"

"Nancy Reagan wears originals."

"You don't own any originals?"

"Your Honor," Eisenberg interrupted, "would the court please instruct Mr. Kraemer to ask the defendant to explain what 'originals' are?"

The judge nodded.

"Originals are somewhere in the neighborhood of five thousand dollars apiece. But take designer jeans. Everyone wears those nowadays."

"Did you tell John Schultz to be careful when he helped you and Fred move, because you had 'designer' dresses that you wanted to move yourself?"

"Not exactly. I said that I would not want my dresses to be piled on the floor of John's van. I said I'd carry them myself."

"Did you make the statement at a dinner party in February that 'I would pay to have Christine Schultz blown away'?"

"No."

"You never said that?"

"No!"

"How tall are you, Ms. Bembenek?"

"Five feet, nine or ten inches."

"Would you step down from the witness stand and put this on for me please?" Kraemer held up the red warm-up jacket that I'd brought to match with the jacket in the black-and-white photograph.

"I object!" Eisenberg said.

"Objection overruled. Proceed."

I looked at my lawyer, then slipped on the jacket. Kraemer instructed me to stand next to him, in front of the jury. He was barely six feet.

"I object!" Eisenberg shouted again. "What is Mr. Kraemer attempting to prove? That he's a small man?"

There was a quiet chuckle, and Kraemer glared at my lawyer as he walked toward us.

"I have three-inch heels on, too," I said loudly.

"Take them off," Eisenberg told me. "Or is the State now suggesting that the defendant jogs in high heels?"

"What exactly are you trying to show, Mr. Kraemer?" the judge asked.

"Your Honor, I am illustrating how easily the defendant could have been mistaken for a man, because of her height. As the jury can plainly see, she is not much shorter than I am."

"Your Honor!" Eisenberg moaned.

"You'll have your chance if you choose to redirect," Skwier- awski told Eisenberg.

Toward the end of the day, Kraemer seemed to be at the end of his list of questions. His previous calm attitude, by this time, seemed to swell to a thirst for conviction. This angry frame of mind, which he made no effort to conceal, finally consumed his better judgment as he launched into a line of questioning which seemed improper to me.

Producing the snapshot that showed me with Fred and the boys at the Brady Street Festival, Kraemer asked me about the restrictions of my bail conditions.

"Isn't it a fact that upon your release on bail you were to have no physical contact with Sean or Shannon Schultz?"

"That's correct."

He handed me the photo. "Do you recognize this picture?"

"Yes."

"Isn't it a fact that you knowingly violated the restrictions of your bail by seeing the children at the Brady Street Festival, as evidenced by this photograph?"

"No!" I cried. Kraemer was dead wrong.

"Objection!" Eisenberg shouted.

"What was the date you were arrested?" Kraemer asked, ignoring him.

"Answer the question," the judge told me.

"June 24."

"What was the date of the Brady Street Festival?"

"In June," I replied, trying to remember the exact date. I knew off the top of my head that it was in the second week of June, but could not recall the exact date.

"When in June?" Kraemer persisted.

"Um ..." I looked at Eisenberg, hoping he could help. I needed to look at my engagement calendar from the previous summer, which was on the table where Eisenberg was sitting, poised to spring like a tiger. He was obviously furious with Kraemer. I looked at my calendar and then back at Eisenberg.

"Was the Brady Street Festival before your arrest or after?"

"Before my arrest—the first or second week in June."

"Are you telling me that you never saw the children after your arrest, in an attempt to influence their testimony?"

"No!"

"You never saw them?"

"I never saw them!" I answered angrily.

"Your Honor!" Eisenberg hollered. "I object to this entire line of questioning on the grounds that the State has presented no proof as to the date of the festival, when it would be easy for them to verify the date of such a large city event. Mr. Kraemer is inferring that the defendant violated the conditions of her bail. He is insinuating that she saw the children to influence their testimony and stipulates that the photograph proves that she did.

"It proves no such thing, Your Honor! Laurie Bembenek was arrested on June 24 and the Brady Street Festival was in fact held on June 17!" Eisenberg waved his hand in the air as he spoke, holding my calendar in his hand. "I request that the jury be instructed to disregard—"

"Mr. Eisenberg, you are out of order. Your objection was overruled and I suggest that you refrain from further argument."

"Mr. Kraemer cannot support his accusations!"

"Sit down, Mr. Eisenberg."

Kraemer smiled and continued down the path of referring to matters not in evidence.

"Do you know a girl named Laurie Futh?"

I thought for a second. "She is a friend of Judy Zess."

"Isn't it a fact that you once showed Miss Futh pictures from your honeymoon?"

"No." I frowned, wondering what Kraemer was talking about.

"No? Well then, are you aware that Miss Futh told the police that she saw photographs of your honeymoon in Jamaica, and that in one of those photographs she remembers the travel clothesline that you denied owning? A clothesline similar to the one used in the murder of Christine Schultz?"

"I never showed Futh any pictures! My honeymoon pictures do not include any with a clothesline! I don't own a clothesline!"

"Your Honor!" Eisenberg interrupted. "Laurie Futh has not testified in this courtroom! The State has not admitted the defendant's honeymoon photographs into evidence! These innuendoes and inferences that are not supported by evidence should be considered inadmissible and I object to them!"

"Objection overruled."

During the recess, Eisenberg informed me that he planned to use redirect examination to clear up some of the implications Kraemer had tried to use.

"I'll bring in all of my photos from Jamaica. That's how positive I am that no such picture exists!" I told my lawyer.

After answering the last few questions Eisenberg asked, I stepped wearily down from the witness stand, expecting the State to rest its case. But once I had returned to my seat at the defense table, Kraemer stood and informed the court that he intended to call two additional rebuttal witnesses. The names were unfamiliar to me.

Eisenberg turned to me in surprise, and I shrugged.

A middle-aged woman took the stand. She wore a vinyl jacket and nervously picked at her hair, teased to resemble Tammy Wynette's.

She identified herself as Madeline Gehrt, and she testified that she owned a wig store on Twenty-seventh Street, called Olde Wig World. She went on to say that I'd bought a wig from her the previous spring.

With this, the prosecution tried to link me to the wig at the last minute. I was appalled at this preposterous testimony. The prosecution had handed Eisenberg Gehrt's business card, and I stared at it. I'd never been in the store! I'd bought my short, blond wig at Gimbels, and eventually sold it to Suzy.

"Can you believe this cheap shot?" Eisenberg whispered. "Watch this."

"Miss Gehrt." He addressed her sharply, stalking up to the witness stand. "When did you come forward with this information?"

"Yesterday."

"Yesterday?" he shouted. "Yesterday?" He paused, glaring at the pitiful witness with apparent disgust. "The day before the last day of the trial? This highly publicized case has continuously hit the media for the last nine months!"

Intimidated, Gehrt glanced furtively at Kraemer.

"Just what inspired you to come forward at this time?"

"It just dawned on me," she replied lamely.

I began writing down some points on my legal pad, hoping Eisenberg would see them in time.

"It just dawned on you. How convenient. Do you deny that you've read about this case in the paper or have heard it on television or radio?"

"I've ... read about it," she said, in a voice that was barely audible.

"You said the defendant walked into your shop last spring and bought a wig from you?"

"Yes."

"Do you know the date this occurred?"

"One afternoon."

"Do you recall what day it was?"

"No."

"Can you at least tell me what month it was?"

"I don't recall."

"How is it, then, that you can come into this courtroom and identify this young girl as the one who allegedly bought a wig from you?"

"When she paid for the wig, I noticed her name on the check."

Eisenberg strolled over to the defense table to see what I had written.

"Are you aware of the fact that the defendant has not had a checking account since 1977?"

"Um, no."

"Then, Miss Gehrt, wouldn't it have been impossible for you to have seen the defendant's name on a check?"

"She—no, um—she paid for the wig in cash. I remember because she said the wig wasn't for her. It was for a man, she said, for a joke."

"If you now say that the defendant paid for the wig with cash, then where did you see her name?" Eisenberg grew sardonic. "She didn't by any chance have on a green jogging suit, with the name BEMBENEK written across the back, did she?"

"When I asked for identification, I saw the name."

"Do you always ask cash-paying customers for identification?"

"No." Gehrt stumbled in her story. "When she paid in cash. I mean, I saw her name on her billfold."

"And you just remembered the name?"

"I remembered the name, because my girlfriend Maria has the same maiden name."

Maria? I thought. My cousin, Maria?

"I called Maria afterwards," Gehrt went on, "and Maria told me that it was probably her cousin, Laurie."

"Do you have a sales slip for this purchase?" Eisenberg asked.

"No."

"A canceled check or carbon copy?"

"No."

"A receipt?"

"No."

"In fact, Miss Gehrt, you have no physical evidence or record of this alleged transaction with the defendant at all, do you?"

"No."

Eisenberg shook his head and sat down next to me.

"Isn't it a fact that you just wanted to be on television?"

"No."

"No further questions, Your Honor."

As if the Marilyn Gehrt performance wasn't bad enough, I was shocked to see that the State's next witness was a Boston Store employee. Her name was Annette Wilson, and she worked as a store security guard nabbing shoplifters.

She was never very friendly with me, unlike the other employees at the store. When she learned that I'd turned in my resignation, she'd seemed resentful. I remembered the conversation in the cluttered coffee lounge.

"So, I hear you're leaving us," she'd said coyly.

I nodded. My friends had thrown me a going-away party in one of the stock rooms, with a cake and punch, and word got around.

"I'm going to be a police officer."

"If you make it," she sniffed.

"I hope to. I don't see why not. My dad was a cop and he has been encouraging me."

"So? My dad is a cop and he thinks women have no business on the Police Department! You'll see."

I watched her now as she stepped up onto the witness stand. She told the court that in 1979 she'd seen me leaving the store after work in none other than a green jogging suit.

"Laurie used to play tennis after work with a stock boy," Wilson said. "We carried the jogging suit she was leaving in. It was priced at sixty-eight dollars. Naturally suspicious, I checked with our Sporting Goods department to see if Laurie had purchased the suit."

I scribbled to Eisenberg: "Jogging suits not popular back in 1979. Don't think Boston Store carried anything other than some tennis dresses and racquetball shorts. Not any for sixty-eight dollars! The Athlete's Foot carried jogging suits—only about thirty-five dollars in 1978 or '79. No way!"

And I added: "I did play tennis after work, true—but in a white T-shirt and white shorts I bought from Boston Store. Stockboy's name is John Mavis. We could subpoena him! He'd stick up for me!"

The witness said, "So I made my report, for security reasons, and I remembered this whole incident because it was so suspicious."

"What was the color of the jogging suit?" Kraemer asked.

"Forest kelly green. It was made out of velour."

I went back to my scribbling: "Forest? Kelly? Which? Same words as last night's paper! Who'd play tennis in velour? She could never stand me! Her dad is a cop!"

Eisenberg nodded, and arose to approach the witness for cross-examination.

"Annette Wilson, do you read the *Milwaukee Journal* or *Sentinel*?"

"Yes."

"Are you aware of the fact that the news media has referred to my cross-examination of the witnesses, regarding the green jogging suit and in particular that my questions were about the shade of green this mysterious jogging suit is?"

"Would you repeat the question?"

"The shade, Miss Wilson. I'm talking about the shade of green that was printed in the newspaper. I had asked previous witnesses about the shade of green that they allegedly saw, and I mentioned forest green and I mentioned kelly green. Did you say it was both, just to be on the safe side?"

"No."

"Are you telling me that you did not read that in the newspaper?"

"I did not."

"You say you remember this so clearly. What year did this occur?"

"I don't know."

"Would it be 1978?"

"I don't know."

"1979?"

"I don't know."

"Do you remember what years Ms. Bembenek was employed by Boston Store at Southridge?"

"No."

"Miss Wilson, isn't it a fact that your father is a police officer?"

"Thirty years!" Wilson said proudly, nodding.

"Isn't it also a fact that you never liked Laurie?"

"On the contrary, we got along well," she said.

Eisenberg stared at her, paused, and his eyes narrowed. I came so close to shouting "Liar!" that I mouthed the word silently.

"You told the court a few minutes ago that you made a report regarding the incident. Do you have a copy of that report?"

"It was a verbal report."

"A verbal report? Oh—I see. Now, Miss Wilson, since you have inferred that Ms. Bembenek was stealing this 'forest kelly green velour jogging suit' from the store, one—I might add—valued at sixty-eight dollars did you attempt to apprehend Ms. Bembenek as she left the store?"

"No."

"Your job is security guard? Store detective?"

"Yes."

"Did you tell your supervisor?"

"No."

"Was anyone else aware of this?"

"I don't know."

"Miss Wilson, did you ever catch Miss Bembenek shoplifting or stealing anything from the store?"

"No, sir. We weren't that fortunate!" Wilson replied, with the surprise of a sniper.

My mouth fell open in shock. She was implying I'd been stealing from the store!

Eisenberg, who had been pacing back and forth, whirled around to face her. "Weren't that fortunate?" he repeated. "Weren't that fortunate?" His voice rose in disbelief. It was so brazen, so outrageous that he lost his temper. I couldn't blame him; it had been a frustrating two and a half weeks.

"Isn't it a fact, Miss Wilson, that you don't like Laurie because she's prettier than you are?"

Spectators in the courtroom gasped and several boos were heard. Annette's face took on a startled look. Skwierawski simply grinned slightly, his eyes down.

I cringed. It was true, but he was wrong to have said it. It hurt us, and played to all the old prejudices.

As Kraemer stood to raise his objection, Eisenberg quickly offered, "I'll withdraw the question, Your Honor."

"One more thing, Miss Wilson," Eisenberg then continued. "When, may I ask, did you come forward with this information?"

"The day before yesterday," Wilson said, sounding like Marilyn Gehrt.

"The day before yesterday? Why?"

"Because I read that she denied owning a green jogging suit."

Eisenberg informed the court that he wanted to recall me to the witness stand so I could refute the testimony of the rebuttal witnesses. I was sworn in for the third time, and explained that I'd never bought a wig from Marilyn Gehrt because I had never even heard of her store. I told the jury what I wore when I played tennis outside after work. Again, I denied ever owning a green jogging suit.

"How do you feel now?" Eisenberg asked.

"Angry," was my honest answer.

"Did you kill Christine Schultz?"

"No! I did not!"

"The witness may step down," the judge said.

Kraemer announced, "Your Honor, the State rests its case."

Court was adjourned until the following day, when closing arguments would begin. I felt like collapsing.

Once I arrived home, I peeled off clothes wet from nervous perspiration. A pile of my dresses had accumulated because I did not have time to take them to the dry cleaners, and I had exhausted my closet.

A real trial is nothing like the courtrooms depicted on TV, I thought, pulling on a robe. No hysterical outbursts allowed. No dramatic scenes or Perry Mason badgering the butler into admitting his guilt. I wanted so badly to jump up and call some of those witnesses liars at the top of my lungs—but I didn't dare. The bailiffs would have hauled me out of there, and I would be sitting in the slammer, with my bail revoked.

The telephone rang, and the floor felt cold on my bare feet as I hurried across the room to pick up the extension.

"Hi. This is Maria," a timid voice said. "Can I talk to your ... can I talk to Uncle Joe?"

"Maria, this is Laurie. Is it about the Gehrt woman?"

"I'd really like to talk to your dad."

"Please ..." I picked up an apple I'd intended to snack on and nervously dug my thumbnail into it, making small, half-moon indentations. "I'm the one who's on trial. If you have something to tell me ..."

Her voice was shaky. "What I want to know is, do I have to testify if I don't want to?"

"Did the police subpoena you?"

"They said they were going to. Let me start at the beginning. This silly girlfriend of mine—Maddy Gehrt—she owns a wig shop, and the other night she was gossiping to some of her customers that she saw you on TV and I was your cousin. She told them that she knew me.

"Well, a cop was in her store and overheard her conversation, and took her to the DA's office that same day. Two detectives were over at my house today. It was all a big mistake, really. I mean—"

"Who was the cop?"

"Alan Miller. He used to be Maddy's boyfriend. Maddy's husband is causing such a stink, because he doesn't want to pay child support on one of his sons that he says is Alan's kid. It's—"

"Miller? How convenient for him to drop in on a girlfriend who just happens to own a wig shop, of all things."

"Well, I told these two detectives just what I told you now, and they said that they were going to subpoena me because they said maybe I could help you."

"No detectives want to help me!" I argued.

"I'm so shook up. I really don't think I could testify—and you know, my sister was just in a car accident and, and—all I want to know is if they can make me come to court?" Maria whined.

"Calm down," I said, irritated. "First of all, you can relax, because the State rested its case today. That means that no more witnesses can be called to testify. The two cops who talked to you today probably didn't realize it was over. But Maria! I should think you'd want to help me! After all—my life is at stake!"

"I'm sorry ..."

■   ■   ■

The following day—the last day of the trial—was a Friday. Kraemer's closing argument was what I expected, but he changed his theory about the Ramsey Street house. He told the jury that I'd killed Christine so that Fred and I could sell the house.

"Isn't it odd, ladies and gentlemen of the jury," Kraemer crooned sarcastically, "that Lawrencia Bembenek has been able to explain away every minute detail of this case?"

If I couldn't explain some of these things, I'd be guilty! What could be odd about the truth? What did Kraemer expect me to do? Not tell my side of the story and go like a lamb to his slaughter? I was filled with resentment.

"It's as if she and her attorney stayed awake nights, working out every last detail of this case, and presented it to you, the jury, with remarkable smoothness! But that's the worst part of this whole case, ladies and gentlemen.

"The fact that this young lady planned and plotted and manipulated innocent people like those poor, helpless children, to believe her incredible story, and subtly brainwashed them to testify that she was not the intruder who entered their house that night and killed their mother. That is what I find deplorable beyond words."

"How can he say such horrible things?" I whispered to Eisenberg, who rolled his eyes.

"You see?" Kraemer continued. "That is why the defendant took the stand in a last-minute effort ..."

"He should talk about last-minute efforts!" I said, referring to the rebuttal witnesses. Eisenberg hushed me.

"... and told this courtroom that she was now angry! Angry, ladies and gentlemen, because the last two witnesses that I called did not fit into her plan. She was not prepared for them. They were a surprise. She didn't have time to prepare her defense against them or her explanation for their allegations."

"I was angry because it was so unfair! We weren't even allowed to prove they were liars!" I whispered. Eisenberg nodded. I cupped my chin in my hand and leaned on my elbow, letting Kraemer's voice trail off. I couldn't listen to another word.

My lawyer's closing argument lasted five hours. He reiterated the reasonable doubt in every piece of evidence the prosecution presented. He was thorough and direct. He stressed the numerous inconsistencies as he systematically took the jury through the testimony of every major witness for the State. He repeated the fact that the only witnesses to the murder testified that the murderer wasn't me, explaining that I had had no time to "brainwash" the children before the police talked to them.

The skyline outside the windows grew steadily darker. Later, I clawed my way through the mob of spectators and cameramen. Eisenberg shielded me from the hungry throng of reporters. My head ached unmercifully from the strain of the days, the weeks, the months of persecution.

The jury was out.

Unable to do anything else, we could only wait.

17

A WORLD WITHOUT COLOR

It was Saturday, March 6, 1982. The weekend was a devastating combination of anxious speculation and pessimistic expectation that made my heart pound every time the phone rang.

I forced myself to avoid thinking about being convicted; I couldn't bring myself to consider it realistically.

I tried to dull my overwhelming fear with the Scotch left over from Christmas, avoiding the disapproving eye of my mother. I thought, often, about suicide.

Fred and I met Don Eisenberg and his wife Sandy at an East Side restaurant. We sat at the bar, still discussing the trial and the jury and the performance of "Perry Kraemer."

The place filled with customers as we sat at the bar. Suddenly a loud, boorish man loomed up behind us.

"Hey, Tony!" he shouted in the direction of the bartender. Our backs were still to him. "Did anybody hear if Bembenek got burned yet?"

I almost choked on my drink, and I looked at Sandy, who gasped. We all turned to stare at this person. I shook a few wisps of hair out of my eyes and watched as the man noticed me. His smile faded.

I was thinking, You arrogant, ignorant slob ...! I spoke calmly, I think.

"You could be the father of someone my age. Would you say such a thing if I was your daughter?"

He mumbled something I didn't catch. "Bartender?" he called suddenly. "A round of drinks here, on me!"

It grew late, and the judge announced he'd no longer accept a verdict that day. The announcement was televised on every channel. The bartender turned off the TV.

We stepped outside. Don and Sandy went to a hotel, and Fred went to fetch the car. I waited under the large canopy.

A couple approached me on the sidewalk, arm in arm against the cold. As they passed me, they paused and said, "Good luck," reaching out to shake my hand. I thanked them, and they disappeared into the restaurant. It was still disconcerting to have strangers recognize me. If I'd chosen to thrust myself into the public eye, like a politician or an actress, I guess I might have been better prepared.

When we got home, my mother got up from the couch in the den and hugged me.

"I'm so proud of you, Laurie."

"Why?"

"You're so brave. My God, I don't know how you can stand it."

Fred walked in, fed Sarge some scraps from a doggy bag, and went upstairs.

The kitchen lamp had a warm glow. I untied the knot in the belt of my dress and leaned against the counter. There was an awkward silence. None of us knew what to say, feeling that any conversation would seem trivial.

■   ■   ■

The following morning, I was sipping coffee and reading the newspaper when the phone rang. I rushed to answer it.

It was Eisenberg. No decision had been reached yet, but he invited us to join him and Sandy for brunch, if we wanted to get out of the house. I went with Fred and one of his brothers.

It was bright and clear out, but the temperature was below zero.

Eisenberg was tense. He wore jeans and a thick, white sweater and drank a Bloody Mary while Sandy read the menu. He explained that the jury's long deliberation could be interpreted as a good sign.

"I've seen juries take less than twenty minutes to return a verdict of guilty," he said. "We may have a hung jury."

"Then what happens?" I asked.

"Then it's like Judy Zess's trial, remember? She had a hung jury, and they dropped the charges."

"But they wouldn't do that with a murder charge, surely?" Fred asked. "Just drop it, if the jury can't reach a decision?"

"Well, they could re-try the case, but I doubt that."

As we were eating, Eisenberg received word that he was wanted on the phone. I glanced at Fred anxiously as my lawyer left the booth.

Eisenberg sat down. The jury had requested to see the apartment complex where Fred and I last lived. Eisenberg said the defense had no objection to the request, but Kraemer had refused. Since both counsel had to agree, the judge had to deny the jury's request.

"Does the judge tell the jurors which side opposed the idea? Did he tell them it was Kraemer?" Fred asked.

"No," Eisenberg said.

"But that's not fair! The jury might think we didn't want them to see the apartment! They might think we have something to hide," I said.

"I wonder why they wanted to see the place," Eisenberg said. "Damn! I wish I knew what was going through their heads."

"So do I. I wish they could see the size of those garbage bins my mother was accused of digging through. We should have taken a photograph of them, with a person as tall as my mother standing next to them."

"They've been replaced with a different kind. The owners contracted with a different disposal company, and they use another type of bin. They aren't the same bins."

By evening, the judge again announced that he'd no longer accept a verdict that day. He refused to declare a hung jury.

"How are you holding up, Laurie?" Eisenberg asked.

"I guess ... I'm okay."

"I know it's tough. Hang in there. If you aren't acquitted, at least we can hope the jury is deadlocked."

I stayed up late and watched a movie on TV with my mom and dad. Fred sat on the couch, with Sergeant at his feet. Even then, a part of me continued to deny what was happening.

The next morning, Monday, I was told to meet Eisenberg at the courthouse because the jury had requested that portions of the transcripts be read back to them. They were still unable to reach a decision, after deliberating since Friday.

"They want to hear Durfee's testimony again, part of yours and part of Fred's," Eisenberg explained. "Obviously, I'm going to object. It's not fair to take testimony out of context."

"Well, if Kraemer didn't want the jury to see the apartments, then we should be able to refuse this request," I said.

As usual, Skwierawski had other ideas. Despite Eisenberg's objections, he said that, though he'd normally deny such a request, this time he'd break with tradition and allow portions of the transcripts to be read back to the jury.

Again, we were overruled.

By the end of another agonizing day, still no verdict had been reached.

Tuesday, March 9, 1982. I was so depressed I could barely get out of bed. It was a dreary, freezing day. The sky was the color of gray flannel.

I took a warm shower, trying to relax the tension in my muscles by letting the water beat on my shoulders. My mom asked my dad to pick up some sandwiches, and then she paced anxiously, in an aimless stroll about the house. We decided to play a game of Scrabble to pass the time. I wrapped my hair in a towel and sat down at the table. It was almost noon.

The extension phone rang softly. I held my breath and picked up the receiver.

"The jury has reached a verdict," Eisenberg said. "Cross your fingers and see you downtown."

My heart pounded wildly and the color left my face. From my expression, my mother knew that the end to the waiting had arrived. My dad returned with the sandwiches, and his eyes showed concern when he saw my face. An intense feeling of dread washed over me.

My mom walked up to me and held my shoulders. "It's going to be all right, Laurie. It has to be."

"But we thought it would be a hung jury," I said, trembling.

"No jury in their right mind could find you guilty."

"Mom! You just don't know! You weren't there for all of it, because you were sequestered. It was so unfair! I have this awful feeling ..."

"Here," she said, handing me her gold wedding band. "Wear it for good luck."

When we arrived at the courtroom, the cameras and reporters were there, but the place was strangely silent. Eisenberg was there. He wrung his hands as I hung my wool coat over the chair at the defense table.

"How are you?" he asked.

I felt as though I'd been suffering from a terminal illness for a very long time, and was about to die.

"I feel like I'm at my own funeral. Why is it so quiet in here?"

"A better question is why are so many sheriff's deputies in here?" Eisenberg asked. "Do they expect a riot?" Officers from the Sheriff's Department lined the walls like trees.

"I don't know what to think," Eisenberg told me. "I've talked to the bailiffs and they claim the jury took several different votes. They kept coming up with different answers. I just don't know."

"Is Skwierawski here?" I asked.

"He will be in a minute. I'll tell you one thing, Laurie. When the jury comes in, if they're looking at you, you're safe. If none of them looks at you, it's time to appeal."

I turned around to see Fred's dad walk in with my parents. They sat down just as the judge appeared, with Kraemer at his side.

"All rise."

The jury walked in.

None of them looked at me.

And then I knew.

■   ■   ■

He sentenced me to life imprisonment.

The rest of my life.

He took my life away.

My life!

My head filled with fog, with gray fog for a gray half-life, gray walls, gray cells, gray places, gray people, gray hours, years of living without life.

A scream rose in my throat, but smothered in the gray, gray fog.

Then they came, and took me away to jail.

■   ■   ■

"Oh!" I heard a male voice say just around the corner. "The new prisoner is here! I didn't recognize her with her clothes on!"

I was taken to another room, where I signed papers I didn't even read. "My purse and my coat," I mumbled, in a stupor. I was in a thin County Jail gown once again.

"You better make any phone call you need to now, because you'll be taken to Taycheedah Correctional Institute tomorrow," the deputy said.

A door opened and I was pointed in the direction of a cellblock. I walked straight to a phone on the wall and tried dialing Fred, twice, but I kept getting a recording. I wondered if my mom and dad were home yet. I realized I had been staring at the phone, unable to use it. The other inmates sat around a table, watching me.

I went to a cot in my cell and burst into heavy sobs. A matron walked in and put a supper tray on the shelf attached to the wall. It looked like dog food with a spoon in it.

I walked back to the phone, and got through to Fred, who was also crying. I told him that I needed a coat and the case for my contact lenses. He said they'd be right down.

The matron walked back in. "Channel four wants an interview."

"No," I said, trying to control my shaking.

I took my contact lenses out and put them in a paper cup with water. Just as I lay down on my cot, a sheriff's deputy came to get me.

"Get dressed," she said.

"Excuse me?"

"Come with me. I'll get your clothes. You're going to Taycheedah right now."

I followed her out, knowing that there was no time to contact my family, who were on their way with my coat. Why did the authorities suddenly feel compelled to rush me out of the Milwaukee County Jail? Some prisoners sat downtown for weeks before being transported in the van to jail.

It was dark outside. I sat shivering in handcuffs and chains that left greasy smudges on my white pullover. I was in the back of a Sheriff's Department squad car, with three officers. The dim countryside along the highway appeared blurry; I had forgotten my contact lenses.

Somehow, though, the blurred world was appropriate, marking a passage from one world to another, far grimmer. A world without any color.

■   ■   ■

So this is what the case against me amounted to:

- A woman whose credibility was suspect, at best, said she'd overheard me saying I wanted to have Christine Schultz "blown away."

- The "motive" was that child-support payments and mortgage payments had put a crimp in our lifestyle, and either I wanted to frighten Christine out of her house in some manner that had gone wrong, or I wanted to kill her so I could move in myself.

- On the night of the murder, a girlfriend of mine luckily canceled a date. Early in the morning, in my heavy police shoes and a green jogging suit, a wig and a mask, I jogged the eighteen or so blocks over to the house. No one saw me. I entered with a key I hadn't known we had, effortlessly bound and gagged Christine, tried to smother the boys, killed Christine and jogged back to the apartment, holding on to the gun. The man the boys saw was a phantom of their imagination, though the jogging suit only one of them had seen wasn't. It wasn't a man at all. It was me, whom the boys had known for some time.

- After I got to my apartment, I cleaned the gun and put it away and got into bed and fell asleep, just in time for a call from Fred.
- I was able to do this because I was a cold-hearted bitch (a former Playboy bunny, after all!) who would stop at nothing to continue living life in the fast lane (like working at Vic Tanny's and as a security guard on campus).

The thing is a joke.

A very sick joke.

The motive:

There is a considerable amount of evidence to suggest that Christine feared someone other than me. Her own attorney, Kershek, told the police shortly after her murder that Fred had threatened to kill her and that she thought she was being followed. She believed Fred was angry over her relationship with Honeck; he had already blown the whistle on Honeck for sleeping with Christine, thereby getting him into trouble at work. He'd then let Honeck believe I'd done the fingering.

Two other friends of Christine's, Dorothy Polka and Joanne Delikat, also said Fred had threatened Christine, and both said he'd beaten her severely several times. Joanne said Christine was afraid of Fred.

It wouldn't be hard to establish that I didn't want that house and never had. Too many people had heard me complaining about it. Nor did I want kids—everyone knew that. It's worth noting that I called Josephine Osuchowski only a few hours after the murder, worrying about having to take the kids.

Fred may have had a motive, but I didn't.

And bear in mind this:

- I was suing the Milwaukee Police Department for sexual discrimination, was to be the star witness in a federal investigation, and had been the target of reprisals;
- I had made public, in the anti-discrimination suit, the very unpopular connections between the cops and the drug dealers who ran the Tracks bar;

- I had opened the can of worms that had some officers dealing drugs, running hookers and selling pornography from their cruisers;
- High officials of the Milwaukee Police Department were involved.

You tell me if you still think this was a clean investigation.

The hairs found at the scene:

The prosecution claimed that a hair found by the medical examiner was retrieved from the bandanna around Christine's mouth. This was compared to hairs from my hairbrush and found to be compatible.

What to say about this?

It was stipulated at the trial that "a hair of light tint" was found on the bandanna. Eisenberg accepted this as fact. In reality, there was no such hair. Dr. Samuels wrote in a letter, after I was found guilty: "... at the time of the unwitnessed autopsy I recovered many brown hairs, along with numerous fibers of non-human origin.... I recovered no blond or red hairs of any texture or length, nor did I recover any hair grossly compatible with fibers from a red or blond wig. All the hairs I recovered were brown and grossly identical to the hair of the victim."

Still, one blond hair, "color-processed," "consistent" with mine mysteriously made its way into the police inventory. Here's the chronology surrounding the hair:

1. The bandanna goes to the Crime Lab.
2. The Crime Lab numbers the hairs one through twenty, *all* of which are consistent with Christine's hair.
3. The bandanna is checked *out* of the Crime Lab by the cops.
4. The bandanna is returned by the cops.
5. The lab discovers additional hairs, which they number twenty-one through twenty-five and Eureka! *one* matches the blond, color-processed hair of Lawrencia Bembenek.

Was it just a coincidence that this happened right after they'd seized my hairbrush and security guard uniform from my locker on campus? It was these phantom hairs that Diane Hanson analyzed and found to be compatible with mine. The jury never knew the stipulation about the hair was false. If they'd known, they might have questioned whether the hair really did come from Christine Schultz's body.

The gun:

Ah, the gun!

The jury said afterwards that the gun was the one compelling piece of evidence that they used to ignore the boys' testimony and convict me. The gun did it for them.

Fred's was the only testimony that connected me to the gun. If he hadn't testified, there would have been no case. If he'd said there was a third gun, and that third gun had been the one in the apartment, there would have been no case either.

I was a cop. I knew about police procedure. I was familiar with guns. Yet the prosecution was asking everyone to believe that I killed Christine with Fred's off-duty gun, and simply returned it to Fred. If I had killed someone with a gun, would I be dumb enough to hang on to it, even after the murder, when throwing it away would have precluded a case against me?

The State's ballistics guy, Monty Lutz, said the bullet, which the jury was led to believe came from Christine's body, was fired by Fred's off-duty gun. That gun was then identified as "the murder weapon."

But was it?

On the night of the murder, Durfee and Fred came home. Their stories about what they then did differ in some respects. Fred said he and Durfee went straight to the off-duty gun. Durfee said Fred and I disappeared for a while, and after that they went for the gun. Durfee did say he examined the gun and it hadn't been fired, but he could not later identify the murder weapon as the gun he inspected, because he never wrote down its serial number. The notebook in which he made this glaring omission was mysteriously missing—he'd lost it or thrown it out.

Others examined that gun, too. There was a meeting in the inspector's conference room at police headquarters, to which Fred had been summoned. They presumably examined it (why else ask for it?) but presumably concluded, too, that it hadn't been fired. They gave it back to Fred to keep, which he did.

Fred didn't turn the gun in until twenty-two days after the murder. No evidence says that the gun shown to Durfee was the gun later given to Monty Lutz. Fred could have changed it. Anyone could have, in those twenty-two days.

And the bullets? Lutz was given a collection of bullets from Fred. Some of them couldn't be fired from either of his two official guns. At no time was anyone questioned about what missing gun these bullets could have come from. If the jury had known about these bullets, and about the procedures involved in handling the gun, they could reasonably have concluded that there'd been a third gun—after all, Fred at one time testified he owned five. They might have concluded that it was this third gun Durfee inspected, and that this was not the murder weapon. I know now that there are significant differences between the autopsy protocol sheet and the Crime Lab sheet descriptions of the bullet. Not only the sets of initials, but the weight of the bullet differs from sheet to sheet and on one sheet it is described as having a damaged nose. But, no damage to the bullet is listed on the other sheet. This means that somewhere between the morgue and the Crime Lab, the bullet underwent a miraculous physical transformation! Who transports the evidence from the morgue to the Crime Lab? Who else? The police!

The bullet Elaine Samuels released for evidence carried three initials. The bullet introduced in evidence carried six initials. Who knows whether this was the same bullet? Just as with the gun, the chain of continuity is broken. The evidence is, at best, suspect.

Was there some other way of verifying whether this gun was the murder weapon, apart from the ballistics, which were not reliable anymore? Could the gun be matched to the wound? It was a contact wound, and a muzzle imprint was left on the body. When you compare the muzzle imprint with the murder weapon, so called, there is a 250 percent discrepancy.

I have support for these suspicions from, among other people, Werner Spitz, the former medical examiner from Detroit, who knows something about guns; and from Dr. Michael Baden, a top forensic guy from the New York State police; and from Dr. John Hillsdon-Smith, the top Canadian expert, a man who usually testifies for the prosecution.

Said Hillsdon-Smith, Ontario's Director of Forensic Pathology: "It's difficult not to conclude that this woman has been railroaded." His own view was that "autopsy records indicated that the impression left on the victim's back by the rim of a gun muzzle was two and a half times as large as the muzzle of the alleged murder weapon."

The discrepancy is so great that it cannot be accounted for—therefore that gun did not leave that mark. Either there was a switch in the guns, in which case Fred did it, or there was a switch of the bullet. In either case, the basis on which I was prosecuted was false.

Further, what about the blood on Fred's own service revolver?

The green jogging suit:

The only person who ever saw this phantom jogging suit was the younger boy, Shannon. Sean, the older boy, who gave the more complete description, called it a green canvas army jacket. He never mentioned anything about a jogging suit. He also quite clearly stated that it wasn't me, and that the person he'd seen was far too big.

So who said there was a jogging suit?

Zess, of course. At the prelim, she said she saw only sweat pants with tight elastic ankles and couldn't say if it was a jogging suit. At the trial she changed her mind. It was now definitely a jogging suit. Years later (as we will see) she changed her mind again. She said she'd been induced to change her evidence by police promises that they'd do everything they could to help Tom Gaertner, in prison on drug-trafficking charges.

Shannon, who first described this suit, said it was dark green. Detective Shaw said he couldn't place the color exactly. His wife said it was lighter than forest green. Officer Faubel called it kelly green, but no one else ever saw me in it. Faubel and his family were known to one of the jurors.

There was Annette Wilson, of course. But her superior, the chief investigator for the Boston Store, went on television to say she was lying when she said she'd reported me stealing a green jogging suit, kelly or forest or any other green and she was *fired* from her job because of it.

And something else: there had been several sightings—six or more—in the neighborhood on the night in question of a male jogger fitting the description given by Sean. This evidence was never introduced at trial, not even by Don Eisenberg. The most significant sighting was probably that of Nurse Barbara Sarenac, who spotted him that night around the time Fred was calling me. She was never called as a witness. None of this was ever mentioned at my trial.

The key to the Ramsey house:

The key I was supposed to have was never introduced in evidence. It had been packed away somewhere in Fred's jewelry box, I was told, but where my mother had packed it I didn't know. Fred had gone looking for it afterwards, I'd thought. But could he have been replacing it? I was confused. In any case, in a police report on May 29 it was said that Fred handed one key over to the investigating detectives the night of the murder, and then opened the doors to the Ramsey house a few hours later. That would seem to account for both keys.

The clothesline:

Throughout the trial it was suggested that Christine's hands were bound with a clear plastic cord. However, the initial report simply states that Christine had it around her wrist and through the fingers of her left hand. The photographs taken at the medical examination support this.

Zess—of course!—said Fred and I owned such a cord. We, in turn, both said the only cord we knew of belonged to Judy. This cord was supposed to appear in photographs taken on our honeymoon in Jamaica, since it was a traveling clothesline. No such photograph exists.

The wig:

Both kids said their assailant was a man with reddish-brown hair in a six- to eight-inch ponytail. Since I was a blond, with hair too short for the kind of ponytail they described, perforce it must have been a wig for me to have been present. (Later I found out that the wig they found was a cascade—a small hair piece—not long enough to be pulled into a six- to eight-inch ponytail.)

On the night of the crime, the police report indicates that a fiber was found on Christine's thigh after the police turned the body over.

It wasn't until a few weeks later, on June 15, that there was any indication a wig was involved. At that time, our landlady, Frances Ritter, told two detectives that a wig had been retrieved from the plumbing drains that were shared by our apartment and another, occupied by Mr. and Mrs. Niswonger and Judy Nitchka. Sharon Niswonger had called the landlady to complain of an overflowing toilet, and a plumber had fished out this wig. The landlady kept it for a while (hoping she could charge someone for the cost of the plumber) but then threw it into a dumpster. The cops retrieved it on June 15.

Yes, but ... what was never placed in evidence was that the last person to use the toilet in the Niswonger-Nitchka apartment before it backed up was Judy Zess! She had visited the apartment unexpectedly and asked to use the toilet. Sharon Niswonger told Kraemer about this, but he never raised it while she was on the witness stand. Of course not—it would have cast doubt on his nice theory. Again, I remind you that Zess later recanted and deposed that she'd been asked to change her testimony as a reward for help for Tom Gaertner.

One more point about this wig. It's hard to believe that some human hair wouldn't adhere to the inside of a wig. Did they ever examine this wig for such evidence? No! Why not? Because they wouldn't have found any of mine.

If the fiber on the leg could have come from the wig, the fact that Zess might have had the thing in her possession and tried to flush it down the toilet was certainly exculpatory evidence. Surely it might have made the jury think?

And the woman who said I bought a wig from her shop? No one now believes her. I bet her own mother doesn't even believe her.

The fingerprints:

Fingerprints *were* found on the bedpost and window frame of Christine's bedroom. They were compared to the fingerprints of six other people, but not to mine. Nor were they compared to the fingerprints of Frederick Horenberger or those of Danny L. Gilbert, of whom more later ... At the time of the trial, I only saw one MPD Homicide Index Report that stated: "Number of fingerprints found at the scene: none." But other reports later found by Ira Robins made references to prints! Fancy that. Conflicting information about something as crucial as fingerprints at a murder scene!

Me and my movements the night of the murder:

My mom and I were packing on the night of the murder, as I've said. Fred slept until about eleven, when he went to work. He phoned at midnight, and again half an hour later.

Stu Honeck logged the call from Sean at 2:26 AM. Before Sean called, he saw the murderer leave, tried to stem his mother's bleeding with gauze, tried to call the operator, and then called Stu.

Fred called me at 2:40.

The house is eighteen blocks away.

Fred and Durfee checked my car when they came by, and its motor was cold. I had no bike. I would have had to jog over.

Nurse Sarenac saw a man matching the description of the murderer shortly after 2:40. An hour later, Fred called again. Shortly after that I called my friend Josephine Osuchowski.

Another thing. On the Memorial Day weekend, our building's front door lock was changed. The landlady, Mrs. Ritter, confirms it. Neither Fred nor I had a key. If I'd jogged over to kill Christine, I'd either have had to buzz someone to get back in—suuuure!—or somehow propped a door open.

And Fred that night?

Fred's and Durfee's reports differ considerably. Fred said he was never out of Durfee's sight. Durfee said it wasn't so. Both of them said they'd worked the whole time. Others admitted to having seen them both out drinking at Georgie's Pub. If they are inconsistent in this, why not in other things?

So we have Fred on the record as lying. Transcripts we received ten years later from Police Department records show that two detectives, Craig Hastings and James Kelley, caught Fred perjuring himself. They recommended proceeding against him—four counts of perjury at unrelated hearings.

They told McCann.

"Do you want Bembenek or do you want Schultz?" McCann asked.

"He's violating the law," Kelley said, stubbornly.

McCann of course ignored him. He wanted me, not Fred.

But *why*?

Without Fred, of course, there was absolutely no link between me and the crime.

None. Not one.

What about my good friend Judy Zess?

Let's recap the main events: she admitted lying about the concert where she was arrested for having marijuana, and lying about me. But she quit the police force. In 1981, she shared our apartment. She then became involved with Tom Gaertner, a good friend of Sasson, an off-duty cop killed by Fred.

July 2, 1981, Zess was robbed by Frederick Horenberger and Danny L. Gilbert. Both men were convicted and sentenced to prison. Both had long records. The owner of Georgie's Pub has testified he introduced Fred Schultz to Horenberger (though Fred has denied knowing Horenberger); they worked together on construction projects. On the night Christine was murdered, one Danny L. Gilbert was found by the police in a truck at the side of the roadway overlooking Christine's home. He told police he was tired and stopped to rest. It's possible this was another Danny L. Gilbert (they have different birth dates according to their IDs) but it's a neat coincidence, isn't it?

The last person to use the toilet before it backed up with the wig was Judy Zess.

Judy Zess told Horenberger she wanted to get me to help Tom.

And another thing. Who took the bullet to the Crime Lab? Detective Frank Cole. Who was hot on my trail? Frank Cole. Who was the prosecution's star witness? Judy Zess. Who was in Judy's bed? Frank Cole.

And Stu Honeck?

Stu was a cop who lived with Fred between his break-up with Christine and his marriage to me. He said he was engaged to Christine, though no one could prove it. He left Christine's house around 10:50 PM, he said. Honeck was the one who got Sean's call and was one of the first cops there. Sean and Shannon both said a strongbox in the house had been tampered with and was open.

In 1986 my mom and dad got a call from Stu. During that call, Honeck mentioned some three hundred thousand dollars worth of drugs that had gone missing from Christine's house the night of the murder. Honeck claimed Fred took them. Drugs were never mentioned during my trial.

What about Frederick Horenberger?

He's dead now—committed suicide after taking hostages during an armed robbery in 1991. The evidence that he knew Fred is pretty compelling. He was convicted of robbing Zess, using pretty much the same MO [modus operandi] Christine's killer had used. He had a long record of violent crime. He could have been the one who pulled the trigger that night. I just don't know.

The murder scene:

The first cops on the scene found Christine face down. Thomas Hanratty, the medical examiner, found her face up when he arrived. Someone had turned her over.

There were bloodstains on the wall at the scene of the murder. Fred told the cops it was probably from the Great Dane that had been in heat. But Christine had got rid of the dog months earlier. The bloodstains were taken to the police lab. Diane Hanson said she was never asked to do an analysis of the blood, not even to see if it was dog blood.

The medical examiner wasn't called until two hours after the detectives arrived, and it wasn't until several hours afterwards that Elaine Samuels, the assistant, performed an autopsy. No police officers were present at the autopsy, in violation of state law. Further, Fred, who was clearly a suspect at this time, went to the morgue with me to identify Christine, and even turned the body over while he was there. Stu Honeck could have made the identification easily enough.

And Judge Skwierawski?

At the start of the trial, he advised both counsel that he'd once acted as a lawyer for Tom Gaertner. No one objected, not even Don

Eisenberg. At the time, Gaertner was in prison awaiting trial on his trafficking charges. Zess, who would later marry him, was the State's star witness.

The jurors, too:

Two of the jurors might have been predisposed. One was a friend of Officer Faubel, the one recruit who believed I'd owned a green jogging suit. The other knew Judy Zess (as a "party friend").

Not to mention my attorney, Don Eisenberg:

Later he was suspended indefinitely from the Wisconsin bar for conflict of interest in another murder trial. My mom and dad paid most of his fees, but Fred chipped in five thousand dollars and signed over his share in the house on Ramsey. He was paid by Fred. Fred was another suspect. Eisenberg had Fred sit in on most of the meetings he had with me. He later appeared on TV with Fred, where both of them said I was guilty.

Great case, right?

18

THE PRISONER

I'd never been to Taycheedah, or even to the County of Fond du Lac, where it is situated. When we arrived at the gatehouse, the deputies were told to remove their gunbelts. I strained my eyes to get a look at the compound but could only make out blobs of light that resembled hungry eyes in the darkness.

"Good luck, Lawrencia," one of the female deputies said.

The next thing I knew, I was in a small room with two shower stalls and a wall lined with shelves that held supplies. I'd been escorted to a large building that was referred to as a "housing unit"—a nice college-dorm euphemism if ever there was one. They made it sound like a condo. A large, male lieutenant named Wood informed me that I would stay in "R&O" (Receiving and Orientation) until I was medically cleared.

The jingle of many keys and locked doors greeted me.

"It's up to you how you want to do your time," Wood said, in a kind of baritone bark. "You can keep your mouth shut, and have it pretty easy—or you can do hard time. It's all up to you."

Hard time? Was there anything else? It had all happened so incredibly fast. One minute I was enjoying the company of my family, playing Scrabble at the kitchen table—and then the metal door of my cell was locking behind me, shutting me in. I knew I'd never forget that iron clang as long as I lived.

I heard the approach of walkie-talkies. Two female prison guards, or "correctional officers," ordered me to remove all my clothes for a strip-search. Humiliated beyond words, I stood there naked, attempting to lessen my embarrassment by staring at the tile floor. I was still crying.

"Turn around, bend over and spread your cheeks."

After the guards watched me shower with a lice shampoo called "Kwell," I was given a thin gown and a cotton robe that smelled of body odor. I wondered who had worn it before me. Then they took me to my cell. My "room," they called it.

I sat on my bed, staring at walls closing in on me. I could still hear the judge's words echoing in my mind, see his mouth moving. I worried about my family, remembering the sobs I'd heard behind me in the courtroom.

My head ached from crying.

Thoughts of God and Hell swirled in my mind. There were no innocent souls in Hell, were there? Not in any theology they taught at St. Mary's. Perhaps they'd got it all screwed up and the universe was run by malevolent devils? I thought of the eternity to come, the years of iron doors and prurient guards stretching into the future, and considered suicide. It would have been so easy! Easy right then to tear strips from my bedsheets and construct a rope long enough to tie to the pipe, hanging there until blessed oblivion came.... It would have been a relief, finally something constructive to do. It was the thought of my mom and dad that stopped me. They'd had enough pain.

■　　■　　■

I found a passage in Nietzsche, years later: "Everything can be acquired in solitude, except sanity." A melancholy truth. The boredom of the days left me with nothing to do but dwell on my misery. I couldn't touch the food that was brought to my cell. I couldn't sleep at night—I didn't even have control over the large overhead light above my bed. I could only guess what time it was.

The same routine woke me every morning. Keys in the lock on the cell door preceded the voice of the sergeant on duty.

"Six AM. Do you want a breakfast tray, Bembenek?"

"No, thank you," I would answer from my bed, turning over and falling back to sleep. The cell door would close and the lock would turn noisily. After about twenty minutes, the door would wake me a second time, with officers collecting the dishes.

"Tray, please."

"I don't have a tray," I would explain every day. "I refused breakfast."

Just about the time I got back to sleep, the cell door would open for a third time, and the guard would announce, "Shower."

No matter how hard I wished for it, I was never lucky enough to find warm water issuing from the battered old shower faucet in the bathroom. None of the old buildings, I learned, had warm water. Every morning, I would cringe under an icy shower, unable to withstand the cold shock for more than a minute or so. Afterwards, I'd get back into bed, my teeth chattering. I'd curl into a fetal position, pull the cotton blanket up to my chin and shiver until I fell back to sleep.

The next event on the unvarying morning agenda was to supply each cell with a mop and bucket. Cleaning was top priority every morning. By that time, I would usually acquiesce and change into the "state-issue" clothing, which consisted of baggy denim pants and a gray sweatshirt. Old white tennis shoes were provided, and white cotton socks.

One morning, after a heavy snowfall, I was lying in bed, listening to some black women shovel the snow just outside my window. I was on the first floor of the building, and my window was at ground level. It was quiet outside, the snow muffling sound. I could hear the women easily, over the rhythmic scrape of the shovels.

"I seen 'dem bring in a whole lot of womens. I bet R'n'O is full."

"That the poh-lice in that room," one said.

I knew they were referring to me, and I wondered what inmates did to former cops in prison.

So many different guards opened my door over the next few days that I felt like a freak on exhibition. I later found out that they were unprofessional enough to parade to my cell, eager to get a look at the "infamous" Bembenek.

It was the sheer arbitrariness of it all that bothered me most at first, the careless inconsistencies between officers. I was given a huge stack of rules and policies that I was instructed to read. Some of the material was outdated. Some of it was just ignored. Contradictions were everywhere. No one would provide clear answers.

I scanned the regulations concerning visitors. The prison struck me as a virtual paper factory. There were hundreds of memorandums, written policies and procedures, regulations and addendums to the memorandums. There were forms to fill out for visiting privileges, with those approved comprising a prisoner's official Visitors List. Only persons on that list were allowed to visit. After I filled out a request for visiting privileges with a particular person, the Social Services Department mailed that person a form to complete. If my social worker approved the person, the name was added to my list, and could not be removed for six months.

There were request forms for writing privileges that had to be completed in triplicate for all correspondence to another institution. There were forms to request phone calls. We were allowed two ten-minute calls per month, and we could call only a person whose name appeared on our approved Visitors List. The call would be placed by the housing unit sergeant, at the sergeant's convenience.

There were forms to request canteen privileges, medical attention and everything imaginable—a world so foreign to me then. I was confused and fearful, aching to know how soon I would be able to see my family.

I read in the stack of policies that "new commitments" (that was me) were allowed to see immediate family after seventy-two hours. I asked a guard at my cell door about this rule, and she verified it.

Another section of the rules stated that inmates in R&O were allowed to mail seven letters a week without stamps on the envelope called "free stamp letters." I used the pencil and lined paper I was provided and wrote to my parents, asking them please to visit as soon as possible. I also wrote to Don Eisenberg, and to Fred.

When my pencil became too worn down, I had to stop. I had to slip the pencil under the door and wait until an officer noticed it and sharpened it for me. I also slid my letters under the cell door for the guards to pick up. Of course, they read everything.

I looked out my window. It was reinforced on the inside with wire mesh and would only open about two inches. I felt claustrophobic. I could see a farmhouse and a barn past the prison fence, about a mile away in the darkness. The blinking lights in town lined the horizon like fallen stars, a constant reminder of another life, another world. I could run that far, if it meant my life, I thought. I'd done it once, years before. When I was thirteen, I ran away from home. I literally ran, cutting my feet on sharp stones, unseen in dimly lit alleyways. I'd give my right arm to be able to run back home now.

Another guard opened the lock on my door. It was mealtime. Biting into a sandwich, my front tooth broke. When the meal trays were being collected, I asked the officer for a Dental Request form and chatted with him, desperate for conversation.

"I can't wait until I see my family," I said. "They'll be here tomorrow."

"You can't have any visitors until you're medically cleared," he said, shifting his weight in his cowboy boots (only the lieutenants wore uniforms). "That probably won't be for another week or so."

"But the other guard, the female at night, said they could see me after seventy-two hours!" I told him tearfully.

"I'm sorry. That's an old policy. She gave you the wrong info."

"I wrote home and told my mom and dad that they could visit! Now they'll drive here from Milwaukee for nothing!" I cried. "It says in these rules—seventy-two hours!" I pointed to the papers I'd been given.

"Those must be outdated manuals. I also have some letters to return to you. You're only allowed to write five free letters a week."

"But the rules say seven!"

"The rule now is five per week, per prisoner, for the first thirty days of incarceration. Then it drops to one per week."

Later, I found out that five was not the correct number either; it was three.

Every shift of guards did things a different way. I was in their hands now, and totally dependent upon them. From their decisions, large and small, there was no appeal.

It seemed to take forever to get medically cleared. The institution's medical staff and equipment were inadequate, and the tests and "bloodwork" had to be mailed to Madison.

I was aware of the new "commitments" being brought in. There were cells on either side of me. I wondered what day it was, because I had lost track. Black women walked in groups on the sidewalk outside, returning to the building. Some shouted "I love you!" up to prisoners on the second and third floors, so I thought, naively, that there must be male inmates in the building. I wondered why some inmates were allowed outside, and for what purpose.

The following week, I began to receive hundreds of letters and donations from people across the state who supported me. All the envelopes had been opened by the prison before I received them. Fred wrote that a defense fund had been established, and it lifted my spirits to learn that strangers cared about me and were outraged at the verdict.

My mom and dad wrote as soon as they were allowed to. On the night that I was convicted, they said, by the time they'd reached the County Jail, I was already gone. I started to cry again, and cried each time I saw their familiar handwriting.

"They couldn't wait to take you from us, my darling daughter," my dad wrote.

I cried again.

Even as I slept, I clutched my father's letter close to my heart, the writing blurred from the tears.

In the morning, I wandered over to the mirror on the wall and stared at myself. My skin looked bloated, pale and unhealthy from crying. Because I couldn't use a cream rinse or conditioner on my hair, the hard water turned it into a cotton-candy frizzle. My eyebrows were growing in. I ran a hand across my face. My fingernails were chewed down to ugly stubs.

I was moved to another floor in the same building. The third-floor cell wasn't much different, except it faced the woods behind the "housing unit." I was finally medically cleared.

The same day, Don Eisenberg arrived, with my family. Escorted by a guard, I walked to another building in the shabby white tennis shoes that were labeled "R&O" in black magic marker. There was snow on the ground.

I was directed down a hallway to an office. Expecting to see my family, I walked in eagerly. Instead, a woman sitting behind a large desk greeted me. She said she was the warden, Nona Switala.

"Well? Is it as bad as you thought it would be?" she asked.

"Yes," I replied honestly.

"You're still adjusting." She was slender and had straight, brown hair. Explaining that she was concerned about the amount of publicity I had received, she informed me that newspaper and television reporters had been flooding her office with phone calls ever since I arrived.

The media circus was continuing.

"They're anxious to interview you, Laurie," she said. "If you don't wish to be bothered, I will do everything in my power to see that they leave you alone. They've just about been camped out at that gate, waiting to get a picture of you. I don't know what they expect! They were asking me if your window had bars on it! You should have heard them."

The jackals, I thought, still feeding on the carrion. But I kept that to myself. I told the warden politely that I preferred to avoid reporters for the time being, and thanked her for her concern.

I was at last allowed to see my family. Everyone was crying, except Eisenberg, who stood by solemnly as I embraced my mom and my dad. Fred rushed toward me and tried to kiss me passionately, but I pulled away, embarrassed.

"It seems as though the jury was highly undecided," Eisenberg said. "I found out the results of the first vote they took: six women voted guilty, and one woman and all five men found you not guilty."

My dad offered me his handkerchief.

"Apparently, that forewoman was extremely aggressive in arguing her viewpoint while the jury was deliberating, and she swayed many to the guilty side. She really wanted to hang you."

We discussed the appeal, and the length of time it would take. Eisenberg explained that he'd already filed the Notice of Appeal. The next step would be to have the transcripts typed from the trial—a lengthy and expensive process.

"How long will this take?" I asked.

"It's hard to estimate. The Appellate Court has six months to reply. They can decide to confirm the conviction, reverse the conviction or order a new trial. At least you'd be released pending the new trial if that was the decision. Skwierawski denied your appeal bond, you know."

"Is this appeal going to a state court?"

"Yes. We have to exhaust all steps before moving on to the federal court system."

"If I can just hang on for six months ..." I said.

"Guess what," Eisenberg said. "There is a God! Annette Wilson was fired from her job at Boston Store. Her supervisor, Scott Nicholson, called me and said she was lying. He offered to give us an affidavit."

Now he tells me.

"We brought you clothes and things, but the prison refused to let it come in," Fred told me. "We got a copy of the property list. I think there are some things we can bring in, but some items have to be mailed."

"There are limits to what we can have," I said. "I believe it's five tops and five pants. I've got State-issue right now. I just spent two days sewing name tags into everything I own."

"No stamps are allowed?" my mom asked. "I brought a book of stamps."

"No. Stamped envelopes, but no loose stamps," I said.

My family promised to visit me again as soon as they could, without a lawyer in tow. They were given a sheet listing the visiting days and hours. Then they left, after tearful hugs and kisses.

I could see the parking lot as I stared out a hallway window while I waited for the guard to unlock a door. I peered out, my face close to the glass. I raised my hand to wave, hoping my family could see me.

"That's unauthorized communication," the guard said. "Stop it."

The car lights drove away into the distance, glowing, receding, dimmer, taking my beloved family with them.

■   ■   ■

Once I was allowed out "in population," as it was called, I could walk to the building where meals were served. Inmates were not allowed to stop, loiter or change the direction we were walking in while going to meals. Following a line with our trays cafeteria style, we were limited to single portions of everything. We were to be seated, filling up the tables from left to right, and we were restricted from talking to any of the women at other tables.

After my arrest, I'd had to learn legal jargon. Now I was confronted with prison slang. During my first meal, I sat at a table with three black women. I listened to their conversation. It seemed to make no sense.

"And whenever he be checkin' his trap, he beats 'doz hoes asses," one was saying.

"He do?" another asked.

A small woman with skin the color of chocolate pudding suddenly looked at me. "You ear hustling?" She sucked her teeth loudly.

"Excuse me?" I said. Whatever that was, I was sure I wasn't doing it.

"Dippin'."

"No," I said.

"You gone to A'n'E yet?" She was referring to Assessment and Evaluation.

"What's that?"

"That board thing. It's like PRC."

"No. Have you?" I wouldn't see the Program Review Committee for several weeks.

"No. I jus' got out of R'n'O, too."

"What are you in for?" I asked, trying not to sound like the late show.

"Aggravatin' a battery," she replied with a smile.

"Aggravating a battery?" I thought to myself, stifling a hysterical laugh.

She turned back to the other inmates at the table. They were talking about things like "MR" (mandatory release dates) and "kites" (illegal letters passed from inmate to inmate). "TLU" stood for Temporary Lock Up. "Seg" was short for Adjustment Segregation. The jargon reminded me of *Clockwork Orange*.

My cell on the third floor of the Addams Housing Unit was small, with a desk and a metal bed and a bulletin board on the wall. The old radiator was warm. A switch inside the room controled a radio speaker that played country and western music.

"I fought the law and the law won ..." someone sang. I turned it off.

The guards enforced a rule that restricted inmates from sitting on their beds with the bedspread on. If you wanted to sit on your bed, you'd have to unmake it first. But there was another rule that prevented you from leaving your cell without the bed made. We made and unmade the beds all day.

A small, porcelain pot, sort of like an old-fashioned chamber pot, with a lid served as a toilet inside the cell, but I could not force myself to use it. It was unconstitutional to lock us down without a real toilet and sink, but that didn't stop anyone. The only alternative was to pound on the cell door and ask to use the main bathroom. Usually, an irritated guard would shout, "Just a minute!" My digestive system was rather consistent, and after I ate a meal, I'd have to use the toilet. However, knocking on your cell door during meals was not allowed. Since the inmates would eat in shifts, that meant that I had to wait until the second meal was over with, and those inmates were back in their cells, before I could knock. We were given twenty minutes to eat. Still, I could no more use the porcelain kettle (which everyone called a "jitney") than I'd been able to use a hospital bedpan in the past.

Sometimes the guard never came to let me out at all.

It didn't take long for the vast amount of lesbian activity at the prison to become obvious. Some of the women, I guess, were always that way, but some had husbands at home and converted either out of loneliness or just to play the game. "Sexual conduct" was against the written rules, of course, but they were rarely enforced, which only encouraged the hesitant. It hardly mattered, when so many of the female guards were also gay. I found myself part of a small, repulsed minority. At first I was shocked at the lesbian activity. Now I view it as commonplace.

The trickle of hot water on the third floor at Addams was so meager that it was ludicrous to expect us to take a bath in the fifteen minutes allotted, because we also had to clean the tub in that time. On our floor there were no showers, so the one antiquated tub was our only choice. Cool water would initially drip out and gradually accelerate into a pathetic, lukewarm dribble. I thought something was wrong with the faucet the first time, and summoned the guard. She assured me the faucets had always been like that. The water was very hard and the pipes were choked with lime deposits.

Five of us were allowed to watch television in a room at the end of the hallway. I looked forward to any type of distraction, even an inane sitcom. We sat on stiff chairs facing the television set, but I could barely hear the program over the commands of the guard.

"Sit with both feet on the floor, ladies! You can't put one foot up like that! No talking! Face the front." She sat at a desk, a few feet away. "Turn the TV down! Who turned that volume up?" Despite her determined vigil, two of the women managed to kiss whenever she turned to answer the phone.

Just as I grew interested in a movie, television time was over and we were ordered to return to our cells.

Several women out "in population" looked as though they belonged at a mental institution. One walked around talking to herself and laughing at nothing. Another was so high on Thorazine that she drooled on herself, staggering like a zombie. They frightened me. I was afraid I'd get to be like that.

There were small fights between inmates occasionally, but most were easily suppressed due to the threat of "Program Segregation," or solitary confinement.

The population was a cross-section of society. There were massive, masculine women and some who resembled lost little girls. Some were handicapped, on crutches or in wheelchairs; some had missing limbs. Most inmates I talked to were serving short sentences for forgery or theft, or were drug cases, but the institution also had its share of lifers, like me. There were those convicted of violent crimes, arson, sexual assault, sex crimes against children, and women who'd killed infants. The sentence disparity was unbelievable; some inmates were serving five years for the same crime others got twenty-five years for. It was an appalling environment.

Many of the inmates made continuous efforts to get high, despite the consequences if they were caught. They smuggled in drugs, using every available body cavity, only to be sent to lock up for "dirty urine" later. (One enterprising inmate tied drugs into a balloon, tied string to the balloon and the other end to a tooth, and swallowed the thing, hauling it up safely later.) We were requested to "drop" urine at random, but if an inmate was suspected of contraband, a urine analysis was requested frequently. At that time, the penalty for dirty urine was 360 days in Program Segregation.

Not all women were lucky enough to get visits. The prison was out in the country, and most of the families were too poor to own a car. I was thankful that my family lived only sixty-five miles away, as they were my support system, and in the beginning, I willed myself to live from visit to visit. One woman I knew never got visits, because her parents lived out of state. She was convicted of "homicide by intoxicated use of a motor vehicle," and was given five years. I remembered Marylisa's former boyfriend, Jeff, who'd received probation for the same offense.

It was an early spring, unusually warm. I was moved into an eight-by-fourteen-foot cell in the maximum security building called Neprud Housing Unit, where I was lucky enough to be blessed with a heterosexual roommate named Laura Zunker. We discovered we were from the same neighborhood, and a friendship developed quickly. Because we were convicted at the same time and we had never been incarcerated before, we shared the same feelings—the horror, the regret, the despair and the anger.

It was wonderful to talk to someone intelligent again. Her childhood experiences were similar to mine, and she empathized with the "culture shock" I was trying to deal with. We were both exhausted. She was serving a three-year sentence for embezzlement.

Three years! It seemed like a day.

The cell we shared was equipped with a toilet—the prison had started to install them after several inmates filed a lawsuit—but I still found it difficult to use one in such close quarters. I was especially self-conscious about the odor, since the cell was so tiny that it was immediately noticeable. Ventilation was inadequate, because the windows were barred on the outside and almost inaccessible due to a locked, mesh grate on the inside. The same stops prevented us from opening the window more than a few inches, even after tediously picking them open with a pair of tweezers pushed through the grate. Greasy smells from the prison kitchen directly below us routinely wafted in. Our only view was a patch of scraggly apple trees, leafless and skeletal.

Room searches and inspection made it mandatory to maintain order and cleanliness in the tiny cell. Cleaning was stressed obsessively, which seemed to indicate that either the female domestic role was being inculcated or the prison staff was anal-compulsive.

One afternoon, Laura and I returned to our cell to find all our drawers overturned. The two boxes we were allowed to store under the bunk beds had also been emptied. It looked like a tornado had struck the room. I was hurt to see that most of the lead in my pencils was broken. Our bedding was undone and thrown about. My clothes were scattered.

The sergeant had left us a note designed to make us feel like naughty children: "You should know better than to have nametags missing from your clothes and dustballs under your bed! Consider this a warning. The next time, you'll both receive Conduct Reports." A Conduct Report results in loss of privileges, or even in banishment to the hole, to segregation. Later, I found out that she had bragged to the other guards about her room search, saying that she intended to show me how "celebrities" were treated at Taycheedah.

Visits were unbearably painful. It was wonderful to see my parents and Fred for the allotted time, but brutal when they had to leave. In those years, visits were held in the prison gym on weekends, and in a classroom and the Harris Housing Unit card room during the week.

I finally got my chance to appear before the Program Review Committee, and I was asked how I wanted to spend my time at the institution. Why did they bother to ask? Lifers weren't allowed anything interesting. I'd heard about several school programs from my social worker and asked if I could take some classes. I was told, in typical corrections jargon, "Based on your sentence structure, you are not an appropriate candidate for educational rehabilitation." One of the committee members said it would be pointless to take a two-year school program and then "sit around for ten years." What was I supposed to do instead? I was told that I could work in the prison kitchen, the laundry, or in cleaning, called "Homecare." Homecare inmates were called "Environmental Specialists."

Cleaning, cooking or doing laundry? Couldn't they get a little more "female"? The prisons for men had programs like welding, woodworking, metal furniture, industries, auto-body work and mechanics.

I wound up in the steamy prison kitchen, peeling potatoes and scrubbing pots and pans for fourteen cents an hour.

Laura and I talked one night, both of us in our beds, in the dark. I had the top bunk.

"It's the strangest thing," I said wistfully, "but I was peeling potatoes over some newspapers today, and the smell of that suddenly reminded me of home so much. Does that happen to you?"

"Of course," she said. "I really miss the simple things. Being able to answer a telephone ..."

"Driving a car."

"Raiding a refrigerator!"

"Or sitting outside at night. I used to love sitting on the front porch on a fragrant summer night ... lilacs. The wind chimes singing in the breeze, the crickets ..."

"Or the feel of money in your hand!" Any cash we received was deposited directly into our accounts by the Business Office. Money transactions were completed with the use of "money transmittals" written in triplicate.

■   ■   ■

But those things weren't the worst. Sure, we missed them. We missed them, and love and sex and walking to the corner store to buy a popsicle. But as I told you at the start of my story, it was the utter lack of privacy that hurt the most. Privacy! To hold some thing, some thought, private! To be utterly vulnerable to the pettiest bureaucrats—that's what hurt most. To have our love letters read, our every moment "authorized," our property and our bodies open to inspection and scrutiny. God! A world without strip-searches, walkie-talkies blaring in the night, the heavy footsteps of the guards, the hourly flash of light through the bars. Privacy! Without it there is nothing, no person, no individual, no Me.

■　　■　　■

One night I was watching the news from a nearby town and heard that a triple murder and suicide had occurred. A man had shot and killed his wife and children, and then himself. There were problems with a pending divorce action and the visitation rights were said to have upset him greatly. There was a time when I found stories like that mind-boggling. Now, after so many months of persecution, I could understand at least the intensity, if not the action.

I thought of suicide again, often.

I think it was only Mike Levine, the psychologist at Taycheedah, who got me through it. Once he said to me, "I will take you and put you under a cold shower until you change your mind and keep you there, keep you there forever if I have to. I'll hold you there until you change your mind!" He would have, too.

Well, after three years Mike Levine left too. Pressure got to him. But I'll always be grateful for his help.

I was given my first Conduct Report from a female guard. I was in the main building, called Simpson Hall, when I received a "white pass" from the Education Office, summoning me to the other side of the building. An enclosed breezeway separated the two halves of the building. I was required, I learned later, to report to the Control Center with my white pass and obtain a blue pass. Instead, I arrived at my destination with the white pass, and was promptly charged with Unauthorized Movement Within the Institution.

A verbal reprimand was given to me by one Lieutenant Sheridan. She was aunt to Officer Sheridan, one of the guards. Her ex-husband was the Recreation Director. Nepotism among state employees was common, and almost always worked to the inmate's disadvantage. For example, if Officer Kahill "wrote me up," the Conduct Report would be reviewed, for its validity, by a lieutenant. But that might be Lieutenant Kahill, her sister.

Laura and I were both moved to the medium security housing unit, named Harris. We shared a cell with two other women, both black. One suffered from epilepsy, and the other was very pregnant.

There was racial tension everywhere. In the prison kitchens it hung over everyone like a death threat. The other inmates turned simple personality conflicts into an issue of color. Tempers were quick in the steamy heat of the work area, and I kept a worried eye on the paring knives and vegetable peelers. We had only one supervisor in a four-room work area. I left work each day exhausted from the tension and stress. We were strip-searched occasionally, to control food theft, or if a knife was missing. Eight hours usually passed like twenty-four.

I always remained silent, even when anger swelled up in me, even when a co-worker yelled at me, "Honky white trash bitch!" I had a rack of cups thrown at me once. I was constantly sick, sick of the purposeless hate and resentment.

In my cell, I would read or sketch, to relax. I read Marx, Lenin, Dostoevsky, Hobbes and Paine. I read Quine, Nietzsche and Freud. Women escaped, went to lock-up for contraband, and were moved in and out of that cell. It felt like living in Grand Central Station. I never knew when some of my stamps or instant coffee would be stolen, as they often were. With three cellmates, one can always blame the others. More than once, a gay inmate was moved into the cell, which made me very uncomfortable because of their aggressive attitude. They were nothing like my gay friends on the street, but along the same vein, the black inmates were nothing like my black friends in Milwaukee, either.

Emotions that I had bottled up inside me for years now flowed uncontrollably. I began to burst into tears at the least little thing. With three cellmates, privacy was impossible.

I tried to be brave, knowing that people in the past had survived worse fates, but I was terrified that I would die and be buried in Taycheedah. I had never experienced anything like it in my life.

■   ■   ■

A friend had mailed me a collection of *Milwaukee Journal* articles describing Taycheedah when I was convicted. They portrayed the place to which I was sent (the place that strip-searched its inmates, that had stinking buckets instead of toilets, that was riddled with racial hatred, violence, madness and petty vindictiveness among the guards) as akin to a "country club or small, private college," because of the "quaint old buildings that housed the residents, with beautiful, mani-cured lawns and luscious surroundings." The college image was fur-thered by the names of the housing units—Addams, Harris and Neprud Halls—and the administrative building, named Simpson Hall after a former warden. In a system literally riddled with euphemisms, cells were called "rooms," prisoners were called "residents," and the mess hall was called a "dining room." Staff always addressed a group of inmates as "ladies," which I bitterly resented.

In some of these pieces the warden emphasized the wonderful programs and explained that the inmates had their choice of jobs or free college courses. She was quoted as saying that an inmate's secu-rity classification had absolutely no bearing on the programs available to them, and that Lawrencia Bembenek would be able to participate in anything she was interested in.

Like the descriptions of the "campus," this was far from reality. At that time, lifers weren't allowed off-grounds school, off-grounds work, outdoor maintenance jobs or even college courses. The newspa-pers might just as well have told their readers that inmates were given free trips to Florida. In any case, their readers seemed to believe all this crap. Citizens wrote angry letters, which were duly printed. Out-raged taxpayers complained that convicted felons were coddled and provided with every luxury. One nice woman wrote that she had sym-pathized with my life sentence, until she saw the photographs of Tay-cheedah (which of course showed the portico, not the cells). Another young woman wrote to say that it was so hard for her to work her way through college that she was considering robbing a bank, so that she, too, could go to school free.

I was—again—appalled.

No reporter visited the Segregation Unit on the third floor of Addams; no one ever wrote about the "Adjustment Seg" cages, which were nothing but a metal platform bolted to the gray floor to which women were shackled. There were never photos of the "jitneys." They just showed the pillars in front of Harris, the exercise yard with its birdbath that was named The Sunken Garden and the lush lawns where the inmates were forbidden to go (unless they wanted to be charged with Being In An Unauthorized Area). They wrote about the fucking *flowers*, for God's sake! (Sorry.) And, of course, it's tough to photograph intangibles. You can't photograph the sexism, the inconsistencies, the inequities or the pain of separation from loved ones. That would take imagination on the part of the press.

Norman Mailer said of Jack Henry Abbott: "He even writes, 'It has been my experience that injustice is perhaps the only ... cause of insanity behind bars.'" So much truth! But injustice is another thing you cannot photograph.

Consider the lifer. Lifers have no mandatory release date—unlike other inmates—which means lifers earn no "good time." Good time can be earned by every other inmate, and if nothing else is a convenient management device. For lifers, however, good behavior is a meaningless incentive. At the time, lifers had to remain in maximum security for seven and a half years, which means no furloughs, no early release program, no off-grounds work or school, no halfway house and no work programs—like inmate driver or outdoor maintenance. At other institutions, male lifers could earn a transfer to the camp system—but there wasn't one for women, naturally!

All of this, because we had exercised our right to a jury trial. Because we believed ourselves not guilty (or, in my case, because I *knew* I wasn't guilty). But we had to live side by side with inmates who had committed the exact same crime, or worse, as what they had accused us of—inmates who had declared themselves guilty in order to plea bargain. Those who plea bargained, by virtue of their shorter sentences, were quickly assigned to medium or minimum security and afforded all the benefits denied lifers.

The jurors from my trial were interviewed afterward, and I read how they complained about the long sequestration order that kept them confined to a hotel. It prevented any contact with their families and friends. One woman commented that she had missed her cat terribly over the three weeks.

■   ■   ■

She missed her cat! I flung the paper into the trash. She missed her poor little pussycat.

And she had taken away my life.

19

THE END OF FRED

Let me dispose now of Fred. In a manner of speaking.

I thought about him a lot those first few months in jail. His behavior, always erratic, began to veer off into the pathological. I was the one in jail, I was the one in that world of long gray corridors, the world governed by the clang of iron gates, but Fred behaved as if he were the one imprisoned, as if his life was the one stolen away.

We seemed to spend most of his visits arguing.

One evening, he told me he'd bought two more stereo speakers for his van.

"Fred! Two speakers weren't good enough? You have to have four?"

"Music is all I have!" he whined. "Everything else has been taken from me—my wife, my kids, my job, my house ... Would you really deny that little bit of enjoyment that music brings me?"

And I used to be swayed by this sort of thing!

"How much did they cost? Probably worth more than your van is worth! What if somebody breaks in again and steals them?"

"No. I bought an alarm."

"How much was that?" I asked, frustrated. I was wearing state-issue clothing to save money, using the toothpaste, tampons and other low-quality supplies that the prison dispensed, while Fred wanted to soothe his aching breast with music.

"Eighty-five dollars," he replied.

I rolled my eyes. "Eighty-five dollars for a car alarm? I'm using a deodorant soap on my face, when I could buy a gentle soap at the canteen, because we agreed to save money! Fred, how could you? How much were the stereo speakers?"

"I need something for myself once in a while!" he argued. "I have to think of myself! After all—I'm in prison, too!"

To this outrageous remark, the only appropriate comment was silence. My parents, who were there, simply stared in disbelief.

■　　■　　■

It wasn't long before my parents suggested that we split up the visits, so that Fred could see me alone. They were becoming uncomfortable with the frequency of our disagreements. But this only presented a new problem.

As I suspected, the three of them were not living together under the most harmonious conditions. Whenever my parents came to see me without Fred, I would hear about his misdeeds. He was spending money on other frivolities—personalized stationery, new business cards. He'd hired a new lawyer to represent him in the custody matter. He subscribed to several needless magazines and papers.

Both my friends and my parents described Fred using identical adjectives: evasive, inconsistent, unreasonable, erratic. Everyone said he eavesdropped. He interrupted. He demanded to be the center of attention, and ended up being obnoxious.

I really needed this.

And they didn't tell me everything—how he was staying out all night with the family car, running up huge phone bills by calling Florida and charging all his building materials to my dad's account. They kept this from me initially, feeling that I had enough stress to deal with.

Fred came to visit one afternoon with news that he'd been accepted in Florida for a police job. He said it would solve the problem of trying to live with my parents. He considered it a "fresh start."

"I've got to build a secure future for us, so that when you win your appeal and get out, we'll be together and you won't have a thing to worry about," he said.

"What about your children?" I asked.

"I can get an extension on the joint custody so we can deal with that litigation later when we're better able to."

Reluctantly, I agreed. Maybe it was a good idea for him to go.

After much bickering about what to take—my stereo, my waterbed, my dog—he finally left. I felt nothing but relief.

Of course, nothing worked. A few days later, I asked him to send me some money—ten or twenty dollars—but none came. His letters were short and sounded forced. When I was finally able to call him, he was drunk. The next time I talked to him, he said he wasn't working at all. He was bored beyond belief and passing the time playing tennis and swimming. I could hardly feel sorry for him.

"What happened to the work you said you had all lined up?" I asked.

"The bottom fell out," he simply said. I was about to demand more explicit details when the officer ordered me to hang up the phone. My ten minutes were up.

Then, despite the promise to wait until fall to visit because of the expense involved, Fred impulsively hopped a plane and appeared at the prison one afternoon.

I stared at him in shock as he entered the visiting room wearing a red T-shirt and a tiny pair of red, satin shorts. His dark tan was intensified by his blond hair, which had grown shaggy and was bleached by the sun. A gold bracelet I'd never seen before glistened on his arm, and he wore new sandals, strolling in as if he'd just walked off the beach with sand still between his toes. I was angry that he'd spent money on a plane ticket after telling me that he wasn't even working in Florida. He had only been gone three weeks.

Of course, he acted crushed that I didn't welcome him with open arms.

This was another of our memorable conversations.

"This is a waste of money," I said.

"I don't think you love me anymore."

"I write to you every single day. Isn't that enough?"

"It's the quality, not the quantity!" Fred said.

"You mean the context?" I asked, unable to follow his thinking.

"Stop trying to use big words with me! I'm not a little kid!"

"What are you talking about? I write to you every day on my break. Still you're not satisfied! What do you want? A sonnet?"

"Don't be sarcastic. You don't give a shit!" he wailed.

"You're insecure and demanding," I said.

"Don't use that cop-out."

"It's not a cop-out. I just don't know what more you want from me."

"It's tough on me out there." He began to snivel. "If I didn't love you," he cried, "I would have divorced you the day you were charged!"

I refused to reply.

"I have to say something to get a response from you," Fred protested. "I don't feel appreciated. You say you write every day but I don't get a letter every day."

"That's because our mail only goes out Monday through Thursday," I said. "I've told you that a million times."

"Are you trying to drive me out of your life? Is that it? Look at me when I'm talking to you."

"Where did you get that gold bracelet?" I asked suddenly.

"It was a gift ..." Fred sputtered. "Laurie! Don't let this place do this to you! Don't let it turn you into a cold person. If this isn't resolved this afternoon, I'm coming back tonight."

"No, you're not. I don't want you using up all my allotted visits for the whole week. My mom and dad are supposed to see me tomorrow."

"Who means more to you? Your parents or me?"

"Don't ask me that, because you won't like the answer," I replied.

"Then give me that wedding band, right now."

"No!" I said, jerking my hand away. "I honestly don't know what you want from me."

"So you're saying that the responsibility of this marriage is all mine? That none of this is your fault?"

"Fault and responsibility are two different issues," I said.

"Don't split hairs!"

"Fuck this! I don't even want to argue anymore."

There was a silence. Tears rolled down my face. The visiting-room guard was getting an earful. The officer sipped her coffee.

"It's too bad," Fred said dramatically. "I could have loved you so much." He stood up, kissed the side of my head and walked out.

A month later, more problems developed. Fred began to lie to me about our savings. I thought he had half of his pension—about six thousand dollars—in the bank. In addition to that, he told me that he and I had made about five thousand dollars from the remodeling jobs. He'd even shown my dad one of the checks he received. He told my mom one of his life insurance policies had matured to the tune of over ten grand. He had also organized a benefit marathon run after I was convicted, from Milwaukee to Taycheedah, where he'd collected several thousand, according to a newspaper article. My dad had worked with him on several different jobs. I talked to Fred one last time on the telephone and asked him to send my mom and dad some money for their hospital bills.

Fred told me he had no money.

"I'm sorry, but I'm not going to send your mom and dad my last fifty dollars."

"What? What happened to all of our money?"

"Bills."

"What bills?"

"Oh, you know—phone bills, electricity, gas, food."

"What about that insurance policy you told me about? You said you were going to get twelve thousand dollars from that."

"Oh, that! That was all a big mistake! That was my father's policy! The company made a mistake, because I'm a Junior. The wrong birth date showed up on the printout and they realized their mistake." I hung up on him.

My parents recounted more money troubles. "When he left for Florida, Fred signed a few of his personal checks and told us to pay for the lumber bills and the phone calls to Florida he made on our phone," my dad told me. "Then the checks started to bounce. I wrote him a letter, and he replied, saying that he had closed that account at the bank! I don't understand!"

"I do," I sighed. "I just realized he forged my name on our income tax forms, and the refund check. He filed jointly. That required my signature! I'm also getting bills because he's using my credit card and not paying."

My mom and dad looked at one another.

"We didn't want to tell you this," my mother said. "We felt you had enough to deal with. But when Fred was living with us, he was borrowing our car frequently, and staying out all night. We think he has a girlfriend." She paused. "There's something else. A friend of yours named Ken called me. Fred bought a handgun from him for three hundred dollars. Fred promised to pay him as soon as he could, but four months went by. Ken wrote Fred, but he never wrote back. I guess Ken is thinking of reporting that gun as stolen."

"Fred should be able to pay Ken now. He got that new job ..."

"What new job? He told your father and me that he didn't get the job!"

The guard announced that visiting time was over.

It wasn't long before the man with "no money" spent another three hundred dollars and flew to Milwaukee again. His brother's girlfriend, Marylisa, wrote to me and told me that he'd stopped by. Later, he met them at a bar with an eighteen-year-old girl on his arm.

He moved all of his belongings out of my mom and dad's house and told them he was staying with his parents. When I placed a phone call to his father's house, his dad didn't even know Fred was in town.

The guard distributed the mail. A letter from my husband simply read: "Good luck. Goodbye."

The man who told the newspapers, radio and television stations that he would "wait for me forever" couldn't even wait six months. I was numb. I felt nothing. I tore up his letters, one by one, scattering the pieces. His smell lingered on my fingers.

I sat down at my small desk and began to write to my lawyer. Then I saw that in the upper left-hand corner of the envelope, instead of writing my correct return address, the prison, I'd written my old home address on Taylor Avenue.

That was when I started to weep in earnest.

■   ■   ■

Fred was gone. I'd met him and married him in a time of despair. I thought I loved him, once—I did love him, once. Then his jealousies and his lies enmeshed me.

He went on national television not long ago to say he was convinced I had, indeed, committed the murder. I was a cold, hard bitch, he said.

I thought of the tears that had fallen, the many, many tears, and felt only sadness.

I couldn't forget, in the end, that it was his testimony that put me here.

20

A NATION OF INMATES

When I first got to Taycheedah I was depressed, but I was also scared, freaked out. As a result, I became totally obsequious, fawningly servile, super-obedient. So, if I eventually became a super-litigious jailhouse superlawyer, they had it coming. They made me what I am today, and I hope they're happy.

As the years passed, I got more and more angry, and more determined to force them to comply with their own regulations. They were breaking so many rules and laws, so many federal standards! There was so much illegal inequity that often I used to think, Wait a minute, they've got the wrong people behind bars! In the end, it was the only sense of autonomy I could find anywhere, having that little bit of legal leverage, the authority to make them comply with their own directives and force them to court.

As the years passed, I grew more mature and more angry, and my anger had to be channeled into constructive causes, positive outlets. It's interesting how people's responses to incarceration will differ. You get radical. You find your best friends sometimes doing some really weird things. In my case, I became a little obsessive about things like exercise, which I suppose was relatively harmless. I also moved about as far left politically as I could. Eventually, though, I found out there's no black and white in the real world. In prison, you don't know that. In that artificial world, everything is black and white, and extreme positions are normal.

Taycheedah was in many ways an archaic facility when I first got there. There was no running water or plumbing in the cells. All this was quite unconstitutional. But the female prison population is more passive than the male—it's their socialization, I guess—and there are fewer of them. In any case, they don't often riot and aren't as violent, so of course they aren't taken seriously.

The women seemed to me to be living under eighteenth-century conditions.

For years the prison had been under a federal court order to install toilets, and they'd just ignored it. No money, they said. Eventually they were installed, in 1984, and they shuffled us about from cell to cell while they put them in.

When I got there, we were allowed only two ten-minute phone calls a month. Requests for calls had to be submitted seventy-two hours in advance, on paper, and we could only call people who were on our Visitors List. Calls had to be made from the sergeant's office, and the guards would insist on doing the dialing themselves. What a waste of time! It was preposterous! In any case, you didn't want to talk to people you got visits from; you wanted to talk to your sister in California, people you never saw in person. Our Visitors List was limited to twelve adults, and we didn't dare waste spaces on people who wouldn't visit.

Well, when I found out that the men had phones in their prison—phones they could use themselves whenever they wanted—you never saw a complaint written up so fast! It was such a blatant inequity that they didn't even want to risk a judicial review, so they simply installed them. In the meantime, though, I'd lost contact with many people, many good friends.

At that time I had made one really good friend—I guess she's still my best friend—named Kathy Braun. Kathy and I were lifers who shared the same socio-economic background. She's ten years older than me, but she's from Milwaukee, so we had a few people in common and I felt comfortable with her. I always felt she was an island of sanity in a sea of madness.

Hers was a typical Milwaukee case. She got a life sentence for being party to a crime, first-degree murder. She'd merely been standing in the room with her husband and the actual killer, the man who pulled the trigger. This man, who later dumped the body in the Milwaukee River, turned State's Evidence against both of them and didn't do a single day in jail. He was given immunity in exchange for his testimony. And his was a premeditated first-degree murder! Kathy was defended by the best Milwaukee talent, James Shellow, and her parents had money, but it didn't help.

Kathy's husband plea bargained and is now out on the streets with their kids. She got life.

Is it any wonder that we lifers are cynical about the justice system?

We tried for a long time to share a cell. There is a long and tedious process you have to go through to get the cellmate you want. You fill out a request form, and then the other person fills one out. Eventually, if you're lucky, you get put on a list to be moved. But of course no one can be moved until there's an empty bed. So it took a while.

While we were waiting, we were both living in the Neprud Housing Unit. My cellmate at the time was finishing a drug treatment program ... I think. As I've said, it's like Grand Central Station in there. All these inmates with piddly little eighteen-month sentences come and go and they use your things and break your stuff and steal from you—of course, they don't want to *buy* anything because they're not going to be there long enough to really justify spending the money. Whenever one of these people moves in with a lifer, it's always, "Can I watch your TV? Use your blow-dryer and your typewriter?" They break things and then they leave. That's why lifers like to share cells.

Kathy had been convicted in the '70s. She escaped for seven and a half years and got brought back to Taycheedah in 1983. We met in one of the classes—we were both taking a program they called PREP, which led to university credit associate degrees. I was the first lifer to get approved for that, after a struggle.

Finally, my cellmate was transferred to a halfway house, and Kathy and I moved in together.

Our cell, our "room," was tiny. One corner was sectioned off for a sink and a toilet. Radiators and other hot pipes prevented furniture placement in some areas. There were bunk beds and two desks crammed into sixty square feet, but we were happy. We didn't have to worry anymore about roommates coming and going.

We thought.

One day maintenance people knocked on the door. They had instructions to move a third bed in. They agreed it looked screwy, but they had their orders. They put a third bed in there, and in came a third body.

I was convinced there was something wrong. Federal standards require so many square feet per prisoner. I wrote to the superintendent, the warden. I pointed out that the cell next door was much bigger yet contained only two people. I thought perhaps they'd got the two cells switched on some list.

But, of course, authority hates to admit error. The superintendent wrote back: No, you're wrong and we're right.

Kathy used the Inmate Complaint System. This provides a sort of ombudsman, who can deal with less important complaints, so that the superintendent doesn't have to suffer through too many judicial reviews.

The Inmate Complaint Investigator had a neutral party re-measure the room, and found, of course, that we were right.

The superintendent wrote back, acknowledging the mistake but refusing to move the bed out. It was a somewhat hollow victory.

That was the superintendent's worst mistake. As a result of her being stubborn over this square-foot issue, we started what I think is the biggest women's class-action in the history of Wisconsin—and it's still going on.

I went to the prison's meager library and read up on as much case law on overcrowding as I could. I didn't want to do anything unless it was well researched. I was looking for federally mandated standards. I found there were many; a number of federal cases had been decided. The most liberal judge decreed that 120 feet per inmate was the minimum acceptable standard. The strictest judge required at least 60 square feet per person. We had three people in 60 square feet! Taycheedah had a rated capacity of 126 inmates, but of course they paid no attention to the legal limits. The population went up to 287; we were being stacked up like sardines.

I found out how to file a federal class-action suit from "guerrilla law manuals," more or less like self-help litigation manuals. And of course you network with other inmates and learn what you have to learn. We had a great case. They couldn't lie about the number of bodies or the number of cells, and so it was obvious they had a population way over the rated limit. Kathy and I and one other person got affidavits from everybody we could. We talked about the plumbing breaking down because of overuse, about the problems of secondhand smoke, about the violence levels going up because of the overcrowding.

Prisoners don't have a constitutional right to rehabilitation, but they do have a right to live in conditions that are not "degenerative." Eventually I filed a motion for court-appointed counsel with a brief in support, and we got lucky. The Federal Court gave us a wonderful lawyer named Diane Sykes. She was a godsend, a feminist, interested in the case and a total professional.

It felt so good to force them to grit their teeth and lose. It was therapeutic for me to direct my anger toward something productive.

This is one of the things outsiders can't understand about prison, this tightly wound anger. It's one of the great dangers of being locked up. When you're in a tiny cell like that, twenty-four hours a day, with total strangers coming from opposite backgrounds, the result can be bloodshed.

People read in the papers how one inmate killed another because he used his toothbrush, and they write these people off as animals, as violent crazies. They don't understand the long history of petty aggravations that took this person to the breaking point. I felt myself on the edge many times. Your self-control has to be phenomenal; you have to keep in mind always that you're only hurting yourself by reacting.

A prison is like a little community in itself; the jail has its own little jail, and if you commit an offense, fighting or whatever, the police come and they handcuff you and they take you to the hole, down to this building called Program Segregation. You can go to Seg for 360 days. This means a year of total isolation, twenty-three-hour-a-day cell time, one visit a week, no property. They hold that over your head all the time, until the threat of going to Seg is worse than the actuality of it. I did go to Seg lockup once, for refusing to shovel snow at 5:00 AM, and when I got there I thought, well, this isn't so bad! It wasn't that much worse than being in jail in the first place!

This was a bleak period for me. I was between lawyers then. I didn't have any appeals going. And then there came another setback.

I was studying in the Pilot Re-Entry Program, needing only six credits to graduate and get my associate of arts degree, when they took the program "off grounds," meaning they would henceforth hold classes elsewhere. There are fewer women inmates in the prison system, and they decided to hold classes in the men's institution. Because I was a lifer and wasn't allowed off grounds, I was cut off from my courses. The program review committee wouldn't approve me or Kathy.

Two full semesters went by before I was able to win a fight to get classes back. During that time I plugged into a data-entry program that was in reality nothing more than a secretarial course, learning to be a typist ... A typical female kind of thing, though better than peeling potatoes.

Eventually, they brought the classes back, and I graduated with a degree from the University of Wisconsin–Fond du Lac.

My mom and dad have a picture of me in my cap and gown. I'm standing with them, and they look so proud! I was the first lifer to be approved for the program, and the first to graduate.

This is what I said in my graduation speech, on July 31, 1986:

> "PREP gave me goals, when being warehoused seemed real useless. It changed my focus and allowed me to survive. The very process by which I was able to respond to

the challenge of the program constituted an exercise in freedom. I had to take responsibility—responsibility for interpreting, analyzing and studying. Like all of us here today, I had to practice self-discipline in meeting deadlines, completing assignments, accepting views different from mine.

"Accepting that responsibility is a choice. Because it's a choice, it's also an exercise in freedom. There is virtually no other aspect of our lives in prison where we are required, much less permitted, to assume such responsibility ...

"... Every semester was interrupted by bad news: either an appeal getting denied, or a family member in the hospital, or another appeal being denied. Not that 'free' students don't have problems, but I believe they have many more alternatives than inmate students. Come on! They aren't strip searched on the way to graduation! And they aren't discouraged by the prevailing attitude that inmates don't deserve a free college education—especially women! Especially lifers!

"... With all that to cope with, PREP was the only way for me to keep my sanity. It provided pathways to the power of knowledge that everyone wants—self-awareness, greater clarity, a sense of place in life. PREP offers the opportunity to realize that you can abandon negative patterns for positive choices! Embrace the risk of self-change! Comprehension is satisfaction ..."

All this seems hopelessly naive now. But I meant it. PREP helped me keep sane.

After PREP I went into a program called ACCESS and worked towards a Bachelor of Arts degree in humanities from the University of Wisconsin–Parkside. ACCESS is a quasi correspondence-course arrangement. It's not for prisoners only, but any non-traditional students. It's a four-year program. You must already have sixty credits to be eligible for ACCESS.

The co-ordinator was a terrific woman named Frances Kavenik, who actually came out to the prison once every six weeks, all the way from Kenosha. In my senior year I wrote papers ranging from an extensive analysis of perestroika, through toxic tort litigation and marine pollution to—my best project—a huge paper on recidivism. After all, I had the perfect opportunity to do primary research!

A cellmate, Sherry, and I started a prison newspaper for inmates called *Inmate Output*. The first issue came out in November 1983. It looked amateur, but I hope its standard of journalism was better than I'd been used to seeing in the metropolitan papers.

I was also a very active member of the Task Force on Women in the Criminal Justice System for almost nine years. The Task Force made recommendations to the Governor's Advisory Council on the Female Offender and was chaired by an extremely dedicated, competent and intelligent lawyer named Victoria McCandless. Vicky is a super person that I admire.

So I survived. After a few years we got several lifers interested in the battered old tennis court on the grounds. We weren't Wimbleton, but a group of us got really serious about tennis, playing as often as we could.

Keep in mind the insurmountable odds you have to go through just to get from point A to point B in prison, the small things most people take for granted. We had to fight for everything. We were given privileges little by little, and given them only because we raised parity issues, because we made—quite literally—a federal case out of it.

Lifers have to work hard for everything. And we get angry when some little clown walks in with a two-year sentence and ruins everything. It happens over and over.

An example: we fought for months for the simple privilege of being allowed fresh fruit from our visitors (if I ever see another can of fruit cocktail again I'll scream). We were *starved* for fresh fruit. Finally, we were grudgingly given permission. But some short-term idiot got the bright idea of injecting oranges with vodka. They thought it was so funny! Of course, the warden's response was to cancel the privilege. They messed it up for everybody, as usual.

We lifers felt the need to make the place as tolerable as we could. Kathy had two kids from a previous marriage, and two other little boys while she was on the run. So she became involved in a program to cheer up the playground where the kids played during visits. Some inmates volunteered countless hours to sit behind the concession stand in the visitors area selling snacks and chips; they bought playground equipment with the proceeds. True, all the profits essentially went back into the institution, and we took some flak for that, but it was for the children we did it. I painted some wall murals for the kids, and I don't regret it. The concession stand project, incidentally, was dissolved when a short-timer was busted stealing from the profits. Yet another example of one person ruining it for everyone.

■   ■   ■

I used poetry as a release. When every aspect of your life is open to scrutiny, you can't keep a diary—it would just get stolen or confiscated. Cellmates are probably going to read it and the guards certainly will. I loved the obliqueness of poetry, the way images could be powerful and allusive and hidden all at the same time. The real meaning would be known only to me. So if there was an issue that wouldn't let go, I'd open the chambers of my heart a little and let the anger simmer in my head for a while until I could sit down and put it down on paper, and then I'd feel better.

This is one of my poems, written in late 1987.

October

It now takes more than one hand

to count all the birthdays I've spent here
Waiting in a dark office one cold morning
I glanced up at tree branches outside
noticing that already they look like
veins stretched skyward
and realized
I can no longer live like this

You would think
that after years of being subjected
to so much dehumanizing
degradation and intrusion, after being
strip-searched while menstruating
        (to the obvious delight of two lesbian guards)
after being forced to use the toilet
in front of many strangers,
after being seized in the middle of the night
to shovel snow or to urinate into a cup—on command

after year upon year of sensory deprivation
        of mental sodomy
of being harassed
blamed
controlled
embarrassed
segregated

confined
humiliated
put-down
accused
criticized
discouraged
threatened and interrogated

you would think
the small punishments could be ignored—
when we are loudly warned
not to let a visitor kiss us again
when we are ordered to do meaningless work
and then lose two days' pay for being late,
when we are helplessly moved from place to place,
when we are denied a package of cookies from home;

but this deathless oppression only grows worse—
becomes more unbearable

I'm tired of wondering
how many fascist assholes read my letters
(and then wonder if they will reach their destination)
of being monitored by cameras
deprived of sex
ruled by a lack of alternatives and the
sound of bells, keys and walkie-talkies.

I can no longer watch the children
outside the fence, crying: "But mommy!
I don't want to say goodbye!"
I have no children, but I feel like that child.
I look quickly away
from the red-eyed women I
don't want to see anymore.
I can't stand the paranoia, the worry and despair.

Sometimes of late
it feels as though I could explode;
but then They would win.
I would trade only my poignant reality

for psychotropic drugs and paper gowns.
So I gather up another armful of resistance
and go on
for now.

■   ■   ■

I did a lot of writing, then. I did a piece I called "Soul Tattoos" for a place called Theater X in Milwaukee, a small place that did experimental performance art. It got some reviews, too. One called it somewhat self-indulgent, but mostly they got what I wanted to say. I used it to attack the issue of how the media treats a female defendant. I got a lot off my chest, too; I was so sick of the myths that surrounded me and my case, the whole "killer bunny" thing.

And there were strange things happening! Christine Schultz's family sued me for three million dollars, did you know that? And Don Eisenberg's firm sued me for thirty-eight thousand dollars in a fee dispute. Imagine! So I declared bankruptcy. I was earning seventeen cents an hour in prison. Everyone wanted something from me.

My friends and family kept me going. Some of them visited me for years. Some still do. But others, inevitably, moved on. You can't fight psychic distancing with long-distance calls, and sometimes I struggled with myself not to blame them. They have lives to live, years pass, they get older, they take on other responsibilities.

Over the years, people die. Because I was in prison, I would find out from a letter or a phone call, but I couldn't be there to share in the grieving process, so to me these people were still alive. I was afraid to scratch them from my address book; it felt like killing so much memory, like a willful destruction of a life lived so long before.

I made new friends along the way. I made a lot of good friends in prison. But it's hard to know whether we were close only because we shared so much so fast; on the outside, I don't think prison friendships would last.

Misery loves company, I suppose.

If there's one thing I'm now sure of, it's that the way the system is set up, you're insane if you don't plea bargain. If I'd done so, I'd be out by now. So what if you didn't do it, if you're not guilty? Pleading innocent only keeps you in jail. Those who are guilty get out more quickly; because they know they're guilty, they have no hesitation in plea bargaining. They therefore draw ten years or less and they're out. There you have it—the most guilty people are the ones doing less time.

Pleading not guilty is an affirmation of belief in the system, believing that justice will prevail. No one who has been where I have been believes any such thing. Raw injustice happened to me. It has happened to so many of my friends.

I ask myself now, would this question of guilt or innocence matter any more after twenty, thirty, forty years in jail? Would anyone care?

My answer is, No.

I counsel anyone going into the system—plea bargain for your own sanity.

So what if you didn't do it? No one will believe what you say anyway. Freedom is the bottom line. After a third of your life in prison, you'd do anything to be free. And if you have to compromise all your principles, well, tough.

But me? I had a naive, ridiculous faith in the system.

21

THE BEMBENEK CIRCUS

*A*mbulance-chasers, sensation-seekers, crazies, the klieg-light vampires of the television wasteland, the riffraff and the lowlife, the ink-stained wretches of what passes these days for the fourth estate, the obsessives and the dogged chasers after elusive Truth—my case seems to attract them all. Why is it that I'm a magnet for all this swirling passion, all these gaudy characters? Why do people either seem to love me or hate me? I don't know. I'm isolated in here, dependent on what people tell me. I just want to be able to go home, but I'm at the center of the Bembenek Circus ...

■ ■ ■

Under Wisconsin law, you have two shots at winning a new trial: either present new evidence or show conflict of interest. For a prisoner, neither is easy. You are dependent on what your lawyers tell you. You have no access to documents. (It wasn't until I was in Canada and my lawyers there gave me a copy of the extradition warrant issued by Wisconsin that I finally saw some of the original police reports in my case.) Lawyers are not crazy about taking advice from a client anyway. Even less so when the jail is hours away by car and the client has to rely entirely on memory. They don't try to make things any easier, do they?

In my case, there was some new evidence. Or, put another way, the original case was starting to unravel.

For example, the medical examiner, Dr. Elaine Samuels, came forward in 1983 to dispute the hair and fiber evidence. She denied absolutely that she'd ever recovered any blond hairs from the body. Because witnesses were sequestered, she hadn't known during the trial that those blond hairs in the police evidence had been attributed to her. She'd read about it only after the conviction. Samuels gave us an affidavit that she had found only hair consistent with the victim, and no "color-processed" (dyed) blond hair at all.

Then, in 1984, Judy Zess recanted her testimony; inconsistencies were pointed out in Fred's alibi; Fred was investigated for three or four instances of perjury; and there were some other things ...

Eisenberg thought the best strategy would be to go directly to the DA, E. Michael McCann, show him the new evidence and ask him to reopen the case. Eisenberg thought there was more than enough to persuade any fair-minded person at least to take another look. The timing wasn't great. McCann was running for a congressional seat at the time and didn't want to do anything controversial. Ironically, nine months went by, McCann lost the election anyway and then announced he wouldn't reopen the case.

After that, Eisenberg decided to file a motion for a new trial. The motion material seemed to be just thrown together. You should have seen this motion! It was a mess. A law student could have done better. He just threw it together and filed this half-baked, stupid thing. And then, a hearing on this motion before Judge Gram was scheduled. Three days prior to the hearing, Don's law license was suspended indefinitely for conflict of interest.

Wonderful timing. A blessing in disguise, I suppose.

I had to scramble to get someone else to represent me and to attempt to withdraw the motion. I was in a complete panic. There were still no phones in the prison at the time; I couldn't persuade the prison staff I needed special dispensation. It was awful. The only thing that saved me was that I was at the time looking into a divorce from Fred who was in Florida, and my divorce lawyer paid me a visit. I told him I urgently needed him to go to court to withdraw my motion for a new trial. He did that for me.

For a new lawyer I hired Thomas Halloran, a Milwaukee attorney.

It takes a new lawyer time to get acquainted with a case, particularly a case as complex as mine. Halloran, however, seemed to me to be a very slow reader. Six months went by. No action. He kept saying he was going to file a new motion, kept saying it, kept saying it ... and more months went by. His marriage broke up, he lost his partners, everything went wrong, every excuse was put forward. Two years later he finally filed the motion, but only because my parents pushed and pushed—this after they'd paid him seventeen thousand dollars.

Two years went by. Two *years*. Nine years and four different lawyers. People wonder how nine years can go by in prison without action! This is how.

Meanwhile, Eisenberg sued me for more money. They tried to garnishee my wages. Good luck, at seventeen cents an hour. He finally ended up in Florida. It must be getting crowded down there.

Then the Joseph Hecht scenario started.

I learned about Hecht from a friend of mine in Madison, a girl I'd gone to grade school with. She sent me some news reports of Hecht's case. She wrote: "This case sounds identical to yours, Laurie. Hecht was a hit man, he fits the description that Sean and Shannon gave, the victim was a cop's ex-wife, the motive was a matter of alimony.... He got into the house, there was no sign of forced entry, he shot the victim in front of her children. He even used the same caliber gun. It was the same MO all around. Maybe you should check into this?"

It did seem almost spooky.

I knew it was a long shot, but it was worth a try. I mean, I was in prison all these years knowing that, since I hadn't killed Christine Schultz, someone else had. I was waiting, hoping, that someone would come forward either to say, Yes I did it, or to say they knew who did it. I was always hoping something would break.

Enter Joe Hecht.

But how to investigate? I could hardly pop up to the men's prison to chat with Hecht. Halloran wasn't at that time up to speed on my case, and Eisenberg was gone. So my friend Bill Roddick, who had helped me so much over the years (he'd written two books on my case, *The Thirteenth Juror* and *After the Verdict*), said he'd see what he could do.

However, Hecht refused to see him, as I'd suspected he would. I'd been in prison long enough to know you don't just talk to anyone who comes by.

At that time, Halloran came up with the bright idea that I should take a polygraph test. Great, I thought. Why now? What will it help? People don't understand that those things cost thousands of dollars and are inadmissible as evidence in court to boot. Why would I want to take one? I had already passed a voice stress analysis that Don had required.

But a prisoner is always suspect. If you refuse, it looks as if you had something to hide. You just can't say no, so I did the damn thing, and passed, of course.

The one thing Halloran did do for me was to dispatch Joseph Broderick, his investigator, to talk to Hecht. And Hecht talked. I guess he was more willing to talk to a lawyer.

Hecht confessed. He said he'd killed Christine Schultz. He told

Broderick. Then he told Halloran. Then he told another attorney they brought in for corroboration. All three times his story was the same.

Was I excited? Of course I was. But I'd been disappointed often enough to preserve some cynicism. After all, I wasn't there. I had to believe what Halloran told me. And Hecht did have one reason for confessing to the case falsely—according to Halloran, he said he was wanted in Texas for another murder, and that state had the death penalty. It could certainly be seen to be in his interest to want to stay in Wisconsin, which didn't.

Still, Broderick set off to attempt to verify Hecht's story.

Everything seemed to pan out. Hecht had been working at a gas station at the time. He said he was allowed only four sick days per year, and took three of the days on May 27, 28 and 29, 1981. Christine was murdered on May 28. Coincidence? His employment records verified his absence, according to Halloran. Hecht said he'd picked up a bag with the gun, a wig and some other stuff in a parking lot behind a carpet store. He described how he'd been told to look inside a stack of giant cardboard tubes used for rolling carpet, and had found the gun in the third tube from the left. Broderick went to check the store. It wasn't a carpet store at all. But when he looked into it, he found that it had indeed been a carpet place in 1981. So that checked out, too.

Hecht said he was paid half in cocaine and half in money. After the murder, he said, he spent a couple of days just partying. He rented a limo and ran it like a taxi, ran it to Chicago and back, partying and doing the cocaine. Broderick said he verified the limo rental. So it all seemed plausible. I don't, of course, know how much of it was true, but it did seem plausible.

One of the puzzles of the case had always been why Christine's legs hadn't been tied. Why bind someone at all if you're planning just to shoot them? Hecht's version of that seemed to make sense. He said he'd been planning to rape her but had been interrupted by noises from the kids' bedroom.

As to who had hired him, he wouldn't say. He had his own bizarre set of scruples. He said his code of ethics wouldn't allow him to snitch. This was consistent with his recent conviction—he would not tell police who hired him in the Madison murder, either.

Still, we thought that with my polygraph, his confession, the deposition from Samuels, Judy Zess' recantation and the other stuff, we had enough for a new trial.

So in we went. Back to the Milwaukee County Courthouse.

And Robert Donahoo, the assistant DA, produced a lunatic convict witness who said Hecht had told him he'd never killed anybody.

As if things weren't bad enough already, Jacob Wissler started to interfere.

■　　■　　■

Jacob Wissler! Where did he come from? Straight from hell. He's an evil, sick man, and he poisons everything he touches.

■　　■　　■

He first came into my life when the *Milwaukee Journal* printed a front page story about me in September 1983. He wrote me a letter. It was a normal enough letter, and we started to correspond. All his early letters were innocuous enough, and interesting in their way. We argued about politics, and I enjoyed that. He was a rightwing Republican conservative, and I blasted every Reagan policy in existence.

He saw me only twice, I believe. I was so distracted. My appeals had yielded up one disappointment after another. Not only was the legal process going badly, but my father almost died of stomach cancer at about that time. Wissler offered to come up and visit me, and I was so down, I was so desperate to see someone, anyone, that I accepted. It was better than no visits at all. My dad was in hospital and my mom couldn't manage the long drive to the prison. Wissler's early letters had been completely rational, and that's how I had communicated with him. Perhaps if I'd been able to talk to him on the phone I could have seen earlier that he wasn't cooking on all four burners. But, because I was filled with grief, I grabbed the chance to have a visit.

So he came to visit. He was just a visitor, not even a friend. I did give him a hug before he left, and said thanks for everything, but it wasn't like a sexual hug, just like you would hug a friend.

Soon, however, it became clear he was utterly obsessed. He claimed to be in love with me. His visit with me, this small contact, built in his mind into something towering, some grand obsession, something sick and twisted and poisonous. He wrote me love letters. Then he told the newspapers he'd sent me gifts and was in love with me. Then he wrote to me and threatened me and my family. He would send me as many as ten letters a day, and hundreds of Western Union telegrams and messages via Federal Express. He also sent copies of all this to my mom and dad, to my lawyers, to Bill Roddick and others, anyone who had anything to do with me.

When I refused to accept his mail, he started sending it anonymously. He even misrepresented himself as an attorney by using envelopes "obtained" from Eisenberg's office.

As I've said, this was happening at a desperately difficult time for me. Wissler was aware of my situation and used it to his advantage. It was obvious he knew a great deal about me and my case, though he always implied that he knew even more. "I hold the keys to your freedom," he would say. He claimed he had tapes that proved my innocence. Don Eisenberg advised me to keep up contact with him— just in case he really had information that would be useful.

What were these "tapes" he was supposed to have? Another product of his imaginings. Finally, my dad had enough, and told him to put up or shut up. Wissler responded by demanding that I first write a letter to him saying how much I cared for him and how much I appreciated his help. Only after getting such a letter would he hand over the tapes to my attorney.

Oh, how powerless I felt! How vulnerable! In order to gain a key to my freedom—*if* such a key existed in the first place—I would have to write to him and gush and thank him and tell him I loved him? In other words, lie? I felt dirty, used. But what could I do? What if he really did have this stuff? The evil man understood my dilemma. He manipulated everyone. I reluctantly wrote the letter he wanted. He responded by returning the letter by the next mail with the words *Fuck You!* scrawled on it. The very next day he began writing romantic letters again, as though nothing had happened. The tapes, of course, never existed.

In the months following, he paid fellow inmates to spy on me. He wanted to know even the most mundane things, like my hairstyle. Any information he had about me gave him the crazy sense that he owned a piece of me. He found out who visited me and harassed them all with calls in the middle of the night. He wanted to cut me off from friends and family, to leave me alone and isolated, so I'd turn to him out of desperation.

He was like having my own personal John F. Hinckley. He was a master of deception and confusion—a scam artist. With him, nothing was the way it seemed, nothing was real.

Through his inmate spies he once "heard" that I was having an affair with the female warden. This ridiculous allegation made him insanely jealous. He even phoned a bomb threat into the institution and was charged and finally arrested.

Where did he get all his money? He had no visible means of support—no nine to five job, no freelance occupation. Did someone hire him to muddy the waters?

Someone, after all, had killed Christine Schultz. Someone was responsible for my conviction. If there was a conspiracy, they could have wanted someone to damage me, and damage my case badly, drive me and my family crazy ... Could he have been hired by the other side? Is that too outlandish? Sometimes an individual can commit acts a government can't.

He once told Bill Roddick that "I hope she never gets out of prison, so the fantasy can continue."

Talk about going through hell! My family didn't need this! I tried everything. At first when he got creepy I responded, and that didn't work. Then I ignored him, and that didn't work. It was only his conviction on the bomb threat charge that finally put a damper on him.

■   ■   ■

Wissler interfered in the Hecht affair, too.

It started when he read that Hecht had confessed to the killing I'd been convicted for. Of course, Wissler couldn't stand it. He immediately threatened me.

"If you refuse to love me I'll pay Hecht hush money to shut up," he said.

I don't know whether he did or not. But he did go to the press and the DA and tell them he'd bribed Hecht to confess in the first place. And that this had been at my urging—that it had been my idea!

When we got to court, Hecht decided to plead the Fifth. Halloran told me that wasn't so bad for our case. Why plead the Fifth unless you have something to hide? But Wissler just wouldn't stop. He wrote letters to Hecht in prison, knowing of course that they'd be read, like all inmate mail. At Donahoo's request, these letters were confiscated by prison guards and tainted my evidence.

Hecht tried to escape before he testified. He almost got away, too, by pulling a gun on two guards who had transported him to a Madison hospital for a doctor's appointment. Or, put another way, he was almost killed, which would have been very convenient for the cops. Too bad for them: he tried to escape across a golf course in Madison, and TV cameras followed the attempt all the way. Wissler, of course, bragged about being involved in Hecht's escape attempt, claiming to have smuggled him the gun.

It was a mess. Halloran was trying to present his motion; Wissler was threatening the judge, threatening Hecht, threatening me; Hecht was trying to escape, then took the Fifth ... What a zoo.

Wissler then changed his tune and bragged that he'd paid Hecht not to testify. But by then he'd so muddied the waters that no one, including the trial judge, knew what to believe.

With Hecht's confession suspect, my chances for a new trial were virtually destroyed.

Wissler is now living and working in the Chicago area and says he doesn't want any publicity!

It wasn't until years later that the rest of the exculpatory evidence began to accumulate.

■ ■ ■

That this evidence did accumulate, and is accumulating still, is due to a lot of people and a tremendous amount of diligent work.

But more than anything, it is due to Ira Robins, my private investigator.

My own personal pitbull.

The persistent, unstoppable, irrepressible, irresistible Ira Robins.

■ ■ ■

Ira Robins has been with me—or I've been with Ira—for so long now I've almost forgotten what life was like "B.I." (Before Ira.)

I first met him through Kathy Braun. He'd done some work in the past for her family, and came to see her in prison concerning her family's company.

I was more or less between lawyers—that is, officially I still had Halloran, but he didn't seem to be actually doing anything.

Ira urged me to hire Attorney Gerry Boyle. He seemed to be a good criminal lawyer. We arranged a meeting, but it didn't go well. He wanted me to agree to questioning under sodium pentathol before he'd agree to represent me pro bono. I was dismayed. For years I had been put in the position of being forced to prove my innocence. Over and over again with every new lawyer, a new lie detector test. If I balked they took it as a sign of guilt. I was weary of it. I'd already taken two lie detector tests—and to what end? They cost me thousands of dollars, were always inadmissible in court and they never got me out of prison. So I thanked Mr. Boyle and said "good-bye."

He walked out, taking his huge belly and perpetual tan with him.

Then Ira hooked up somehow with Marty Kohler and that's how I got Marty as a lawyer.

■　　■　　■

What's motivating Ira? At first, he was interested, and when Ira gets interested he gets tenacious. Oh, is he stubborn! But I saw a turning point in Ira when the assistant DA, Donahoo, tried to make a fool of him, tried to attack his credibility, paint him as some kind of a nutbar. That was a big mistake. Ira began to take my case as a personal challenge after that, to the point of obsession. He lives, eats and breathes this case now. I needed an Ira, and there he was. He'll always have my gratitude for that.

Someone asked him on TV when he'd give up.

"The only way they're going to stop me is to ice me," he said.

That's a very Ira sort of thing to say.

■　　■　　■

Some people say he's fanatical. But oh, how I needed a fanatic, needed someone obsessed! The years went by, the weary years, and time rolled on and people changed; unless you're a victim or a villain or a saint, it's so hard to keep the white heat of anger burning for so many long, tired years ...

■　　■　　■

My good friends were now starting to fade. Even Bill Roddick, bless him, who was such a good friend, who did so much, who did so much to help keep costs down for me and my family, even Bill got to the point where he just gave up. I could see it in Bill about 1985 or so. Finally, the enthusiasm just wasn't there. I could tell even from his conversations. At first he would talk about "when you get out of prison," but then a point came where "when" wasn't said anymore; he seemed resigned to the fact that I'd spend the rest of my years without ever getting out. I found this transformation in him depressing and discouraging, but I never blamed him, even then. He'd just reached burn-out.

Luckily for me, that was just when Ira was getting fired up.

Ira and I have been together so many years now, I know him like

I'd know an old shoe. We've had our differences. He's not the easiest guy to get along with, believe me. He's prickly and quick to temper and has very strong opinions, and he pushes, pushes, pushes. But he's been through so much, he's suffered personally and financially, he's been evicted several times, his bills pile up, the phone gets cut off, he gets bounced from one place to another. The Milwaukee authorities humiliate him when they can. And sure, he complains. Ira is not one to suffer in silence. My parents paid him, I don't know, only about four hundred dollars initially, and every time he gets really hard up he hits them for a couple of hundred more. But he deserved it and deserves it, because he's earned it many times over.

There are friends of his who grow weary of his constant borrowing. They say, Ira, nobody told you to do the Bembenek case full time, you *could* go get a job. But he just can't stop.

I've thought about him a lot. When I escaped and was unable to contact him, I hoped he didn't hate me. I thought, my case was his life, and now that I'm gone he doesn't know whether he'll ever see me again, and maybe he's really crushed ... I didn't *know*. I wanted to call him and I couldn't.

Many people assume he's in love with me. What an easy out! Every time someone's on my side, they diminish it by bringing in sex. It's the easiest way for McCann to discredit a person on my side. "Oh, he's in love with her, what can you expect?" This infuriates me more than anything; it is a last poisonous residue of the "killer bunny" image—men who are on my side must be there because I've ensnared them sexually and not because the evidence of my innocence is overwhelming. I hypnotized them, manipulated and charmed them. From prison yet!

In Ira's case, it's just not true. I've known Ira for years. He visited me socially for a while, but only because it was easier for him to get in that way than through arranging "professional visits." He and I talked about things other than the case, and we came to understand about each other that we're polar opposites.

■   ■   ■

Ira has threatened to quit a million times. He can be a bit of an emotional terrorist, believe me. Every so often he'll say, that's it, I'm gone, I've had enough ... But he never does.

Some people have asked me what he'll do when I do get out of prison. What'll he do when it's all over? And of course I don't know.

If something has become your life, if someone's cause is your life, is your primary motivation just to ... continue it? Could it be that Ira ... wouldn't *want* me out? I hated myself for thinking this way, but hey—I have my paranoid moments after all I've been through.

So I've looked for signs like that. And found nothing.

Nothing. No such signs are there.

I was ashamed of doubting him.

Ira has never, publicly, berated me, unlike my fair-weather friends—Fred and Eisenberg. When they love me, I'm innocent. As soon as an argument ensues, they run to the media to announce my guilt. Ira and I have had our personal arguments, our private disagreements, but he's never repeated anything to the media, he's been utterly loyal, he always defends me.

As I have defended him.

■　　■　　■

Marty Kohler helped me get my case going again through the courts.

By the time I acquired him, I was dead in the water. The storm of publicity had died down; I was in my sixth year in prison, and nothing was happening or seemed about to happen. I felt like I was trapped inside Beckett's play "Waiting for Godot." Kohler took a look at the case and, in his phrase, "it didn't pass the smell test," by which he meant he felt intuitively that my conviction has been wrong. He began to explore what remedies I had left.

I had already tried to get a retrial under the "new evidence" provisions, and that road was now closed. You get only one kick at that can, even if you get even more new evidence. Just in case some court thought differently, Donahoo tried to insist that any such new evidence must have been presented within a year of the trial. Why? Is an old injustice more acceptable than a recent one? He never said. The court ignored him, in any case. And then they denied the motion on other grounds.

I was left with proving a Conflict of Interest. Under federal law, there was a two-part test for conflict. First, you had to prove a conflict existed, and then that the conflict damaged the defense in some way. The state law was much tougher, and better for the defendant: all you had to do was prove the existence of a conflict. The state supreme court had ruled that a lawyer cannot accept money from one suspect to represent another suspect. In other words, you can't represent two suspects in one case.

Fred was paying Don Eisenberg. And clearly Fred had been a suspect.

Kohler asked me how many attorney-client meetings I had had with Eisenberg with Fred in the room. It would be easier, I said, to say how many I had when he wasn't there. He was there for most of them—all but two, I think. Kohler was appalled. He was even more so when I pointed out that most of our meetings had been not in chambers or private spaces but in restaurants and bars.

Kohler also argued that Fred should have kept away for no other reason than that he was an active member of the Milwaukee Police Department. But of course I hadn't known that. Eisenberg hadn't told me. And Fred surely didn't. I thought he was there to help. And he was helpful—there were so many questions Eisenberg asked that I didn't know how to answer, specific things like which child would be the more credible witness? Was there an alarm in the house? It was Fred's house, Fred's kids, Fred's ex-wife—his world. I had no answers.

Marty Kohler seemed pretty good. And it helped that he had an associate lawyer named Ann Reilly, who was a wonderful help. I think women tend to think differently, and can communicate on a different level. I appreciated having her around. She was a caring, compassionate attorney.

Because Eisenberg had been a Wisconsin lawyer, and under Wisconsin law we would only have to prove that a conflict existed, not that it damaged the defendant, we thought we'd developed a compelling case. It should have been enough. No one denied that Fred was a suspect.

Marty filed the motion. We got a good judge, and Marty was pleased until Donahoo objected and pointed out that state law required us to go before the trial court. To my dismay, Donahoo was able to require us to reappear before the original trial judge, Judge Skwierawski.

And it happened again.

We'd been promised two full court days for witnesses, but the motion was fragmented into seventeen different appearances, and the impact of the argument, the logic and the force of it, were utterly diminished.

It was so expensive! We had three expert witnesses who were to testify on my behalf. One was a member of the board of the lawyers' self-regulatory organization, the Board of Attorney's Professional Responsibility; another taught ethics at Marquette Law University.

But we had to pay them, get them together, get them back again, over and over. Eisenberg and Fred flew up from Florida. That motion took months. It was so frustrating.

One of the things we were alleging was a connection between Fred and Horenberger. Fred denied it, but we had evidence that they knew one another, and it was certainly possible that Horenberger was the man who'd actually pulled the trigger that night. We pointed out that according to a MPD written report, one Daniel L. Gilbert had been found near the scene and that Gilbert and Horenberger had later robbed Zess. These are two seriously bad people. So, imagine how I felt one day when the van that brought me to court, handcuffed to a chain around my waist, stopped and the sheriff loaded Horenberger and Gilbert into the van. Wonderful.

My motion was denied, of course.

22

IN THE NICK OF TIME

I met Nick, Dominic Gugliatto, through his sister, Maribeth. She was in Taycheedah, serving a fairly short sentence. When I was doing my Bachelor's degree work I spent every afternoon from one to four in the prison library, and it was there that Maribeth approached me. She knew who I was. She was very friendly and bubbly and we chatted, and we seemed to get along. Later there were press reports that we'd been cellmates (another myth becomes "fact"), but we didn't even live in the same housing unit. She lived in the one I facetiously call "Tara"—it's got big white pillars—and soon afterwards she was transferred to another institution. Anyway, she was pleasant and we got along.

I saw Nick first on a Sunday.

I'm pretty much of a materialist and I don't believe in much hocus-pocus, but those who believe in fate will say something was "meant to be," that you'll meet someone if you are meant to. I do know it was unusual for me to have a Sunday visit. I usually avoided them because during the week, visits are three hours long. They're only two on weekends, and the weekends are more crowded, to boot. But for some reason, I was sitting there this Sunday with a visitor.

We were sitting outside, in a grassy area with picnic tables scattered about, and this guy passed by our table on his way somewhere.

He had on white tennis shorts and a white shirt, like a tennis outfit, and my testosterone radar went off right away.

Oooooh, who's *that!!!*

I watched and saw him sit down at Maribeth's table. There were a number of people at the table, so I didn't know who he was.

Maribeth and I just happened to finish our visits at the same time, and we walked out together.

"Who was the guy in the white shorts?" I asked her.

"That's my brother Nick," she said.

And I said, "Well, is he gay or is he married?" Because, you know, at my age that's all I run into.

"Neither," she said. "And, by the way, he noticed you, too."

I told Maribeth to tell Nick that if he wrote to me, I'd write him back. But he had to write first, to make the first move. I didn't want to seem like the proverbial pathetic, lonely prisoner, because, alas, it was only too true. I had my dignity. I wasn't going to write anybody first.

Maribeth called home and told Nick what I'd said, and he started to write to me, and one thing led to another, as it does in these matters.

I was kind of pleased about it, to tell the truth. I was flattered. And excited, too—I was having fun. Nick asked me to call him, and I did, and then we agreed he should begin visiting, and I put him on my Visitors List, and he started to come up.

Oh, was I surprised! Surprised and delighted that I was, after so many years, still *capable* of feeling happy—that these long-dormant (or long-suppressed) feelings were still there. There was a joyous reawakening going on; I had lived so long in isolation. Ironically, only a few months before I had staunchly, emphatically (and a little defiantly) defended my solo life, my living without a male presence in my life. I'd told Kris Radish of *Wisconsin Woman Magazine* that I had come to the conclusion once and for all that there was no way to have a loving relationship in prison, and that was that.

Well, I'd just finished saying how impossible it was, and here I was. It was ridiculous, but delicious, too.

I had tried to get interested in one man or another over the years—there were a couple of times and a couple of different guys— but it just never worked out. Why? I was in, and they were out. I'd call them and a girl answers the phone, you know—stuff like that inevitably happened. I had adjusted to my small, little life and I was comfortable with it that way, like an old shoe.

In retrospect I can see how I was defending myself from more heartbreak. Maybe I was getting a little warped, I don't know, but I was dealing with it.

I'm certainly not sexually interested in women; after all these years I would know by now.

So I reveled in my new emotional state.

First I grew to like Nick, and then I felt myself falling in love with him. It's a wonderful feeling, a giddy feeling, but ... I was still a prisoner.

I remember one day I was walking back to the housing unit after a visit and through the fence I could see his truck driving away down the highway and I started to panic. I thought, "Oh no, here I go, I don't want to have to yearn for somebody, not here, I don't want to want someone I can't have, I don't want to do this, to put myself through this ..."

In prison, it's a survival trick to try to eliminate from your life all the things you desire, so it doesn't hurt that badly. You put your life on hold, you freeze-frame your feelings, you shut down your heart.

I thought I had done that.

But here I was—my heart hadn't dried up and blown away as dust after all. I was shocked! And delighted. And worried. All my pals noticed a change in me at once. I was a lot more open, a lot happier. I was no longer acting as if I had PMS thirty days a month. I was just a lot ... nicer.

People would say to me, "You must be in love or something," and I would just smile. At the same time I was fighting it because I knew what it would mean. I knew for a lifer, falling in love was ridiculous.

Finally, Nick told me he loved me. I'd been waiting for him to say it first. So then we talked about my future—if I would ever get paroled, and he didn't seem to care about any of that. He asked me to marry him. He'd been hinting that if I got out of prison he was afraid I wouldn't need him anymore; he seemed to need the marriage to make himself feel more secure. So I wasn't really surprised when he popped the question.

When I broached the subject with my mom and dad they were concerned. They didn't want me to marry in a place like that, and we quarreled.

"God, no, don't do this, don't do this to us," my mom said.

"You don't understand," I'd respond. "This is the one little thread of happiness I've had in ten years, and you want to deprive me of it. Why can't you just be glad? Even if this is temporary, it's bringing me happiness now, and that's all you should care about ..."

We were all being unfair, I think. It was difficult.

Prison weddings are strange, of course, a peculiar version of the real thing. I've been to a few. Most prison marriages don't last. The prison system requires that you take counseling if you're contemplating marriage; they want to make sure you know exactly what you're doing, what you're getting involved in.

I argued that I was getting to know Nick in a way that I might not have on the outside. Outside, when you're dating someone, you might go to a bar, or go dancing, or to a movie, but you don't necessarily ever really just sit and talk like you do on visits.

I pointed out that when I married for the first time it was to someone I didn't even know. But when a person visits you in prison three times a week for three hours and you do nothing but talk, with no phones ringing and no TV on, no distractions, you can get to know that person very well. We wrote letters. We phoned every day, and talked. There's more contact than people realize. It was a good argument, anyway.

Well, wrong again.

I now understand that you can't know someone really well until you live with them, until you see them in daily routines, see whether they stay drunk or sober, see them under stress, see how they behave with others. On prison visits, everything's wonderful, everyone puts their best foot forward.

A couple of friends of mine tried to tell me this, but I didn't want to listen. "I don't care," I said. "I might be in prison for the rest of my life, and this is making me happy now." I was also thinking of my parents getting older, and of the burdens they had taken on, and of their weariness. I needed so much help all the time. It was always, "Can you send me this, do this or that for me ..." I thought perhaps a husband could take over some of these small duties, and that would make their lives a little easier.

I had several long talks with my mom and dad. They were being really protective, as usual.

"I know what you're objecting to," I said, "but I have to go on, I have to hang on to something, because I haven't been living, really, I've just been existing, and now I feel I'm alive again."

They thought it over, and it wasn't easy for them. But they liked Nick when they met him. They weren't too happy with the fact that he was divorced with several kids, but then their generation worries more about divorce than mine does.

Nick even offered a prenuptial agreement, whatever I wanted, whatever would make things easier for them. He seemed sincere enough. I thought if he wanted to marry me in prison then he really loved me.

We went ahead, and I bought a wedding dress from a catalogue; we would have been married in the prison chapel, and in the pictures it would have looked just like any other wedding, like any normal wedding. We went ahead on the assumption that my appeal would be denied. If it was denied, we'd get married in prison; if not, we could do it "out there."

■　　■　　■

But while my emotional juices were flowing again, and I was squeez-
ing out increments of happiness like wringing water from a damp
cloth, in the veins of the legal system there ran only acid.

Acid that seemed to eat away at my future.

Again.

They were pinching off avenues of emotional escape, and that's
why I was led to contemplate a real escape.

■   ■   ■

It was a difficult summer.

First, the Wisconsin Department of Corrections arbitrarily
changed the classification of all lifers. This was like tying us down
and beating us on the head with a shovel.

Without warning, they changed the system for lifers retroactively.
It was obscene. It was like Nazi Germany. They went round to all the
institutions, all the camps, seized all the lifers at four in the morning and
took them, in shackles, back to maximum security to be reclassified.

By this time I had a network of other lifers, and it wasn't just me.
We were all in the same boat.

Legislatively, they amended the Wisconsin Administrative Code
to reclassify all lifers into various categories and created subjective
criteria that the institution's review committee would apply to us to
decide how dangerous we were. If the victim of the crime was bound
or sexually assaulted, for example, that would put the lifer in Category
One, which would add about fifty years to her sentence. The one U.S.
Constitutional Right that has always been honored, is the right of a
prisoner to never be arbitrarily incarcerated for longer than whatever
sentence the judge imposed. A person sentenced to five years, for
instance, could never have the term increased to fifteen years. Yet this
was, in effect, what they were doing to us. Category One lifers were
required to spend a minimum of fifteen years in a maximum security
prison, then a number of years in a medium security facility and then a
number of years in a minimum security prison.

We filed a Class Action against this horrid new law, but there was
no hope for me. The light at the end of the tunnel had turned into an
oncoming train.

The reclassification was eventually overturned by a higher court,
but I couldn't know that would happen. At the time I was being told
that I would never get out of prison.

Then we had a lockdown for two weeks.

A lockdown happens when, for reasons best known to themselves, the prison authorities decide to cancel all routines. They "lock down" everyone—lock them into their cells. Meals are brought to cells. No one moves. Nobody goes to work. All recreation is canceled. All study is canceled. The place screeches to a halt. You just wait.

There was no communication. They told us nothing. They brought in drug-sniffing dogs, the whole thing. It was really melodramatic, really stupid. They'd been watching late-night television too much. Everybody felt pushed to the brink.

After the lockdown, they began giving me a particularly hard time in the visitors' room.

You must understand the arbitrary nature of prison authority. They can, in practice, do what they want. You're allowed visits, but if they decide you shouldn't have them, they'll find a way to cancel them. They will fabricate Conduct Reports, make up infractions, change the rules so you can't help but break them, because you have no idea what they are this month, this week, this hour.

There is a rule against sexual conduct anywhere in the institution, of course. There are good reasons for this. The whole issue of consent becomes difficult in prison. If you find two people in bed, well, perhaps they want to be in bed together, but one might just be stronger than the other. If a woman has a strong arm around her neck, she'll be prepared to smile and tell the world she's enjoying it. In order to prevent rapes that result from grotesque power imbalances, prisons try instead to prevent all sexual conduct whatever. So prisoners cannot kiss or hold hands with another prisoner or you risk being charged and thrown into the hole.

Of course, people do it and get away with it, but officially it's prohibited.

This prohibition carries over into the visitors' room. And, depending on the personality of the guard, it can get insanely picayune and hyper-technical. You're allowed to hold hands with your visitor, and when the visitor walks in you're allowed one hug and one kiss. Again, when they leave, one hug and one kiss. This kiss is a fast little smooch, too—no standing there for fifteen minutes.

Naturally, people try to get around the rules. Understand, these are people who have been deprived of sex for three, eight, ten years; when you get a visitor and you're in love, it is only human to want to snuggle, to hug, to touch. Always under the watchful eye of the visitors' room guard.

One particular guard refused to use the common sense and judgment of some of the others, who used to look the other way unless the conduct was utterly outrageous. What's the difference if someone has an arm around a loved one? But the guard watching over us was like a hawk. You couldn't have your hand anywhere, on any part of your visitor's body.

Once Nick had his hand on my back, between my shoulder blades, and the guard said, "Bembenek, that's a warning!"

"What do you mean, that's a warning?" I said. I was genuinely puzzled. A hand on my back, in the middle of a crowd of other people?

"That's Sexual Conduct. Take his hand off your back."

I argued. "Wait a minute! The administrative code does not define 'back' as a sexual part. It defines sexual part very clearly. Breast, buttock, scrotum and vagina—you cannot have your hand on any of those—but I don't think back is defined as a sexual part."

"I'm giving you a warning," she said. "This is going on your card."

I was stupid to argue. You can't win. After two warnings you get a Conduct Report, and then the guards have the power simply to remove a person from your Visitors List.

I warned Nick. I told him how arbitrary they could be, how once they get an idea in their heads they'll never let it go. I had to keep warning him. It was depressing. Here was someone I loved, and I spent so much time saying, "Watch it, don't, don't do that ..." But it's hard for someone who hasn't been in prison to understand. He didn't take it seriously.

One day in the spring (it was still cold enough for me to be wearing long jeans and a denim jacket), the guard saw Nick with his hand on my hip. We must have been goofing around or something, because I don't even remember the incident, and there was certainly nothing sexual about it. But I got a Conduct Report on the incident anyway.

I sent it home to my mother, using it as stationery. It was stupid and petty and mean-spirited. But petty as it was, they gave it to me with both barrels. They denied me the use of the library; they forbade me to use the telephone; they prevented me from playing tennis on the beaten-up old tennis court; I wasn't allowed to jog; I was allowed no recreation at all.

I complained to the superintendent about this. It didn't help, of course. Complaining never helps, but I can't stop myself—the ability and willingness to complain was the only sense of "self" I had left, and I wasn't going to give it up without a struggle.

Complaining about sexual conduct was even more than usually useless. The guards tolerated lesbian behavior. I don't know why exactly—perhaps because lesbians don't get pregnant—but the institution consistently discriminated against heterosexuals.

You think I'm making this up? Not at all. I watched it closely for nine years, and I know.

I pushed and pushed. I wrote to the superintendent: "Why is it that you have lesbian couples visiting, and they're all over one another, kissing and doing this and that, but you don't enforce the rules? Why?"

She wrote back and said: "If you can't conduct yourself in the proper manner I can have your visitor removed from your list."

Great, I thought, now she's threatening to remove someone I'm supposed to get married to next month.

Nick found all this hard to believe.

"Behave," I said. "They're looking for an excuse to remove you from my list."

"They can't do that!" he said.

And I said, "Not in America, right? Maybe we're living in the Soviet Union after all, maybe that's where this prison is ..."

He was offended.

I began to wear a little metal button on my jacket, a likeness of Lenin. After *glasnost* there was this catalogue of all these cool things from Russia. I had a little Red Army button with a hammer and sickle on it. All the other inmates were shocked. *Oh, Bembenek, the Communist!* After that, inmates would come up to me and say, "Who's that?" And I'd say, "Lenin." Puzzled, they'd say, "John?" I'd say, "No! Vladimir!"

■   ■   ■

One of the Last Straws of Summer:

The other disappointment was this: I had worked six years to get my BA—I would be the first female prisoner in Wisconsin to earn a university Bachelor's Degree. After I finished my course work, my professor from Kavenik entered my name on the list of graduates, so the crazy newspapers printed an article about not only getting "first degree" but a "college degree" as well (sick humor). I looked forward to attending graduation with the AA graduates from PREP at the end of July. But as "Bembenek luck" would have it, my prof discovered I neglected one of my BOK (Breadth of Knowledge) requirements for graduation: two years of a foreign language. Still on the list to attend graduation, I hurriedly finished Russian 101 in two months and began Russian 102, working on it eight hours a day.

Kathy tried to cheer me up. "Don't worry about it, Laur," she said. "There are three other PREP students who are currently finishing their summer course, but the warden is letting them go to graduation."

"Yes, but they aren't me," I replied pessimistically.

"Switala will let you go," Kathy said. "And by the way, stand up straight. You're slouching again."

I had begun to walk with my shoulders rounded, hunched over— a physical manifestation of oppression. Show me a round-shouldered prisoner and I'll show you a prisoner doing life.

The warden refused to let me attend graduation. Now that's what I call positive reinforcement for productive behavior.

■   ■   ■

This was the sequence: First, the lifer reclassification. Then the lock-down. Then they blasted me with this punitive action in the visiting room. And, to top it all off, I couldn't attend the graduation ceremony.

"I can't stand this," I told myself. "I can't live like this anymore."

Then my appeal was denied.

That was it. The last hope. The tunnel had caved in completely.

■   ■   ■

I remember a conversation in the visitors' room with Nick.

"Let's say everything fails," he asked. "How much time are we talking about? How long will you still be in?"

"Nick," I said, "I've never tried to mislead you. I've tried to explain. I don't know whether you had stars in your eyes or if you really believed this appeal was going to happen, but I'm telling you, we're in for a long haul. A long, long haul. Lifers have no mandatory release date."

He just ... How to explain where an idea comes from? He thought about it, and I thought about it, and gradually we came to understand that the only way I would ever live again was to go over the wall. It was a mutual decision.

■   ■   ■

It's important that you understand. I didn't just wake up one day and decide to take off, decide that I really wanted to get it off with Nick and hit the road. I'd been desperate for so many years, but there had always been one last chance, one last, slim hope that the system of justice would come to its senses, would understand that a travesty had been perpetrated in the name of the law. Instead, like a strangler in the night, they kept hauling the garrote tighter and tighter until ... until it was breathe, or die.

■   ■   ■

I know there are people saying that I was the one who talked Nick into helping me escape, that I manipulated him, somehow, into going against his judgment. They like to portray me as having this strange sexual allure, as if I can make men do anything I want, as if I am this Svengali-like figure. (You'd be so disappointed! But I guess the truth is really boring.)

I don't know why two lovers planning an escape to freedom wouldn't be just as good a story as a man being sexually hypnotized against his will, but there it is. We just wanted to be together, and we thought of it together. We were in love!

Nick, I think, was a romantic. He wasn't very happy with his life at the time. He'd been working at the same factory for about eleven or twelve years, and the job was going nowhere. His ex-wife was giving him problems. He saw this, I think, as a chance to start all over again. It was a romantic thing, to run away together ...

And it was, and it is, romantic, not just for Nick, but for me, too.

I was at the point where I couldn't *not* escape. I came to believe that I'd try it, even if I knew in advance I'd have only one night of freedom. That would be enough. I'd add five more years to my sentence for one free night. I needed it that badly. It was juvenile, of course, I know that. But it's how I felt. The letter from the superintendent was the last straw.

Only one thing gave me pause: what if I didn't make it? What if I got caught within the compound? What if I never made it over the fence? I'd be going to the hole for 360 days, and for nothing ...

Most prisoners, most women prisoners, don't try to escape because they have kids, and they wouldn't be able to see them again. That's a major controling factor.

I just hoped to God everybody would understand. I worried about my parents and about Ira. Maybe everybody would be really mad at me. I didn't know; I only knew I had to try in order to survive. As it turned out, they weren't mad at all. Most of them said afterwards, "That was the best thing you could ever have done."

Run, Bambi, run!

The last day was terrible. I knew it was the last time I would see these people, my friends ... and yet I couldn't act as if anything was wrong, or anything was different. I couldn't tip off the prison officials. I'm generally very private and stoic about my emotions, so when I do cry my friends know there is something seriously wrong. I'm generally embarrassed about public displays of emotion.

So when my parents left for the last time ... There was a baseball diamond in the yard in front of the housing unit, and I walked out into the middle of the field and I broke down and sobbed, I wept and wept, the tears staining my shirt. I had a good cry, then I put my sunglasses on and walked back to the housing unit.

My parents mean everything to me. But if I had to wait ... how long could they keep going? How long? It was hell for them, too. By leaving, I was going to free everybody else. I knew them well. I knew that if I was free, they would take comfort from that.

And I think, honestly, my mom was glad I wasn't going to be married in prison.

If I looked out of sorts that last day, at least I had an excuse. My friends blamed love. "Oh well," my good friend Debbie laughed, "she's in love, she's a little distracted ..."

Every Sunday afternoon I played tennis, so on this Sunday I had to play as usual. Everyone knew I lived for tennis, and I couldn't, on this day of all days, do anything out of the ordinary. In the middle of the first set, my doubles partner Laurie Fox said sharply to me, "Laurie!"

It was my turn to serve, and she'd caught me staring into the middle distance, my mind miles away.

The escape was going to be that night.

23

ON THE LAM

When you're in the same place for nine years you get to know everything, every inch of every room, everybody's routines. Human beings are creatures of habit, and one of a prisoner's habits is watching the watchers. You get to know which guards head for the kitchen for coffee as soon as they come on duty, which ones bury their noses in newspapers or gab on the phone for hours. When you're planning an escape, you have to know who is going to be on shift. It would be riskier with some people than others. I had to think all that through.

And even then, you have to be flexible. Someone may call in sick, they might switch jobs without notice. You have to be prepared to cancel your plans at the last moment.

In truth, I could have taken off at any time during the last eight years or so, but I needed the psychological push, the sense that I had, truly, lost all hope of ever being free again.

Every summer I worked on the outdoor maintenance crew. Although we eventually got tractor mowers, at first we used to mow the lawns by hand. What a sight—a crew of women, side by side, with hand-mowers. Monday we'd start at one end of the prison compound and by Friday we'd be at the other. These were big lawns, over two hundred acres of them. Because of the unvarying nature of the routine, every Thursday I found myself at the North Gate. I mowed away by myself. Near the gate was a dump for garbage and cut trees and whatnot. The highway was beside the dump. I used to stand and watch the beer trucks drive by. Mostly, I was there alone, not even within sight of the cameras (we all got to know the cameras, and how far they could see). There was a supervisor who checked on our whereabouts periodically, but I knew that if someone met me on a Thursday, I could just ... go. There is always a crack in any system. Always. If you wanna go, you can go.

I thought it all through. They say prison is a crime school, and this is so true! I learned a *lot* over the years. I'd seen people escape before, often enough, and nine times out of ten they'd go right back to where they came from, to their children or their families or their homes. And, of course, they were picked up right away. I knew that if I left, I'd leave Wisconsin for good. The best thing would be to go, just to go immediately, and not to stop.

■ ■ ■

I finished my tennis game in the late afternoon.

I knew there was a 5:30 PM "count." Everything revolved around these counts.

They did "counts" all the time, checking to see that we were all accounted for. We had counts at 7:30 AM, 12:30 PM, 5:30 PM and 9:30 PM. So I had to go either well before or just after a count, otherwise they would know I was missing immediately. The count at 9:30 PM was no good—after that, they counted every hour on the hour, all night long. The guard shift changed at 10:00, then they patrolled the corridors and went past every cell with a flashlight, walkie-talkies blaring and keys jangling while we tried to sleep. The rule was that the guard counting us had to see skin. I learned to sleep with one foot hanging out of the blanket.

After the 9:30 count cleared, we had several options. We had access to a basement card room in the Housing Unit, but I hated the noise and smoke. Or, until about 11:00 PM, we could take a shower or use the telephone in the hallway. But every hour, on the hour, we were all counted.

There were some women who escaped through the windows in their cells. I had once lived in a cell where that would have been possible. On some floors the windows had no bars, but the window stays prevented anyone from opening the windows more than about four inches—just enough for some rather inadequate ventilation. In a cell I once shared with Kathy Braun, the window just flew right open. The stays were broken, or perhaps they were never put on by mistake. I certainly could have escaped from that room. Other women who sawed through the stays, tied their sheets together and out they went.

I remember two women who went to great lengths to get out. They stole a file from maintenance and cut through the bars. They worked at it for a long time. And when they'd escaped, what did they do? They hitchhiked to Madison, an hour and a half away, went immediately to the first party they could find and bragged about what they'd done. Someone from the party called the police and they were caught the same night.

So I knew what *not* to do. No parties. Take off and keep going!

If I'd waited until 9:30 it would have been dark, but there was that matter of the hourly count. I decided on that odd time between dark and light, dusk, when you can see, but not very well. Better than dark, in some ways.

Ironically, two things actually helped my escape. The Security Director insisted that when a prisoner was doing laundry she had to stay in the laundry room until she was done. Of course, this was done to inconvenience everybody; how boring to sit and watch a dryer going round for hours. Most people would otherwise have gone to the card room instead. It worked to my advantage in this case, because it allowed me to be absent from my floor, the third. They would simply assume I was doing my laundry for a couple of hours. And to help me further, the Captain was conducting a white glove building inspection that evening. All the guards were preoccupied with dustball reports.

Right after the 5:30 count, I signed out with my floor officer and told her I was going to the laundry room. This was consistent with my routine. I carried my sweaty tennis clothes with me.

There was a window in the laundry that was not secured. Who knows why? Maybe they'd painted it and forgotten to put the stays back on. But there it was, calling out to me like one of the sirens.

It was not as small as the newspapers reported the next day. I think the prison exaggerated the smallness of the window to minimize their fault, and implied I had somehow wriggled through a hole about six inches square. Actually, it was about two feet by two feet. It was high off the ground, but I was in wonderful shape because I'd been running five miles every day and doing aerobics four nights a week, not to mention my tennis matches.

There I was, pushing myself through the window, on my way Out.

I can honestly say I've never been so scared in my entire life. My heart was pounding so hard it was like drums beating in my ears.

Security vans patroled the grounds, but they, too, had their routines. Through simple observation I'd learned when they had deliveries to make and other things to do.

I was afraid of them, of course.

I was also afraid of the screwy inmates. Someone could easily have spotted me. Of course, anyone with half a brain wouldn't have said anything, but prisons are full of the other kind, too—people who will blurt out anything that comes into their heads. "Hey, everybody! I just saw somebody!" They would! There are people so bored they have nothing to do but look out the window. You have to anticipate that.

There was an apple orchard behind the housing unit, and I knew the cameras couldn't see past it. If I could only get into the woods past the orchard, I'd be safe. Well, maybe not safe, but cool ...

In the first few seconds after I got out I paused in the woods behind the Housing Unit to catch my breath and make sure no one had seen me. There is a large stone grotto with a statue of the Virgin Mary. So much for separation of Church and State.

I wore a leather jacket, to protect me from branches in the woods, so I got through the woods without a scratch. I'd never been in those woods before, and it was scary. Woods at night are always creepy, and when you're in a hurry, even more so. I didn't want to lose an eye to a low-hanging branch; nor did I want to fall into a hidden ravine and break a leg. I didn't know whether there were any ravines. The woods sloped generally uphill from the housing unit to the highway beyond. To freedom.

I was still within the perimeter of the fence.

It was hot, and very dark in the woods. I sweated profusely; I had the hood of my sweatshirt over my head. My heart was pounding. I was afraid I would hyperventilate because I was panting like a horse. The air seemed thick and rank. I just wanted to get through those woods!

I went up, and farther up, and eventually I could see light at the end of the woods, I was running toward the light, scrambling over fallen trees, crossing one small ravine on a deadfall bridge, like a balance beam, but I just went, driving myself, trying not to panic, trying to keep going.

I reached the fence. It was tall, maybe nine or ten feet, with barbed wire at the top. I wrapped my belt around the barbed wire and I pulled it taut, and no sooner had I done so than I heard a car coming.

I didn't know if it was Nick, but I couldn't risk being seen at the top of the fence, so I jumped down, ran for cover and waited. It could be a prison van doing a perimeter check.

When the truck had passed, I tried again.

This time I became hooked on the barbed wire. It snagged my pants, and I felt it tear into my leg. I yanked at it, and the barbs raked my leg, but I freed myself.

I left half my pant leg on the wire. Talk about fiber evidence!

Later, I saw three or four big gashes in my leg. It looked as though I'd been attacked by a mountain lion—four big claw marks in the flesh. I worried about infection, but it healed eventually.

I was out!

I had to run for cover.

The truck that had passed hadn't been Nick after all. We two amateurs had got the timing down pat. Nick showed up right on time.

A witness at his trial later swore he'd seen Nick parked near the fence where he picked me up. It still amazes me what lies people will tell, just to get into the papers or on television. Nick *never* parked anywhere—we had worked that out ahead of time. Drive up and down twenty times if you must, I'd warned him, but don't ever stop, it will only attract attention. He'd agreed, and did as I suggested.

He pulled up, I jumped in, and we sped off. To freedom!

I'd made it! It was an amazing feeling. My heart was still going. My adrenaline levels must have been off the charts! Ecstasy mingled with fear.

I scrunched down and started peeling layers of clothes off to cool myself. I took my leather jacket off, then my sweatshirt, down to a tank top. Hand in hand, with Guns 'n Roses blasting on the tape player, we just drove straight through to Canada. It took us all night.

■   ■   ■

We reached the Canadian border, and I looked across at Another Country beyond. The trees looked the same, and so did the roads. The highway signs had little crowns on them, but everything else looked the same. I knew, though, that it wasn't so. I knew that beyond that gate the Milwaukee Police Department had no jurisdiction, no weight, no authority. It was a place that was Donahoo-free. Skwierawski had no say there. They had never heard of McCann there. It was a refuge, a place empty of malice.

It was our first big test. Nick gripped the wheel, but looked otherwise relaxed—good old happy-go-lucky Nick! I was so nervous! We'd driven all night but I was wide awake, running on pure adrenaline. We couldn't get stopped here, surely? We just couldn't! Not after all our efforts!

We pulled up at the border crossing post.

The officer approached Nick's side of the car. "Hi!" he said. "Where are you going?"

■   ■   ■

Would the word have been out by then? I thought we'd still be pretty safe. They'd do a thorough search of the grounds before they even notified the sheriff. I had looked into it surreptitiously earlier, and discovered that they generally delay issuing an APB for something like forty-eight hours, to allow a thorough search of the immediate locality. But I wondered if all those years behind bars had made me ignorant of the new high-tech systems available. After all, I had never even seen a fax machine. What if news of the escape had been sent by fax to the border?

It was mid-morning by the time we got to Canada. There were some things in our favor. I was in good shape and I was suntanned, so I didn't look like the stereotypical jailbird. We were sitting there holding hands like an ordinary couple.

"What's your business in Canada?" the border officer asked.

Could I have told them an earful! Refuge, I wanted to say.

"We're on honeymoon," I said.

"Okay then, have a nice time," she said, smiling and waving us off.

Freedom! I rolled down the window and let the breeze speed through my hair. The sun beat furiously over the tops of the pine trees. The sky was a brilliant blue.

I looked over at Nick and said, "Well, maybe there is a God." Me, an unwavering atheist for so many years!

■   ■   ■

Even had they demanded our ID at the border, we would have been all right. Nick had come prepared.

It turned out to be surprisingly simple. In Milwaukee County they don't cross-reference birth and death certificates. Every baby gets a birth certificate, but if that baby dies in infancy the death certificate isn't cross-referenced to the birth certificate. The trick, therefore, is to go to a cemetery and look for a child who died young but who would have been about your age had she lived. You write the name and birth date down. Then you have to consult the death notice in the newspaper to find out the mother's maiden name. Death notices commonly say something like, "Beloved daughter of so and so, née so and so." You have to have the maiden name to apply for a copy of the birth certificate. It has to be a baby, unfortunately. Most adults have other identification that is cross-referenced to birth dates; if you apply for a birth certificate for someone who also has a social security number, they can trace you easily enough.

Once you have a birth certificate, you can apply for a real social security number under that baby's name—which means you can get a job.

We got "our" birth certificates. I was Jennifer Lee Voelkel, a name from a tombstone, and Nick was Tony Gazzana.

Later, some people expressed outrage about what we'd done. It bordered to them on the sacrilegious, the morbid. After we were recaptured, the newspapers published a picture of the dead baby's tombstone, which did seem morbid, and went to the parents for comment. We didn't mean to be hurtful. It was the only means we had to acquire ID.

Afterwards, the parents of the real Tony Gazzana became our friends. Nick met with the Gazzanas after he was deported and apologized. They even signed a petition we sent to Canada's Immigration Minister, Barbara McDougall, to dispute her ministry's contention that I was a danger to the Canadian public. "We don't find Laurie a danger here, please don't in Canada," they said. They came over to our side.

The Voelkels were upset with me, and I'm sorry, but I meant no harm. I hardly ever used the name, anyway. Nick and I were posing as husband and wife, so I traveled and worked under the alias Jennifer Gazzana.

■   ■   ■

It's true, it was illegal to acquire false ID. It was the only illegal thing I did all the time I was on the run. The Canadian immigration and justice lawyers for the ministry, trying to establish that I was a menace to public safety, made much of the fact that I had got jobs under false pretenses. What did they want me to do? Say, "Hi, I'm Laurie Bembenek, I'm a fugitive, can you give me a job?" But Nick and I never stole anything. We never robbed banks, held up gas stations, pilfered from newspaper boxes, short-changed anyone, drove without a license or even jaywalked. I worked at two jobs, six days a week to survive, and we lived frugally in Thunder Bay. Never for a moment did we consider committing a crime.

I never want to commit a crime.

I want desperately to be ordinary.

I want to work, and pay my own way.

■   ■   ■

Meanwhile, in Milwaukee, the cops, in typical Milwaukee fashion, wiretapped my mom's phone, opened my parent's mail and waited outside my parents' house for me to come "home."

For months afterwards they waited there. They were so obvious! They would sit in front of the house, and my mom and dad felt like prisoners in their own home. One time a large furniture truck pulled up across the street, and before you could turn around it was surrounded by squad cars. It was as if they'd dropped out of the sky.

What goes through their minds? Did they really think I'd come home in a furniture van posing as a sofa bed? My mom and dad thought that was a real hoot.

■   ■   ■

You know what my dad said, when they asked him on television how he felt about my escape?

"I hope she's safe," he said.

Then he added, "If I saw her I would tell her to keep on running, because it may not be freedom but at least it's a taste of freedom ..."

■   ■   ■

I can't tell you how hard it is living on the run. It's like being on guard at all times. You have to be aware of everything you say, everything you do. For twenty-four hours a day you have to be another person. If somebody calls you Jennifer you have to respond right away. You have to remember to call yourself Jennifer. I might be telling you a story and say something like, "I said to myself, now Laurie, smarten up ..." But I had to learn to say Jennifer instead of Laurie. Usually when you sign your name you do it without thinking. On the run, you have constantly to think the idiotic question: "Who am I?"

To everyone but me, the escape itself seemed astonishingly easy. So much so that most people assumed I'd had lots of help. They accused Kathy Braun of giving me tips on how to escape—but it wasn't like that at all. Nobody advised me. I couldn't do that to my friends, implicate anybody, so none of them had even an inkling of my plans. They could all take a polygraph test and pass easily. As far as they were concerned, I just had to disappear one night. I hated having to do that.

And in Thunder Bay I missed Kathy and my other friends from Taycheedah. Nick didn't have a clue what I was going through. How could he? Only another prisoner would have understood what things were like, how the little things affected me. Like the price of cigarettes. I'd been in prison for a decade, and then had the double-whammy of going to Canada, where things are incredibly more expensive. Cigarettes were about a buck and a half in the U.S., and about six bucks in Canada. Nick smoked over a pack a day, which meant over two hundred dollars a month going up in smoke! We argued about that constantly.

I lost so many simple skills. I'd lost any ability to figure out directions, east and west, north and south. It took me weeks just to figure out how to take the bus to work in the mornings. I know that sounds absurd, but when you're in the same little compound for years and years, and when you do go somewhere you're taken by the police, you don't have to take responsibility for anything. You wouldn't believe how many bus stops I waited at for buses that never came.

I also lost the ability to make choices. You're not presented with any choices in prison. You're told when to eat, what to eat, what to do ... you don't get a variety pack. I drove Nick crazy. We'd go to a restaurant and I'd keep looking at the menu, and I'd say "I want this. No, wait, I'll have this. No, no, can you come back in a minute?" I couldn't decide. We'd go to a grocery store and I couldn't decide what to buy. There were too many choices.

■　　■　　■

Jennifer and Tony Gazzana spent the day looking for a place to stay. Wide-eyed, I looked around. So this was the outside world! Hot dog vendors, people shopping, kids on bikes. So this was life! I slipped off my sandal to feel the warm cement of the sidewalk under my foot. I kept thinking I was dreaming. We finally bought a newspaper and went to a coffee shop to mark off some likely prospects for apartments. We did that right away because you need a permanent address to apply for a job. And we needed to work—we didn't have much money.

That night we stayed in a hotel. Fortunately, they never asked for ID. We paid cash. Hotels made me nervous. Nick said I was paranoid. Prison does that to a person. So we bought some beer and a pizza and looked for news of my escape on TV. Nothing was reported.

One of the things the cruder reporters always seem to want to ask me is: "Did you make love all night?" And you know what they're thinking: "Did you have good sex? Did you screw like minks? You'd been without for nine years—what was it *like*?"

They always want to ask me about sex.

Once, years before, I'd made a facetious remark to a reporter. She'd asked me about the first thing I'd do after I was released, and I said, "Have sex." I was joking, for God's sake! But the quote took on a life of its own, and eventually made its squalid way into *People* magazine and, of course, taken out of context and blown out of proportion, it winds up making me sound like a nympho.

So we were in love, and we went to bed, and in the morning we went and found ourselves an apartment.

A woman named Jenny Beck rented us a place. It was a basement apartment, small and somewhat dark. Jenny had done all the work herself—from the paneling to the plumbing. She is a very small woman, and the place was built for midgets. I once went to a rummage sale and saw a beautiful sofa for fifty dollars. I wanted it, because the apartment only had two chairs so Nick and I couldn't sit and cuddle. We measured the sofa and it wouldn't fit through the damn door. I wanted to cut it in half!

I picked up the first job I could get. I was scared. I was scared all the time, in fact. I was scared of starving, of going through all our money. I didn't want to end up as a public charge at some shelter someplace. Especially after seeing the prices. So four days after we arrived, I got a job in the Fort William side of Thunder Bay, as a cook in a Greek restaurant.

What a joke! That's one of the things I would have loved to have shared with Kathy and my friends. A cook! I have a domestic deficiency. I don't know how to cook! I've been locked up for ten years. I can barely fry an egg. Even before I got sent up, Fred did the cooking.

But the Columbia Grill and Tavern trained me. They showed me how to make souvlaki and gyros and Greek salads.

After a while, because I was still obsessed with this irrational fear that we'd starve and because everything seemed so expensive to me, and because Nick wasn't working, I got a second job, in a gym. I'd go home, change into my aerobics clothes and walk to my second job. I couldn't drive; I didn't have a license yet.

I wished constantly that I had Kathy there to share things with, the small things that mean so much to a prisoner. Every animal I ran into on the street I would bend down and pet. I'd attract stray cats. We got a cat of our own. I'd walk barefoot in the grass, go for long walks in the night, smell the air, watch the stars, stand in the rain, walk down the hill to the convenience store at night and get something, anything, a popsicle.

Very simple things were so wonderful. Jenny had raspberry bushes in the back yard, so Tony/Nick and I had fresh berries on our breakfast cereal. She gave me a homemade apple pie one day and as I baked it, the most delicious smell filled our apartment. I hadn't smelled anything so good in years! I even made grape jelly one evening and really thought I was the cat's pajamas. I know these things sound silly to the average individual, but another lifer would understand.

I worried about so much. About running out of money. About seeming conspicuous. About saying the wrong thing, asking the wrong question. I was worried about getting drunk and blurting something out. I became very conservative about drinking. Apparently, over the years I have turned into a control freak. I had to be constantly aware of what was going on and who was saying what.

For weeks I'd keep my ears open, listening for news of our escape. I looked at the supermarket tabloids. Nothing. Thunder Bay seemed like a million miles from Milwaukee. Nobody had even heard of me. People at work would talk about this and that, and occasionally the topic of prisons would come up, but the only U.S. prisoner they seemed to know was Charles Manson. Most mornings cops would come in for coffee, and I would serve them thinking, *"Act normal, Bembenek!"*

I didn't try to change my appearance too much. It would have been too expensive for one thing, and it would have meant frequent trips to the beauty shop. I didn't want to go back to being blond, anyway. Over the years I've been everything—short brown hair, long brown hair, blond hair—I didn't know what to do. So I left it alone.

Why, I was asked later, Thunder Bay? There was no particular reason. We just landed there. I barely knew how we got there. I just let Nick drive. But I loved Thunder Bay. It was so beautiful. I was seduced by it.

Of course, that was easy. I was suffering from sensory deprivation. In prison you're so starved for beauty, for anything natural. I could see Mount Mackay on the way to work every morning, and in the other direction, in Lake Superior, there is a huge mound called the Sleeping Giant. Up the hill from our apartment there was a beautiful little hilltop park, with a gorgeous view.

Everything was gorgeous to me.

Thunder Bay was a good choice, I think. It was small enough for me to handle. If we'd gone directly to Toronto, I would have been lost, unable to cope. The pace would have been too frenzied. We heard about Toronto in Thunder Bay, and all the stories were negative: its cost of living was outrageous, its people harsh and unpleasant. People in Thunder Bay certainly implied that no one in their right minds would want to live there.

■   ■   ■

"Tony" had a real driver's license. I'm an artist, so I bought some art supplies and made up more ID for him, (it looked quite authentic when laminated, I must say), and with that and his birth certificate, he got himself a real Ontario driver's license under the name Tony Gazzana, with picture ID and all.

The next thing we had to do was get rid of our car. Not so easy, that. We couldn't sell the damn thing without returning to the border and filling out some forms. Obviously we didn't want to chance that. So we bought a Canadian Datsun. After that, if we'd been pulled over by a cop, we had legitimate papers. I wanted every last detail to be worked out.

You have to think of everything. It's complicated finding out the simplest thing, getting the simplest questions answered. In the U.S., everyone has a Social Security number. I knew they likely existed in Canada, but I didn't know what they were called. How can you ask? You can't stop someone on the street and ask them. And how many digits should it be? We had a three, a two and a four in the U.S. How many in Canada? Fortunately, I found a place that let me take an application form home to fill in, and I saw there were nine little boxes for the Social Insurance number. You have to think of all this just to get a job. And it's hard to get a job without a phone, but you can't get a phone without a job. It's a circular process. If you're legal, of course, none of this is a problem.

■   ■   ■

And Nick? Nick and me?

I don't want to say anything bad about Nick. We were in love, and he was there when I needed him. He helped me get out, and I'm grateful for it.

But I learned that you can't get to know someone in prison.

We were both naive, I think.

I had been in prison for too long. That was years of learning to live without material possessions. I learned actively to reject any attachment to possessions; in prison, attachment leads surely to disappointment. Someone would steal your goods, or break them accidentally or maliciously, and if you had allowed yourself to care, the loss would hurt you. Successful prisoners learn to live entirely internal lives. So I wanted to talk, and to hug, and to take walks, and to go to the park and sit quietly, listening to the silence, taking pleasure in freedom. I needed no music but the wind. I had no desire to watch television, no need for a phone, no urgent need at all to fill the blessed silence.

To me, silence was not an emptiness but a peaceful relief. Silence was a rich part of my freedom.

Nick, on the other hand, was like most people—immersed, saturated, in the material world. He was unhappy without a phone, without a VCR, without a stereo, a television, expensive fishing, golfing and hunting gear. He had to have the best brand of coffee, he's gotta have his White Russians. He was the kind of person who wouldn't mind hiking, but he was uncomfortable without the best hiking boots money could buy. Being penniless, as we were, depressed him.

I tried to warn him before we escaped. I didn't want him to participate blindly. I was afraid he'd blame me. I told him how hard it would be. I told him, "You're going to be homesick. You might lose the custody of your kids. If we get caught you're going to jail, you could do five years." He just kept saying, "I don't care, I love you ..." He treated it as a romantic escapade and never really realized how much he'd have to do without.

Until he was immersed in it. Then, oh, Mr. Unhappiness!

But, as I said, we were both naive. And we hadn't known how unalike we were.

When he got back to Milwaukee, he told some friends, "Laurie has been in jail too long. She's forgotten how to have a good time. She never wanted to go dancing or have fun. She just wanted to go sit in a park and talk."

He never understood that for me that *was* having a wonderful time.

We were penniless, and I got two jobs so we could get by; I was determined to be a good citizen. At first, he went to a lot of job interviews, but he never managed to land one. I never knew why. Something always went wrong. It was never his fault. After a while, he stopped trying so hard. He went fishing several times a week, then he wanted to go moose hunting. He wanted to play, to have a good time. I couldn't figure out why he didn't want to come home to me. I slept alone in prison, and now I was sleeping alone again.

Eventually he got a job selling vacuum cleaners, but it didn't last. It seemed to cost him more in gas than it brought in, anyway.

We had lots of fights, I'm sorry to say. One night, a Sunday night, I was standing at the bus stop in the rain, weary and footsore. Nick was off fishing, I didn't know where, and it slowly dawned on me "What is wrong with this picture? Is this why I escaped from prison? Oh, I'm having so much fun!"

Nick didn't get back until one in the morning. I was terrified he'd been in an accident, had been arrested. I wondered whether I should pack and get to the bus station. But he came back, saying he had been delayed because he had stopped to help a truck out of a ditch. He later admitted that it was a lie.

I guess it was just that he hadn't been inside, hadn't been a prisoner, that he was careless. He used to hang out with friends at a local hardware store, and he once told his friends there that it was my birthday. But it was August—Laurie Bembenek's birthday. Jennifer's birthday is in January! It caused trouble later when we were at a party and people started talking about jewelry with Zodiac signs on it. Someone asked me what my sign was. I had to say Capricorn, and some woman at the party said, "But Tony just said it was your birthday last week?" (I'm a Leo.) Luckily she was half in the bag, and it just went away. How easy it is to get trapped by something so seemingly insignificant. Tony/Nick just thought I was being paranoid when I worried about it.

My main priority was to make Nick happy. I never wanted him to regret what he'd done. I was so grateful to him for helping me. Because of him I was free.

Many times I wished I'd escaped with another inmate. A convict would have understood.

24

RECAPTURED

I never saw the program that did me in.

We did have a TV—Nick insisted on it, so he bought one at a rummage sale. But the last thing I wanted to do after nine years in prison was to watch more TV; I wanted to see the outdoors, to be outside as much as I could. Our set wasn't the best in the world—it only got a couple of channels and we didn't have cable—so if there was indeed something on "America's Most Wanted," I didn't see it. I went to work the next morning as usual.

We'd been planning to move. I knew we were pushing our luck staying in one place as long as we did. One day in the early fall I saw an ad in the newspaper for Banff National Park. They were hiring for the winter ski season and listed a whole range of jobs. I was sure if we went there we could *both* get work. And if Nick and I were on the same schedule and both working, life would be easier and we'd get on better together. I typed up letters of application and mailed them off.

Everything's in the timing, isn't it? We'd been planning to go right away but decided to wait another week, to see what Banff's response would be. If there was no response in a week ... off we'd go.

By September, it was getting colder, already a touch of winter in the air. I took the bus to work as usual. I remember standing around after the breakfast rush with the other waitresses, waiting for the lunch crowd to come in. We were gossiping and laughing when a man in a suit and tie walked in.

He walked toward us and asked to see the owner. Louie wasn't there—he usually came in a little later—and so Ann, a waitress who had worked there since I was in rubber pants, said she'd give him a message. She assumed this person was a salesman. Instead, he asked to talk to her privately. Thelma, another of the waitresses, said to me, "These salesmen are so damn pushy, eh?"

We could see this fellow talking to Anne at the rear of the

restaurant. He showed her something and I could see her shaking her head, no. I didn't think anything of it.

Then he came back to where we were all standing. Oh God! He showed me his badge and said, "Can I talk to you for a minute?" He was a Thunder Bay cop.

Well, let me tell you! Talk about a heart attack! I almost had a massive coronary on the spot. Of course I knew at once why he was there.

I thought, Calm down and it'll be okay, just calm down ... My life was flashing before my eyes and I was thinking, Okay, this is it, it's over.

We went to a booth and sat down. He spoke first.

"I asked if anyone from the States was working here, and you're from the States?"

"Yes," I said, stating the obvious.

"What are you doing here?"

Nick and I had several stories prepared. It had gotten somewhat complicated because to some people Nick had said that I was a Canadian, and to others that we were both Americans and he'd been transferred to Thunder Bay. Different people heard different stories, and it was sometimes difficult remembering which story was which, and keeping track of the different versions. Oh God.

I said, "My husband got a job transfer."

"Oh? How long have you been here?"

"Oh, since about June, or something like that."

He asked me for identification, and I dug it out of my purse. Oh God. Oh God.

"What's your date of birth?" he asked. Cops always ask you for your date of birth, even when you've just handed them a birth certificate.

"January 7, 1961," I said, remembering to be Jennifer.

"Where are you from?"

"Chicago. I was born in Milwaukee but I moved to Chicago when I was a baby." Everyone at the restaurant thought I was from Chicago.

He didn't ask for my work permit, which was just as well because I didn't have one. Nor did he ask for my visa, which was also just as well, for the same reason. He asked my husband's name and my address. At first I was going to lie about my address, but I made a split-second decision—what happens if he asks someone on the way out where I live, and they tell him? So I told him.

Then he pulled out The Picture.

It was a fax, a poor reproduction, but it was definitely me and Nick. I was just dying.

"Have you ever seen this before?"

I tried to look thoughtful, and squinted at the picture.

"No," I said, "Nooooo ... I don't think so."

"Is that your husband?"

"Not at all," I said. I had a curly perm by now, so I looked different.

"Okay, I guess I'll tell them we got the wrong girl," he said, and got up, and walked to the front of the restaurant.

But by then Louie was at the cash register and the cop pulled the picture out again. I saw Louie shaking his head, no, no ... He must have asked him the same question. After another minute, out the door he went.

Well!

I was thinking, Oh my God oh my God oh my God what am I going to do? I couldn't just run out of there. Everybody in the restaurant would then know.

Think, Laurie, think!

The first thing was to reach Tony, Nick, I no longer knew what to call him. Was he home? Noooo! I called all over Thunder Bay looking for him, and he was nowhere to be found. I finally called the hardware store where he usually hung out and left a message.

"It's extremely important, it's an emergency, if he shows up tell him to call me immediately, okay?"

How long should I wait? Maybe they've got him already? In the States, the cops would "sit on" the restaurant; they'd park nearby, and if the suspect went flying out of there, that's your man. Surely that's what they were doing right now? Meanwhile, the lunch crowd came in, a real stampede, everyone wanting food right away. Suddenly I had twelve tables to wait on and no time at all to think.

My mind was spinning. I didn't know my left hand from my right. I gave people menus, took orders—God knows what I served them. The refrain was going through my mind: oh my God oh my God oh my God oh my God! I was trying to act normally, whatever that was. I didn't want to panic, because when you panic you get stupid, do something stupid, like flying out of there.

The phone rang. Anne answered and called me over.

"Jennifer, it's Tony."

I talked quickly. "Look," I said, "we've got to get out of here right now, come and pick me up immediately, it's the cops, we've got to get out of here ..."

"Okay," Nick said, and hung up.

I guess I had a troubled look on my face, and one of the waitresses asked me what was wrong.

"Look, I'm sorry, I had a death in the family," I said. "I have to go." What an old excuse! I hated lying to them because they were my friends, but what could I do? Louie gave me an odd look.

I put my coat on, and since it was raining outside I put my hood up, and left out the back door. I looked up and down the alley and saw no cops. With my hood up I don't know whether they would have noticed me anyway. I walked to the corner and looked around. Nick wasn't there yet.

I waited. After a minute he arrived. And what did he do? He pulled up in front and leaned on the horn! *Beep beep beep*! Why not just let everyone in Thunder Bay know you're here, Nick? Why not rent a giant neon sign?

Up the block I waved and he saw me and pulled up. I got into the car, by this time completely panicked.

I said, "We've got to get out of here right now, right away, don't even pull over, let's go!"

And he said, calmly, "Now wait, wait a minute, explain to me what happened, don't panic. Let's decide what to do."

I told him about the cop and the picture.

After a while he said, "So let's go to Banff."

"Okay."

But there was a problem. I'd been making our fake ID at the apartment, and there was incriminating material lying around. If they got a warrant to search the flat they'd be able to trace us easily. Not only would they have our aliases, but they'd know for sure who we really were and how we'd done what we did.

What bad timing! We'd been planning to get rid of the stuff, but we hadn't quite finished with it. Worse—the Wednesday after we got busted we got Canadian ID, the real stuff. A week later and we'd have been free and clear. One week later! I could have screamed. The only way they could have traced us after that would have been through fingerprints. We could have worked normally, lived normal lives. Oh, the might-have-beens!

And that's all I ever wanted to do, to be legal.

I didn't want to commit any crimes or rob banks. I just wanted to be legal, be normal, like everybody else. Get a work permit, work, earn money, have a real life. One more week ...

But this scrambling ... collecting all this stuff takes time! You can only do things so fast. People don't understand. They would say, "You were there for three months! Why didn't you go to Europe?" I'd say, "Because we were waiting for passports. You can't get passports overnight. You need paper to get paper."

■   ■   ■

So many times I'd sit on the bus and look at all the people around me and think, God, I'd trade places with any of them, just to be normal and legal and legitimate, and not have to look over my shoulder, worrying about my actions, my words. Any face, any of those faces on the bus would do. I'd trade my life with any of them.

Any day, at any time, they could come and take me away.

■   ■   ■

We sat in the car, arguing. I didn't want to go back to the apartment, and he did.

"You're panicking," he said. "If they really thought that was you in that picture, they'd have picked you up right away." That sounded reasonable. But what if they were sitting on the house?

"Okay," I said. "We'll drive up High Street and look down our street. We'll be able to see the whole block, and if there are any strange cars outside the house, we're taking right off, we're not going in."

Even then Nick argued. "I can't leave my fishing rods! Those are nine hundred dollar fishing rods! And the boat motor! I have to return Charlie's boat motor!"

Meanwhile, he was driving toward the apartment. *He wants his goddamn fishing rods, he tells me I'm panicking, we should fetch the incriminating stuff* ... So I said, "Okay, maybe you're right."

Of course, we should never have gone home.

Looking back, it seems obvious.

There were no strange cars anywhere near our apartment. After more discussion, I persuaded Nick to park in the garage—at least that way our car wouldn't be quite so obvious. I went in to begin throwing things together in suitcases, and to change into my jeans.

It took the cops a while. The Thunder Bay cop went and had lunch or something, and only called the RCMP after that. Then the RCMP called Immigration to see if there were work permits in the names of Jennifer and Tony Gazzana, and of course there weren't. So the Mounties, while they didn't know who we were, figured they at least had a pair of illegals on their hands.

Nick took some of our things from the apartment out to the car. But he left the back door open.

In a basement flat, you can't look out to see if anyone's there. I heard a little *tap tap tap* on the back door. I assumed it was Nick, though I was puzzled—is he carrying something back into the house and he can't get the door? It was just a little *tap tap*, not like a true knock on the door. I peeked around, and saw nothing. I came out of the apartment and peered up at the outside door. If the door had been closed I'd never have answered. They could have waited all day. (Though Nick, of course, was still at large, in the garage.) I'd be holed up in the basement and we'd tunnel out—or something! Nick had left the door open, and an RCMP cop was standing there.

I thought, Well, game over. At the same time, I didn't recognize the cop. It wasn't the same person who'd been at the restaurant.

He was very polite. "Are you Jennifer Gazzana?"

And I said, "Yeeah," cautiously.

I was thinking, Oh, holy shit!

I knew if he went in it would be the end. We had been frantically packing, and there was stuff all over the apartment. The place looked trashed. It wouldn't have taken a genius to see that someone was trying to leave in one awful hurry. The Thunder Bay cop arrived, smiling.

I thought, If he comes in, that's it, that's all.

I didn't know if he needed a warrant or not. I didn't know Canada's laws.

"Can I come in?" he asked.

I said nothing. We stood there for a moment.

"We do have the right," he said. "We *can* come in."

I wasn't in a position to argue. I just didn't know. Nor could I afford to seem uncooperative. He started saying something about work permits and I was thinking, Oh man ...

And then Nick came in.

That was the end of that. I had told Nick to shave his mustache off, but he has a distinctive face; he's got this big nose and there's no hiding it, not much you can do to change his appearance. The cop looked at the pictures and said, "That's our boy! Now, who are you?"

All of a sudden everybody was there—the RCMP, the local cops, the Immigration officers, three jurisdictions.

Ohhhh man, I thought, it's over.

You know, I was so exhausted that there was almost a sense of relief. Finally, we can relax.

I can't tell you how exhausting it was to live like that. I felt like the horse in Orwell's *Animal Farm*. It was way too much for me.

We walked into the apartment, and the Thunder Bay cop who'd been at the restaurant earlier looked around and said, "Hmmm, looks like we're in a hurry to leave," or something like that, and I sat down at the table and I thought, Oh well ...

It was so low-key! In the States, the cops would have been busting down the door with sawn-off shotguns, screaming, "*Hit the floor! Freeze!*" (the Kent State approach). But not these guys. They were quite casual.

The Thunder Bay cop asked me, "Could I please see the ID you showed me earlier today?"

I dug into my purse. Now, I could have had a gun in there. I didn't, of course—we didn't own any weapons and I wouldn't do something like that anyway—but he didn't know that. I also dug into a couple of drawers to pull out some clothing. I mean, I could have had an arsenal in there! If I'd been the desperate criminal everyone thought I was, they'd all have been dead, for real. I was shocked, to tell the truth, at how casual they were.

One of the cops looked at me and said, "You used to be a cop, didn't you?"

And I said, "Yeah."

"*Run, Bambi, Run!*" he said, and started to laugh. Hysteria.

I just sat at the table and said to myself, Great, this is just great! Oh God!

They radioed for more people. I looked at Nick and he looked at me and we just shrugged. They wanted to know all kinds of things—when we came over the border, our previous address, how long we'd been there.

We had a bank account, and they went through it carefully. How did we get this money? Did we commit robberies?

"Not at all," I said. "There was a payroll check from both my employers deposited on a weekly basis, the same amount, you can easily see we didn't do anything like that."

"Do you have any weapons?" they asked. "Drugs? Stolen property?"

We said no, and they said, okay. Again, in the States they would have been tearing that place apart, looking for who knows what, creating more problems than they solved, wrecking the poor place. Not here. They just politely asked us questions. I was quite surprised.

Finally, they formally placed us under arrest—the RCMP, the cop from the restaurant and the Immigration officer.

I watched all this in wonder. These guys were really nice! In the States, we would have been in shackles, in separate cars, on our way to jail in minutes. But not here. One of the Thunder Bay cops asked me what we wanted to do with our cat—he was really concerned about it. The cat was walking around being friendly, not knowing what was going on. I didn't want to just leave him. The cops let me write a little note to my landlady asking her to take care of our cat and saying how sorry I was. What would Jenny think? Oh God!

Then we went outside, to the squad cars. We came out into the air, and there were cops in the front and back yards. The weather was dramatic, strange—it was snowing, but there were also flashes of lightning and rumbles of thunder.

Nick and I were together in the same squad car on the way to the local jail. That was another thing they'd never do in the States. There, they would have separated us at once, so we couldn't talk. But they let us travel together in the same squad, and we chatted quietly as we drove. I promised I would never make any incriminating statements to the police against him and warned him not to talk to any cops until he got a lawyer.

That night the news went over the wire, and the next morning I woke up and the tiny Thunder Bay jail was surrounded. Every tripod and satellite dish in the world was there. *People* magazine was there, all three networks, TimeLife, "20/20," "60 Minutes," "Hard Copy," "A Current Affair" and "Inside Edition." It was a mess. The poor jail didn't know what was going on. They'd never seen anything like this before; they were just shocked.

Of course, the media people were demanding to be let in.

No, they said, this is Canada. I don't know where you people are from, but you don't get in.

It was just a little rinkydink bucket anyway, a very tiny jail, but they wouldn't let anybody in. Good for them.

■　　■　　■

But—and this makes me sick at heart, this is how institutionalized I have become—I didn't feel normal until I was back in jail.

When I was back inside, I thought, I'm home again ... I know how to do this, I can do jail ...

All the time I was out there, while I was free, I wanted to keep pinching myself, I felt like I was dreaming, I felt unreal, I was disoriented. So often I would stop myself and think, No, I'm going to wake up any minute now, this isn't real.

Jail feels real to me. Freedom doesn't.

When I finally got back in, I lay down on my bunk, took a nap and thought, So I'm back in. That's normal.

I hate this. I've become like a caged bird who can't handle freedom. It sickens me.

Perhaps, I comfort myself, three months of freedom wasn't enough. Perhaps being on the run isn't really being free. Perhaps with more time my sense of self would return from where I have hidden it. Perhaps there is still a chance I can become me again. I don't know. I hope so, but it terrifies me that perhaps the "me" of myself has shriveled and died ...

■   ■   ■

As I lay on my bunk, small things filled my head. The little things that others would not have noticed. For instance, every day after an eight-hour shift at the restaurant I would have a bagful of loonies, dollar coins, from tips, and we'd go grocery shopping. We'd be at the cash register and I'd hand over a fistful of loonies. It used to drive Nick crazy. "Laurie," he said (forgetting to call me Jennifer), "will you stop this? It looks like we've been panhandling all day. Stop paying in change!" He thought it was socially inappropriate behavior. It was just money to me.

That would happen all the time. I never got the hang of acting normally. I kept asking Nick, "Am I acting weird?" Mostly he would comfort me, tell me I was doing okay.

■   ■   ■

I don't usually believe in fate. I'm not a spiritual person. But, what happened next ... Matters got rather strange ...

I hadn't thought through my legal situation very well. I just assumed I'd be returned at once, that I'd be on the next plane out and back in Taycheedah the next day. That's certainly what the Immigration people implied. I knew I had to go to a hearing, but I didn't know what for.

"Is this a hearing where I need a lawyer?" I asked.

"Oh no," they said. They'd rather I didn't, of course.

Okay, I thought, I won't bother.

Thunder Bay doesn't have a major-league jail. It's a twenty-foot by seven-foot cellblock for women, with a picnic table bolted to the bars, a little black-and-white TV in the corner, three cells with three bunks each, a shower and a little table in the corner where they stack *True Romance* magazines. That's it, that's all—you eat, sleep and shower in that little cage and you don't go anywhere. The only pleasant aspect is the view; there's a pretty view of Lake Superior from the window.

There are no phones, no exercise treadmill or bicycle. Nothing.

The cops came the next morning and said, "You're going to a hearing. Are you dressed? You're going to court."

I brushed my teeth and waited and waited. Two hours went by, and nothing happened.

So I thought, Wait a minute! The misinformation is starting already. I'd better get myself a lawyer.

A tiny guard called Debbie came into the cellblock. She was really nice, a very pretty woman, a pleasant person.

I asked her, "How does a person go about getting a lawyer if we can't make a phone call? I'm not from here so I don't know any lawyers."

She said, "Oh, we'll call a lawyer for you. We have a list of legal-aid lawyers. I'll call Mary Kelly for you, she's really good, everyone seems to like her."

I was impressed. A woman lawyer, good!

About four hours later I was less impressed. Nothing had happened. No one came. I was thinking, Yeah, right, you'll call a lawyer for me. Already the lies are starting.

But I was wrong. Debbie had been calling all over, looking for Kelly. Kelly was at her cottage and didn't return the call. Finally Debbie returned.

"I can't find Kelly so I'll call the next lawyer on the list," she said.

And that was Dave Dubinsky.

Now Dave was six months out of law school, twenty-six years old. He is such a doll, like a brother to me, I just love this guy. He looked fresh-faced and sweet as he walked into the lawyer visiting room. It was pretty overwhelming for him. By now the papers were printing their garbage and the media circus was in full cry. He fought his way through the scrum to get to me. Dubinsky was so young and dressed so casually that he didn't look like a lawyer, and they didn't bother him.

We talked for a while, and he said, "Let me talk to my partner, Ron Lester, and we'll come back tonight."

So they did. And it all fell into place for me. Without me even trying.

Understand this, what it felt like. For nine years I'd been clawing and scraping and doing everything in my power, begging and borrowing, to try to get out of jail, calling and writing and hounding people, trying everything, exhausting myself. And now, for the first time, I sat back and did absolutely nothing and people helped me anyway. It blew my mind.

What an incredible sense of relief! I couldn't get Legal Aid because I'm not a Canadian, but these lawyers didn't care about money. They recognized that a terrible injustice had occurred and wanted to help.

Ron Lester and Dave Dubinsky gave me back a bit of myself. And I love them for it.

Lester came in with a copy of the Immigration Act, and he said, "You know, this might be a long shot, but I think you have a legitimate refugee claim."

■   ■   ■

My parents and Nick's parents flew up to join us. The Immigration Act requires a hearing within forty-eight hours after arrest, and the ministry assigned someone from its Sault Ste. Marie office and from Mississauga, near Toronto, to act for them. Ron told us from the start that Nick didn't have the same case; he was being deported right away.

My lawyers warned me that the refugee-hearing process might take a very long time, and that the time I spent in jail in Canada would not count against my sentence in Wisconsin.

"Well," I said, "what have I got to lose? I already have a life sentence. And the longer I'm away from that horrible place the better." I wasn't in any hurry to go back.

Nick was deported November 16, 1990. He got bailed out December 1, 1990, and he had his preliminary hearing December 6, being bound over for trial. The charge? Aiding and Abetting Escape from Lawful Custody. They set his bail at one hundred thousand dollars! Wisconsin is really insane. His sister borrowed money for him.

I tried to tell him to plea bargain at once. I pleaded with him.

"Believe me, Nick, I've been through this system for nine years, listen to me. You're guilty, so don't even think you're going to be acquitted. Plea bargain at once, and get it over with."

Instead, he entered a not guilty plea.

Nick fired his first lawyer, who had wanted to blame me for the whole thing. It was the old Svengali defense—this manipulative woman had somehow hypnotized him, somehow forced him to do this from prison, had held a (metaphoric) gun to his head and forced him. Nick didn't buy that. He knew it had been a mutual decision.

I argued with him again. I said, "Just get a public defender, plead guilty, and you'll get a nice little deal. And by the time I'm done in Canada you'll be out." But noooo! He wouldn't listen.

They found him guilty anyway, just like I said they would. He was convicted on September 4, 1991 and went to jail. In November 1991 Nick stopped writing to me.

■　　■　　■

I spent five months in the cellblock of the Thunder Bay jail. Jenny Beck, Louie Kabezes, and other local friends faithfully visited me, including my co-workers from the restaurant and my other boss, Debbie Pedre from the fitness center. All were very supportive and encouraging and kind. A regular customer, Doug Smith, even got a group of carollers together at Christmas and they sang outside beneath the jail windows.

It was a long, tough five months, not knowing what my future held, alone and heartbroken. With no access to cream rinse or conditioner for my new perm, my hair looked like a psychotic gerbil's nest. With no access to Vaseline or Chapstick, the jail's dry heat turned my lips into a chapped, cracked and bleeding mess. The other problem was that smoking was not allowed anywhere in the jail for the staff with the exception of the cellblocks—so they'd all come into our cellblock to smoke day and night, which bothered me. The canteen list was very limited and offered only Old Spice deodorant—which reminds me thoroughly of my dad—but no women's products at all. We received a change of clean clothes once a week, consisting of one pair of panties, socks, a bra, some sweatpants and a sweatshirt.

Soon I was disappointed to learn that only the male inmates were allowed to work—not women. The men also had a separate cellblock for mentally ill prisoners, but the women did not—so we occasionally shared the cellblock with women from the Lakehead Psychiatric Hospital across the street. I caught a nasty virus from one of them because she failed to cover her mouth when she coughed. With no access to cough drops or cough syrup, I waited five days to see the doctor and coughed all night every night. The other women, for the most part, were Native Canadians (aboriginals). I never did see one single black person in Thunder Bay, but there seemed to be a large Native population.

The days *crawled* by. Like a Sumo wrestler (held in a cage and force fed), I managed to put on ten pounds in five months because the food was dynamite. While in Canada I acquired a taste for gravy on my french fries—like they don't have enough calories already—and the jail gave us a snack at 9:00 PM like tea and big chocolate macaroon muffins, still warm from the oven!

■   ■   ■

In Thunder Bay, we went back and forth to court a couple of times. The U.S. media was raising hell about not having access to the hearings. Normally, immigration hearings are closed to the public. The media can petition for access provided they don't disrupt the proceedings. Initially, they were not allowed in, and it was driving them wild. So the first couple of hearings dealt mostly with that.

Dave Dubinsky stood up in court. "We have a tradition here in Canada," he said. "We try people in the courtroom, not in the newspapers."

No wonder I love this guy!

Ron Lester had been approached by the Justice Ministry about becoming a judge. He'd been looking at it for a while, and told me he was thinking of accepting. He was feeling burned-out by practicing criminal law, and he wanted out. At the same time, he said, he didn't want to leave me in the middle of my fight without a good lawyer.

I believe it sincerely bothered him, and this was really a switch. I was so unaccustomed to concern, especially from lawyers. It had become clear to me that in the U.S. a good lawyer won't even talk to you if you don't have three hundred thousand dollars in your pocket. They just don't seem to care. If you have the retainer, fine, if not, goodbye.

But now—an ethical lawyer! A lawyer with a conscience! A lawyer who cares about his clients! I couldn't believe it!

It was Ron that picked out a refugee claim as a possible defense.

When he told the case presenting officer that this is what he was going to do, alarm bells went off in the Justice Department. Or I suppose they did, because shortly after that the Minister of Immigration and Citizenship, Barbara McDougall, issued a certificate calling me a danger to the public. Ron Lester then knew that he urgently needed someone who was a criminal lawyer with a knowledge of constitutional and immigration law.

Ron called his friend David McCombs, a criminal lawyer, in Toronto.

"No, I can't do this," David told Ron. "She needs *the* expert on immigration. Let me call Frank Marrocco. He wrote the book on immigration—literally. It's called *The Annotated Immigration Act.*"

■   ■   ■

Frank Marrocco showed up at my next hearing in Thunder Bay, and the Immigration Department adjudicator just about fell off his chair. They wanted to ship me back right away, and having Frank Marrocco walk in was an unpleasant surprise for them.

I had hearings in December, and that same month I took a polygraph test, a thorough examination of my veracity conducted by a well know Toronto firm called International Corporate Investigators Inc. The specialist they used was John J. J. McClinton, a certified forensic polygraphist. His conclusion was pretty clear: "It is the final opinion of the polygraphist," his report said, "based upon the polygraphic interview of the examinee, that Lawrencia Bembenek was telling the truth when she denied shooting Christine Schultz in her home with a thirty-eight caliber handgun on May 28, 1981. This truthful polygraphic opinion is substantiated by the statistically significant total examination scores of +8 recorded for Lawrencia Bembenek ..."

Bear in mind that a total score of -6 or lower, means the subject is not truthful; a score between +5 and -5 is inconclusive; and +6 or greater means a judgment of truthful.

There were more hearings in January and March. On March 26, 1991, I got a change of venue and was sent to Toronto.

I have been in Toronto ever since. It's where I write these words.

■   ■   ■

From my jail cell in Thunder Bay, I wrote to my mom:

Dear mom
Did you ever think for one second
after I was born
that the baby you carried home in your arms
would someday be a cop, a convict, a refugee?
You just don't know how many times
I looked out a window
at an ordinary woman walking down the street
with a bag of groceries or a small dog
and wished I was that woman—
wished I was anybody but me;
just someone plain, anonymous, legitimate
normal and free.
Did you ever think for one second
when you saved me from drowning
in Canada twenty-three years ago
that someday
Canada would in turn
try to save my life?

I love you and dad so much!
Laurie

25

FREEDOM FOR A DAY

I was transferred to this grim place, Toronto's Metro West Detention Centre, in March 1991. Population: over six hundred. One morning, in September, I went out, as usual, for "Yard" (a kind of outdoor "airing" given prisoners in this otherwise recreation-free environment).

I wasn't expecting any trouble. After all these years, I know how to live with women, how to get along, and I seldom had any problems.

I was sitting by myself in the sun when four women came over and sat down beside me. I mean, *right next to me*, a deliberate provocation. Oh oh, I thought, I don't know these people, something is about to go down. I knew that whatever it was, it would be something ugly.

The woman closest to me was covered with homemade tattoos and pus-filled needle track-marks. I found out who she was later—a hard-bitten old con who had spent time in the Pen. Most people knew her as an old lesbian junkie prostitute from the Parkdale area of Toronto. She was a truly repulsive person. I heard her bragging about stealing from her dealer and then stabbing him fifteen times. "Yeah, well, I stole twelve grams of heroin from the fucking goof ..." A true gem, a charmer.

But these are the people you have to live with.

She'd read about me, and for some reason something clicked in the mush the heroin had made of her brains.

She started in—"You fucking copper ..."—and she began to spit at me. Her three friends joined in.

This, I didn't need. I normally remain passive in these situations. I'll defend myself when attacked, but I won't throw the first punch. It's seldom worth getting into any kind of fight, and here even more so. I have too much to lose. Although it took everything I had not to react, I remained still. I'm particularly vulnerable here, I thought. The last thing I need just before one of my hearings is to get into a physical altercation in Yard. What if I accidentally hurt this woman? There would go my refugee claim. There was a concrete floor out there. If she fell and cracked her head ... I could already see the headline: "Bembenek kills Canadian inmate."

People don't understand what jail is like, what the provocations are. Any incident would be torn out of context, and I'd be portrayed, again, as a violent, crazy person.

I didn't feel physically threatened, because I can take care of myself, but I didn't want to have to, I wanted to avoid it. So I struggled not to react.

They pushed me. People like this always feel powerful in groups.

So all I said was, "Give me a break, eleven years ago I was a cop ..."

She just sneered. "Once a cop, always a cop."

"Look," I said, trying to be reasonable, "I've done more time than all you clowns put together."

It was unpleasant, but there was no violence. Still, I stopped going to Yard after that. It was the only time I had all day to get fresh air, and now even that was taken away from me.

A few days later the guards intercepted kites (unauthorized letters) these people were writing to each other. They were full of death threats. You should have seen them: "We'll kill her, we'll stab her in the shower, I'd be proud to go to Seg for killing a cop ..."

The institution moved fairly swiftly; they didn't want an incident any more than I did. They moved her to another range, where we wouldn't bump into each other. I was blamed, of course. I was the rat because they moved her. The inmates' golden rule is, "Don't go to the cops for anything."

I agonized over this. Should I continue going to Yard? If I don't go, they'll have won, they'll have dictated to me. If I do go, there's going to be a fight, I know it. I wrestled with myself, not knowing what to do.

It was at that time that they let me out.

Cruelly, cruelly, for a day.

And then they put me back.

■   ■   ■

It came out of the blue, one Thursday afternoon while I was at "hobbycraft."

I lived for hobbycraft. I was not allowed to work because they were convinced I was Houdini, so the only thing they allowed me to do in this prison was go to the hobbycraft room twice a week—Tuesday afternoons and Thursday afternoons. There I could get out my brushes and my paints and, using whatever surface I could find— some old cardboard, scraps of plywood or particle board—I'd try to lose myself in my painting. (The *Toronto Sun* later published a page of my paintings under the heading "The Artful Dodger." *Please*!)

Wouldn't you know, of course, that the Immigration people would choose to hold their weekly review of my detention every Thursday, too? Under the terms of the Immigration Act, detentions must be reviewed every seven days, but it didn't really matter which day it was held. It seemed perverse of them to insist on holding it on my hobbycraft day.

The hearing cannot be waived. Everyone knows it's a waste of time and money, but they hold it anyway. It usually takes only a few minutes. An adjudicator and a case-presenting officer go to the prison; the CPO tells you what a jerk and a menace to the public you are, and then they leave. It doesn't do much for morale, let me tell you.

That Thursday, the art teacher came to pick me up as usual. The hobbycraft room is on the men's side of Metro West, a good five-minute walk away. Of course, you can't go anywhere unescorted. As with any art class, it takes a while to set up, get the paints ready and jars open and canvas in place and so on, and so you don't have very much time for actual painting. No sooner did I start that day, September 12, 1991, when the guard arrived. "I need Bembenek for Immigration."

The teacher said, "Well, when you're finished, could you bring her back?"

I begged the guard to wait for me. "It only takes thirty seconds or so," I said. If he left, I wouldn't be able to go back to my painting.

"Okay," he said.

But when we got there, only one person was in the room—Terry Mackay, the adjudicator that day. There was a national civil servants' strike going on, and they hadn't been able to find a CPO willing to cross the picket line. A CPO must be present for a detention review.

Mackay explained the problem. "Thanks," I said, and left.

"You weren't kidding about the thirty seconds," the guard said.

He took me back to hobbycraft.

About twenty minutes later, another guard showed up.

"We need Bembenek again," he said.

It was maddening. I went stomping back. I stalked into the room, and there was a new person there, a CPO I'd never seen before. I stood, waiting for the wham-bam-thank-you-ma'am, but he just sat there. Then the adjudicator said, "I want to ask you some questions."

I thought, That's odd. What's this? It's a game you learn to play in prison: Do I get my hopes up? No! He doesn't mean anything by it. You have to struggle to maintain mental strength, and not getting your hopes up is a basic strategy—you have to come to terms with the fact that you're not going anywhere.

I was thinking, Nah! It can't mean anything!

Mackay spoke quietly. "There is quite a lot happening in the U.S. right now regarding your case. Would you be more willing to return there if they ordered a new trial?"

I suppose rumors of the John Doe investigation they had launched in Milwaukee had been circulating. But this left me in something of a pickle. I'd applied to stay in Canada as a refugee. That meant I was maintaining that I mistrusted the U.S. judicial system, that I believed it would not give me a fair trial. I couldn't now say I thought it would treat me fairly. On the other hand, his question was innocent; he was thinking of granting me bail, and he wanted me to say that I wouldn't flee. I was between a rock and a hard place. I gave him some outrageous two-step answer, babbling for twenty seconds without really saying anything. A hypothetical answer for a hypothetical question.

Then he said, "Well, let me ask you this: if bail was granted, would you return for your hearings?"

"Of course," I said, meaning it fervently. "If someone put up money for me for bail, there's no way I couldn't return. That would be a real slap in the face for that person. I wouldn't do that to anybody, anybody."

And I added, "In any case, where am I going to go? When I first came to Canada, no one looked twice at me. Now, my face is all over. There's no place I *can* go. The point is, I want to stay.

"People from the Justice Department say to me, 'We can't let you out because you have a history of escape.' Well, no kidding! How do you think I got here? But it's a circular argument—when I escaped the first time I had absolutely nothing to lose, and nor did anyone else. I didn't compromise anyone. And no one lost money because of me.

"You can't compare that to the situation now.

"Since then, a great deal of exculpatory evidence has been documented. If I ran now, I would lose everything—the faith that my lawyers have in me, and all my supporters, the growing presumption of my innocence. There's simply no way I could contemplate taking off. I'd have to be crazy—I have a very good chance now."

Mackay said, "I have the tendency to agree with you, Miss Bembenek, and I'm going to order your release."

Well, I just about fell off my chair.

He looked at the CPO and asked, "Do you have any submissions on this?"

The CPO said, "No submissions."

I was numb. Once a week, very formally, they sat me down and told me what a horrible person I am, what a danger to the public, how I'm an escape risk, a fugitive, a runaway who would never come back, a real menace that no one could trust. On and on they'd go.

This time this person just said, "No submissions."

What was this?

He said nothing more, just looked down at his papers.

My heart was thumping. I couldn't believe that somebody, after all this time, was ordering my release. A tear rolled down my face.

Metro West was a very punitive environment, really tough. The year I had so far spent there was harder than nine years at Taycheedah. Metro West was just a holding tank, a detention center, never meant for long stays. It's not equipped to hold inmates for years like prisons are. It has no humanity. You can't go anywhere, you can't do anything, you can't have anything—any of the little creature comforts that you might have had in other prisons are forbidden here. Three or four times a week they get everyone up and line us up, and you think you're at Dachau or something. You get strip-searched, then they search your cell and take away the one pen more than you're supposed to have, tip through all your stuff, take whatever they feel like. We're allowed virtually no possessions.

People weren't supposed to stay there as long as I had.

I was thinking about all this, about this awful place, and tears were running down my face. I was just stunned. The CPO left to take a phone call, and I said to Mackay, "Honest to God, you will not regret this decision. I'll not do anything to make you regret this. I've been begging to be allowed to live in a less punitive environment. Can I shake your hand, can I please shake your hand?"

I wanted to hug the guy! I wanted to have his baby! Let me hug you! Please!

I shook his hand.

"I've been thinking about this for a long time," he said. "You're right, where could you go? You've got a good chance right now."

"I know," I said. "That's the other point, I want to stay in Canada."

I thanked him a thousand times, I think, in about a minute.

He set the conditions on my bail: stay at the Elizabeth Fry Society Halfway House, do volunteer work at the Salvation Army (I wasn't allowed to work without a work permit), ten thousand dollars cash bail and ten thousand dollars surety. He also added the stipulation that I report to the Immigration office every day.

"I'll report ten times a day if that's what it takes, if that's what you want," I said. "It's okay, I'll do anything."

So he signed the papers and started to walk out.

I called after him, "Don't I get a copy?"

"No," he said, and left.

■   ■   ■

They returned me to my cell, my mind utterly boggled. I didn't say anything to anyone. I couldn't. I had nothing to prove this had really happened, nothing tangible, no copy of the release order.

Just then one of my lawyers, David Liblong, came by with a reporter from CBC TV. I went down to the visiting room, my mind spinning. David walked in and picked up the phone on the other side of the glass wall.

"David!" I said, trying not to look agitated. "You won't believe what just happened! They just ordered my release at a detention review!"

Liblong's eyeballs popped. "Holy shit!" he said. "Please, don't tell anyone!"

The reporter was asking me questions, and I didn't know what I was saying ... I must have sounded like someone who ought to switch right away to decaf. It was unreal!

I couldn't think. I couldn't sleep. I paced like a tiger. I lay awake all night. It was so unreal. I was sure there was someone in the background with authority over Terry Mackay who would put a stop to this as soon as he heard about it. On the other hand, they were on strike, so maybe it was going to happen.

I called my mom and told her, and I was crying, and she said, "Should we come up, Sweetie?"

"No," I said, "don't come, just wait, it's too soon, too much can happen."

Of course, they didn't listen, they were on the next plane. I was afraid it would fall apart, and I didn't want them to take on any more pain. On my own, I could handle it.

I didn't pack anything in the morning. I didn't tell anyone. What was I to do? I tried to call my lawyers at home, but no one was there. They weren't in the office, either.

Then the superintendent came to my cell and she put her hand through the bars, and she said, "Well, good luck, Laurie ..." And then I thought, If she's heard about it, it must be true!

I bundled my little possessions together, my few precious little things, my Russian studies book, my Immigration Act, my law course, a few toiletries, some lotion, a little shampoo. I put them into a pillow case, because I didn't have a bag.

Nine o'clock came. I went out for Yard and played ping-pong for a while because I couldn't sit still, and then a guard came and hollered, "Bembenek!"

This is it! They don't come to Yard unless it's important.

I went running in and they took me to A&D—Arrivals and Departures—where everyone gets processed. That's where all your money and possessions are, and the paperwork gets done. I had some paintings I'd done and two boxes full of junk. Some of it I'd never seen—sometimes people would send me stuff and the prison would simply confiscate it. I had to carry all this stuff—the paintings, these boxes, my little bag of possessions.The only clothes I had to wear in Canada were the dress and high heels I'd been wearing to hearings. I didn't want to be teetering around on these golf-tees carrying boxes and paintings, so I asked if I could wear jeans and my prison-issue top. "No," they said, "if you have clothes you must change into them here."

The International Center, where the Immigration Ministry is headquartered, had sent Pinkerton guards in a van for me. They had to wait until I'd changed into my dress.

Bad, bad timing. In the five minutes it took me to change into my dress, the guy at the desk got a phone call.

He came up to the Pinkerton sergeant and said, "Can I talk to you?" in that "Oh no!" tone of voice that you learn to recognize, that all prisoners know and love. They whispered together for a few minutes. The Pinkerton man came back with a stunned look on his face. "You're not going," he said.

I was standing at the door, waiting for the electronic gate to open so I could get into the van. I was in my dress, carrying my boxes.

"I don't understand," he said. "I've got your release order right here, this is as good as a court order. But ... we were told to return to the International Center without you."

And I thought, I knew it! I knew it I knew it I knew it!

And so they left.

The superintendent didn't know what to do with me. She put me for a while in the little bullpen near the entrance. I sat there in my dress, in this filthy and horrible place, cold concrete ... She said, "I don't know what's going on, Laurie. If we knew, we'd tell you. I don't know what game they're playing. But we have to take you back upstairs."

They took me back up to the range, one step farther away from the door, away from freedom. I was still in my dress. I couldn't call anyone, because they turn the phones off over lunch.

I was just hanging by a thread.

What were they trying to do? After ten years, this was the first time I'd be out legally, and they were telling me, Yes, No, Yes, No ...

I tried to eat, but my stomach was in knots. About an hour went by, I think—I don't really know because we are not allowed clocks. Then they came for me again.

They said, "Let's try this again, Bembenek."

"Are you sure this time?"

We went back to the main floor, I signed out my money, and this time I made it out the door. I was in the van, driving away. They had sent three Pinkerton guards to come and get me. One of these swash-bucklers looked down at me—I was in nylons—and said, "Oh, these shackles are really going to hurt your ankles ..."

I was being released, and she wanted to shackle me? Please! I imagined teetering along on high heels, in shackles, carrying boxes and paintings. It was ridiculous, and eventually she saw it, too. She left the shackles off.

We arrived at the International Center, and they wouldn't let us in. Civil servants' strike. Pickets. It was the media circus from hell—satellite dishes everywhere. Crowds of picketers rushed the van and wouldn't let us go.

The van engine was turned off and we sat. It was very hot without the air-conditioning on, 100 degrees or so, and we sat sweltering. The cameras zoomed up to the van, attaching themselves to the window like flies. Picketers circled outside, chanting, "Even Bambi eats better than we do! What kind of justice is that?"

Finally they agreed that management could escort prisoners across the picket line. But management was out to lunch, and didn't come back for another hour.

Inside the International Center, more hours went by. I sat in some kind of waiting room, doing nothing. The Pinkerton guard dozed off. Other people, guards, workers, came by. It seemed every person on staff made some excuse to come look at me. They'd stand there and just stare! I didn't know what to do. I was reduced to some kind of zoo animal. They were deliberately stalling. They wanted as long a delay as possible while they figured out ways of stopping my release.

Isn't it interesting that when a court order is in their favor they insist on implementing it at once?

My lawyers were almost reduced to violence, they were so frustrated. They were about ready to punch someone.

At 4:00 PM, it was over. David Liblong and John Callaghan rushed in. "That's it, you're released, let's go!"

We bulldozed our way out through the media crowd. They were chasing us down the hallways. I'm surprised they didn't go ass over teakettle, walking backwards with those giant cameras. I bet they could land planes with those lights.

There was considerable confusion when we went out the wrong door and we had to hunt through the parking lot looking for our car, a scrum of reporters following us. Frank Marrocco was in the back seat, and we zigzagged our way through the crowd of reporters as Callaghan drove out of the lot.

Frank smiled at me. "Well," he said, "you made it."

"I told you you should've let *me* argue," I laughed.

We pulled out into the street. I rolled down the window and I breathed in the air ... the free air.

■   ■   ■

The lawyers had rented a conference room at a nearby Holiday Inn to get away from the reporters and regroup. I followed Frank into the Holiday Inn, thinking, Oh God the next headline is that I head right for a hotel room with Frank Marrocco as soon as I'm out on bail! Michelle Nash and John Callaghan and other members of the legal team came, and my dear friend Louie, my employer from Thunder Bay, who was putting up the surety. We heard my parents had flown in, but we didn't know where they were.

I looked around at everything, as delighted as a child. The Holiday Inn looked like a palace! I was delighted with the mineral water, with the coffee in neat little cups, with all the ordinary things that were extraordinary to me. John Callaghan asked me how I felt. "Freaked out!" I said. I didn't even know. I gave Louie a big hug.

But of course it wasn't over. The lawyers were huddling over in a corner, and I heard the words "extradition order." "What extradition order?" I asked, and they all looked at me, with that look on their faces. My heart started to constrict.

"No," someone said, "no, it's impossible, you can't extradite a refugee claimant. How can you? The claim hasn't been determined yet."

Frank, who knew better, reached for a phone and called a colleague, Doug Hunt. He handed the phone to me.

"Hi," said this voice. "I'm Doug Hunt. Do you want me to represent you?"

I was confused. I didn't know what was going on. Represent me in what? Didn't I already have lawyers? "What are we talking about?" I asked. "What's happening?" I didn't know. It hadn't registered that the State of Wisconsin was already seeking extradition.

■ ■ ■

The blood started to thud in my brain. They would not leave me alone! They had heard I was being released on bail—were the fax machines humming while I sat there during the delay at the International Center—and they wanted me back inside. A year had gone by since my capture, but now they decided it was "urgent" they extradite me. I could hear them laughing. I could hear the shrill vindictive laughter echoing down the years. I thought of all the mean, pinched people who wanted to control my life. The idea of my freedom seemed to give them all nightmares. I felt the dead weight of the State on the back of my neck. This wasn't supposed to be how America was!

■ ■ ■

John Paul Barry and David Liblong took me to Elizabeth Fry. I went through orientation, reading the house rules, getting a lock for a locker, figuring out what the curfews were. They assigned me a room.

It was so quiet! The silence was deafening. That was my first impression. Jail is so noisy! Sometimes, when I talk to people on the phone, they hear what sounds like someone getting macheted in the background, but it's normal prison noise. The TV is blasting and people are yelling over it. The silence was wonderful. Everything was carpeted, soft and pretty. Oh God, I thought, my own little bed, with its own little nightlight so I could read before I went to sleep. I could turn it off when I wanted to! There was even a little kitchen, and you could go in and make your own stuff. My roommate, who was also American, was baking lemon meringue pies for everyone.

I kicked off my shoes, because I can't walk in real shoes anymore—nor can I walk on carpeting, because I keep tripping. I was walking around in my pantyhose. I was exhausted. I hadn't eaten anything all day. I was sweaty and wanted to shower.

The lawyers had left. I was trying to make my bed and get situated, poking about at all the wonders—a cabinet, a little closet, drawers, a mirror, places to put things.

Then the residence staff told me my parents had arrived.

We sat in the lounge, my dad with his arm around me. It was so wonderful, but I was exhausted, and they saw that.

They stayed for about an hour, I think. My mom took pity on me and said, "Well, we've got time now, we can talk a lot. We'll let you get some sleep and come back tomorrow. Shower and change and sleep and we'll be here for a week if necessary."

So they left. There was a bowl of fresh fruit in the kitchen—fresh fruit is like gold in prison—and I grabbed a green apple. And then the lawyers came back with a suitcase of clothes. Lawyer Arthur Jacques' wife had gone out to get me clothes ...

I had a lump in my throat. I probably didn't thank them enough. Everyone was being so ... nice ... I didn't know how to act. I'd become so accustomed to harsh treatment—the normal inmate-guard relationship—that being with pleasant people who seemed to like me was quite disconcerting and upsetting. I changed clothes. Some of the stuff in the suitcase I couldn't figure out—fashions had changed in ten years. I put on a top and pants made out of T-shirt material.

After I'd changed, we used the phone in the Elizabeth Fry office for a conference call to Doug Hunt. He needed information: he had to go into court the next morning on the extradition matter, and he had to be prepared.

That's when it started to sink in.

Shit, they're serious. Court in the morning.

Even so, I was more cynical than the lawyers. They were still saying, "This has never been done before, this is unprecedented ..." and I was thinking, Yeah, story of my life ...

One of the things I liked about Hunt was that he gave me straight information. Right until the end, Don Eisenberg kept painting a rosy picture. Don's favorite comment was, "We'll talk about that after the acquittal." You're not mentally prepared if your lawyer keeps insisting nothing bad will happen.

Doug Hunt pointed out that the criteria they had to satisfy to get an extradition warrant was extraordinarily simple. They had to prove a conviction, which was easy, and make a positive identification, which wasn't so hard. Doug warned that the judge might feel compelled, using those criteria, to issue the warrant.

J. P. Barry called David Liblong at home, got him out of bed and down to the office. "We've got to go over the case," J. P. told him. "Work all night to be prepared."

This is how these guys worked for me. They're incredible! I kept saying, "Thank you, thank you!" I was so grateful. I still find it hard to believe ...

I went back up to my little room and sorted out my stuff. There were all kinds of things I hadn't seen. I hung a few things up and figured out what to wear to court. It was like Christmas—three or four pairs of shoes!

In my boxes from Metro West was all sorts of odd junk. The most exciting part was, I got to open my own mail for the first time in ten years.

I fell asleep an hour or so after midnight.

I wanted so much to stay there, it was so quiet ...

■   ■   ■

The next morning they picked me up at six, and we went over to Doug Hunt's office, on the thirty-eighth floor of one of the bank towers. The morning had a dreamlike quality. I had never met Doug Hunt, but he was now to be representing me in court, trying to stop them from sending me back. We sat for a few hours and went over the information again.

At nine, my herd of lawyers and I got into the elevator—that's what it felt like, this whole legal entourage. There was Doug, with five assistants. John Callaghan and David Liblong and John Paul Berry were there. Frank showed up, too, and we walked over to the courthouse, a whole regiment of legal talent.

We walked up York Street toward the courthouse. I was thinking, Oh no, please, I don't want to get arrested again, I don't want to go back in that place.

The judge was Patricia German, a tiny little woman. Doug Hunt told me she was sympathetic but felt compelled to issue the warrant because of the ease of meeting the criteria.

She insisted on doing the bail hearings right away, and that took all morning.

She was pleasant. She called me "young lady" and offered to let me use the bathroom in her chambers (it was a Saturday and the others were closed). On the way out, she told the RCMP, "Now make sure she gets a nice lunch." She seemed to be going that extra mile to show me she was sympathetic.

The RCMP were ticked off. "We've got better things to do with our time than this bullshit," one of them said. They refused to cuff me. Clearly they thought the whole thing was ludicrous. I was finger-printed again and we went to lunch in the staff lounge. They picked up ribs and fries and we sat around and had lunch. We chatted about the case. They had read about the gun, the so-called murder weapon, and what procedures had been followed.

"A bullshit case" was their verdict.

■　　■　　■

Once again the Justice Department lawyers made a big production of the fact that I'd worked for a living in Thunder Bay, using false ID! They implied that if I'd used false ID there was nothing I wouldn't do. I still don't understand what they thought I should have done. Of course I wasn't using my real name. Would they rather I'd robbed banks for a living?

Around 6:00 PM we adjourned until the next morning. Doug Hunt asked if I could go back to Elizabeth Fry for another night. The judge made an approving sort of face, as if she was going to go along with this idea, but the Justice Department lawyers went wild.

"Your Lordship! This is a convicted killer! The most horrible crime imaginable, in Canada as well as the U.S."

A whole tirade. I looked at them, wondering what was going on in their heads. I wondered if they heard the wounds their words caused, and whether they cared. Perhaps they armored themselves in some way against feelings. I wondered if their husbands and wives and children and sisters saw this side of them, or whether they had simply somehow persuaded themselves I was some subhuman monster. I hoped they could live with themselves in the mornings.

The judge said she would have to remand me back to Metro West.

My heart went cold.

I went over to my dad and hugged him and I started to cry. I cried and cried, I felt so desolate, sobbing and holding onto his shoulders, those shoulders that were now so much more frail than when we had started this awful journey, ten years before. I felt the bones of his shoulders and it all poured out, the frustration and the sadness, and he just stood there and hugged me back. The courtroom was so quiet you could have heard a pin drop. Even the reporters were quiet, for once. I think they felt the desolation, too. How could they help but feel it? It was choking the air.

I went back, and it was really bad. When the door opened and the guards saw me, they just shook their heads. They couldn't believe I was back. "What the hell is going on here, you just got bail yesterday?"

I felt worse than I had when we were caught in Thunder Bay. It was such a cruel joke. To put up with this horrible place for all these months, and then get that one, short, tantalizing night—it would have been better not to have left at all. I had made the prisoner's fatal mistake. I had allowed myself to hope.

■   ■   ■

There were three of us in my cell, now. One was a crazy girl, burned out from cocaine, crazy and hyper and restless, sitting on my clothes, pressing on my space, filling the air with craziness ...

Please, please, oh, let me out of here!

But no one came.

26

THE RETURN

Well, it's over.

I'm back in this ... this place.

For months, for so many months, I simply endured what they did to me. They would take me to court, then take me away again. I went to a hearing, and then they put me back in jail. I came and I went. Lawyers argued, judges listened (typing away on their little computers), prosecutors ranted. It was a routine. It wasn't a life, but it was a routine.

For months I went to court in the little death box on wheels they call a Metro Police transportation van. One week ... they had seventeen women stuffed into the back of one of the police wagons, five on either side, handcuffed together. I was in my suit, and nylons, but there was no room, and the policewoman said, "Too bad. You're gonna have to sit on the floor." There were already four other women on the floor—and then they wonder why we look like criminals. You do everything in your power to look presentable in court, but you're filthy and wrinkled and there's nothing you can do about it. They get us up at 5:30 AM, I'm in court at 9:00, it's over by 10:30, and I sit in the bullpen until 6:00 PM. In the evening, on the way back, they picked up a woman who was obviously mentally ill. She was in her underwear—no shoes or socks or pants, and this in December. Couldn't they have found her some pants? What is she going to a jail for anyway? She should be going to a mental health facility.

But why should they care?

And so "home," to that grim place, and to bed.

Again, and again.

For all that time, my lawyers were fighting for me. They spent hours, days, weeks, months fighting for me. I became a little legal cottage industry all on my own—these guys used to have other clients! They fought because they thought what had happened to me was outlandish, and because they liked the idea of justice and because—well, let's face it, they liked the challenge, too. Frank is a chess player, and he understands intricate moves.

I watched them in the hallways sometimes. They argued and gesticulated, getting angry at the obstinacy of the other side—*Why can't they see it the way we can?*

But it's over now. The shining towers of freedom I thought I saw in their arguments were just a mirage after all. I thought Canada could be my home, a refuge; I wanted so badly to become a citizen of some place where I could be free! But it was not to be. Mirages are just dreams, after all, and dreams are dangerous for inmates, because they let the daylight in, and you can see the bars and the bare concrete, stretching down the years... If I am to win my freedom, it will have to be here, where they first took it from me. So I came back, of my own accord, to continue the fight.

■   ■   ■

I have many memories of Canada, good and bad. Among the bad are my memories of Metro West Detention Centre and their strip searches, the most pointless and dehumanizing of all prison procedures. Some jail rules are at least understandable—making us eat spaghetti with a spoon at least helps cut down stabbing incidents among inmates—but strip searches make no sense at all except to humiliate people. In Thunder Bay and Toronto they routinely stripped and searched inmates during cell searches, a completely purposeless activity. In Toronto, you could be stripped three times a day. Wherever you went in prison, you were strip searched afterwards. Cell search in the morning: strip search. After work in the laundry or kitchen: strip search. After hobbycraft: strip search. After Elizabeth Fry volunteer visit: strip search. After a lawyer's visit: strip search. Come back from court: strip search. And the guards looked on the activity as normal, not even caring that male officers were present; they only looked puzzled when I complained that I was not an exhibitionist and hated taking off my clothes in front of strangers. Most of the guards just shrugged, and said they didn't like strip searching people either, but they were just following orders. Orders! There's an excuse familiar from history!

But of course I have good memories too, and among them were the friends I made and the people who worked so hard on my behalf.

A friend told me how Frank Marrocco really got involved in my case (I was too timid to ask Frank directly).

At first, I was told, Frank wasn't too impressed when McCombs called him. Frank's been around a long time, and believes that plenty of guilty people insist they're innocent. So he believed that if he was going to get involved at all, it would be to give me a quick opinion, for a good fee, and then take himself out.

But the thing that struck him immediately was the testimony of the boys—twelve-year-old Sean insisting he'd seen the murderer and it wasn't me. That made him think.

Also, Frank is of that rare breed, a criminal lawyer who knows constitutional law. And the Immigration minister's certificate offended him constitutionally. It was such a circular argument the minister was making—she declared me a danger to the public on the basis of the very conviction I was claiming gave me a good basis for a refugee claim! I was claiming that my conviction was erroneous. She said I was dangerous because I was convicted. Frank agreed to argue this at the hearings.

So he flew to Thunder Bay to meet me. And I guess he saw I wasn't a complete wingnut. Then he spent two thousand dollars on Xerox bills and took all the documents away with him. He read everything—transcripts, police reports, everything. And again, what struck him was that at first everybody had been looking for a man. All the police reports mentioned a male suspect.

He began to get interested.

Immigration Minister Barbara McDougall, confronted with a challenge, withdrew her certificate and asked for submissions for both sides. Frank prepared a brief to her outlining all the exculpatory evidence that had been uncovered in my case to date.

She re-issued the certificate, once again declaring me a danger to the public. But at least Frank's brief was now on the record. Finally, somewhere, I had on the record some of the evidence that supported me.

We were challenging the validity of the second certificate when Ron Lester was called to the bench as a judge. Suddenly I was without a lawyer. So, almost by accident, Frank found himself arguing the merits of my case and not just its constitutional aspects.

This is what he told my friend:

"So I started to get into it. I could have turned it back, and told her it was none of my business, that it was an American case, and nothing to do with me. But I thought, I have to live with myself. If one day I was to wake up, and she was fifty-five instead of thirty-three, and she's lost her adult life instead of just her twenties, and she is then proven innocent, or someone eventually confesses, well, that would have haunted me for the rest of my life.

"I believed in her and I just couldn't do that ...

"I'm no saint, God knows, but if I could have done something to save her and refrained ... no, I couldn't do that."

Many law firms would have insisted he drop the case, or at least get paid for it. But by this time he was in, and bringing his friends and colleagues in, and the firm not only allowed but encouraged it.

I still find it all hard to believe.

So I then had Frank and John Callaghan for the immigration (refugee) case, which was being held before a two-man tribunal of the immigration department, not a judge. Frank looks like a lawyer. He used to be a Crown prosecutor, on a per diem basis, and he can't always get the prosecutor out of his bones. Sometimes when he was questioning me I'd say, "Frank! What's this cross examination!" He kept asking me about stuff that's ten years old, and I didn't mean to give fuzzy answers but I couldn't always be positive. Then he got a prosecutorial sort of expression that said, "What do you mean you don't remember! You were there!" He wanted me to remember so badly.

Frank's a chess player and was always thinking a couple of moves ahead. For instance, at the immigration hearings (unlike court-rooms in Canada) television cameras were allowed. So Frank was playing to two audiences, the immigration tribunal, arguing my case there, and the television audience back in Milwaukee—they played my evidence in full on air there, and this was finally helping to turn public opinion in my favor.

And John Callaghan? He didn't look old enough to be a lawyer. I had to laugh every time I saw him in court, in his robes (in Canada lawyers wear robes), looking like a kid, with a face like Tom Hanks. But *smart*!

Doug Hunt, of Fasken Campbell Godfrey, was my counsel for the extradition matter, before the Ontario courts. He's a desert storm all by himself. The immigration proceedings gave rise to a habeas corpus application—that was David McCombs, of Carter McCombs and Minden. (There was another habeas corpus application attached to the extradition case.) Then there was Arthur Jacques, a colleague of Frank's, who is a barracuda. David Liblong and J. P. Barry were student lawyers, and then there was Michelle Nash, who knew everything about the case there was to be known and ... oh, there were others: the Milwaukee chapter of the National Organization of Women applied for intervener status in the hearings, and retained a lawyer named Michelle Fuerst. In the U.S. I had Sheldon Zenner out of Chicago, who was (and is) acting for me in the John Doe action. And Mary Woehrer, in Milwaukee, who was helping me by representing Ira Robins. She is formally counsel for the applicants for the John Doe—Dr. Irwin, who was the chief medical examiner at the time of the murder, and Ira. She also assists Zenner.

A regular industry, no? All these actions—the extradition case, the refugee hearings, habeas corpus actions arising from both, the John Doe.

A John Doe hearing is sort of like a one-person Grand Jury. This one has a specific frame of reference, which is police misconduct—they are looking for proof of evidence tampering. The prosecutor is investigating the investigation; that is, he's looking at police procedures rather than my guilt or innocence. All these proceedings had one basis: my apparent inability to get justice in the courts that tried me. The prosecutor will probably report about mid-year 1992.

Frank believed I had a strong case in the immigration hearings. Although one side effect of stringing out the Canadian hearings was to give the John Doe hearings more time, that wasn't why they strung them out. They did so because they thought they could win.

At least, in our many submissions and petitions and motions in the various Canadian tribunals and courts, we slowly got on an official record some of the exculpatory evidence no one had ever recognized before. At least people now know what kind of "evidence" convicted me. They can now begin to see how oddly intransigent the Milwaukee authorities were about re-opening my case.

My Chicago attorney, Sheldon Zenner, wrote to the DA before the Canadian immigration hearings started, and suggested letting the FBI look into the case. The DA refused. Why? During the course of my trial, they didn't hesitate to call in the FBI about evidence like the mysterious clothesline.

The Justice Department in Canada complained that my lawyers used the immigration hearings just to retry the murder case in Canada. But I had to try to establish that I might have been framed as a consequence of my attempts to expose corruption and police misconduct in the Milwaukee police force. We had to get someone to pay attention to the facts.

And, as Frank put it, "You can't be blind to that fact that the Special Prosecutor may find someone, someone who will just walk through his door ... I believe someone, whoever, down there in Milwaukee will wake up to the fact that the best thing he can do is make a deal ... After all, *someone* did the murder."

Frank also told a friend of mine this:

"The ultimate objective of all these actions, of everything we do, or every argument, is to get the door open and let her walk out.

"How we do that, and where it happens, is not material.

"We can't let our own egos get in the way. It would be grand to win here in Canada. But if the best way to get her free is to let her do so in the U.S., so be it. You can never afford to ignore the moral dimension, to forget that it is her freedom that is the real issue. I can't afford to let the process get in the way of her fate. Winning a good case, setting a good precedent, is not the point of this. Prying open the gates for her is the point."

In February 1992, he advised me to come back. And here I am.

■   ■   ■

My friends held rallies for me in Milwaukee. There was a jog-a-thon to raise money for my defense, there were bake sales and craft sales and fund raising drives, there were write-in campaigns and telephone drives and mail drops and ... people worked so *hard* for me. It's not just my parents and my sisters, Colette and Melanie, and Ira and my old friends, Donna and Wally, from the Boston Store days; there are hundreds of others and I hope they know that they have been sustaining me, that their efforts have been keeping me alive, that I love them all for it with a fierce affection, and that if I get out—when I get out— it will be partly because of them, who have kept the long vigil and not given up.

My parents have mortgaged their house twice for me.

And yet—what do they say?

"It's not the money, because money is just money, but it's her youth, how do you put a price on that? On ten years? You can't replace it. So we've been fighting for her ..."

Their loyalty makes me weep, for all that has been done to *them*.

The last time they came to visit me in Toronto, the airline clerk insisted on changing their tickets to first class because "you need a little tender loving care." He asked them to tell me that "she should hang in there, we're all pulling for her, remember to tell her that ..."

Maybe things *are* changing.

■   ■   ■

Of course, there are people who will believe whatever they want—that Elvis is still alive, despite a mountain of evidence. There was a bumper sticker in Milwaukee after my escape, which said, "Bambi's with Elvis."

Too true!

Once, sometime in 1991, reporters called Fred Schultz to get his comment about something, some trivial matter. The man who cleans his pool answered the phone. Fred didn't want to be bothered. "Say I'm in Kuwait," he said. So the man did.

What did the press do? They printed it, of course. Every news outlet in Milwaukee ran with it. Even my Canadian lawyers asked me what Fred was doing in Kuwait.

I knew right away that he wasn't of course. It was just common sense. So I said to them: "Get outta here! He is not!"

And they said, "He is, it was on the news ..."

"The news! You believe the news! Please!"

They were pretty embarrassed.

It's not always as benign as that, however. You must understand how vulnerable I am in prison. People feel they can say anything they want, and they do!

Recently, Fred Horenberger, who was (and is) a prime suspect for Christine Schultz's murder, committed suicide in the course of an armed robbery. He got caught, took hostages, and killed himself after a standoff.

What happens? Horenberger's brother goes on television and says that Judy Zess and Horenberger and I had frequent sex orgies together. Not to worry that I never once met Horenberger, never mind that in Horenberger's own handwriting there is a document admitting Zess was fabricating allegations against me, and several documents that proved I had never met Horenberger. None of those things prevent this cowardly creep, Horenberger's brother, from libeling me all over again. Why doesn't the press feel it necessary to check? Why do they allow lies like that to be broadcast? Is it enough to have Ira Robins on afterwards denying it, but identifying Ira as one of my partisans, when the facts were checkable?

Why can anyone come off the street and say anything they like about me, and they'll print it? Why does the press feel cavalierly free to manufacture stories when the facts don't say what they think they should? No one should be that vulnerable.

What am I supposed to do? I get so angry at this stuff. The

lawyers always advise me to do nothing, because reacting to a libel only draws attention to it—those who hadn't seen it the first time will surely see it then. But why should they get away with it? I'm not for censorship, just for some responsibility, for some professional standards.

Well, maybe things are changing, now. I even have some of the media on my side.

But I still don't know how long my fight will take, or whether I'll ever be free again.

I'm back where it all began. The struggle continues. The love of my family and my friends, and my inner knowledge of my innocence, sustain me.

Those things, at least, are not mirages.

■   ■   ■

Well, now you know me a little better.

As I said at the beginning, I'm no Joan of Arc, no cringing virgin, no saint. I was something of a wild child, and I made lots of mistakes. I'm also mouthy and independent and, I think, I have become quite strong.

But I'm also just an ordinary person, like your sister, or your daughter.

I'm just a person who would like her life back.

Is that so much to ask?

I have learned so many things I wish I'd never had to learn. I learned about the system of justice; I learned that it protects its own, cannot bring itself to admit its mistakes, that many of its practitioners seem more concerned with process than justice.

So much heartbreak, so much despair, so unnecessary, so many lives broken on the wheel of crude ambition and coverup, on the rack of process ...

I will be out, soon, I hope. But I will never recapture any sense that the system is benign. It has taken ten years of my life, and every day I listen to its partisans demanding to take more, more, more.

Going on is possible.

Survival is possible.

Even happiness is possible, I hope.

But I'm not at all sure about forgiveness.